THE ART OF
Arabian Costume
A SAUDI ARABIAN PROFILE

THE ART OF
Arabian Costume
A SAUDI ARABIAN PROFILE

Heather Colyer Ross

arabesque

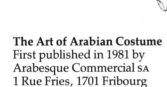

The Art of Arabian Costume
First published in 1981 by
Arabesque Commercial SA
1 Rue Fries, 1701 Fribourg
Switzerland

Phototypeset in Palatino by
Tradespools Limited, Frome, England
Printed in the Netherlands by
Royal Smeets Offset BV, Weert

Photography Heather Colyer Ross
Design and production Anthony Nelthorpe MSIAD
in collaboration with Arabesque Commercial SA
Colour illustrations Sheila Talbot
Black and white illustrations Elizabeth Finnie
and Heather Colyer Ross
The Publishers wish to thank Mary Gostelow
for permission to reproduce the drawings
on pages 144–147 from her book
The Coats Book of Embroidery

Page 1: *Dramatic shape and curious embellishment
combined in an indigo hand-dyed dress from Yemen.*
Pages 2 and 3: *Incomparable splendour in
gossamer-thin pure silk billows to the length of the
evening shadows on the Dahna. The appeal of this
Najdi* thawb *lies in the spectacular dimensions of the
evolved* kaftan, *the chosen textile and the brilliant
embellishment. Red, green and gold sequins edge the
broad cuffs in motifs of crowns and crescents. The
under-arm gussets are royal purple laced with gold
metal-thread which creates palm trees and crossed
scimitars.*
Pages 4 and 5: *Artist's impression of the* tawb
aswad, *worn in the Najran Oasis and in the far
north.*

Contents

Acknowledgements

Knowing where to begin in thanking my helpers is difficult. The kindly Bedouin trader, Umm Muhammed, who saved her special garments for me is obviously as important as the informative Textile Department of the Victoria and Albert Museum in London.

My faithful friend, translator and travelling companion, Georgette Kashisho, was ever ready to help, just as Elizabeth Finnie, Angela Cooke and Ascaloo Burhu cheerfully devoted hours to whatever tasks I set. I am especially indebted to Mary-Margaret McLernon and also to Mobil Oil Company.

Dr. Fouad Abdul-Salam al-Farsy, Deputy Minister of Industry, Kingdom of Saudi Arabia, was a continual source of encouragement, and Dr. Abdullah H. Masry, a Deputy Minister of Education, contributed valuable time and expertise, as did Professor Abd al-Rahman al-Ansary, Chairman of the Archaeology Department, Faculty of Arts, University of Riyadh. I am also indebted to Faiza al-Khayyal, Şirley Bedikoğlu, Cary Cavness, Betty Vincett, Leyla Alireza and her family, Marjorie Phillips, Doreen Sharabati, Jenny Cook, Bonnie Shawaf and the Al Nadha Philanthropic Society of Riyadh, Joni Shelton, Chris Hill, Dr. Muhammed Hasan Bakalla, Linguist, Faculty of Arts, University of Riyadh, Joyce Zaple and Khalil Ghindi.

For the assistance of the abovementioned, and the many others unnamed who gave encouragement and support, I am truly grateful. It remains for me to thank three people who made this book possible. First of all, my mother, for I grew up with a knowledge of gussets, gores and godets – as a skilled tailor, she taught me about textiles and sewing, so garment construction is not a mystery to me. Secondly, Dr. Abdulaziz H. al-Sowayyegh, Assistant Deputy Minister of Information, Kingdom of Saudi Arabia, because he approved my work and supported the project. Then, my best friend, my husband Barry, who gives me freedom to do research and has constantly supported me in my creative endeavours since we first met in 1959. I thank them most sincerely.

Heather Colyer Ross

Author's Note

The garment which began my Arabian costume collection is a Najdi "wedding" dress – so called because it is the gown traditionally worn by Central Arabian women at festive events, most of which happen to be weddings.

It was purchased at the same place that I discovered Arabian Bedouin jewellery – in Riyadh's Dira market complex at the "Women's *souq*" where the traders are, uniquely, all women. In this fascinating market, new garments are also sold, alongside spices and cooking utensils.

New dresses do not have openings for the head, proving that they are truly unworn. The purchaser must have the neckline cut. Although these neatly-folded, machine-made Bedouin dresses – stacked in piles – barely resemble their traditional counterparts, they are eagerly bought by local women and visiting Westerners. For me, they do not compare with the old hand-made, hand-embroidered garments which spill forth in brilliant disarray from the depths of great chests in the recesses of each Bedouin trader's booth. From the moment I first saw these gorgeous gowns, in 1969, I felt a child-like impulse to dress up in them.

Naturally, each of my purchases needed careful cleaning and some had to be repaired. In caring for these ethnic garments, many of their secrets were revealed. For example, I discovered how many times the embroidered sleeves had been re-used by uncovering layers of sleeve appliqué (on a section which traditionally matches the body of the garment); and, using a razor blade to carefully remove silver bells from the cuffs for cleaning, I learnt how many times they had been transferred to new sleeves.

One sad revelation was that the embroidery thread dyes were not colour-fast. After washing, the garment's subsequently faded colours were not unattractive and recalled the beautiful mellow effect which serves to enhance old Oriental rugs. But, needless to say, I never again washed another of these garments. Hand-drycleaning is the most desirable method of cleaning, especially when there is beadwork, sequins or metal-thread embroidery.

It was initially bewildering to find my specialist drycleaner unwilling to touch one particular gown. Their explanation was curt and unclear via the reception desk, but it was sufficient to lead me to enquire about indigo, the most popular dyestuff used in the Arabian Peninsula in the past. As it turned out, the refusal to clean the dress was fortuitous because the hand-dyed textile was so steeped in blue indigo that any attempt to treat it would have resulted in turning the exquisite natural-coloured embellishment to blue.

Collecting costumes, like collecting anything, is interesting enough, but in modern Arabia, the search for traditional garments is also an exciting treasure hunt. I have only recently, after ten years of searching, found a hand-made, hand-embroidered Asir Province dress. Traditional dresses from this region have been machine-embroidered for at least several decades, it is said.

Curiosity about traditional Arabian costume has led my investigation through fascinating books and into a search for old prints. It has also been necessary to visit ancient Middle Eastern fashion centres such as Damascus and Istanbul – and India – for very little has been written about the dress of old Arabia.

I became keen to draw attention to the subject by writing down all I could discover and by exhibiting the clothes. I am not an anthropologist so my work does not pretend to be scholarly. Knowing that the complete subject could fill many books – one covering each region – I proceeded because there was a need for someone to begin.

It was somewhat daunting to learn that, for several hundred years, the taxes levied by the Ottoman Empire had made inroads into Arabian wealth – a situation which would leave many with little to spend on their wardrobes. This thought, and the fact that the tribal-structured society had been breaking down since the formation of the Kingdom of Saudi Arabia in 1932, prepared me for the discovery that regional differences in costume are now partially obscured and sub-tribal variations have been practically obliterated.

In retrospect, this project has been an enjoyable adventure, albeit demanding. The heat of Arabia requires tenacity. And, the work calls for perseverance, especially since most Arabians are pre-occupied with the future, and, until very recently, only a few people showed interest in Arabia's ethnic costumes. Also, all gathered information needed to be screened and hearsay had to be verified by direct observation when at all possible. There still remains, of course, the possibility that more facts will emerge. Possibly this publication will draw forth valuable details.

It is hoped my book will serve as a basis for future work. For me it represents the culmination of several years of effort, exposing beautiful Arabian garments which lay almost un-noticed while Arabia thrust its way into the twentieth century. The pleasure of dealing with the subject exceeded the many harassments – those difficulties that are to be expected when attempting to research a previously undocumented subject. Overall, it can be recommended as a gratifying activity for any devoted hobbyist like myself.

The ultimate benefits of having a book about traditional Arabian costume are manifold. Knowing that encouraged me to continue in the latter laborious stages of the venture. The sense of accomplishment is of course great but the feeling that the work is useful gives much more satisfaction. Western fashion houses will have a richer store to draw from when Arabian costumes are catalogued. They can then conveniently, from time to time, refer to the various garments for inspiration as fashion spins along the pathway of clothing history.

Furthermore, the Arabian people, who are the most impor-tant beneficiaries, may bring forth more old costumes and thereby assist in preserving an important aspect of their cultural heritage. It is hoped that a complete collection of Arabian costumes of bygone ages will be housed eventually in a national folklore museum in Saudi Arabia.

Heather Colyer Ross
Riyadh
SEPTEMBER 1981

Introduction

Of the many fascinating facets of desert culture revealed to the world since Arabia's emergence from obscurity, none is more interesting than traditional Arabian costume. Clothing, it has been said, reflects the aesthetic sensibilities of man, and is therefore revealing. So, in taking a closer look at Arabia's costume traditions, there is an opportunity to learn more about Arabs and their culture.

The word "Arabia" has generally conjured up romantic images. Long before Arabia stepped into the centre of the world's stage after the discovery of oil, the romance of this largely arid land with its mysteriously veiled past captured the imagination of scholars and adventurers. It is not surprising, therefore, that since greater opportunity now presents itself, the West has begun to exhibit interest in the Arabian Peninsula from an historical point of view.

It has been said that the increased interest in Arabian garb is merely the result of the petrodollar. It is also claimed that the world of fashion, through a natural course of evolvement, is independently rediscovering classic forms. While both arguments are valid, the fact remains that the Crusaders of the eleventh century were so impressed with Middle Eastern costume that they took the styles home with them, an action which is recorded as having influenced Medieval European dress for centuries. Also, in 1911, Paul Poiret, the most famous French couturier of his time – inspired by Islamic miniatures and the ballet "Scheherazade" – launched his haute couture versions of Middle Eastern fashions. Today, Yves Saint Laurent, an equally influential Parisian couturier, habitually includes an Arabian touch to his couture and ready-to-wear collections.

Despite this, traditional Arabian costume has not been documented. It has merely been noticed. For instance, crafty London boutiques currently sell an assortment of Arab gear gained from the increased traffic with Arabia, but it is generally sold without knowledge. Unfortunately they don't know much about what they are selling, and the buyer is attracted merely by the exotic quality rather than the traditional and historical value, and it is bought without any desire to wear it as it should be worn.

Interest is heightened when Western women, who have lived for a time on the Arabian Peninsula, cause a stir by wearing authentic Bedouin dresses. The appeal of desert garb is instant. The glamour of some is unmistakable. These gowns have a magic truly their own.

While the first garments ever created by man were undoubtedly utilitarian, prehistoric art confirms that costume underwent artistic evolution no less than painting, sculpture and jewellery. Accepting this, and knowing that Islamic art has influenced crafts such as jewellery, it becomes intriguing to learn how important Islam has been to Arabian costume by maintaining ancient style features.

Costumes of bygone ages, echoing romantic origins, hold a strange fascination for modern man. It is this interest that has led many countries to carefully preserve their traditional dress which is sometimes worn for special festivals. In Arabia, traditional costume is still an integral part of everyday life, but the garments worn now are merely styles evolved from the true traditional costumes, and because they have been accepted so readily by the world at large, there has been a danger of entirely losing the genuine article.

There are many misconceptions about how Arabians lived and dressed long ago, due to the scanty reports made by the few early explorers. Reports were also biased because they travelled in Arabia's difficult times causing them to see superimposed austerity rather than the evidence of an opulent past.

For the romantics among us, desert life conjures up visions of spacious tents with exotic, dimly-lit interiors, richly decorated with Oriental carpets. The inhabitants recline or pad about noiselessly, wearing diaphanous, flowing robes and priceless jewels. Outside, against a background of undulating sand dunes and clear desert skies, gallant Arabs stand, their splendid robes billowing. In the background, long, colourful camel caravans move on, loaded with trade treasure. Literature tells us of this facet of Arabian life as well as the harshness of a desert existence. Whatever the reality, which lies somewhere in between, we can see for ourselves traces of past grandeur in garments, jewellery, tent and camel accoutrements, all displaying a wealth of style and colour and suggesting a rich ethnic heritage.

Despite three hundred years of Ottoman rule, the life Arabians led in the deserts before this century, surprisingly, did not mean a totally spartan existence for all. Great and wealthy tribal *sheikhs* as well as rich townsmen were well able to clothe their ladies and themselves in fine garments. Particularly in the period when camels were in demand and trade was prospering, well-to-do Arabian ladies could wear fine fashions from Baghdad, Damascus and other far away places. They received gifts of beautiful Chinese silks often embroidered for them in India.

Some traditional Arabian dresses were sewn and embroidered within the Arabian Peninsula from locally-spun and hand-woven textiles, while others were made up from plain or pre-embroidered imported dresslengths. Since ancient times, exotic and utilitarian textiles have been carried along the trade routes for the settled, semi-settled and nomadic Arabians.

Very few foreign people who have lived in Arabia since the discovery of oil have had the opportunity to see the indigenous people in their captivating desert attire. Neither has it been possible to read about this aspect of their culture since the early explorers paid little attention to costume, particularly pertaining to women – no doubt discouraged by Islamic modesty. And there are indications that, even in the nineteenth century, hard times were having an adverse effect upon Arabian handicrafts.

Since that time, desert women have acquired sewing machines and handwork has all but ceased. A further contributing factor to the decline in crafts was the introduction to Arabia of wheeled transport which increased the pace of life. As a consequence, the Arab woman has less time for such things as needlework. Furthermore, stepped-up trade with the outside world has resulted in the ready availability of inexpensive factory-made garments. Beautiful home-spun, hand-woven, hand-sewn and hand-embroidered Arabian garments are increasingly difficult to find. Locally-spun, hand-woven textiles are very rare indeed, and it is inevitable that needlework, as part of a woman's domestic skills, will also cease. Only in remote pockets of Arabia will we find settled, semi-settled and nomadic people wearing the totally hand-made traditional dress of their tribe.

Traditional Arabian garment styles, as well as their textile and embroidery colour combinations, are beautiful and enduring fashion-wise. Yet, these exciting styles are being supplanted by Western gear. Even in those parts of Arabia where nomads still wear regional dress, inter-tribal influence has now modified the pure forms and the threat of progress is ever encroaching. It is inevitable that old Arabian costume will totally fade into history. It has left the cities and most of the towns and crafts have vanished from many of the villages. It is expected that the last vestiges of Arabian traditional costume will disappear along with the hand-loomed tents which gave shelter to those stoic women who chose to wear bold silver and gold jewellery and hand-embroidered dresses.

It is likely that the world is witnessing the end of the old Arabian way of life and its costumes as a functional aspect of daily life. It is encouraging to learn that the Hasa *thawb nashal* still appeals to the fashion-conscious women of Saudi Arabia. This fact, and the appreciation of these garments by many Western women, will help to keep alive at least the interest in costume. If nothing else, it is essential that these treasures be recorded and preserved as items of historic interest.

Ideally, the complete traditional costume of each town, and tribe and sub-tribe should be housed in a museum. It is unfortunate that many garment styles cannot be found.

The vast changes which have swept Arabia into the twentieth century are appreciated by the people. There is no doubt that they now enjoy a broader role in community life, as well as an increased opportunity to live comfortably. Young men who have availed themselves of the opportunities of government-sponsored university and technical training abroad, have returned to help develop their countries on the Peninsula. While the progress is worthy and exciting, it would be a pity if it were gained at the cost of losing ethnic costume traditions. It would be as well to ponder the words of Walter A. Fairservis, Junior:

"The aesthetic loss to the world of the unembarrassed, full-fledged, and prideful use of splendid costume traditions is a great one but what that loss means locally in terms of self-identity, security, and progress is incalculable."

Artist's impression of a
northern dress featuring
exquisite embroidery. The
motifs include stylized trees
and plants. Full details in
Embroidery.

Foreword

Traditional costume is part of Saudi Arabia's national folklore and, as such, is an important aspect of our cultural heritage. It is a facet of Arabian culture that was almost passed over in the Kingdom's drive towards modernity; despite the unquestioned beauty of these colourful costumes, few people sought to preserve them and very little was written about them. The author introduces this fascinating subject at a time when traditional Arabian costume is passing into history. In the future, there will be folklore museums established throughout the Kingdom and collections of costumes from bygone ages will stand beside other traditional Arabian handicrafts and artistic works. We therefore appreciate the perseverance of the author in her efforts to document this passing phase of Saudi Arabian culture.

It is acknowledged that costume reveals a great deal about the wearer and this book therefore presents an opportunity for the reader to learn more about the people of Saudi Arabia. As a reference book, it will be of particular benefit to the world of fashion – an industry that has already acknowledged the originality, versatility and fascination of Arabian styles.

With the focus presently on the Middle East, this book is welcomed as it conveys the role of Islam in the costume and customs of traditional Arabia. The author points out how Islam has maintained ancient costume shapes – and is responsible for preserving modest attire for both men and women right up to the present day – particularly in Saudi Arabia where the population is totally Muslim. Islam is not only a ritual of worship but is also a philosophy that deals with all aspects of human life – regulating the relationship between God and His believers, and man's relationship with his fellow man. The author conveys how Islamic art has played an important part in the story of Arabian costume and it is without a doubt the right moment for traditional Arabian costume to take its place with other forms of Islamic artistic expression and achievement.

In conclusion, I would like to thank the author for her interest in our heritage. This is manifested in this book and in her previous book about Bedouin jewellery. I believe The Art of Arabian Costume *is an excellent book which will serve as a basis for further work – perhaps separate books covering the costumes traditional to each region of the Kingdom. For the moment, the book stands as an introduction to the subject and will undoubtedly result in the emergence of additional information.*

Abdulaziz H. Al-Sowayyegh
Assistant Deputy Minister of Information
Kingdom of Saudi Arabia
SEPTEMBER 1981

Appearance

The English explorer, Charles Doughty (1843–96) who travelled in the north-west and west-central Arabia, recorded the famed appearance of Arabian women: "There are none more comely women than in the Arabian Peninsula. They appear gracious in the simplest garments".

H. R. P. Dickson, a noted Arabist who served in eastern Arabia as the British Political Agent in the 1930's, writes that Bedouin women were "as vain as women the world over, loving above everything to deck themselves out in fine clothes".

It would seem that Arabian women of the past were just as fashion conscious as their modern counterparts. The immediate differences are that today, instead of keeping their garments neatly folded in great wooden dowry chests, Arabian women hang their gowns in built-in wardrobes and their labels read "London", "Paris", "Rome" and "New York". Women's social gatherings in Arabia today further attest to a love for beautiful attire, as they are fashion shows in themselves.

Another obvious similarity between Arab dress of the past and that of the present is its total coverage. Despite progress, the women of Arabia still dress modestly, adhering to Islamic lore by choosing flowing and flattering but unrevealing gowns. The Prophet Muhammed's teaching encouraged maidens and matrons alike to maintain modesty in attire as well as behaviour. The resultant mystique is undoubtedly ultra-feminine. If it can be said that modesty, mystique and haute couture are the ingredients for allure, then the women of Arabia have justifiable claim to it.

As for high fashion, Paris has for decades given close attention to Arabian apparel – producing chic French translations of classic Arab shapes. The West has long admired the *kaftan*, *kuffiyyah* and the turban too.

In the Middle East, since ancient times, it has been the custom to cover the entire body except, perhaps, parts of the face, hands and feet. This was done to protect the body from the elements. Suntanning, a relatively recent Western fad, never attracted oriental people. It was introduced to the West by the famous fashion model Coco Chanel in the 1930s.

From time immemorial, costume in the Middle East has had a loose, flowing quality and a distinctive element has been headgear. The various headcloths serve to present an aesthetically pleasing appearance while offering protection from the strong sun and blowing sand.

As with jewellery and other forms of body ornamentation, clothing indicates appearance consciousness. Within Arabia, it has steadily maintained its importance through thousands of years of turbulent history. Clothing is especially appreciated by the Bedouin – colourful costumes are still one of their main luxuries. Many of their tra-

ditional celebrations call for new clothing and guests at a wedding may change garments two or three times as the festivities progress over a period of days. The special dresses brought out or newly made for such an occasion by the female guests are sometimes known as wedding dresses for this reason. In fact, there was often very little difference between the gowns worn by the bride and guests, at least in cut.

Professor Motoko Katakura described the Bedouin women of Wadi Fatimah, Western Arabia, as "elegant in their traditional clothes". Her eyes saw them as "appealing in colourful animation . . . interacting in their daily lives before the monochromatic background of the harsh desert".

Professor Katakura spent enough time with the Bedouin to observe how important dress was to the womenfolk at the time of a wedding. In wadi Fatimah, on the day before the wedding, all the *hareem* (married women) don their special dresses for the luncheon banquet party. The unmarried girls, also in new dresses, are not permitted to sit with the married women at this party but remain with the bride screened by a special curtain.

Again, around noon on the wedding day, the *hareem* assume new finery especially for the wedding party. The bride then changes into a pink or red dress and, after a brief meeting with her betrothed, joins the *hareem* for the first time and is entertained with singing and dancing to the accompaniment of music played by women. The donning of the garment would seem essential to the full enjoyment of the ritual.

Most Arabian women also make a new dress for the *Eid al Fitr*, the festival following Ramadan, the holy month of fasting; and for the *Eid al Adha*, the festival of the Pilgrimage to Mecca. The menfolk and children also wear new clothes on these occasions. The men of Arabia enjoy dressing in fine new garments for special occasions just as much as they enjoy a feast with family and friends.

Hospitality, for which the people of Arabia pride themselves, is conspicuous at weddings. On this important social occasion guests can number many hundreds, which tends to make the festivities tumultuous. Women dance indoors wearing their finest garments and displaying their jewellery – their appearance presenting a moving kaleidoscope of colour. In traditional Arabia, men and

Above: *Artist's impression of a Central Arabian fustan which is commonly cut from floral cotton today. Although the seams are often machined, the tribal pattern embroidery is still hand-done. The silk patches are invariably cerise and orange. Silver balls trim the cuffs. The style of Bedouin dress confines its embellishment to the sleeves which are displayed when worn under the wide-sleeved thawb. Full details are given in the sections dealing with the Najd and under Embroidery.*

women danced and sang on separate days, beginning with the day for men to celebrate, usually out of doors, when they performed the sword dance to the accompaniment of drums. The men wear their best which, although uniform today, looks spectacular en masse.

In days gone by, when an Arab met a stranger, he could tell at a glance a great deal from his appearance, especially from his weaponry, for even a townsman wore a dagger of some sort. A tribesman could be placed by his cartridge belt buckling, while the traveller conveyed whether he was from the north or the south by the coconut fibre or palm-frond pad under his camel saddle. The way he wore his head-cloth, loosely or more closely wound, the stitching on his shirt, the folds of his loin-cloth, the leather cover of his rifle, the pattern on his saddle bags, the way his rug was folded above them, and even the way he walked would reveal his identity.

Tribal society structure fostered appearance traditions and signs were particularly manifest in the embroidery and decoration on garments and trappings. Although much of the tribal and sub-tribal variations in costume have been lost forever, it is still possible to place old Arabian garments regionally.

Bedouin appearance is created by a combination of dress, ornamentation and tribal custom involving hairdressing and beauty culture. However, the old ways are rapidly mellowing and appearance is no longer revealing. Today, clothing and hairstyles, especially for the men of Arabia, are almost identical throughout the Peninsula.

Jewellery was traditionally worn in profusion by the women and jewels were also appliquéd to garments and entwined in the hair. Bedouin body ornament included kohl for the eyes, henna to stain the skin, and tattoos for more permanent beauty marks.

Throughout the Middle East, there is similarity of appearance amongst the nomadic peoples. There is also a resemblance to be seen in the traditional dress which used to be worn by the townspeople who tended to give up traditional ways sooner than their rural counterparts.

Village women in Arabia, like their nomadic sisters, favour their loose-fitting, ankle-length dress with long sleeves. The sleeves vary from straight and slightly narrowed at the wrists to wide and sometimes flared. The latter kind, which usually end with a deep lappet, are worn wrist-length or much longer than the arm, as a rule, with the lappet often reaching the garment's hemline. These sleeves are usually pinned to the shoulders or knotted together and dropped over the head to be worn behind when greater freedom of movement is required.

The cut of the Middle Eastern *kaftan* does not hinder domestic activity – flared side panelling radiating from under the arms to ankle-length or calf-length hemlines allows comfort and freedom of movement – in active as well as squatting or reclining positions. It contrasts cleverly with cumbersome gathered garments which form part of the traditional costumes from so many other lands.

Arabian women's traditional dresses are entrancing – exhibiting great visual appeal. The colour hues in harmonious combinations serve to make Bedouin costume unique. Embellishment is generally exotic. Most Bedouin women's gowns are still richly embroidered today and even when the work is machine-done, it is handsome.

Each region's embellishment varies and within each area there are further variations. Even when there is a determined tribal style, there are subtle differences within the traditional rules for designs and thread colour juxtaposition as each embroiderer applies his own artistic interpretation – this results in highly original versions of age-old formats. The stitchery is generally extremely fine and sometimes quite exquisite – often good enough to equal the finest Victorian samplers. Although necklines, bodices, cuffs, hems and side gores can be accented with embroidery, traditional placement varies from region to region. Imported traditional dresses often carry metallic thread work and sequins on each pattern segment as well as over each seam.

Bedouin costumes provide a striking contrast to the desert background – the rich colours creating a beautiful impression, particularly when several women are gathered together for a festival. Dress materials of the prosperous Bedouin have always been silk, brocade, satin and velvet, while cotton and wool are worn by the poor. Rich or poor, a love of colour prevails, and the simplest indigo-dyed calico garments often feature exotic appliqué and embroidery and are sometimes bejewelled.

It is surprising to hear people exclaim that it is a pity Arabian women always wear black. This is a very superficial observation, obviously the result of the false impression conveyed by the black outer cloak which women wear when venturing outside the home. It is true, however, that darker colours are considered more acceptable for elders while light colours are generally reserved for the young.

Because Bedouin women love colour and glitter, they can often be seen carrying out the most mundane chores clad in magnificent materials. The nature of metallic-threaded satins and brocades allows their dresses to maintain some splendour despite heavy use. The predominantly favoured colours are crimson, cerise, rose, purple, orange and green.

The outer garment or mantle which Arabian women find fashionable today is plain black and unembellished. In the past, a townswoman's cloak was also black as a rule, but embellished with gold embroidery and gold tassels. Sometimes the mantle was a plain or striped sheet, clutched about the body – the plain black versions decorated with silver, mother-of-pearl, appliqué and embroidery. For the Arab man, the modern cloak is edged with gold braid which looks rich and even opulent contrasted with some of the alternative colours that range from beige, honey and cinnamon to black. In the past, the man's mantle was often quite colourful.

Although the man's *kaftan*, the *thawb*, is made of a plain textile, which is generally white, self-coloured braid and soutache is often used to enhance the garment. *Thawbs* invariably look impeccably neat because of the simplicity of design. The entire outfit of *thawb*, cloak and headcloth presents an image of rare sartorial elegance.

14

The Historical Background

The first known Arabian civilizations are believed to be three coastal settlements and the oldest evidence, so far, of civilized man on the Peninsula was found on the north-east coast, dated 5000 BC. The artefacts found on this site are identical to those of the Ubaid culture of Mesopotamia – the valley between the Tigris and Euphrates Rivers – on the east side of the Fertile Crescent which arches across the northern borders of Arabia.

From about 4000 to 2000 BC it appears that the Dilmun civilization dominated the eastern coast of Arabia, extending sixty miles into the interior to the oasis of Hofuf and including present-day Kuwait and the island of Bahrain. At its zenith, in 2000 BC, Dilmun controlled the route to the Indies and was the trading link between the civilizations of the Indus Valley and those of Mesopotamia. In Oman and Abu Dhabi, further south, remains of other civilizations have been found which may well prove to be related to Dilmun.

Some historians theorize that Arabia was only sparsely populated in the interior until about 3000 BC and that thereafter people began to migrate there from both north and south. It is also believed that as climatic conditions changed and deserts encroached upon arable land, those who remained developed a way of life suitable for desert living which has been maintained to this present day. The lifestyle of the settled people living on the periphery of the Peninsula is also believed to have been constant through centuries.

Archaeological evidence suggests that approximately once every thousand years people migrated from the Arabian peninsula to the more tenable lands around them. There were apparently several major migrations to Egypt in the fourth millennium BC, at the same time that others would seem to have turned east to amalgamate with the people of Sumer who were later known as Babylonians. It appears that, in the third millennium BC, migrants from the Peninsula merged with the Fertile Crescent Canaanites and the Phoenicians (collectively known as Amorites). Further migrants settled in Syria in the second millennium BC, and were among the ancestors of the Aramaeans or modern Syrians. The others, who are believed to have settled in southern Syria and Palestine, would be among the forebears of the Hebrews.

Sometime in the third millennium BC, the peoples of Mesopotamia and Egypt discovered that southern Arabia possessed two desirable gum resins, frankincense and myrrh. Egyptian records describe expeditions to Dhofar to collect them. Both of these commodities had a large market in the ancient world. Frankincense, *boukhor*, was the chief incense burned as an offering to the many "gods" and was also used lavishly in cremations. Myrrh, *morr*, was a major ingredient in many cosmetics, perfumes and medicaments. Until quite recently, it was believed that foreigners initially monopolized this trade until Arabian descendants returned from eastern Jordan and southern Iraq. This theory accounted for evidence of the early use of technology known in the north, since they are believed to have returned with irrigation techniques, metallurgical and ceramic skills, an alphabetical script and a developed art. In any case, it appears that the southerners formed a confederation of states out of their Kingdoms of Saba (Sheba), Qataban, Hadramaut, Ma'in, Himyar and Ausan.

A huge and complex commercial network comprising both land and sea routes was established by the people of southern Arabia. In addition to exporting their own fruits, rare spices, a coveted coffee, cotton and heady perfumes, they became middle-men for trade between India and the Horn of Africa. Southern Arabia was bountiful. It was self-sufficient in food and other basic goods and the people had only to import luxury items.

Not having rivers, they designed an ingenious irrigation system which used seasonal rain. Dams were built to direct water to irrigation canals. The unique Marib Dam in particular testifies to the high degree of technical skill and knowledge attained by southern Arabians three thousand years ago.

Excavations of ancient sites reveal that the cities were unwalled, leading historians to believe that the people enjoyed a life free of threatening elements. This fact, and the belief that all the goods in which the Arabs traded were products of southern Arabia, led writers of old to coin the name "Arabia Felix", happy and prosperous Arabia.

Since navigation in the northern Red Sea was dangerous, Arab traders usually avoided it. Instead, goods came by ship from points east across the Indian Ocean and were unloaded at the port of Aden. From there they travelled overland through Arabia to the markets of the western Mediterranean coast, Mesopotamia and Egypt. The system developed with the domestication of the camel which was best able to carry heavy burdens over difficult terrain.

Caravan cities sprang up along the overland routes further north, becoming virtual colonies of southern Arabia. The early cities which gained

Overleaf: Long ago, Arabia was the hub of a thriving network of trade routes. Arabs controlled most of these routes which reached out to link up with traffic from China, Phoenicia and the land of the Vikings. These paths traversed territories inhabited by a myriad of races. Trade was the portal through which influence passed. Through commerce, men were able to develop ideas and their costumes took on overtones from a mixture of civilizations. The textiles ranged from coarse cotton from Egypt to sumptuous silk from Cathay. Costume embellishment could have been pure gold from the heart of Africa, precious gems from Sri Lanka or fabulous furs from Northern Europe. Overland, the camel became the most important beast of burden because it could survive with little water. On the sea, the Arabs held trade supremacy for centuries, and transported treasured commodities from far-away lands together with their own prized frankincense and myrrh.

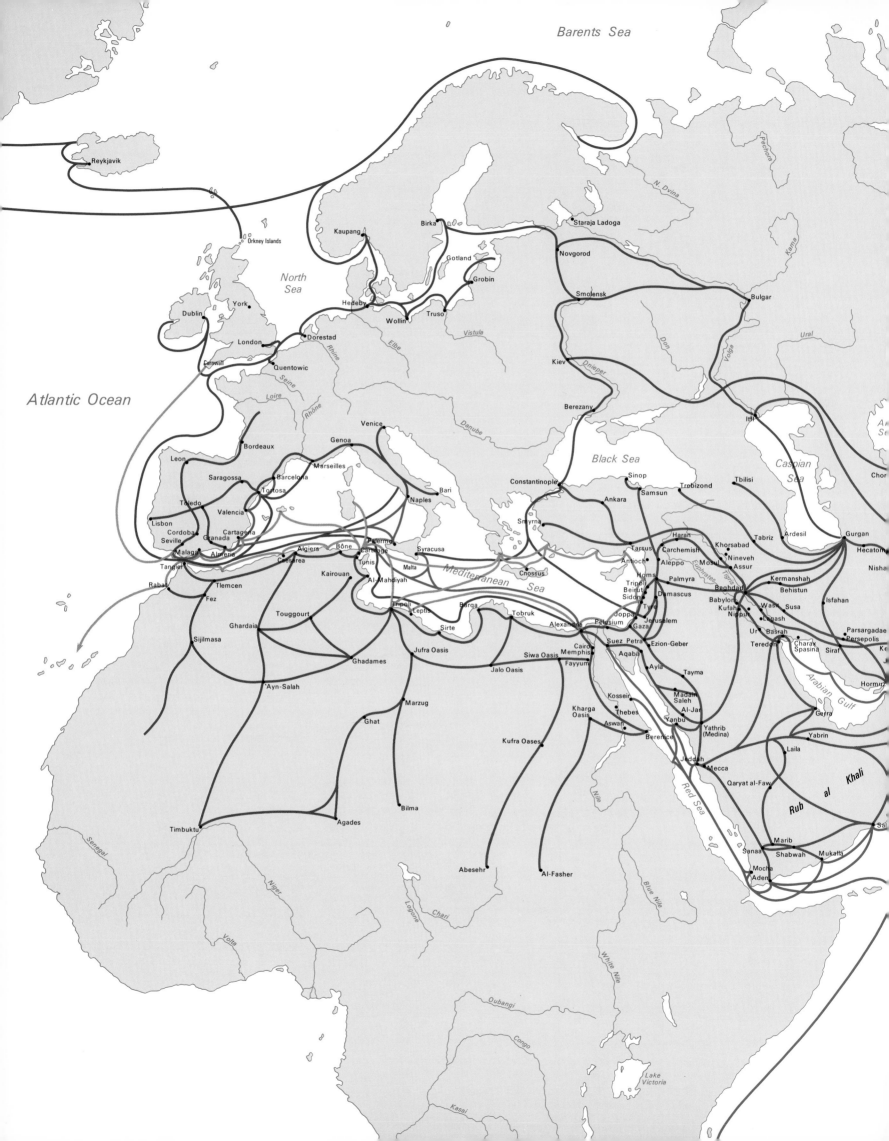

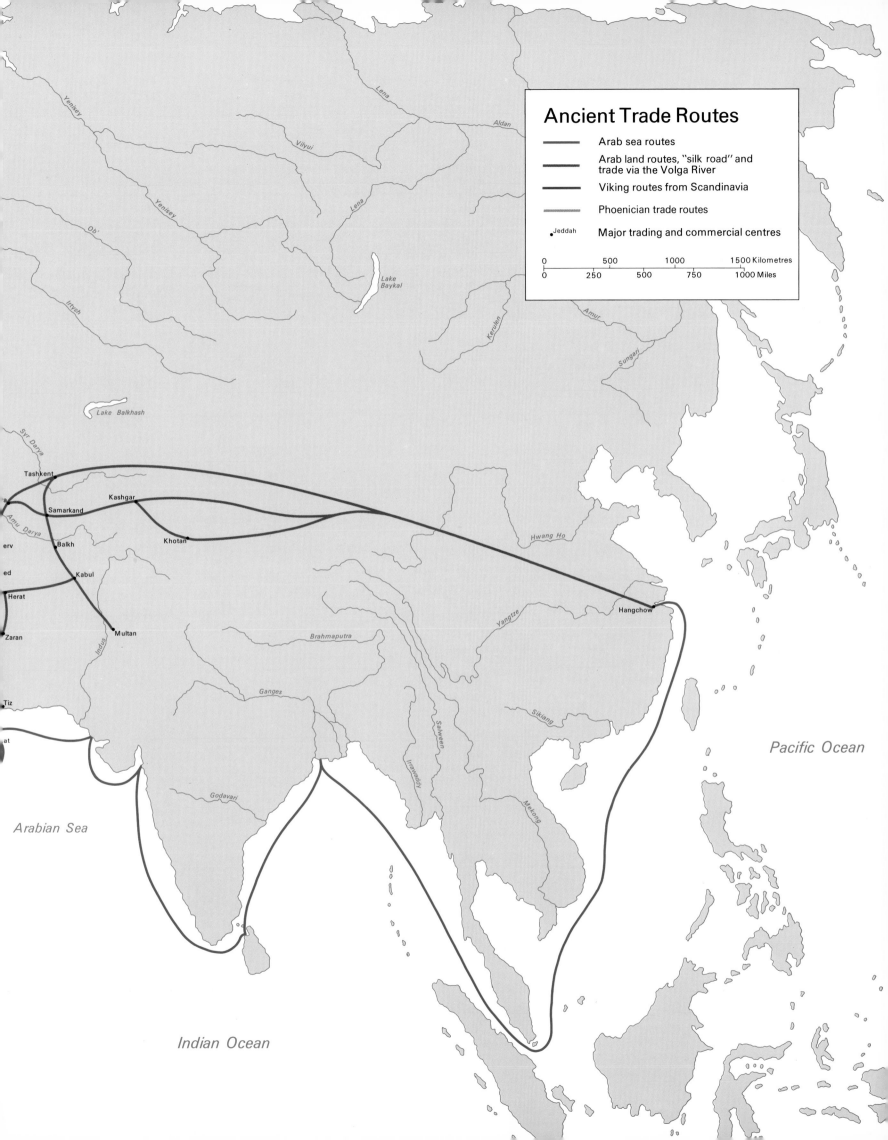

Ancient Trade Routes

Arab sea routes

Arab land routes, "silk road" and trade via the Volga River

Viking routes from Scandinavia

Phoenician trade routes

•Jeddah Major trading and commercial centres

| 0 | 500 | 1000 | 1500 Kilometres |

| 0 | 250 | 500 | 750 | 1000 Miles |

Yenisey

Yenisey

Ob'

Irtysh

Lena

Lena

Vilyui

Aldan

Lake Baykal

Kerulen

Amur

Sungari

Lake Balkhash

Syr Darya

Tashkent

Amu Darya

Samarkand

Kashgar

erv

Balkh

Khotan

ed

Kabul

Herat

Multan

Hwang Ho

Zaran

Indus

Brahmaputra

Yangtze

Hangchow

Tiz

Ganges

Godavari

Salween

Irrawaddy

Sikiang

Mekong

Pacific Ocean

Arabian Sea

Indian Ocean

importance in the medieval period were Mecca, Yathrib (Medina), Palmyra and Petra.

A most interesting northern Arabian kingdom was that of the Nebataeans, whose capital city was Petra in present-day Jordan. The Nebataeans, recorded as an Arab tribe of the Hijaz, gained control of the northern caravan trade at the end of the first millennium BC. By the first century BC their influence spread deep into the Peninsula and the beautiful city Hijr was built, rivalling Petra. It is now known as Madain Saleh. This centre was important for trade during the Hellenic and early Roman periods about 350 BC and about 100 AD respectively. Today, Petra is affectionately known as "the rose red city, half as old as time". Madain Saleh, deserted centuries ago, is the subject of Bedouin legends, but her beauty lay silent until quite recently as this majestic city was secreted away in a desolate place.

In the fourth century AD, the civilizations of Arabia Felix began a slow decline which some scholars believe started as early as the first century BC, heralded by an attack in the north by the covetous Romans. As southern Arabia's trade monopoly weakened, the various caravan cities began to assert their own control with trade tolls. Competition had begun in the third century BC, when the Ptolemaic merchant marine had re-opened the Nile–Red Sea Canal. When the Romans captured Egypt in the first century BC this competition intensified. Then Petra, Palmyra and north-west Mesopotamia were incorporated into the Roman Empire.

Greek shippers eventually learned the secrets of the monsoon winds and were able to travel successfully between India and Alexandria. It was then discovered that many goods thought to be of Arabian origin were from other lands.

The final crushing blow to happy and prosperous southern Arabia came in the fourth century when the Roman Empire accepted Christianity and simple burials without frankincense and myrrh were ordained. Various historians believe the collapse of the Marib Dam in the sixth century also contributed to the demise of Arabia Felix. The Marib Dam, which had irrigated four thousand acres of land, collapsed from massive silting. Its destruction justified the departure of many Arabs who sought homes in Syria and Mesopotamia.

From around the fifth century, north-west Arabia fell under the influence of the Ghassanids who claimed descent from the southern tribes of Arabia. They, in turn, were under the influence of Byzantium at that time. Trade had not ceased with the decline of the south. The northern markets still existed and the Hijaz prospered as a result, growing in importance. About this time, north-east Arabians, the Lakhmids of the Kingdom of Hira, were under the protection of the Sassanid Persians. In the south, the remains of the Himyarite Kingdom were controlled first by the Christian Abyssinians and later by the Persians. The Kinda tribe of Central Arabia were meanwhile making the first attempts to unite the interior of the Peninsula and gained brief power over Hira, only to be suppressed by the more powerful northern Arabian kingdoms.

Ancient Mecca is thought to have been a small-ish community centred about an artesian well and in close proximity to the *kaaba*, the local religious centre to which pilgrims came regularly. It was an active trading centre which blossomed as the south faded. In the seventh century, the Prophet Muhammed, born in Mecca (approximately 570), preached the religion Islam, meaning submission – to the will of God. After persecution in his birthplace, Muhammed migrated to Medina in 622, the year which marks the beginning of the Islamic calendar, *Hejiri*, referring to the migration.

Late in his life, the Prophet's message was widely accepted throughout Arabia. After death, the *khalifate* (singular *khalifa*), or successors, continued to expand the Islamic faith, spreading the word of God throughout the Middle East, North Africa and much of southern Asia.

The first four caliphs who succeeded Muhammed were called orthodox caliphs and were chosen from among his immediate followers. They controlled the expanding State of Islam from its first capital, Medina, from 632–661. After the assassination of the last orthodox caliph, the caliphate passed into the hands of the Umayyads, and the capital was removed to Damascus. The Umayyad Caliphate (661–750) came to an end with the rise of the Abbasid Caliphate (750–1258) led by Abbas, the Prophet's uncle. The Abbasid Caliphate transferred the Islamic capital to Baghdad, where they ruled for five hundred years in spite of political dischord which pervaded that epoch. Fragmentation of the Islamic Empire set in, although the spiritual authority of the caliph was usually acknowledged.

Ruled from Baghdad, the Islamic Empire rejoiced in what is now known as the Golden Age because art, science, philosophy, mathematics, literature and the creative skills of the hand developed and flourished, reaching their zenith in the ninth to tenth centuries.

Since the capital of the Islamic Empire had moved to Damascus and thence to Baghdad, the Arabian peninsula was virtually a cultural and economic backwater, yet it was revered because therein lay Islam's two holiest cities, Mecca and Medina, and the *Kaaba*, to which pilgrims made their way annually.

Toward the end of the ninth century, dissidence began to develop within the Peninsula. The Abbasids grew progressively weaker, and eventually this encouraged Arabia to defy the authority of the caliphate. The rebels were not successful and thereafter disunity prevailed throughout the Peninsula, except in the Hijaz where the *Sherif* (the governor, first appointed in 966) kept control.

At the beginning of the thirteenth century, the eastern part of the Islamic Empire experienced the destructive holocaust of the Mongol invasion, which was later repeated, bringing to an end the Abbasid Caliphate in Baghdad.

This dramatic end of the Islamic Empire was barely felt on the Peninsula. The Meccan Sherifate continued to prosper, remaining virtually autonomous throughout five centuries.

Mecca's growing importance led the Ottomans to install a *Grand Mufti* (leading religious and legal official) in 1539, to oversee their interests and limit Meccan expansion (the Ottoman Empire had proclaimed western Arabia part of its dominions after conquering Egypt in 1517). From this point in history, differences grew between Arabians and Ottomans. In time, as the Ottomans became engaged with wars externally, their power within Arabia weakened. During this period, the enterprises of the Hijaz merchants spread throughout the Peninsula.

The Portuguese were responsible for a quickening of interest in the Hijaz at the end of the fifteenth century. They began to compete for the Red Sea trade but proved to be a lesser influence upon the region than the Ottomans.

In the east, trade and traffic in the Arabian Gulf, already in decline after the fall of the Abbasid Empire, came under the dominance of the Persians and they successfully ruled the Arabian shores and islands.

Egypt's inclination for commerce between Europe and Asia further accelerated the decline in Gulf trade, compounded in 1507 when the Portuguese captured Hormuz and seized control of the Omani coastline. Despite Egypt's advantage and Ottoman presence in Arabia, the Portuguese retained their strongholds in the Gulf and elsewhere in Oman and Muscat for two centuries.

Portugal was the first European maritime power to establish its presence in the peripheral states of the Peninsula. Effective control over its territories was limited however. The Portuguese held out against the Ottomans but eventually Dutch and British intrusion and the efforts of the local Arabs drove them out. In 1650, the Omanis alone defeated the Portuguese forces in their own region.

Mecca was the most important city in Arabia at that time. It was the place where northern and southern people converged. It was also the logical city for indigenous and foreign Muslims to come and enjoy themselves – to exchange ideas as well as commodities. Its growth had taken firm root in the significant remains of the ancient trade route and blossomed progressively each year with the pilgrimage and the fair at Ukaz, site of an annual poetry reading contest.

Mecca's sister city, Yathrib (Medina), three hundred miles to the north, was originally a date palm oasis along the spice route and grew, like Mecca, into a trading centre. Almost as important to the Hijaz was Tayif, six thousand feet above sea level – the summer resort of aristocratic townspeople and a rich agricultural spot which produced a variety of fruits, nuts and flowers.

Northern Arabians had developed over the centuries into great warriors. They had invented a camel saddle which gave the rider efficient control and a definite advantage over the enemy. This saddle, lodged on the camel's hump, allowed the rider to tower above them. Armed with swords and spears, these Arabs became formidable foes. Subsequently, the northern Bedouin started breeding a greater number of camels to meet their twin needs of transportation and riding.

Although the camel was necessary for survival in the desert, many considered the horse superior because it was faster and more easily manoeuvred. For this reason, Arabs also began to breed horses and this became a profitable business. Yet, for the most part, these were lean centuries for many people on the Arabian Peninsula. The turning of the tide came with the rise of the House of Saud.

Around the mid-fifteenth century, the Saud clan moved from the Qatif Oasis to the Najd and gradually branches of the family spread throughout the central region. Eventually the Sauds ruled the Najd, the "Empty Quarter" to the south, the east and the west. The Ottomans were less than pleased with the situation, particularly at losing power in Mecca and Medina. They prevailed upon their viceroy in Cairo to crush the Sauds. As a result, both Mecca and Medina were taken and the Sauds were pushed back to the Najd where Diraiyah was razed. The Najd and the east subsequently suffered Egyptian occupation. The Ottomans, still in control of the Hijaz, reached out and took over from the Egyptians, occupying the land while the Saud family weathered internal strife and the growing opposition of the Rashid family who governed the northern province of Jabal Shammar from Hayil.

Muhammed ibn Rashid, the administrator and general of Jabal Shammar had much of the Najd under his control when he forced the Sauds from Riyadh. The family lived thereafter in exile in Kuwait. Among them was Abd al Aziz, the young boy destined to restore the Najd to the Sauds and found the Kingdom of Saudi Arabia.

In 1902, Abd al-Aziz ibn Abd al-Rahman Al Saud, aged twenty-one, recaptured Riyadh with a band of less than fifty men. His father abdicated his title of *amir* in favour of his son who became known far and wide as Ibn Saud. Ibn Saud was successful in ousting the Rashidis and their Ottoman allies from Hasa and re-established Saudi rule in the Najd. Although blackmailed by the Ottomans into submitting to their suzerainty for a time, Ibn Saud eventually freed the Central Province, following this feat by eliminating them from Hasa and the area from Kuwait to Qatar in 1913.

The First World War brought the Ottoman Empire to an end and their garrisons gradually left Arabia. In 1924, Ibn Saud entered Mecca for the first time and the following year re-opened the country to other pilgrims, guaranteeing them safe passage to the Holy Cities. In 1926, he was proclaimed King of the Hijaz and, in 1927, he became King of the Hijaz, Najd and its dependencies. Finally, in 1932, Ibn Saud proclaimed that his united realm was to be called the Kingdom of Saudi Arabia.

The Kingdom accounts for approximately eighty percent of the Arabian Peninsula, estimated at between 864 and 869 thousand square miles. The Peninsula's other countries comprise a sultanate, an emirate, an island sheikhdom, and republics.

The world has come to know more about the Arabian Peninsula in the last few decades because of oil. The oil industry has been developed since the early thirties, and today the Kingdom of Saudi Arabia, Kuwait, Bahrein and the United Arab Emirates are mentioned daily in international media. Arabia's fabulous past has faded to almost total obscurity. The slate was wiped clean for history to paint in the new scene – the bustling, burgeoning modern cities where Arabians are prospering once more.

Influence

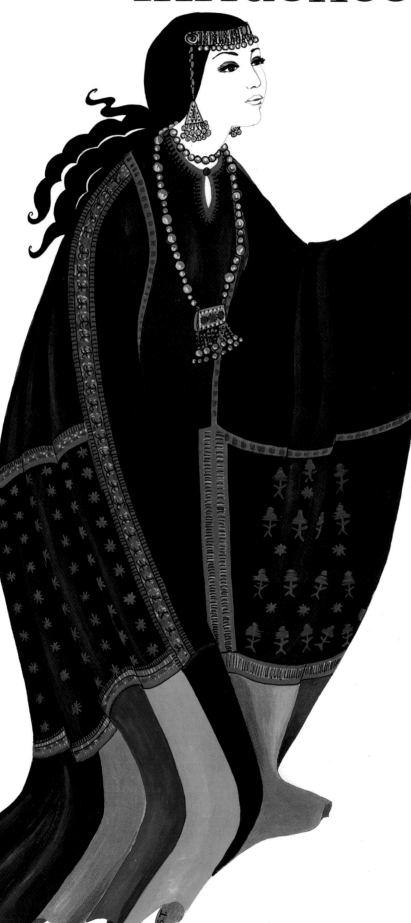

At the dawn of history, just as now, the uneven distribution of natural resources brought men together. The beginnings of trade saw one civilization influence another. But, even before men began to trade, they were influenced by their immediate world.

For clothing, at first man had to use those materials he could easily obtain and the topography of his region influenced him in how he made them up. Once adapted to his surroundings, pride and awareness would see him experiment and modify his garments, improving upon earlier decisions, especially after being exposed to foreign influence.

Wars, including both tribal scuffles and great

Artist's impression of the traditional Najdi thawb. Graceful folds form modestly elegant lines.

territorial clashes, modified ethnic costume. Throughout history, invasions and migrations were greatly responsible for cross-influences upon garment styles. When documentation is available, either in the form of rock art, written records, prints, sketches, paintings or photographs, it becomes possible to clearly trace foreign influence. Writers from 400 to 700 AD, describe foreigners in the Middle East as wearing close-fitting garments and trousers – a style of dress believed to have originated with the nomadic people of the Mongolian Steppes and other cold east Asian regions. Among these nomadic people were the Huns (ancestors of the Turks and Monguls) who may well have been responsible for bringing the fashion for wearing long pants to the Arabian Peninsula.

Many details about costume influence in recent times were unearthed through the memories of the elderly and it was first of all necessary to establish exactly what was traditional Arabian costume. In a tribal society on a large land mass such as the Peninsula, it was to be expected that the varied topography within the different zones would produce marked differences in ethnic costume, and, as the people shared a common heritage, it was logical to expect a unifying theme throughout the regions.

As tribal society structure weakened on the Peninsula, especially during this century, it has become increasingly difficult for ethnic groups to maintain their traditional costumes. Progress has totally obscured regional differences in many parts of Arabia already, especially in the east. It is said that Arabian women, even in remote areas, ceased to make their garments by hand several decades ago when the sewing machine reached them. Fortunately, these women so enjoyed their traditional garments that they continued to perpetuate old styles.

Although the basic garment and the mode of dress throughout the Middle East are similarly based on those from times past, varied life-styles have wrought individual changes, establishing differences between the garments worn by townspeople, nomads, mountain dwellers and by those from arid desert villages. At first glance, therefore, the costumes sometimes look dissimilar, but this impression is misleading. Close observation confirms their similarity in that they all provide total coverage and comfort whether the wearer is sitting, reclining or moving. The secret is in the shared basic pattern.

From the time that the ancient trade routes were established, men from widely separated lands were able to influence one another, not merely by mutual exposure but by trading textiles, trimmings and ready-made garments. Visitors to the Peninsula would sell their commodities and use the proceeds to obtain what they needed, or thought their home market might desire from Arabia's surplus. From the earliest times cargoes included lengths of textiles which ranged from the most

Cerise, gold and green silk appliqué combined with bold embroidery to enliven indigo blue/black cloth.

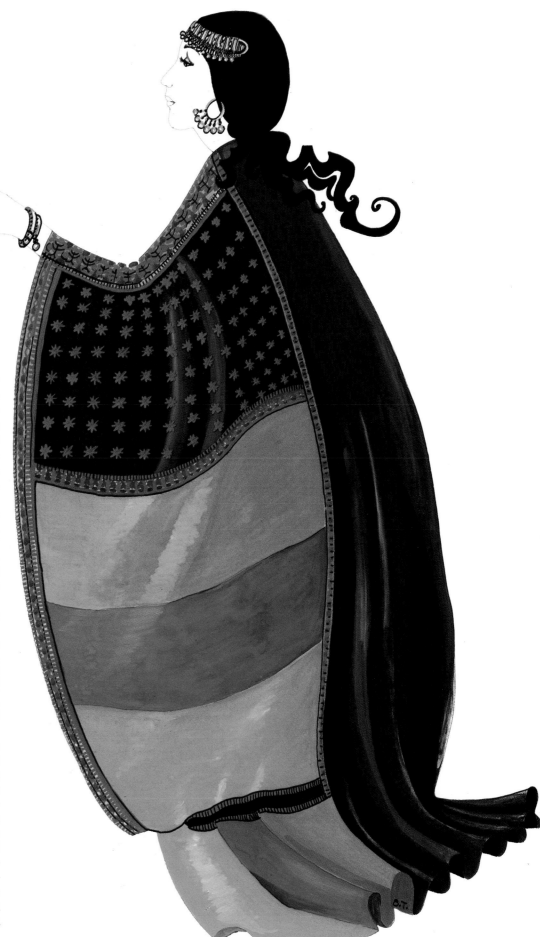

practical to the exotic. Silk from China was worn in Egypt and cotton from Egypt might return to China. The Arabian Peninsula imported cotton and silk because it had only wool, camel and goat hair and a little cotton. In return for the esteemed frankincense and myrrh – and it was the finest – the Arabs could obtain almost anything their hearts desired.

With the spread of Islam in the seventh century, the two holy cities, Mecca and Medina, not only received pilgrims from afar but also began to attract settlers because of the religious importance and flourishing nature of these centres. Garment styles were more or less uniform throughout most of the Islamic world but the superficial differences which existed no doubt insinuated themselves upon traditional Arabian costume with the arrival of peoples from other Muslim lands.

In the mid-nineteenth century, according to the Finnish explorer, Georg August Wallin, customs in western Arabian coastal villages reflected many Egyptian customs, while further inland, he felt a Syrian influence was apparent. In the Najd, it seemed to Wallin, there were traces of the Mesopotamian civilization.

In 1761, Carsten Niebuhr remarked that the people of distinction in Jeddah dressed like Turks. At this time, it is written, the poor wore only a body shirt. The Bedouin, according to Niebuhr, wore lengths of cloth wound around the lower half of their bodies. Bedouin women and the women of the lower ranks of society wore flowing *kaftans*, voluminous drawers, and a veil. Full-cut *sirwaal* and veil were elements of Turkish costume.

To some extent both Niebuhr's and Wallin's observations still hold true today, although the clear-cut images their accounts conjure up have been greatly obscured in recent decades. Yet, the mark of influence remains indelible on the traditional items of apparel which have survived. The cause of these manifestations of influence was trade: through the ages western Arabia depended heavily upon Egypt for grain and cotton; Damascus and Baghdad were chief sources of commodities desired in the Najd and Hijaz; and the Turkish occupation of the Arabian Peninsula brought some of the opulence of the Ottoman Empire into the lives of Hijazi townspeople.

The Influence at Work

Throughout history, Arabia was usually represented on maps as being approximately bounded in the north by the Fertile Crescent which curves upwards from the east, beginning at the head of the Arabian Gulf, and ends in the west at the Gulf of Aqaba.

In the days of the Roman Empire, this border for Arabia was considered accurate enough for it shut out the Bedouin tribes of Arabia from arable Mesopotamia. However, the Arabian nomads reached out, so the Euphrates was not the real boundary of Arabia. Jordan, southern Syria, Iraq and Kuwait formed an homogenous whole with Arabia, uniform in physical features and indigenous peoples. The total area is therefore the homeland of the Arab.

For costume study purposes, the Fertile Crescent is divided into two separate areas because the eastern half, Mesopotamia, and the western half, the Levant, show separate costume evolution, clearly the result of ancient regional cultural differences which have in turn been affected by varying spheres of influence.

The Levant

On the Western tip of the Fertile Crescent lies Canaan, ancient Palestine. As an important part of the route used by caravans between Egypt and Mesopotamia, Canaan was a major site of historic events.

The original inhabitants were nomadic herders from the Arabian deserts. When famine struck in about 1400 BC, they emigrated to Egypt but returned after two hundred years. Subsequent history saw their land split into two kingdoms which, like Egypt and Mesopotamia, were ruled by several empires.

Although a relatively small country, Palestine has a variety of climatic zones. To the south lies the Negev desert, primarily a nomadic area, while the rest of the land includes towns and villages scattered through plains and hills. Both climate and terrain have dictated the life-styles of the inhabitants.

The original designation of Palestine would appear to refer to the coastal area which was settled by non-Semitic people. In the late second millennium BC, Greek and Roman writers included the land to the east as far as the Arabian desert. Its borders varied through the ages, and at one time merged into the Arab Nabataean Kingdom which included the Negev desert and had its capital in Petra (now in Jordan).

Canaan, in the broadest interpretation, is part of the area which became known as the Levant. In the north of the Levantine region, along the coast, was Phoenicia, and inland and north lay Syria. Both were blessed with abundant timber and good harbours. Because of the Levant's unique geographical position, at the crossroads leading to Asia, Africa and Europe, it was subjected to two thousand years of invasions.

Palestine was particularly subject to invasion and was almost continuously under Persian influence until the introduction of Islam. Throughout the turbulence, the Levant received caravans laden with rare goods from far-off lands. The market places of Phoenician cities such as Tyre and Sidon were beehives of activity.

The men of ancient Phoenicia (modern Lebanon), having insufficient fertile land, became skilled craftsmen, clever merchants and expert seamen. To increase their sources of wealth, the Phoenicians set up trading posts throughout the Mediterranean world. They exchanged goods with many different people and, as middle-men, were able to influence the various cultures with whom they came in contact.

Phoenician ships carried home-dyed, woven and embroidered textiles, glassware, carpets and fine metalwares. Returning, they brought English tin and Baltic furs, amongst a myriad of other commodities, which helped to make the Levant a more sophisticated region. From central Africa, Phoenician caravans brought ivory; from Egypt came linen and glassware; perfumes and spices came along the Arabian trade routes to meet up with the Levantine traders.

It is the Phoenicians who are responsible for the colour "royal purple" which is the name derived from their original purple dyestuff known as "Tyrian purple", a stain extracted from shellfish. This colour was in great demand for royal robes in ancient times. It is the same colour we still have which has retained kingly connotations.

In the seventh century, when Muslims poured out of the Arabian Peninsula to spread the new religion of Islam, Palestine became a province of the Islamic Caliphate. It remained so except possibly during the Crusades (end eleventh to end thirteenth centuries).

Trade, which existed between the Islamic World and the West prior to the Crusades, was stimulated by the three hundred year intercourse between Muslims and Christians. Levantine ports flourished, and continued to do so after the departure of the Crusaders.

Palestine continued under Muslim rule until after World War One when it was cut off from the crumbling Ottoman Empire and made a British Mandate. This Mandate was originally to include Jordan. However, in 1920, Transjordan became a separate Emirate or what was the Hashemite Kingdom of old. With Palestine under British influence and Lebanon and Syria under French hegemony from 1922, it remained for the Emirate to preserve what it could of traditional society while ethnic aspects began to fade in Lebanon and Syria.

Palestine was held in great respect by early Muslims because it was the home of prophecy of the two earlier monotheistic faiths. In the *Koran* it is referred to as "the Holy Land". The second Caliph of Islam had come there in 637 from Medina (then the capital of Arabia) to pray and accept the submission of Jerusalem, thus confirming Palestine's importance to the Muslim faith.

The Umayyad Caliphs (661–750) chose nearby

Damascus as their capital, but continued to hold Palestine in particular reverence and honour. It did, however, decline in importance when the Abbasid Caliphate (750–258) moved the Islamic capital from Damascus to Baghdad in Iraq. For nearly one hundred years Palestine was under Egyptian control until the anti-Caliphate Muslims – the Shi-ite Fatimids – rose in North Africa (909–1171). Thereafter, it was taken over by the Seljuk Turks who ruled in the name of the Abbasid Caliphate.

The shifting of the Islamic seat of government to Baghdad began five hundred years of cultural evolution that provided the world with a rich source of artistic material. Although the importance of the previous one hundred years (during which Damascus cast influence over the Islamic world that extended from Spain in the west to Central Asia in the east) is generally eclipsed by the following Golden Age, it is a fact that handicrafts were highly developed in the Levant from early times. It was a relatively sophisticated area and it is therefore logical that this brief period in history caused momentous advances in the refinement of Arabian costume.

Throughout the Levant, for the average person, the basic garment had been an ankle-length, long-sleeved and loosely cut gown for both men and women whether villagers, townsfolk or Bedouin. The type and quality of textile and the embellishment revealed social class and wealth rather than racial origin.

It was part of the traditional way of life in the Levant for the rural woman to gather wool, spin, weave, sew and embroider. The common mantle was usually made of woven camel and goat hair. Palestinian cloaks were generally produced in and around weaving centres such as Nablus where the women created a special textile on primitive looms. Many Levantine men's and women's cloaks were produced in Iraq, and truly splendid examples came from the Syrian towns, Aleppo and Hamma. The commercially produced mantles worn in Arabia today are usually Syrian-made.

In the Levant's traditional range of clothing are long pants, *sirwaal* or *libas*, for men and women. These vary in style and are sometimes cut along the lines of Turkish pants which have a capacious crotch gusset. This gives the trousers great fullness.

Ottoman influence in the Levant began to fade about the time of European penetration in the early eighteenth century. Imported English textiles were thereafter adopted for traditional clothing. This was a rather subtle change in dress customs but, nevertheless, an effective destroyer of the pure traditions.

Fortunately for traditional Palestinian costume, the native textile industry revived during the last quarter of the nineteenth century, and even flourished when it was seen that locally produced cotton was more durable. Handicrafts such as weaving and embroidery, aided and encouraged by educational missions thereafter, took on a new

lease of life.

One traditional Palestinian front-opening overgarment, the *qumbaz*, worn by both men and women, resembles a dressing-gown and is said to be of Persian origin. It is virtually the same as the Arabian *baalto*. Another Levantine coat, particularly popular in the nineteenth century in both Palestine and Syria, is the *yelek*. It bears a close resemblance to the eastern Arabian *zibun* for men and women and Hijazi *zabun* for women. *Yelek* is a Turkish word for coat and the garment was possibly introduced to the Levant during Ibrahim Pasha's occupation between 1831 and 1841.

Yet another coat worn by both men and women throughout the Levant, is the *jubba*, a long *kaftan* with a centre-front opening. Such an overgarment was once worn in Arabia. The sleeves vary from narrow to wide, the latter often extending downwards from anywhere between the elbow and wrist. These sleeves can be seen still on western Arabian Bedouin dresses.

One description of the traditional male costume of Palestine might easily fit the Hijazi costume of yesterday. The male cloth belt was often cashmere in winter, and muslin in summer (heavy cotton was also a substitute). Silk items were usually embroidered in Syria. Light colours were generally worn by the young while darker shades were preferred by the elders.

In another parallel, Palestinian women's costume differed in the past only in superficial appearance for the most part. The most famous traditional dress is the *thawb malak* or queenly dress. Although recorded as the traditional Bethlehem wedding dress, it is cut approximately along the lines of the standard wedding dress patterns from various Palestinian areas. The West has come to know this gown as the Bethany Dress.

The *thawb malak* was customarily provided by the bridegroom, either complete or as an embroidered bodice panel, *qabbeh*, to be completed by the bride's family. The embroiderers of Bethlehem were famous and the wealthy could hire a specialist to complete the robe. The traditional textile was silk and the garment was made in two colours: orange or red with green or yellow. The embroidery threads were orange, purple, fuchsia, dark green, light green, pale pink and yellow. Often gold and silver metal-threads were added.

It is intriguing to note that appliquéd silk patches of orange, green and cerise are traditional additions to Central Arabian dresses, and that all the above coloured embroidery threads are also employed collectively by the Arabian Bedouin. Moreover, in the Hijaz, one style of Bedouin dress features an ornate bodice panel of high-quality workmanship that generally exceeds the standard of sewing on the main body of the garment. It seems likely there is a link between these dresses. Certainly the wide sleeves with deep lappets on the *thawb malak* are strikingly similar to those on western Arabian Bedouin dresses.

In olden times, Palestinian ladies wore a bonnet-like hat trimmed with coins, known as a *smaada* – a name shared with an Hijazi men's head cloth and one Hijazi outer wrapper traditionally worn by rural girls. There is also a coin encrusted Palestinian dowry hat, *shatweh*, with two pendant side ornaments – each hanging from above the ear – that are similar to pieces of Arabian headgear. Bonnets resembling both the aforementioned were worn by little girls in traditional Arabia, although without the heavy decoration. The colourful face masks worn in the Levant and western Arabia are similar, too, and both often display Ottoman coins.

In Syria, despite the fact that there are at least forty different traditional costumes, a basic *kaftan* shape applies to many of them. Damascus, the renowned centre of Middle Eastern couture, and for centuries the centre of Syrian and foreign costume influence, continues to produce, today, the classic *kaftan* for appreciative markets worldwide.

Syrian *kaftans* for export, range from the most elegant of gowns, embroidered with silk, gold and silver, to inexpensive stiff black cottons decorated with colourful embroidery. The favoured embroidery stitch on the latter garments is cross-stitch – as it is on many Palestinian traditional dresses. There is an obvious correlation between these Levantine ethnic dresses and those from Arabia although the embroidery stitches employed are not the same. The cross-influence responsible may have occurred in the earliest times, as waves of immigrants traversed back and forth between Arabia and the Levant. For example, it is believed that after the collapse of the Marib Dam in the sixth century, Peninsula people sought the arable lands of the north. The blending of the cultures is illuminated by means of traditional costume.

Since the dawn of Islam, the ties between the Levant and Arabia have grown stronger, yet as traditionalists, each cultural grouping has staunchly retained its individuality in costume embellishment throughout centuries.

Mesopotamia

The Mesopotamian plains, today's Iraq, are the site of many ancient cities where there were once magnificent palaces as old as the Egyptian pyramids. Egypt and Mesopotamia were contemporary civilizations, sharing almost the same period, circa 4000 BC to the sixth century BC.

Mesopotamia was a land where immigrants and invaders came, influencing and enriching with their various cultures. It was a place where ideas could be exchanged. Unlike Egypt, which ruled itself, Mesopotamia was variously controlled by the Sumerians, the Babylonians, the Assyrians and the Chaldeans. After the Chaldeans, it was dominated by many different empires including that of the Persians. After capture by Cyrus the Great in 539 BC, Mesopotamia was subject to foreign rule for more than a thousand years and was generally important as a province of an empire.

Disunity invariably sapped the energies of the Mesopotamian empires and was the cause of their

demise in 539 BC. However, as in the case of the Egyptian civilization, that of Mesopotamia is considered still alive because other peoples built upon its ancient foundations.

Although archaeologists continue to discover secrets of Mesopotamia's early history, much is still unknown. Sufficient evidence has been unearthed to confirm that the people of the Arabian Peninsula contributed greatly to the advancement of this northern land, both in the supply of new blood and in ideas. As a vigorous and perpetually changing civilization there is no doubt that it in turn influenced Arabia.

Mesopotamia felt the greatest impact of Arabian influence when Islam surged forth from the Peninsula in the seventh century. For more than one hundred years thereafter, it was a province of the Arab Empire, governed from Medina in the Hijaz and later from Damascus in Syria. When the Abbasid Caliphate was founded, Baghdad became the new capital of Islam in 750 AD, remaining so for five hundred years. Despite the common bond of Islam between the peoples of the Arabian Peninsula and of Mesopotamia, the magnificent court life in Baghdad, with its gorgeous robes, in no way resembled that of the early caliphs whose attire had been relatively simple during the time when Islam ruled from the Hijaz.

Ancient Mesopotamians, like the early Arabians, wore simple garments. From relief carvings it can be seen that the Mesopotamians wore a single ankle-length linen or woollen garment. This tunic was fringed at the hem and bound at the waist by a broad belt. The well-to-do wore jewellery and elaborate headdresses, and they carried walking sticks with engraved seals adorning the handles. Bindings of narrow strips of cloth served as cover for the legs and sandals were worn by all.

Mesopotamian merchants had made full use of their twin river highways, the Tigris and the Euphrates – the latter in particular providing ready access to the other ancient civilizations of Egypt and India. During the period when Mesopotamian trade flourished, costume tended to become extravagant. After the devastating Mongul invasion brought this to an end in 1258, the ensuing several hundred years under the Turkomans, the Persians and then the Ottomans, saw their fortunes vanish. It was finally a destitute province of a tottering Ottoman Empire, remaining dependent on agriculture for a thousand years.

Egypt

Egypt was one of the major crossroads of the ancient world. Circled by three continents, Europe, Asia and Africa, it was conveniently located sharing the Red Sea with Arabia, while enjoying a prime location on the Mediterranean Sea. Merchants found the coasts advantageous. Inland, Egyptian traders were fortunate because the Nile River served as a magnificent water highway.

Because of the rich harvests, not everyone had to farm in Egypt, so many became skilled carpenters, metalworkers, glassblowers, potters, paper-makers and weavers. Outgoing Egyptian cargoes consisted of linen, jewellery, glassware and wheat. Imports included Syrian tapestries, horses, Babylonian copper, decorated vases from Cyprus, Yemeni coffee and gold and ivory from the African countries to the south.

In antiquity, the Egyptians were active in the frankincense and myrrh markets in Arabia. When the Arabs controlled these markets, much of Egypt's wealth found its way to Arabia in return for these precious commodities. Also, in return for the Arab's famed Mokka coffee, beautiful beads and colourful striped textiles were taken to the Peninsula. After the collapse of the frankincense and myrrh market and the subsequent rise of Mecca as the major trading centre within Arabia, Egypt became Arabia's chief food supplier.

The Egyptian Empire, 1580–525 BC, said to be the world's first, ruled Ethiopia, Palestine, Phoenicia and Syria in its early centuries. Yet, from 1100 BC, it became victim of one assault after another until 525 BC, when it was conquered by the powerful Persian Empire. Since then, Egypt was dominated by many empires until this century when it became independent.

Through the ages, Egypt remained important to Arabia. When the Hijaz was relegated to the role of province of the Islamic Empire in the eighth century, the political units thereafter, which kept it secure, were usually Egyptian-based. Egypt remained an important country for the age-old reason that it held a strategic eastern Mediterranean position.

Although the *Khedive* of Egypt, in financial straits, sought British and French involvement (culminating in British control in the late nineteenth century) Egypt technically remained part of the Ottoman Empire until the end of World War One. This did much to bind Egypt to Arabia through the shared faith of Islam.

A single cotton or linen garment and sandals were enough to clothe the average ancient Egyptian in his hot climate. Noblemen dressed themselves in the finest linen which was embroidered and bejewelled according to rank. The use of socially distinctive textiles and ornamentation also applied to women.

Egyptian grooming in the earliest recorded times included frequent bathing, shaves, haircuts, manicures and pedicures. The women's makeup included lip and cheek rouge, green eyelid shadow and orange colouring for the nails. Eyebrow pencil was used by both men and women. Women's elaborate headdresses, often worn over wigs on shaved heads, were usually held in place by carved ivory pins.

It is impossible to establish exactly who was first to wear the floor-length shirt-like garment in the Middle East. Quite likely a basic body shirt was worn everywhere, evolving to suit regional requirements and finally being absorbed into the first pure-cut *kaftan*. Later, individual refinements giving characteristic regional identity would have taken place.

The traditional men's long robe of the Egyptians is called the *galabia*. The original version is ankle-length and unadorned, loose-fitting with slightly flared sleeves which curve under the arms to join side gores that contain vertically-slit pockets. It resembles the modern Arabian male *thawb* although the original Egyptian body shirt had a deep U-shaped neckline, and was designed to be worn over another body shirt which had a banded collar similar to the modern Arab *thawb*. The undergarment was generally white cotton while the *galabia* was often made from a striped textile.

Cording, and knotted buttons made from cord, are often added to the *galabia* – either in the form of self-cording made from bias-cut pieces of body textile or soutache, a cording which is slip-stitched closely into the crack of seams, particularly where yoke meets the front at the centre-front opening – and at the hem of each sleeve. Soutache is also used to form ornate loop fasteners. This decoration is occasionally seen on Arabian *thawbs* today, though with a more restrained application.

Egypt has played an important role in the history of traditional Arabian costume. Major contributions were cotton and linen. Her cotton textiles were, in fact, the backbone of the Arab wardrobe for centuries. Poor Bedouin wore cotton percale and unbleached calico from Egypt while the rich were dressed in fine Egyptian linen and delicate muslin. Gauze was also sold to Arabia where it was made into scarves, veils and babies' garments.

China

The Chinese civilization is remarkable because it has had a long, unbroken history up to modern times while other civilizations have risen and fallen.

The Chou Dynasty, circa 1122–255 BC, is considered China's golden age because it was during this period that the firm foundation for Chinese culture was laid and China's two greatest philosophers lived: Confucius and Lao-tse. Beautiful silk and fine bronze vases were also produced during the Chou Dynasty. In the following Ch'in Dynasty, circa 246–206 BC (which gave China its name) the Great Wall of China was begun.

During the Han Dynasty, circa 206 BC–214 AD, an overland caravan route was opened between China and Europe, carrying silk and other Chinese products across central Asia to the north of Persia. This camel path became known as the Silk Road and along it merchants of India, Persia and the Middle East, took goods to Greece and Rome after having the silk dyed and embroidered. Chinese caravans returning home were laden with precious stones, jade and ivory for carving, and horses.

Before the opening of the Silk Road, China was noted for being totally pre-occupied with its own culture. The trade route was responsible for bringing the compelling forces of influence to China, effecting a major change in Chinese dress. Hitherto, the Chinese had worn a full-length coat, outwardly similar to a *kaftan* yet constructed from many narrow segments. This was worn belted. The addition of pants to Chinese traditional costume came by way of the migrating Huns (ancestors of the Turks and Monguls) when they arrived between 700 and 800 BC.

Long before Islam, Arab traders were engaged in regular trade with the East, exchanging aromatics and perfumes from Arabia for Chinese silk, porcelain, gunpowder, saltpetre and paper. Most of the silk, *hareer gazz*, was destined for Rome but there is evidence to suggest that Arabian *hareems* glittered with this Chinese textile. In the heartlands of Islam, it is recorded, Chinese silk was coveted and made into splendid garments.

Arab traders carried the secrets of silk production westward and Arabs cultivated mulberry trees themselves in southern Tunisia to feed their own silk worms.

Perhaps the most curious thing about China was the people's persistence in making things by hand as their ancestors had done, even when machines were within their reach. Paradoxically, their contributions to the modern world, such as paper and ink, were revolutionary.

In the earliest times, the average Chinese wore coarse garments, first made from hemp and later from cotton. For warmth, jackets were generally heavily padded. Later, when silk was developed, it was reserved for Mandarins and their families' colourful, richly embroidered, flowing robes. While the button on a Mandarin's hat indicated his rank, the embroidery designs on his silk robes distinguished his civil service branch.

At one time, China included Mongolia, Turkestan and Tibet, as well as the area of modern China. It is therefore not surprising to see occasionally shared design elements between China and central Asia. In Tibet today, there are costume design elements which are similar to those of a few Arabian dresses. The narrow-panelled Tibetan *kaftan* coat traditionally includes shoulder sections cut from contrasting cloth. These sections are also a feature of western Arabian Bedouin ladies' gowns. The Tibetan reliance on many contrasting patches of different coloured and textured textiles for distinctive beauty, is also echoed in Central Arabian dresses.

Furthermore, it is traditional for a Tibetan actress to wear a garment with sleeves much longer than the arms. This indicates her high status by showing that she does not need to do physical labour – such sleeves hampering menial activity. In the Islamic world, these identical sleeves are said to be tailored thus to cover a woman's hands modestly during prayer as a mark of respect. The trade routes are undoubtedly responsible for the shared costume design feature which is supposed to have originated in central Asia.

China's contribution to Arabian traditional costume is undoubtedly silk. Up until this century, this esteemed textile remained the preserve of the rich Arab. Its lustrous quality brings to mind romantic images of precious cargoes containing fragrant incense and sparkling gems that were borne along the Silk Road and the spice routes by camel caravan from southern Arabia. Small and precious silk segments appliquéd to the dresses of nomadic Arabian women are important forms of garment embellishment. They have a strict colour code on traditional dresses although the reasons for their colour selection and placement are forgotten. Perhaps, apart from the intrinsic value of a piece of silk, these may originally have been added as badges of rank and/or provenance.

Legend has it that the first delicate and precious piece of silk was a royal secret in China five thousand years ago. Only princesses were allowed to rear silkworms and unwind and weave silk. It first reached other countries as gifts to foreign princes in the ancient world. Although it could have been a lucrative export commodity, China refused to divulge the secrets of silk production for centuries and the death penalty was exacted from anyone attempting to take silkworm eggs or cocoons out of the country. There are many tales about how the secret first leaked out and how the Arabs came to control silk production eventually. History books reveal that it was the Arabs who introduced silk to Spain and old records are laced with evidence to confirm their appreciation for China's gift to the world.

Persia

High mountains, forbidding deserts and huge uninhabitable salt marshes discouraged cultural unity in early Persia. Consequently, its population did not form a homogenous whole. Prior to 2000 BC, it was occupied by peoples with a variety of cultures and its history as a nation did not begin until the middle of the second millennium BC. Even then, it remained a highly regional society.

Near the end of the second millennium, small groups of nomadic horse-riding peoples moved from central Asia to Persia and the new nation took its name from one of these groups of immigrants, the Parsua. They eventually joined with another major group of settlers, the Medes. As they rose to power together, Median and Persian strength combined with the central Asian Scythians and the Babylonians to level the Assyrian capital Nineveh. Their empire then spread towards the eastern shore of the Caspian Sea, greatly expanding in the seventh century BC. Despite the fact that the Persians were at the time vassals under the Medes, control eventually fell to a Persian prince, Cyrus the Great, who established the most extensive empire known in the ancient world.

By 546 BC Cyrus had defeated Lydia and secured control of the Aegean coast of Asia Minor (Armenia) and of the Greek colonies along the Levant. Moving east, he took Parthia, Chorasmia and Bactria. He captured Babylon in 539 BC. By the time of his death in 529 BC, the Persian kingdom extended as far east as the Hindu Kush in Afghanistan.

It was the son of Cyrus who subsequently took Egypt in the name of the Persians. The boundaries of the Persian Empire were withdrawn to Asia Minor, however, after conflict with the Greeks at the battle of Marathon in 490 BC. Then Darius the Great, the succeeding ruler and a member of the empire's Achaemenid family, raised the Achaemenids to greatness through his sound and far-sighted administrative planning, brilliant military manoeuvring and a humanistic world view.

The revenue of the Achaemenid Empire came from agriculture, tribute and trade. Darius made use of the relatively new invention of coins and struck gold and silver pieces. He also established a central capital at Persepolis, "city of the Persians", but his empire began to fade as Persian trade and tribute systems were inefficient due to the vast expanse of its territories.

The end of ancient Persia came when the Macedonian, Alexander the Great, was accepted as the leader of the Greeks in 334 BC. Alexander swept through Persia's Asia Minor, Egypt, Babylon, Suza, Ecbatana and Persepolis. Persia was thereafter Hellenized and one may still see its effect upon Persian art as a result of this cultural stimulation from the West.

Eventually Persia fell to one of Alexander's generals, Seleucus, who also ruled Babylon. The Seleucid kingdom gradually gained strength despite internal revolts until, eventually, in the second century BC, one group, the Parthians, began to encroach until finally Persia was theirs.

During both the Seleucid and Parthian periods, the Achaemenid heritage had been preserved and even nurtured, particularly in one Persian state where a descendant of a revered citizen, Sassan, grew powerful. He eventually overthrew the Parthians and thus began the Sassanian Empire 226–641 AD.

Although the democratic way of life was replaced by an immensely powerful caste-system, ancient Median costume styles continued to be worn.

The character of the costume is distinguished by wide, full-length garments with long pointed sleeves. The Medians, who were great horsemen, wore more suitable riding garments besides these grand voluminous robes.

Elements of Median costume which reached the Middle East via the Persians have been preserved by Islamic people and long pointed sleeve lappets in particular, seen in various Arabian costumes, served their needs of modesty and reverence by covering the body totally during prayer.

Arabs and Persians knew each other through trade prior to the introduction of Islam. Thereafter, the Islamic army, in 637 AD, after defeating the Byzantine army at Damascus in 635, occupied the Sassanian capital, Ctesiphon, renaming it Madain. Although the Sassanians outnumbered the Arabs, they were no match because their strength had been sapped by constant battles with the Romans. Also, since they had been familiar with Arabia as a tribally orientated society, they were caught totally by surprise when the seven-century Islamic campaign was launched against them.

Thereafter, the north-east of the Arabian Peninsula, old Sumer, and Babylon – which had been tenuously held by the Persians – fused to become a strong Arab state in close alliance with Persia. By then most of Persia had adopted the Islamic faith. By 650 Muslims had reached and conquered all the Sassanian domains and Arab influence flooded Persia.

During the post-Islamic period – although the main Gulf trading cities were on the Persian coast – Arabs were usually in control, ruling independently unless there happened to be a well-organized Persian government, in which case the Arabs paid tribute.

The presence of Persians in Oman and of Arabs in Persian territory produced an ethnic mixture which still prevails along Arabia's Gulf coasts. The fall of the Abbasid Empire in the thirteenth century gave the Persians the opportunity to control Gulf trade, and Persia in her turn ruled Arabian shores and nearby islands such as Bahrain.

Gulf trade declined in the late fifteenth century because Egypt regained the function of middleman between Egypt and Asia. This decline was further accelerated when the Portuguese captured Hormuz in 1507, thereafter doing little to encourage Gulf interests.

It is interesting to see that embroidery stitches used in the heartland of Arabia are identical to those used in parts of Persia, rather than any of those stitches popular in the Levantine countries.

India

Archaeologists' excavations in the Indus River Valley reveal that northern India had a sophisticated civilization five thousand years ago when Britain was still in a state of savagery. These early Indians lived in brick houses, in well-planned cities with drainage systems similar to ancient Egyptian and Sumerian in the third millennium BC.

They knew how to write, make pottery, work with various metals, cultivate, domesticate animals, weave – and they rode in wheeled transport. From the fragments of madder-dyed, finely-woven cotton found at excavations in the Indus Valley, it has also been concluded that the production of hand-spun and hand-woven textiles is among the oldest of Indian art-crafts.

Although technically India is part of the continent of Asia, its natural boundaries separate it; so much so that it was once necessary to travel by sea to reach the sub-continent. The southern point of this triangular-shaped land dips into the Indian Ocean. Along the eastern coastline lies the Bay of Bengal and on the western, the Arabian Sea. Despite the world's highest mountains, the Himalayas, protecting India in the north, the region was often subject to invasion.

In about two thousand BC, India was invaded by the Persians who remained and became known thereafter as Hindus. In the sixth century BC, north-west India became annexed to neighbouring Persia. Then in 326 BC trade with the outside world was stimulated when Alexander the Great led his soldiers into Indus River territory, thus linking India with the Mediterranean. Thereafter India's fine muslin, silken shawls, carved ivory and delicate gem-studded jewellery were eagerly sought by China, Babylonia and Greece.

Through trade India was able to influence many civilizations; her sphere of influence was remarkably varied as well as far-reaching. Much of the sculpture and architecture of Siam, China and Japan was born in India. Indian numerals reached the Arabs through trade and were thus transmitted to Europe.

When Alexander left India, a local prince set up a successful empire in the north, but the rest of the land suffered from strife due to various conflicting religious philosophies.

The sub-continent of India is a land of amazing contrasts. It comprises some of the world's thickest jungles and some of the most barren deserts and torrid plains which are continually whipped by severe winds that prevail throughout the year. The climate varies from fiery heat to icy cold, and for eight months of the year India suffers from excessively dry weather while the other four months bring torrential monsoon rains.

Because of the climatic conditions, Indian clothing is simple. Traditionally, men wore a loin cloth in the form of a long piece of material wrapped around the thighs and hips, often drawn between the legs from back to front to be tucked in the front waist. To protect them from the sun, Indian men wear cloth wound around their heads in turban fashion. Most Indian women wear a colourful sari – a long piece of textile wound around the waist, across one shoulder and generally draped over the head. This is traditionally worn over a form-fitting, brief bodice of several designs, or a waist-length, short-sleeved blouse not dissimilar to the Arabian *sidaireeya* of the Hijaz region. This popular style of dress, handed down from the ancients, is still considered the most suitable, graceful and convenient style for the country.

The motifs appearing on sari textiles present some surprises. In British India, many European motifs were produced, probably under the direction of the East India Company. Yet weavers still wished to make traditional designs for which Hindu ladies also showed a preference. These traditional Indian motifs were, in fact, Islamic, suggesting that lengths of textile with such motifs might have been originally produced for Arabia as much as for the Muslim population in India. In the State of Oudh, for instance, passages from the *Koran* were interwoven into muslin for Arabia, and also for Muslims on the sub-continent.

The embroiderers of India today are generally Muslims and their skills have been passed down through countless generations. Many of the stitches they work in the far north-west of the sub-continent are identical to those worked by Bedouin women of the Arabian Peninsula. They are also traditional stitches of Pakistan, the Islamic state formed in the sub-continent in the 1940s.

From the earliest written records, mention is made of India as an important centre for the crafts of spinning, dyeing, weaving and for the production of gossamer-like muslins and rich sumptuous brocades glittering with gold thread. In the fourteenth century, five hundred expert weavers were employed to weave silk and gold brocades for gifts to ladies of the royal court. These textiles were said to outdo anything produced by China, Persia or Europe.

Today, most Indian villages maintain a diminishing colony of caste weavers who continue to produce traditional textiles. Despite a current flicker of interest in hand-loomed textiles, especially in raw silk, it is recognized that economic factors are contributing toward the ever-decreasing demand for hand-woven material. As the years pass, the number of power looms increase and despite desperate efforts to revive the hand-loom industry, it is not expected to recover completely.

In India, textile and garment production is an integral part of life. Today, along with traditional cotton, silk and cashmere, the range of materials includes mercerized cotton, rayon, nylon, orlon and various other man-made fibres.

Animal fleece was never considered sufficiently clean for anything but outer wear in India, and was therefore never woven to any great extent. The exceptions are the famous shawls of Kashmir which are judged to be works of art. The most superior example is made from the soft, silky and warm fleece of the Asli Cus wild goat. It is gathered from shrubs and rough rocks against which the animals rub off their wool as summer approaches.

The most coveted Kashmir shawl is known as a "ring shawl" because it can be passed through a man's signet ring. The origin is quite ancient and the early examples formed part of India's trade treasure. Arabs in the past wore Kashmir shawls as alternatives to fine Indian figured muslins for turbans and waistbelts.

India's contribution to traditional Arabian costume is immense. Even before Islam, Indian craftsmen produced textiles and carried out embroidery for the people of the Arabian Peninsula. Rustem J. Mehta believes the most beautiful piece of embroidery ever done in India in the post-Islamic period, was a cloth commissioned for the tomb of the Prophet Muhammed at Medina. Sir George Birdwood, the author of *The Industrial Arts of India*, wrote of this pall: "It is composed entirely of inwrought pearls and precious stones, disposed in an *arabesque* pattern, and is said to have cost a crore of rupees. Although the richest stones were worked into it, the effect was most harmonious. When spread out in the sun it seemed suffused with a general iridescent pearly bloom, as graceful to the eyes as were the exquisite forms of its *arabesque*."

Well-to-do Arabian ladies of the Central Province recount that some of their finest gowns were made and/or embroidered for them in India. Some dress-lengths arrived pre-embroidered – a custom in the Orient.

Violet Dickson, the widow of Arabist H. R. P. Dickson, for years the British Representative in Kuwait, confirmed that the Arabian "dowry" chests, known as Kuwaiti chests, were made in India. These cedar chests were so-called because Kuwait as the convenient Arabian Gulf port was where they were initially bound. In these chests, Arabian women of the past kept their garments and other personal items, as well as household linen.

The evolution of costume continues on the Arabian Peninsula while trade with India increases, not only bringing ready-to-wear garments designed to blend with traditional Arabian costume, but also carrying over India's modern influence. This is particularly noticeable in the south today where women often wrap themselves in a printed Indian sheet of *rhassab* instead of in an Arab cloak. Men of Yemen today wear Indian textiles in the form of a length of plaid material used as a wrap-around skirt or sometimes in loin-cloth style, echoing Indian dress.

The cross-cultural ties between India and Arabia have always been strong. Apart from the formation of Pakistan on the Indian sub-continent in 1947, to create a nation for those of the Muslim faith who live there, Indians over the past centuries have settled in Arabia while Arabs have lived for generations in India.

Central Asia

There may be no clear definition for Central Asia but there was little doubt in the thirteenth century that it was a fearful place. Tartary, as it was known, was the homeland of the Mongol horde which ravaged all before them. On the positive side, after their conquests, East and West could mingle as the region was freed from the Ottomans who had infiltrated and become entrenched. This awesome land of forbidding terrain holds fascination for many because it has been virtually isolated from the gaze of the curious for centuries. It is the home of the legendary and ancient Scythians – the warlike nomads who eventually settled on the shores of the Caspian and are known for their fabulous gold ornaments.

Central Asia is primarily Muslim and the area overlaps several countries such as southern Russia, western China, northern Iraq and Iran and includes Afghanistan.

In medieval times, Central Asia was studded with great Samanid cities. The Samanids 874–999, succeeded the Abbasid Caliphate in Samarkand and Bukara, the most important of the early independent Muslim states in the east, which was notable for encouraging the revival of Persian language and literature.

The Samanid cities and the Khwarism region of Central Asia became important trading centres, bringing great wealth to the Islamic world as part of a booming commercial network. Many Muslims, as a direct result of this trade, amassed wealth from transit tolls and customs dues imposed upon foreign merchants passing through. In fact, it was the only way they could grow rich as their region was barren and lacked natural resources.

This was a fortunate period in history for Central Asian Muslims directly due to their prime location, but it was never to be repeated. They sat at the crossroads when the riches of north, south, east and west passed through, and adventurers from the far reaches of the known world sought treasures from remote lands. Then, around the turn of the tenth century, their prosperity began to wane due to various factors which are still matters for conjecture. From that time Central Asians have mainly lived in hardship, yet, as Muslims and traditionalists, have fought to maintain their ancient values.

There is an obvious cultural link between the people of Asia and those of Arabia, without doubt strengthened by the shared Islamic faith. Because of their annual pilgrimage to Mecca, Central Asians have cast some influence on the Peninsula people. The cross-influence began in pre-Islamic times, in the days when the ancient trade routes were active. Arabia's costume today exhibits aspects clearly traceable to ancient Central Asia. It was the nomadic Asians, for instance, who invented pants.

The origin of pants is traced back to the nomadic tribes of Central Asia and other East-Asian regions – back to the time when fur and leather were worn and weaving was unknown. Pants were worn then probably for warmth, perhaps evolving from strips bound around the legs. When horsemanship arrived in Europe in about 2500 BC, trousers were already an established garment and were quickly adopted by riders as being ideal for comfort while on horseback.

Among those ancient Asian nomads were the Huns, ancestors of the Turks and Mongols. Their riding costume, consisting of a jacket and trousers, had fitted sleeves and trousers fastened tightly at the ankles for protection against the cold.

The district around Lake Baikal in Central Asia is considered to be the place where the Mongolian and Turkoman tribes originated. They were the forebears of the Ottoman Turks. Also descended from these ancient people were the Tartars, taking their name from a Chinese dialect. The Mongols were the rulers over various tribes – Turk-Tartars, Yakutes, Tarantshes, Dunyanes, Usbekes, Turkomans, Kirghiz, and Avares – in the empire known as Tartary.

Within the nomad tribe of Turkomans, there was a progressive branch known as the Huns. It was the Huns – migrating along the ancient Silk Road – who supposedly took to China the Asian custom of wearing trousers under a costume. After being defeated by the Chinese, the Huns turned toward the West and founded an empire at Lake Aral in the first century BC. One branch of these

Huns, the Uigures, remained in the south-west of Lake Aral and developed a powerful empire, spreading as far as the Oxus River circa 1000 AD and eventually submitting to Ghengis Khan, the Mongol chieftain, in the period between 1162 and 1227.

Ghengis Khan was fourteen years old when he became chief of the many nomadic tribes of Mongolia in east central Asia. Like many conquerors, he believed that it was God's will that he should conquer the world. He began by leading his barbarians, mounted on wild horses, to break the Great Wall of China, and succeeded in capturing the city of Peking. Westward, he swept across all Asia and into Europe as far as the Dnieper River in western Russia, founding an empire, notable for being the largest connected one in history. Ghengis Khan's success lay in the fact that his well-disciplined armies moved with amazing speed in battle due to their incredible horsemanship.

His grandson, Kublai Khan, founded the Mongol dynasty, creating for China a new capital at Peking. It was the fabulous tales of Marco Polo and others thereafter which led Europeans to trade with China, then known as Cathay. They were enticed by visions of Cathay's luxurious courts, advanced government, excellent roads, bridges and canals. Inspired men began to search for new routes to capture Chinese trade.

Despite Kublai Khan's advanced ideas, he permitted his armies to kill millions. Similarly, Halugu Khan, in 1258, seized Baghdad and killed the last Abbasid Caliph. He was fortunately repelled by the Egyptians in Syria.

Although the Mongol invasion left the people of the Arabian Peninsula relatively unscathed, it did bring about the end of a thriving Islamic Empire. Enormous areas of fertile land were laid to waste, magnificent cities were razed and untold thousands of Muslims were slaughtered. The Mongol's destructive force was felt again between 1393 and 1402 under the leadership of the infamous Tamerlane. Thus afflicted and cut off from the advantages of rich neighbours, who made the annual pilgrimage to Mecca and Medina, Arabia receded into virtual obscurity and straightened circumstances, suffering further from frequent internal strife. Evidence of the early intercourse can still be seen on the Peninsula. There are parallels in folk costume, customs and jewellery.

The wide sleeve with the deep-pointed cuff, which is said to have been worn originally in Asia, has become an established part of traditional Arabian costume. This style of sleeve can be seen on traditional costumes in several parts of the Middle East – in places where the ancient trade routes passed by. They are worn by people who are accustomed to performing mundane activities. In Arabia such elongated sleeve lappets are worn by nomadic and rural women who knot the ends behind the back when ease of movement is required. In some areas the sleeve points are pinned back to the shoulders.

In the deserts of Turkomenia – one of the Soviet Republics – Turkman tribes centred in west-central Asia still produce hand-woven textiles from the wool of their own animals as did Arabia's Bedouin. The garments they make still follow traditional lines and the home-dyed hues, in harmonious combinations, are remarkably similar to those of Central Arabia. Even the cut of their robes is similar. Although Turkman garments are generally more richly embroidered than most Arabian styles, the embroidery placement is the same: at the neck, cuffs and hem. In the case of the Turkmans such application is believed to be effective in repelling evil spirits from these openings. The triangular motif, typical of Asia and of Afghanistan's ethnic embroidery in particular, is an ancient amuletic symbol, also appearing predominantly on crafted items throughout the Arabian Peninsula.

In Central Asia, the nomads make felt and woollen materials while the townsfolk weave silk. Weaving is a woman's craft, produced on a primitive hand loom. The yarn is usually dyed red, green and deep blue but within these three basic colours, there are a variety of hues. Preference is given to red because it symbolizes for them the colour of life's blood.

Garments are still produced in Asia from strips, approximately 35 centimetres wide, according to the limitations of the loom. This technique is echoed in Arabian garments although these are no longer fashioned from hand-loomed textiles. In both cases, side panels are sewn to central panels, and sleeves also are formed from strips. As in Arabian costume, a variety of textiles are often combined to make up an Asian nomad's dress. The garment is primarily of one colour such as a blackish or red cotton over which colourful patches of printed cotton, silk or velvet are appliquéd. There are strict colour and colour placement codes for both Asian and Arabian women's dresses.

Asia Minor

The peninsula of Asia Minor, modern Turkey, has been called the bridge between Europe and Asia because it was the route of warriors, traders and immigrants for thousands of years – and the core of a major trading zone where Asians and Europeans could interact. It was, in fact, through this passageway that Middle Eastern culture reached barbarian Europe.

Asia Minor's northern coastlines are washed by the Black Sea and by the Mediterranean in the south. Between lies Ankara, the site where the ancient Hittites established their capital, heading a civilization which eventually rivalled those of Egypt and Babylonia.

By about 1500 BC, using iron weapons, the Hittites became competitors with the Egyptians for control of Western Asia. Yet, constant warfare so weakened the Hittite Empire, that in 1200 BC, they were conquered by European barbarians. Subsequently, waves of other conquerors were to crisscross the territory until the Romans took possession in the second century AD. Then in 330 AD the Roman Emperor, Constantine, moved his capital there – to Byzantium. He renamed it after himself and thus Constantinople became the last bastion of a diminishing Roman Empire.

Commerce in furs, timber, textiles, gold, spices, gems and slaves made Constantinople rich and famous, and thus a rich prize when it fell to the Ottomans in the fifteenth century. This Asian tribe renamed the city Istanbul. When the Ottoman Empire (based on the existing Graeco–Roman cultural foundation) eventually stretched from Abyssinia to Vienna, reaching its peak in the sixteenth century, an enriched culture passed into the Islamic world.

The centre of Islamic power moved from Medina to Syria in the year 661, with Damascus becoming the capital of the Umayyad Caliphate. From there in 750 it moved to Iraq where the Abbasid Caliphate ruled from Baghdad.

Within a century after the Prophet Muhammed's death in 632, almost all of Arabia's wealth was reliant upon the *Haj*. She depended heavily upon Egypt for grain and was frequently a political appendage to that country. When the Ottomans conquered Egypt in 1517, they were recognized rulers of the Hijaz, proclaiming Western Arabia as part of their dominions. The *Sherif* of Mecca sent his son to pay homage to the victor and to present him with a silver key to the Holy Shrine, the *Kaaba* in Mecca. At this time the Ottomans carried off the mantle and banner of the Prophet and the Sultan in Istanbul subsequently declared himself Protector of the Holy Places. His successors later claimed the Caliphate and the Ottoman Empire manoeuvred to control the Arabian Peninsula.

Ottoman rule from Istanbul was strengthened by their installation in 1539 of a Grand Mufti, a leading religious and legal official. This marked the beginning of tension between Meccans and Ottomans. As the Ottomans engaged in various external wars which weakened their power in the seventeenth century, the Arabian Peninsula was left to fend for itself, resulting in a difficult period for most of the populace. The Hijazi merchants and traders prospered, however, and extended their interests locally.

Throughout this period of Ottoman turbulence, within the environs of Istanbul at Topkaki (the palace city) Turkish sultans held court from the fifteenth to the nineteenth centuries. Their exotic way of life was shared with five thousand dependents who were housed within Topkapi's walls. The rest of the country had a predominantly agricultural economy and this produced a village orientated society. Since this region was the gateway between Europe and Asia, many different peoples were to be found there although Turks were and still are the most numerous.

The traditional costume of Turkey consists of *charwal* or pantaloons; *entari* or chemise and the *kaftan* or body shirt. Women traditionally wore the *yashmak*, a face veil, specially favoured by Muslim women. It was also the custom for Turkish women to remain secluded as well as veiled. Men traditionally wore the *fez*, a red skullcap, and some-

times added a waistcoat to their costume. Both men and women customarily wore an outer cloak, although it is said this became prevalent only after Islam.

Long sleeves, falling far below the hands are typical of Turkish traditional costume and betray their Asiatic origin. The *kaftan*-like outer coat worn by the Sultans and men of rank from the sixteenth to the nineteenth centuries in Turkey features sleeves seen in Turkoman and Tartari tribal costumes and is echoed in the garments worn by Arabian men in olden times.

As late as 1916, the Ottoman Empire held sway over virtually the whole of the Arabian Peninsula, as well as over Iraq, Syria, Palestine, Lebanon and Jordan. The history of Arabia and Turkey are so particularly entwined through the brotherhood of Islam and subsequent presence on the Peninsula, that it is not surprising to find Arabian costume exhibiting some Turkish influence, especially in the Hijaz and Yemen.

In overall observation, it can be seen that the Middle East – so vital in ancient times as the crossroads where Europe, Africa and Asia met and the throbbing heart of the great Arab Empire – fell into lethargy under Ottoman rule. The classic simplicity of Middle Eastern garb blossomed and became over-blown in parts of the Islamic Empire during this period. It is fascinating to see it revert to simple lines today.

Lady Anne Blunt, the English aristocrat who visited Arabia to buy horses in 1880, recorded that the Ottoman pashas were largely responsible for eroding traditional ways. She writes that they boasted that the power of the Bedouin tribes (Anazah and Shammar in particular) had been seriously checked if not broken within the previous twenty years. Vast numbers of tribesmen were being claimed by settled life in Mesopotamia. Lady Blunt observed that "true Bedouin must retire to the Najd or abandon their independent life".

It seemed that the main flaw in the Ottoman system in the desert was one which, in fact, adversely affected the whole Empire, and that was heavy taxation. Peaceful shepherding tribes under the protection of the great Anazah and Shammar were virtually impoverished as a result. Large tribes remained thoroughly independent of the Sultan, it is true, but it was necessary for them to strive very hard to maintain their ancient character in order that the traditional way of life might remain unchanged.

Byzantium
The Occident, or the area west of Asia, developed much later than the Orient, eastward of the Mediterranean. Yet, by 500 BC, Greece and Rome in the west were making rapid progress.

Ancient Greece, the first democracy, began citizenship and men were encouraged to use their freedom and express ideas. The garments they wore reflected this philosophy in that the traditional costume, consisting of two unseamed lengths of cloth, could be wound around and thrown about the body as desired, expressing personal taste and establishing individuality.

The seemingly idyllic civilization was doomed to end due to internal strife and continual wars with the Persians; thus weakened, it was conquered by the Macedonian warrior, Alexander the Great in the fourth century BC. He also conquered the Middle East and merged the Orient with the Occident. Then Alexander the Great and his successors built scores of cities such as Alexandria in Egypt and Antioch in Syria, where many races mingled and traded. Into Alexandria's harbour sailed ships laden with Arabian spices, Chinese silks, Russian furs and ivory, pearls, and raw cotton from India. In Alexandria there were glass-blowers, perfume-makers, paper-makers and excellent linen weavers.

Greek styles of clothing were popular and many Greek customs were observed, yet, Alexander, King of Macedonia, Master of Greece, Pharaoh of Egypt and Emperor of Persia, preferred the more luxurious Persian robes. Known for his vanity, Alexander allowed his classic Greek costume to absorb Oriental overtones. The vastness of his influence can only be guessed.

In 31 BC, the Romans conquered the entire Mediterranean area and thus the stream of civilization flowed on to the rest of Europe. For over one thousand years, the Byzantine Empire thrived amid various cultural influences and became the centre of artistic innovation.

Prior to the emergence of the Roman Empire in 27 BC, the Romans had presented an austere appearance, wearing a simple body tunic and sandals and an outer wrap. Greek costume had an immediate impact upon the Romans and thereafter their traditional costume affected grandeur – the garments notable for their deep folds and rich, draped textiles.

Romans did not have to worry about losing buttons. Like Greek clothing, theirs was loose-fitting and simple – their mild climate allowing them to get along with two main garments: the tunic, a short-sleeved, long shirt, bound at the waist and the toga, an outer garment which was a long white woollen robe worn draped about the body. The embellishment and quality of textile often totally transformed the appearance of its classic lines.

Purple stripes sewn on the tunic were a sign of rank. For example, a senator wore a wide purple band down the centre while victorious generals wore all-purple togas trimmed with gold embroidery. Women's garments resembled men's except that they were often more colourful and of finer linen or silk. Prosperous women wore jewels, furs and cosmetics imported from the East, while the poor were forbidden to wear anything but black or brown.

The Byzantine army was defeated by the Islamic army at Damascus in 635, at a time when its empire was culturally and socially bankrupt – weakened physically by unremitting war.

While the two great empires of Rome and Persia had ruled Europe and the Middle East in the early part of the millennium, the Arabs of the Arabian Peninsula had remained fairly uninvolved – their intercourse with Byzantium being one centred on trade. Trans-Arabian trade had decreased and southern Arabian trade had begun to fade as a result, among other things, of Rome's declining demand for frankincense and myrrh. Yet, the Peninsula's northern markets still existed. Arab merchants were thus chiefly responsible for continuing cross-influence as they maintained trade with the markets to the north.

There is a curious similarity between early Graeco-Roman costume and the Islamic *Haj* male costume or *ihram*. *Ihram* consists of two seamless lengths of white textile – one wound skirt-fashion around the lower half of the body with the other thrown loosely over the shoulder. While *ihram* is claimed not to be from this source, it is true to say that these costumes are remarkably alike.

It is known that in Alexander's time, Hellenism came to the Peninsula through trade. After his death, the Greeks continued to found trading cities. The island of Failaka, off the coast of present-day Kuwait, and the excavations at Faw, in the middle of the Peninsula, are but two cities yielding Hellenic artifacts. The search continues for legendary Gerrha on the east coast – this city may reveal the link between ancient Greek and Arabian costume.

Northern Europe

In the ninth and tenth centuries, prayers throughout the settled European world asked for deliverance from a flood of ferocious men from the north. These Norse raiders were swift and ruthless and came in long-ships, soon becoming the scourge of Europe.

In retrospect, there were some constructive elements in their adventuring which spanned three hundred years, from about 790 to 1086. This period was known as the Age of the Vikings. For example, it is possible to see massive alterations in the pattern of European history, such as the linking of the known world with the far north. The Baltic became a highway along which merchants, priests and pirates could travel – from north and west to Novgorod, Smolensk, Kiev, Constantinople and as far south as Baghdad.

The term Viking probably means "man of the fjord", referring to the Oslo Fjord which was known as Vik. However, modern historians describe all Scandinavians on expedition of that period as Vikings. The Arab historian, Ibn Fadlan, writing in 922, described the Northmen as Rus. He claimed never to have seen people more perfect in physique, "standing tall as date palms" with reddish hair and fair skins. They wore neither shirts nor coats with sleeves, but wore cloaks with one end thrown over the shoulder, leaving a hand free. According to Ibn Fadlan, every man from the north carried an axe, a sword and a dagger and was never seen without them.

They were also known as Norsemen and Normans. At home, the Rus were self-sufficient farmers whose lands dictated that they would become skilled shipbuilders, navigators and seamen. The geographical character of the countries of Scandinavia – the harsh northern sea, deep-sea inlets, mountains, trackless forests and a multitude of tiny islands – required that ships be built to establish a means of communication.

Navigation was allowed to develop inside sheltered archipelagos, away from the battering sea. The geography of sea and land, so intricately interlaced, motivated the Vikings to become skilled sailors, able to cope with rough waters.

Despite the bounty of some cultivated areas, the men of the north were eventually forced by politics, poverty and overcrowding to go out into the world. Pioneers, seeking land, fought and settled throughout western Europe. Traders, seeking wealth, developed commercial centres in Scandinavia at Birka, Kaupang, Gotland and Hedeby – Viking towns which became gateways for foreign goods and riches.

The seafaring Vikings became hardy warriors. As conquerors and adventurers, their voyages and achievements were colossal. Their brilliant nautical invention, the keel, made them masters of the sea. Vikings built up a vast trading network embracing the Mediterranean countries and the areas of Asia accessible by caravan routes. Their traders went down rivers into the heart of Russia and to Byzantium, taking with them fine gold jewellery and inlaid silverwork which exhibited a high degree of craftsmanship.

The traditional Viking battle-axe handle is decorated with silver-strip inlay resembling that on some firearm butts made in Arabia in olden times. The European term for this work is *Tauschieran*, said to be derived from Arabic.

Viking merchandise includes hides, furs, birds' feathers, whale-skin ropes, amber, walrus, narwhal tusk ivory and more. These were exchanged for luxury items such as silk and other costly textiles and gold, silver and slaves. Fruit and weapons were also taken back to the north, as well as copper, utensils, jewellery and silver coins. Viking women did weaving and produced cotton and woollen garments. However, their graves yield remains of finer fabrics which had been brought back by their commercially-minded menfolk.

Commercial relations existed in the eighth century between Islamic Spain and the Frankish Empire but what Muslims wanted at that time were the furs which came from beyond. Yet, it was not until the turn of the millennium that the Vikings reached Byzantium by river to develop the trade. Arab writers begin to mention that there were Scandinavian traders in the late ninth and early tenth centuries at the trading post of Bulgar.

Bulgar was an important trading post because it was convenient to a number of tribes, and located strategically on the edge of the vast Asiatic steppes, a toll-free area for traders. From Bulgar, the Silk Road stretched due east through Turkish-speaking territory for most of the way to China. Silk found in Viking graves must have travelled through Bulgar. Vikings bartered wares with many Eastern peoples including Turks and Khazars.

A flourishing trade linked Arabia with the distant north during the period when the Abassid Caliphate reached its cultural zenith in the ninth and tenth centuries. Viking hoards in the north reveal many Islamic coins, found over a vast northern area, providing corroboration for accounts of Muslim trade with the Vikings. Occasional camel bones further serve to plot the ancient northern caravan routes.

Arabs also traded frankincense and myrrh for furs in the early Islamic period. Fur was in great demand to trim the garments of the rich, even in the warmer Arab lands. It is recorded that, in the heartlands of Islam, furs were considered a precious luxury and coveted as such. The Islamic civilization avidly sought sable, ermine, mink, marten, fox, beaver, squirrel and otter fur, and it became a basic unit of exchange, although Northern amber, too, was highly prized.

The Burtas, people from the land of the Finns, dwelling in the forests along the banks of the Middle Volga, derived great wealth from fox fur. Books tell us that black fox pelts were esteemed by Arab kings in ancient times, and they took pride in wearing black fox hats, and *kaftans* and mantles lined with this fur as it was considered not only the finest but the warmest.

Fur and skin cloaks remain popular in the western highlands of Arabia today where nights are cold and the weather generally is cool for most of the year. Tribesmen in these areas do not wear imported fur but make attractive cloaks from sheepskins which are artistically edged and otherwise decorated with hand-sewn red leather strips.

The flow of Arab silver to the North ceased around the turn of the millennium, possibly as a direct result of an attack by a Kiev prince who is thought to have been a Tartar or Slav. It has also been hypothesized that the dramatic end to trade was linked with the decline of the Samanids of Central Asia. In any case, about the end of the eleventh century, the introduction of Christianity to Scandinavia saw the proud and independent Viking culture destroyed.

Africa

Until recently, because of its mystery, Africa was referred to as the Dark Continent. It has been said, too, that the darkest thing about Africa has always been people's ignorance about it and this is not surprising considering that books about Africa rarely agree – not even on such facts as the continent's total area.

John Gunther who travelled through Africa in the early 1950s, in an attempt to document facts about the land, talked to pygmies, giants, kings and slaves, white settlers, black insurrectionists, prime ministers, nationalists, sultans, emirs, pashas, mahdis, a kabaka, an asantehene, a mwami and peasants. He decided that Africa was best considered in two groupings – north and east and south and west. He also noted that the northern coast of Africa was like the southern coast of the Mediterranean and was much more a part of Europe than truly African.

Africa is a vast continental mass surrounded by the Atlantic, the Mediterranean, the Red Sea and the Indian Ocean. As the most impregnable of continents, it is logically the least developed. Not only is the periphery difficult to penetrate but so is the interior plateau. Africa is also the most tropical of continents and much of it is desert, brittle grassland and heavy rainforest with less than ten percent of arable land. However, it is rich in raw materials such as diamonds, gold, copper and other valuable minerals in large quantities. Yet Africa remains, by and large, poor.

The people are divided into a fantastic number of tribes which are astonishingly varied. They speak approximately seven hundred different languages. The single unifying factor throughout much of Africa is the faith of Islam.

The original African has obscure beginnings but some historians believe Africa is the birthplace of the human race. Only North African history is clear. For the main body of the continent, written records do not exist and there are only too few tantalizing rock paintings upon which to formulate ideas about the costumes and customs of Africa's earliest people.

The first coastline explorer was a Phoenician. Then, Hanno, a Carthaginian explorer, got as far as Sierra Leone in 520 BC. While bold Greek explorers sailed right around Africa, none could penetrate. Eventually, there were exploratory expeditions by the Portuguese, and thereafter by Dutch, Danish, Spanish, French and British voyagers and traders.

From about 1562, to the early nineteenth century, slavery was a dominant note in Africa's history. Yet, ninety percent of the continent was still unknown, readily proved by the best maps available at that time. It was described by one authority on Africa as "a coastline, not a continent".

In the early nineteenth century, the French and British penetrated the Niger area and two Portuguese crossed Africa. In the latter half of that century, the world at large became fascinated by the adventures of Livingstone, Speke and Stanley. Christian missionaries entered Africa at this time and anthropologists were able to learn some of the diverse ways of its inhabitants.

The African countries known to the world today, came into being within approximately thirty years beginning in the 1870s. Thereafter the continent was largely in the hands of Great Britain, France, Belgium, Italy, Portugal, Spain and Germany. It was carved up like a melon in the interests of commerce and politics. As a side effect of this ravaging, Africa was laid open to the influences of the modern world. During this process, ethnic heritages were not completely destroyed because the land was generally still under the control of its native leaders.

Trade with Africa began long ago. It was known to be rich in the various luxury commodities – such as gold, ivory and spices – which were desired by peoples to the north and east. Arabs sailed to the Horn of Africa for these treasures. They also travelled overland beyond Egypt to Tangier and Timbuktu, and crossed the Red Sea's Strait of Bab-el-Mandeb. The whole of North Africa became laced with Arab trade routes. In medieval times Arabs controlled the north African coast. They followed the ancient Egyptians, Carthaginians and Romans and ideas as well as goods were exchanged.

The best known traditional outer garment of North Africa remains the capacious *burnous* which varies greatly in colour and textile from region to region. The classic North African *burnous* is woven from creamy white lamb's wool or the hair of a baby camel. Its loose, flowing quality likens it to Arabian costume.

Traditional clothing throughout the main body of Africa is often limited to a loincloth which is ideally suited to the hot country. The size of this garment varies from brief to mid-calf length. In many parts of Africa, mere lengths of home-made cloth, sometimes intricately woven or dyed, are draped about the body in much the same way as in ancient Greece. For the rest, the voluminous *kaftan* derivative is traditional – a garment which outwardly would seem to be made from two large squares, when in fact it has the same component parts as a classic *kaftan* with some sections enlarged many times. This gown is remarkably similar to the women's *thawb* from Central Arabia.

The influence of Africa upon Arabian costume is particularly evident along the Red Sea littoral. Coastal-plain thatched villages in Yemen and the Asir are African in appearance, and crafts in this area and further north exhibit a colourfulness, as well as design elements similar to those of Africa, due to the continuous cultural contact throughout the centuries.

Arabia and Africa are separated by a narrow stretch of water at the point of the Red Sea Straits of Bab-el-Mandeb. This narrow gateway to Jeddah and the Suez Canal marks the point where ancient Egyptians crossed into Arabia to collect the prized resins of southern Arabia. This was also a portal through which Arab traders extracted gold, ostrich feathers, ivory, slaves and monkeys from Africa. And, in days gone by, immigrants from Ethiopia, Djibouti and Somalia used this route to cross over into Arabia where they made their home.

Islam

There is a verse in the *Koran* which reads:

"And say to the believing women that they should lower their gaze and guard their modesty; that they should not display their beauty and ornaments except what must ordinarily appear thereof; that they should draw their veils over their bosoms . . ."

Sura 24, aya 31

Although the basic Arabian costume including headgear existed in the Middle East prior to the Prophet Muhammed's Revelation, Islam is responsible for maintaining modest attire for both men and women to the present day. In most countries, progress has seen fashion lead men and women from one form of dress to another, while, in parts of the Middle East where the population is predominantly Muslim, basic costume styles have been constant throughout the ages.

In the beginning, it was wise to cover the head in Arabia against the heat and to veil the face for protection against blowing sand and harsh sun. In biblical times covering the head was also a sign of modesty and respect for both sexes. Islam saw wisdom in these practices and sought to encourage them by enjoining true believers to adhere to the customs.

Clothing styles have changed in the West for reasons other than fad or fashion, of course, and there is the likelihood that the same pressures will come to bear upon Arabian costume as we know it today. Already the sleeves of the man's *thawb* have been reduced in size for convenience in business life.

One of the main reasons why people in the modern world cannot always dress in the comfortable robes of times past, is the impracticality of the garments for many of today's pursuits. Nevertheless, modesty marks the difference between the garments considered acceptable by Islamic countries and those worn in countries under Western influence.

There are no priestly vestments in Islam because there is no priesthood. And, strictly speaking, there is no "Muslim" clothing apart from that worn for the *Haj*. Muslim costume is not subject to the *Shariah* (the law based on the *Koran*). In general, it is based firstly on the *Hadith*, the sayings of the Prophet Muhammed, and secondly, on the *Sunnah*, or traditions and practice set by the Prophet. This stipulates that clothing be suitable for the movements and positions adopted for the prescribed prayers. It must never cling to the body, and it should conceal while conforming to every movement.

The wearing of special clothing during the pilgrimage has a symbolic reason. By donning them, it is impossible to distinguish rich from poor, symbolizing the belief that all men are equal in the sight of God.

The Prophet Muhammed wore various colours on occasions but he showed a preference for the beauty and dignity of simple white textiles. He enjoined men not to wear gold ornaments and he discouraged them from wearing silken robes, reserving these for women.

Although not proven, it is believed that Muslims throughout the Islamic Empire adopted the turban from the nomads of the Arabian Peninsula. It is logical that Arab costume should have spread with Islam from Arabia because the Prophet is known to have welded into a spiritual ordinance certain aspects of dress worn within the Peninsula during

the seventh century. For instance, the seamless cloth for the heads, shoulders and chests of men, and the headscarf for the lower parts of women's faces were considered by Muhammed to be items of apparel which bespoke reverence and modesty. Both of these headcloths are said to have originated with the Arabian Peninsula nomads.

The Prophet Muhammed was probably responsible for modifying the component parts of the basic *kaftan* pattern, such as large sleeves of Asian origin. Lappets reaching below the hands are said to be Islamic in that their purpose is to cover hands during prayer.

Apart from maintaining the modest formlessness of the *kaftan*, Islam has encouraged the continued use of the black cloak, *abaaya* and black veil, *taraha*, for women. This apparel is worn when a woman leaves the house, and is considered to be the perfect foil for the colourful dresses worn underneath.

The superficial appearance of traditional Arabian costume for women has also been affected by Islam. For instance, the geometric and stylized floral embroidery patterns reflect the Peninsula people's acceptance of Islam's precept which discourages the representation of the human form. This has led to the development of *arabesque*, the Islamic form of decorative art.

A similar art existed in primitive form in pre-Islamic times. It was borrowed from earlier days by the Greeks and Romans and reached Muslim designers who adopted the style because it conformed to their beliefs. Islamic calligraphers utilized their talents to produce the richest abstract motifs that could possibly be conceived by the human imagination. They developed some of the greatest patterns ever recorded in the history of art and accomplished, during the Golden Age of Islam, the most exquisite renderings ever achieved in this style of decoration.

Essentially, *arabesque* is a linear ornament with an interlaced pattern based either on pure geometric relations with a variety of angles, movements, or on endlessly flowing curvilinears – sometimes displaying leaf, flower, and animal motifs. It is the strength and harmony of linear design and the mathematical lucidity that has made *arabesque* unique and outstanding among other styles of art.

The simple life in Arabia during the early days of Islam, saw *arabesque* used in a variety of motifs – mainly abstract – to decorate all flat surfaces in the home. It gained such wide acceptance on the Arabian Peninsula that Muslim women embroidered these motifs on their traditional costumes.

Islam has been a major factor in perpetrating cross-influence throughout the Middle East, fashioning the superficial appearance of various ethnic costumes in different countries. From the earliest days, when the new religion surged out of the Peninsula, to the present time when the yearly pilgrimage to Mecca brings Muslims together from every corner of the Islamic World, Islam's influence has been constant.

Traditional Arabian Costume

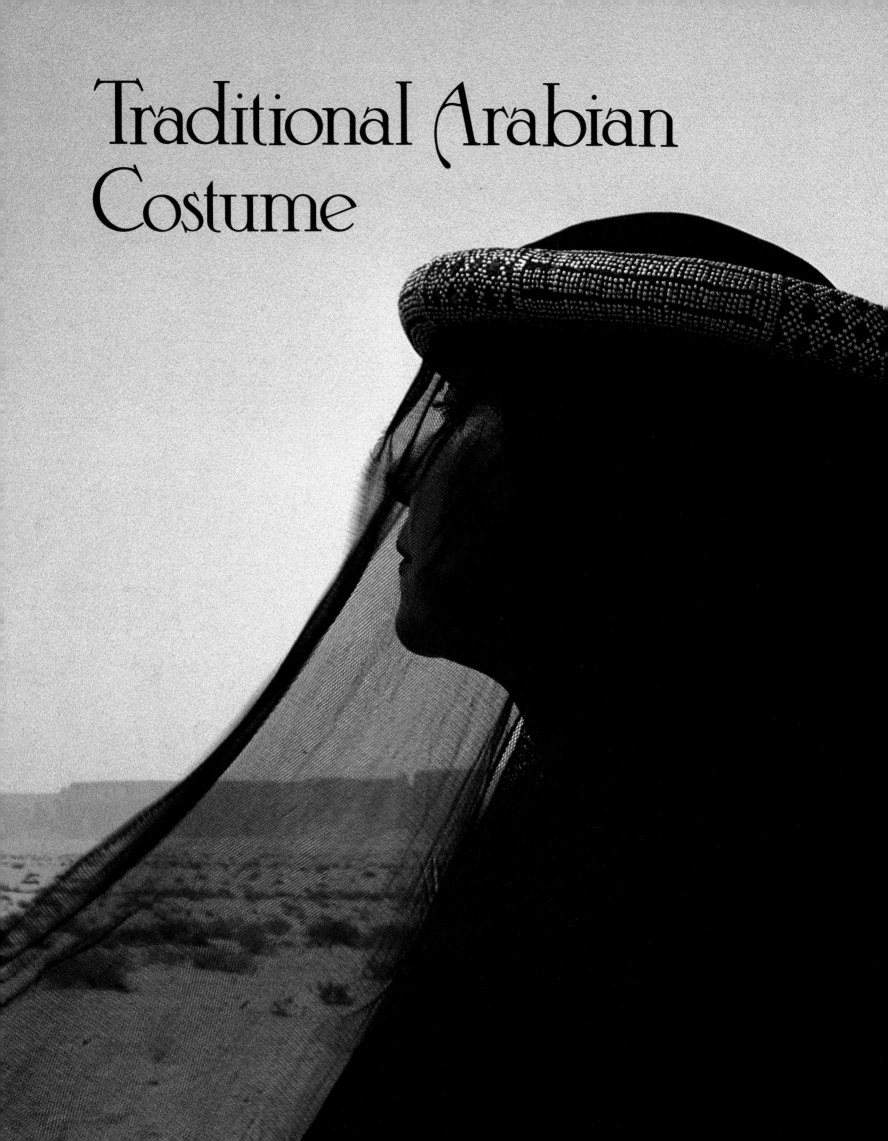

Through the incredible and often dazzling variety of Middle Eastern costumes there exists the unifying theme of layering. Since time immemorial it has been the custom to wear layered clothing to conserve body moisture. These garments were also designed to cover the body almost totally as protection against strong sun. Face veiling and headcloths, too, protect the complexion and prevent inhalation of sand, whereas the camel has the natural protection of thick eyelashes and flexible nostrils which act like shutters in a sand storm.

From man's earliest history until this century, clothing worn by the people of the Arabian Peninsula has changed only slightly, and there is reason to believe that some design facets reach back well into pre-history. These items of apparel have endured for good reason – they are sensible and flattering.

Practical clothing is essential for a life-style dictated by a land of hot weather and largely arid terrain. In the early days people were mostly nomadic because their life-supporting herds required an endless search for pasture.

As there were few suitable trees on the Arabian Peninsula with which to make furniture, even for the townspeople, it was the custom to sit or recline on carpets or soft, transportable furnishings. Quite naturally, garments were designed to be comfortable, but it was also necessary that they afford the wearer modesty.

It is immediately apparent that Arabian garments worn in the cities today still cover almost the entire body with the exception of parts of the face, hands and feet. Although they were primarily meant as a shield against sun and sand and an insulator, these practical aspects became Islamic custom, and now total coverage of the male and female form is a well-established Muslim tradition.

Before Islam, covering the head was a sign of modesty and respect in the Middle East. In the past, many women wore elaborate face masks and headcloths and, even though these garments are fashioned more simply today, the importance of headgear is still strong and it remains an essential part of traditional Arabian apparel – for men as well as women.

Although Arabian women's dresses are almost completely enveloping, their stunning design concept is unsurpassable in elegance. The gowns worn in the past by the ladies of the towns, and their desert sisters, presented a vivid and graceful spectacle. Flowing, voluminous, fine cottons and wools with colourful appliqué, silks, satins, chiffons, floral and plain cottons richly embroidered with bold pink, orange and green geometric patterns; brilliant hues enriched further with massed silver bells attached at the wrists; turquoise and silver or gold buttons at the throat would unfailingly enhance any woman's appearance.

The same grand, flowing quality is seen in Arabian men's garments. In construction, for the most part, there is little difference between traditional garments for Arabian men and women. Both wear layered clothing, the basis of which is the body shirt. The outer mantle, like other garments, changes its name in different regions but the pattern is the same. The most obvious difference between the basic garments worn by men and women in olden times is colour.

Arabian women love and exploit colour. Long ago, men also wore colourful robes but today they are plain. Women wear a plain cloak today but wore richly embellished versions in the past.

The *kaftan* is the basis of traditional Arabian costume. In pure form, it is an ankle-length, long-sleeved tunic devoid of darts, zippers and collar.

Vast stretches of arid land look out towards the silent pinnacles of fossil-embedded cliffs. The Bedouin come in search of sparse vegetation.

They wander throughout the land tending their herds. A woman walks in the heat enveloped in flowing robes – a circlet anchoring headgear.

Head circlets, asayib, *were once many and varied. Left, plaited leather threaded with silver makes a rich roll over a core of packing.*

Nevertheless, the garment is tapered and flatters the figure. It is the most versatile of garment styles – the pattern easily adapted to make a vest, a jacket, a coat or gown. Colour of textile and embroidery often transform the *kaftan*, and dramatic changes are made by modifying the pattern's component parts. The common *thawb* for men today is simplicity itself but flattering and innovative because the gores flair cleverly on each side and secrete vertical slit-opening pockets.

The *kaftan* has a long history, and perhaps it originated in Arabia itself. However, it is generally accepted that it took final shape in Turkey long ago, spreading from there through the Islamic Empire and evolving independently in the various regions. It is interesting to note that the weather is mild in Turkey, unlike all other Middle Eastern countries.

The *kaftan* was originally a body-shirt in a society where layered clothing was the custom. The wealthy often had four or five layers of clothing while the poor had only one. Basically, there is the body-shirt, over which an enormous wide-sleeved *kaftan* may be worn poncho-fashion. Added to that, or as a replacement, rich women for special occasions would usually wear a sheer version of the larger garment. For outerwear, a *kaftan*-cut jacket or long coat might be worn. For venturing out of doors a mantle is customary. Undergarments were also worn in the form of long pants and a vest with short sleeves. Poor folk would choose to add the mantle to the basic body-shirt and get by with two garments only.

It is claimed that the evolution of the tapered cut derives from frugality. Originally, the textile was woven on a loom of a given width so the segments were simply that wide. Each Arabian garment is made from sections of cloth cleverly placed for a certain shape. This panelling conserves cloth and suggests the original designer gave great thought to the pattern, realizing that the effect he or she desired could be achieved economically by radiating wedges of fabric, or gores, from a point. In the march of time, even with the availability of wider textiles, this design aspect was not lost on the Peninsula, perhaps because the Arabian people are such traditionalists.

Arabian *kaftans* generally incorporate under-arm gussets, usually diamond-shaped sections of textile added to the pattern to make body movement easier when there are fitted sleeves. These practical inserts are always unobtrusive in Western garments but never so in Arabian women's traditional outer-wear. Elaborate under-arm gussets even appear in loose-fitting gowns when there can be no motive other than decoration. They are generally cut from cloth contrasting in both colour and texture and often edged with braid, occasionally embroidered and/or lavishly encrusted with sequins. Under-arm gussets are often the most predominant decorative feature of traditional female costume. It is typical of Arabian costume design that all shape and form elements be confirmed by means of embroidery, soutache, braid, strips of appliqué, sequins and other methods.

Clothing is important to all Arabs and new clothes have long been one of their main luxuries. From an early age, girls in traditional Arabia

learned to make garments and customarily assisted in the making of their own trousseaux. On special holidays, husbands and masters traditionally doled out *kiswa* (an assortment of textiles in various lengths) to their wives, dear ones and servants.

The delight and enjoyment Arabian people feel when receiving and wearing new garments may have roots as ancient as the garment styles themselves. Perhaps there is an inveterate instinct which rouses elation – echoing the joy felt in ancient times when a long-awaited camel caravan arrived bringing fabulous textiles from far away.

Although the best dressed gentlemen usually choose a white kufiyyah *with subtle-coloured embroidery, the souqs offer a myriad of colours with exotic embroidery. There are several styles and some are crocheted. Above, a typical array of skullcaps for sale in a Riyadh souq.*

Men

"The nomad kerchief, cast loosely upon their heads, is girded with a circlet band which is the dignity of the Arab clothing," writes Charles Montague Doughty (1843–96).

The internationally familiar Arabian headgear is virtually the same today as it has been for centuries – no doubt because it is a very practical arrangement for Arabia. The head and neck are protected from the scorching sun and it insulates by trapping air within the folds, allowing the wearer to retain moisture and a bearable temperature. This *ghoutra, shaal* or *ihram* is a sufficiently large cloth to allow it to be securely wound about the face or twisted into a turban – a fashion which was once very popular in Arabia. It is a square cloth, generally folded diagonally in half to form a triangle, with a pressed peak formed at the middle of the fold and worn centre front – the sides falling equally to just below the shoulders.

Red houndstooth check versions are worn throughout Arabia today as well as plain white headcloths. The latter are worn during the hottest part of the year and for "best". The checkered variety is known as *shmagh*. This style is also available in black and white, brown and white, green and white and blue and white, but these colours are not so popular. The quality of headcloths varies tremendously as does the edging which is sometimes hemmed instead of being fringed or braided and tasselled. The lengths of the fringes and tassels also vary.

The headcloth of the past (*imaamah*) was larger than the present-day examples. It could be made into a very large turban. In the Hijaz in olden times, a gentleman's fine muslin headcloth was often beautifully hand-embroidered and worn turban-fashion over a skullcap. Sometimes it was pale coloured and the usual shade was lemon. The textile also varied. The turban remains popular in rural areas, particularly the west, south-west, south and south-east regions and colourful printed and embroidered "squares" from India and Pakistan are favoured.

The *ghoutra* has been put to many uses in the past. In 1914, T. E. Lawrence, better known as Lawrence of Arabia, noted that the Peninsula Arabs wore on their heads red shawls which sometimes served as a pillow and at other times doubled as a sack. H. R. P. Dickson observed that every Bedouin went to battle with his headcloth wound tightly around his face, the ends tucked into the *igaal* on top of his head to prevent possible recognition. Only his eyes could be seen. This also kept sand out of the mouth.

The *igaal* is the head circlet, generally a double coil, bound with wool. This covering used to be a combination of black goats' hair and sheep's wool. The circlet is sometimes trimmed with two small tassels which are usually worn at the back of the head. The *igaal* has the purpose of holding the headcloth in place. The word *igaal* is said to have evolved from the same word used for the nomad's tethering rope, and indeed sometimes a simple piece of rope suffices to secure the headcloth of a poor man. A headcloth circlet is sometimes called

Headgear for the Arabian male consists of either one, two or three pieces. The widely accepted traditional arrangement today is a combination of skullcap (kufiyyah), headcloth (ghoutra), and head circlet (igaal). (There are other names for the three pieces.) The kufiyyah *is the basis for correct headgear. The* ghoutra *is folded to a triangle and draped over the* kufiyyah. *It is held in place by the* igaal. *Above, an old skullcap,* kufiyyah mugassabeh, *is heavily embroidered by hand with gold metal thread. Skullcaps are invariably embroidered. In the olden days, the* kufiyyah *was generally washable white cotton with self-coloured silk embroidery. The fine hemmed white cotton and polyester* ghoutra *shown is commonly worn in the cities and during the hotter months. Beneath can be seen the gold edging on a* bisht.

A: *The headcloth (ghoutra) is a square-shaped garment which is folded diagonally to form a triangle. It is worn correctly with a peak pinched at the centre-front of the forehead, and the kufiyyah is barely visible if at all. The black wool double coil igaal serves to hold the ghoutra in place. In the past this circlet was trimmed with two small black tassels which were worn at the back.*

B: *The headcloth varies in quality and type of textile, and the name also differs. Whatever the style, it is common to see men wearing this garment with one or both side ends tossed back over the head.*

C: *In olden times, it was usual for the men of Arabia to twist and wind their headcloths into a turban. Today, it is worn thus generally only by rural men and those who perform menial work.*

shattafa in western Arabia and various other kinds of circlets, *asayib* (some worn without headcloths) are known as *isaaba* (singular). One type is merely a textile head binding called *osba*.

Asayib often seem to have no real purpose other than decoration. They do help shape the growth of hair of some tribal men in the south-west, while most circlets serve only to hold colourful and sweet-smelling herbs and flowers or pendant ornaments. *Asayib* were made from various mediums in the past including pure silver. In remote regions many are made of leather decorated with silver. Others are fashioned from wire-bound straw. To the extreme, is the *igaal gassab*, which is bound with gold metal thread and has knots of black wool at four corners on a double ring. In times past, royalty sometimes wore a four-bar *igaal gassab*. The golden *igaal* is reserved for special occasions today – even for royalty.

Correct Arabian headgear consists of three parts, the final component being a skullcap, *kufiyyah* or *taagiyyah*, which is worn under the headcloth. Sometimes skullcaps are not worn under the headcloth. These caps have often been called "prayer caps", possibly because it is the Muslim custom to cover the head during prayer. In fact, they are more likely "sweat caps". Their original purpose is claimed as practical in that they kept natural hair oils from spoiling the headcloth. Skullcaps in the past were made of cotton and laundered easily. They are invariably embroidered and known as *kufiyyah magassabeh* if the work is lavish.

Embroidery on the skullcap is often white silk but sometimes gold thread and other colours are employed – the most elaborate being decorated with precious gold metal thread. Occasionally, today, crotcheted versions are seen but these are imported, mostly from Pakistan. In times past, especially in Mecca, a gentleman's skullcap was taller – similar in height to the Turkish *fez*. The Meccan version is white cotton, stiffened with starch and known as the *kufiyyah belladi*.

An interesting story about skullcaps confirms that they were regularly manufactured on the

Above: *Checkered headcloths are available in many colours and qualities. Most are made in Japan. The most popular version is red and white, known as* shmagh. *Townsmen prefer to wear it in the cooler months.*

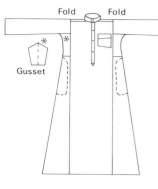

Left: *The present-day men's* thawb *is often tailored with shirt collar and cuffs. The textile is usually white or cream-coloured cotton and polyester or a similar fine textile for summer. Darker coloured worsteds are worn in winter. The side pockets are stitched onto the inside of the* thawb *and the vertically-slit openings to these are in line with the side seams. Another pocket is generally placed on the front left breast today.*

* *The underarm gusset fold is indicated by the centre line.*

Below: *Men's old-style body-shirt of Greater Arabia. It is variously known as* merodan, woniya *or* shillahat *etc. The textile was commonly unbleached calico for the average Bedouin. It is tailored from fine cloth today and reserved for special occasions.*

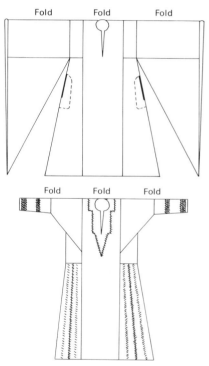

Arabian Peninsula. Around 1500, a shipwrecked sea captain, Gregoria de Quadra, was imprisoned at Zabid by the King of Yemen – thereafter he earned a living making skullcaps.

Some peasant folk on the Peninsula present the exception with regard to customary headgear; in several parts of the land they wear palm-frond hats, especially in the areas where palm trees are plentiful. Fishermen on the Red Sea coast, near towns where palm frond crafts are practised, also wear them. The styles vary sufficiently from place to place for the hats to be a means of identification.

Men who wear palm-frond hats, and other peasants, usually wear a loincloth, *izar*, or a *fouta*, or both. The *fouta* is a colourful length of textile that is wound around the lower half of the body, the end pleated and tucked securely in at the waist. It is generally worn with a belt, but sometimes the *fouta* is simply formed into the style of a loincloth by bringing the end through the legs to tuck in at centre front waist. In fact, it has virtually taken the place of the loincloth, the ancient style of Arabian men's underwear. Instead of a body-shirt, these men often wear the *fanilla*, a short-sleeved, high round-necked shirt.

For the average Arabian male, the basic item of clothing is a *kaftan*, the ankle-length, shirt-like, long-sleeved garment without darts or zipper, and known today as a *thawb*. There have been superficial variations down through the centuries and it

Above: *An Asir Province men's body-shirt tailored in unbleached calico. it is unique in that the sleeves are narrow – possibly because of the cooler Asir climate. It is similarly cut to Asir women's dresses – the notable difference to garments worn in other parts of Arabia is the shape of the under-arm gusset. This segment is much larger on the men's version. The sleeves are also different in that they are fashioned in two sections to allow a fitted* forearm segment and roomy upper arm section. The centre panels, front and back, are cut from a single length which has been embroidered by sewing machine prior to making-up the garment. Side gore and sleeve embroidery is also carried out before joining up the component parts of the pattern. Although there are only two side gores at each side, dividing lines of chain-stitch give the impression of twice the number. The thread colours are red and black.

has been known by several names, but it remains a simple, practical garment. Ludovico de Varthema, who visited Mecca in 1502, aptly described it as a "loose vesture".

The Arab body-shirt, tunic or *kaftan*, can be seen today throughout the Arabized world, where it has been worn for centuries and there is debate about its origin. Although a long body-shirt is a very ancient garment, it seems likely that the Arabs, who went forth in the eighth century from the Arabian Peninsula to spread their Islamic faith, were responsible for influencing tailors. Wherever they went, they apparently assimilated and enriched the indigenous cultures of the lands they entered.

In the past, the body-shirt was known as *woniya*, *shillahat* or *merodan*. It had large, open sleeves with an under-arm seam forming a point which reached the floor. This style is reserved for special occasions today. The modern *thawb* has straight sleeves, and the body of the garment is less full than its predecessor. The *merodan* lost favour in the forties when men took jobs in Ministries and found this style cumbersome and impractical.

Basically, the *merodan* and *thawb* are the same garment. The side panels give sufficient fullness for every movement, as they radiate to the hemline from a rectangular under-arm gusset. These side gores have an inset pocket with a vertical slit opening at each side – a common design feature of Middle Eastern ethnic outer garments. The neckline is high and round, generally with a banded collar (*aga*) and the buttoned opening at centre front reaches to the middle chest. Variations include a normal shirt collar which is matched by shirt-sleeve cuffs.

For most of the year, the average *thawb* is worn in white or cream cotton or silk mixed with synthetic fibres. In cool months, the *thawb* is worn in a variety of fine worsteds in "quiet" colours. In the olden days, the body-shirt was often coloured. Although the *thawb* is a one-colour garment, braid and piping or soutache can make this simple item of apparel very handsome. Sartorial splendour can be achieved by adding beautiful *uzrar*, shirt-front studs and *kabak*, cufflinks.

Outdoor Arab costume throughout the centuries and down to this present modern age is completed only when an outer mantle is added. The men's cloak is known in Arabia as a *bisht* or *mishlah* and it is identical in concept to the version worn by women and differs only in textile, colour and embellishment – and, of course, in the way that it is worn. While women drape the *abaaya* from the centre of the crown, men wear the *bisht* cloak fashion on the shoulders. Today only men's cloaks are embroidered with gold and sometimes a little silver. This metal thread work is secured with yellow thread to form a band about the neckline ending in two small decorative, tasselled tie-cords. There is also gold soutache trimming along the shoulder line and around the hand openings. The textiles range from camel hair and wool to cotton and synthetics. There are many qualities within these categories and the colours may vary from black, brown, beige and "camel" to cream.

Charles Doughty once saw a homespun mantle of tent cloth worn by a Bedouin but he "never saw

Left: *Typical Arabian men's costume worn early this century. It consists of four layers and is among the costumes of King Abd al-Aziz Ibn Saud. The under-layer is made up of long pants* (sirwaal) *and a body-shirt of fine creamy-coloured cotton similar to the* thawb *worn over it. Both garments are heavily worked about the necklines with self-coloured embroidery thread. On top is worn a felt* kaftan-*cut coat and felt jacket.*

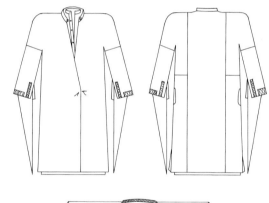

Below: *The front and back view of one of the costumes worn by Ibn Saud, King Abd al-Aziz, founder of the Kingdom of Saudi Arabia. The wide and deep-pointed sleeves of the* merodan *protrude from the slit sleeves of the ankle-length coat known as* baalto, qumbaz, zibun, *etc. It is fastened by two sets of tie-cords – one inside and one outside as shown. The side seams are slit up from the hemline to display the full skirt of the body-shirt. The textile is paisley-patterned brocade in yellow, green, blue, black and white.*

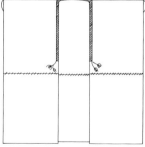

The essential item of attire for men – after the body-shirt and headgear – is the outer mantle. It is mostly known as bisht *or* mishla. *This cloak serves as another protective layer to conserve body moisture and insulate by trapping air in its folds. In olden times it was used as a ground sheet or blanket when resting or sleeping on the sand while travelling. Colours range through pale cream, honey, beige, brown and camel to black. They were more colourful in bygone days. The women's* abaaya *is identically cut and both are taken up along the horizontal centre seam rather than the hem if they must be shortened. The men's cloak is decorated with gold which is confined to the neckband, soutache running along the shoulder line and around the openings for the hands, and small decorative tassels at each end of the neckband. The finest examples are made in various weights of camel hair cloth, wool, cotton, and synthetic fibre textiles.*

Right: *Damascus, an ancient Middle Eastern fashion centre, continues to provide exotic-looking garments such as this jacket* (furmilaaya or saaya) *just as it did when commodities had to come by camel train along the ancient trade routes. Such jackets are also called* cote *and* damir. *They are worn today when performing the ceremonial sword dance,* ardah. *Lavish* aghabani *embroidery stiffens the rich velvet – in the past, felt was common. The young man attempts to sell the author his wares in a Riyadh souq.*

the like on another nomad". Shepherds throughout Arabia ideally own a heavy sheepskin-lined cloak known as a *farwah* in which they sleep on cold nights. Old photographs indicate that there were once coarse woven wool versions of the *farwah* such as Doughty described. Townsmen also wear the *farwah* in winter but it is usually a much grander garment, exhibiting at least two colours, generally black and dark blue and decorated with black braid.

Coarse, woven wool jackets are also worn. Jackets of various kinds form part of the Arab male's wardrobe although it is said they were introduced only a century ago. In the past, most were made in Damascus – the garment usually collarless and tailored from felt and richly embroidered with gold. Today, these jackets, *furmilaaya* or *saaya*, are made of velvet and generally reserved for evening wear on special occasions. A superb effect is created when this jacket (which is usually black or some other deep colour) is worn with a gleaming white *merodan*. Dickson records a similar jacket, *damir*, that was worn in the far north-east of the Peninsula. In the Hijaz in olden times, townsmen often wore, under the mantle, a jacket called a *cote*. This roll-collared short coat resembles a Western dinner jacket or tuxedo. Names for jackets are more numerous than the basic styles – the word *cote* is probably a loan word from English.

Also worn in the Hijaz and various other parts of Arabia in times past were two long coats, one a front-opening gown which fastened with twin ties just below the waistline – with one tie inside and the other outside. This cross-over garment, *zibun* or *baalto*, looks like a Western dressing gown. It is worn over the body-shirt and under the mantle. The sleeves are slit on the under-arm seam, which allows it to properly display the long pointed sleeves of the traditional body-shirt. The two side seams are also slit deeply to the hem which reveals the full skirt of the *merodan*. Similar slits are also featured on the gold-embroidered velvet jackets and the other style of full-length *kaftan*-cut coat known as *jubba*. King Abd al-Aziz Ibn Saud, the founder of the Kingdom of Saudi Arabia, wore these long coats although they are not considered to be originally Arabian.

Wilfred Thesiger relates a circumcision celebration of a southern Arabian tribe in which ritualistic costume is worn. He mentions the garb of the initiates as peculiar to this one occasion in their lives: "The young boys don short, tight-sleeved, red jackets and baggy white *sirwaal*." It would be interesting to discover what these jackets were made of and to know if they were embroidered and, if so, by whom.

In Lewis Pelly's report on his trip into the Najd in 1865, there is mention of leather garments being part of the traditional range of Arab clothing for men at that time. There also seems to be some ritualistic purpose to one garment. Pelly's guide was reminiscing about an incident in his youth, and recalled an event when he was very young, prior to his donning the deer-skin shirt. His story suggested to Pelly that the leather jacket was a ceremonial garment, signifying the boy had reached puberty. The piece of clothing is variously described as a shirt, a coat, and a gown which does not assist further research.

Sheepskin garments are still an important part of Arabian costume today, especially for shepherds in rural areas. In the high mountainous regions of the Asir, Arabian men and women wear capes and sections of hides over their shoulders. These wraps, affixed at each side of the neck by a chain, have decorative red leather work on the natural-coloured skin, worn to the outside. Most of these skin garments are without sleeves and openings for the arms.

All forms of Arabian men's outer-wear is designed to fall open at the front. The possible reason for this is that, traditionally, an Arab is considered properly decked out only when wearing weapons.

Below: *Throughout the cooler parts of the Peninsula, especially the highlands, men wear a sheepskin-lined overcoat,* farwah. *This capacious coat is very heavy and serves the shepherd or traveller as a blanket or bedroll. The outer layer is a tightly-woven woollen or* cotton textile in at least two colours which are divided by braidwork usually black and dark blue trimmed with black. Old examples often have colourful patches appliquéd. Today, souqs offer a variety of sombre-coloured basecloths decorated with bright braid.

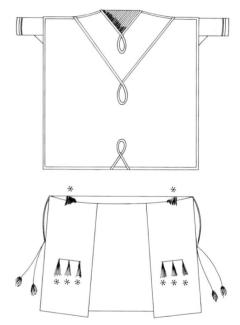

Above: *A sleeveless coarse woven wool jacket from the Asir. Similar jackets were worn in the past by Bedouin in other regions. The wool has been dyed dark red and orange and the triangles of* embroidery* are worked with reddish-coloured wool of a finer gauge. The tasselled pendants are made of orange-coloured wool. Henna or indigo may have been the dyestuff.

Arms are worn to the front – to be "at the ready" it would seem. Arabian arms are usually elaborately decorated and consist of a sheathed dagger, generally known as *jambiyyah* or *khanjar*, and a sheathed sword, the *saif*. Some Meccan men once carried a small sheathed dagger known as a *sikeena*, while Arab tribesmen customarily carried a dagger, knife, sword and spear. The rifle eventually replaced the spear. Ceremonially, daggers are only worn with a jacket but this garment was often impractical with full gear and a battle to be fought.

Wilfred and Lady Anne Blunt, visiting Hayil in

1878 described the Amir, Muhammed ibn Rashid, as "gorgeously dressed, carrying gold-hilted daggers and a gold-hilted sword adorned with turquoises and rubies".

There are two popular swords in Arabia: the double-edged straight blade and the slim single-edged scimitar. The latter was probably introduced into Arabia after the expansion of the Islamic Empire into Asia during the eighth and ninth centuries. The earlier swords were of the double-edged, straight blade type.

Long ago fine swords and daggers were made in many places on the Peninsula. Najran and Yemen are known for producing good blades. Old records mention the Banu Hanifa and Banu Asad tribes as excellent blade-makers and several Omani towns are famous for weaponry of distinctive styles and embellishment. In the past, many swords were

West of Abha, some valley tribesmen carry a dagger nearly a metre long, to protect themselves against leopards, they say.

Many daggers are made for the Arabian market by Indians and Iranians. Wherever the weaponry is made, it is acknowledged as an integral part of traditional Arabian costume. The buckles, belts, bandoliers, hilts, scabbards and powder horns are often richly ornamented and pride of ownership is commensurate with the level of ostentation. Both

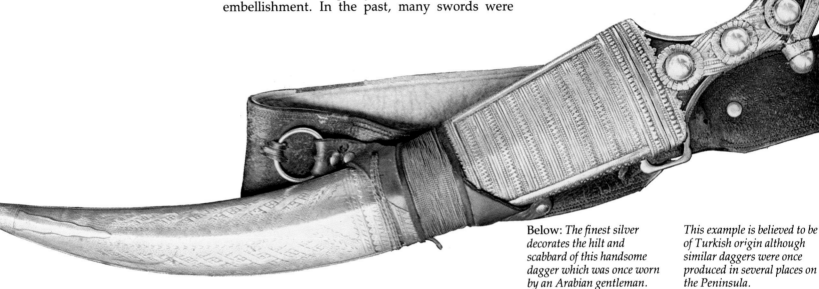

Below: *The finest silver decorates the hilt and scabbard of this handsome dagger which was once worn by an Arabian gentleman.*

This example is believed to be of Turkish origin although similar daggers were once produced in several places on the Peninsula.

Above: *Embossed silver and brass combine to make up the scabbard of this fine Najdi dagger. The blade slips down between two pieces of wood, the insides of which are lined with red cotton. A strip of leather is glued to the back of the scabbard where another small sheath is attached to house a knife. This leather scabbard is richly ornamented with tiny silver beads. The felt-lined leather belt is strongly secured and lashed to the metal scabbard with twisted brass wire. The hilt is horn clad with silver, and the double-edged blade is superb steel, sharp enough to divide a hair.*

imported from Damascus, Basra and India but the decoration on these was usually carried out by specialized Muslim craftsmen. Today, most of the sabres worn on the Peninsula come from India undecorated, to be embellished locally. Many skilled weaponry jewellers are located on the island of Bahrain.

Royalty and the well-to-do often have their names inscribed in artistic calligraphy and many swords also carry Koranic phrases, the names of craftsmen and date of manufacture. It was the custom in Arabia to offer visiting dignitaries presents of swords and daggers, many of which were engraved. The Imam of Najd, in 1865, presented the explorer Pelly with a magnificent "gilt pistol and sword made to please Arab taste". Pelly recorded that the sword was much admired.

The Arabian dagger has a broad double-edged blade, bisected lengthwise by a salient spine along the full length of the blade. It is slightly curved and tapers from the middle towards a spiky point. The hilt is made of horn, bone, wood, plastic or ivory with a T-shaped crown. The scabbard is made from special wood covered with silver. The traditional southern scabbard has a U-shaped end and all others are curved to a much lesser degree. The blade of one Arabian dagger, commonly referred to as the "Gulf dagger" is thirty-three centimetres long including the hilt. The best-known Central Arabian dagger is a little shorter.

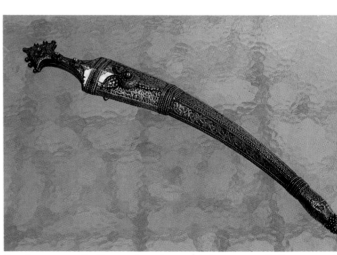

the brass and silver sheaths and horns and the silver pieces on belts and bandoliers exhibit the jewellery-making techniques commonly employed to make traditional Arabian women's ornaments.

Firearms were introduced in the late eighteenth century when metalsmiths began using their skills to decorate them also. Long flintlock rifles were commonly embellished with silver on the barrel and stock and teeth of the gazelle or oryx appeared on the butt. Gazelle hide padding was used to finish the butt.

In the cities today, arms are only worn for ceremonial occasions. *Thawbs* today are conse-

Right: *This waistbelt (hizam), is claimed to be a men's style and from the south-western region, the Asir. Pendant bells are usually more common to women's belts.*

Far right: *Traditional style of waistbelt worn by men in the Asir. Variations fall within the design boundaries illustrated by this example. Asir belts are constructed from stiffened calico and one-third centimetre diameter silver beads are closely stitched to cover the surface. Loop fasteners made from strings of silver beads hook over modern buttons. Original buttons were probably formed from knotted cord. The "buckle" patch is invariably formed from appliquéd red cotton and oversewn with beads and shirt buttons. Possibly the forerunner of the latter was mother-of-pearl.*

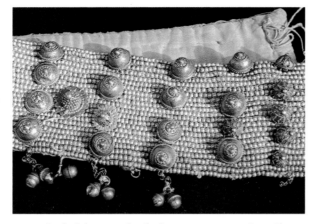

quently beltless – the belt was worn primarily to hold knives. Since the advent of firearms, a crossed bandolier is also worn – with a belt – the harness-like arrangement snugly secure even during the wildest chase on horseback. This double bandolier crossing the chest holds ammunition and has become part of male traditional costume worn for the ceremonial war dance, *ardah*, and other special occasions.

The production of sword belts and bandoliers is a developed craft on the Peninsula, often involving woven gold and silver metal thread work. Many are also imported from Syria.

The waistbelt, *hizam*, is an important item of apparel in the traditional sense. Apart from their use as a means of securing arms to the body, belts contain money and other items. *Hizam* were made from various mediums in the past. Charles Doughty, in his book *Arabia Deserta*, writes that tribesmen in western Arabia wore a "girding lace of leathern plait" which was known as a *haggu*. Belts such as these were worn, according to Thesiger, under the

thawb to support the back when riding camels for great distances. Also from the west and south-west come beautiful webbing belts for men, literally covered with shining silver.

In the past, a waistbelt often took the form of a large square of some fine cotton textile which was bound around the body. This garment is known as a *bugsha*. Pockets could be formed in the *bugsha* to hold money and objects. Although convenient, it is rarely worn today. It is also a sensible accessory to wear in a hot country as it is both absorbent and soft.

In traditional Arabia, men also carried sticks. Townsmen in the Hijaz possessed a decorated stick called a *shoon*. Bedouin carried camel sticks made of cane, known as *asa*, *mishaab* and *baakura*. It was common also for the nomad to carry leather bags called *mizuda*. This name also applies to the woven woollen versions. *Mizuda* are colourfully decorated with beads, tassels and cloth appliqué, and hold anything from Koranic verses to a small supply of coffee beans, dates or money.

Right: *This multi-stranded plaited leather belt is probably the "leathern cincture" described by Wilfred Thesiger who traversed the Empty Quarter. He said the Bedouin wore it beneath their clothes to support the back. The example here was purchased second-hand in the Hijaz where it was claimed to be from the Beni Salim tribe. It may have been common throughout the Peninsula.*

Far right: *Delicate silver beadwork and neat leather plaiting on calico form a most attractive waistbelt from around Tayif, located in the Hijaz. Tayif actually lies at the northern end of the Sarawat Mountain range and has costume styles more typical of the Asir highlands. Fine beadwork is seen in both the Hijaz and the Asir. Red, black, yellow and green embroidery often serves as dividers and geometric shapes placed between silver beadwork.*

Left: *Long and thin plaited leather and silver thong sashes with tasselled ends are claimed as belt styles worn by women of the Beni Salim tribe in the Hijaz. These people have a great reputation for high-quality leather work. There are accounts of a similar item to this belt, and it is worn in Oman by tribesmen who plait one end into their long hair before* *coiling the length seven times around the head. In most parts of Arabia in the past, women donned a waistbelt only for dancing. These belts were silver and studded with semi-precious stones or glass, and silver coins. Pendant bells jangled gaily in rhythm with the dancer.*

45

Women

Listing the Arabian woman's traditional costume in a general fashion from head to toe, and from outer layer to inner layer, puts headgear first. This is ideal as headgear is generally considered to be the most distinctive element of Arabian women's attire.

European travellers passing through the Islamic world from the seventeenth century onwards, frequently mention women's veils. Evidence suggests that the custom for wearing the veil saw a great revival in the Middle Ages.

Face veiling is recorded as having begun with the Assyrians as far back as 1500 BC. Covering the head is also an ancient custom. In the Middle East it has long been a sign of modesty and respect but since the dawn of Islam, the custom has taken on an added dimension for women. Since then, and particularly during the hey-day of the Ottoman Empire, it has been considered virtuous to wear a face veil and headcloth. In any case, in the desert, without the practical aid of sunglasses, these various face and head coverings have a distinct advantage. The incredible glare on the bright sand can cause sun-blindness and do irreparable harm to the eyes, and continual exposure of delicate facial skin to the sun's rays can take a harsh toll. Sun is also harmful to the hair and sand is an irritant to the scalp.

In the past, intricate and costly veils and headgear were made. Today they are much simpler. Throughout the Peninsula at present, women's headgear generally consists of two pieces – sometimes three. It once varied distinctly from province to province and occasionally within a given area because of sub-tribal customs. There was also variance between the headgear worn by townswomen, village women, peasants and nomads within a given region. Yet the differences are only superficial.

Headgear of the past was sometimes a simple arrangement of soft textiles. At other times, it included a stiff mask, *burga*, elaborately constructed on a textile base from pieces of leather, silver coins and charms, pearls, beads, shells and small white buttons. Some masks were made entirely of leather and handpainted in gay colours. Most masks have pendant tassels. Between tribe and sub-tribe, especially in the past, the length of the mask, design elements and mediums employed served to convey the wearer's provenance.

Colonel H. R. P. Dickson, author of *The Arab of the Desert* and *Kuwait and Her Neighbours*, writes that, roughly speaking, Bedouin women south of a line drawn across Arabia from Aqaba to Kuwait wear the *burga*, with the exception of the Shammar and some Hijaz tribes; those north of the line do not wear the *burga* but merely wear the thin black veil, *milfa*, drawn across the lower part of the face only. According to Dickson, certain north-western tribal women, notably the Bani Sakhr, Huwaytat and Bani Atiya do not wear even the *milfa*. He writes that all wear the *umm raugella*, a rectangular black cotton scarf constructed from four segments, worn over the hair and hanging down over the neckline of the *thawb*. A similar black veil known as

Left: *Head circlets* (asayib), *of various kinds are worn by both men and women in parts of Arabia. They usually have the purpose of holding the headcloth in place. In the case of women, they also serve to support decorative pendants. Along the west coast of Arabia, in the Hijaz, Asir and Yemen, some circlet styles have pendants attached. This particular style is a padded roll of leather which is decorated with tiny silver beads. Silver-coloured beads fall in strands to support silver-plated thimbles and woollen tassels. Shirt buttons and cowrie shells are additional. There are seven main pendants, one each side of the face and five at the back of the head. Two metal rings join the ends of the circlet roll at the back of the head to support a bar formed from a triangle of cloth.*

Left: *In several parts of Arabia, women do not wear a veil, particularly in the south-west. Frequently, women wear hats, most of which are woven from palm fronds such as the one shown here. Usually, these women wear a headcloth underneath which protects them further when bending to tend their crops.*

The most popular face veil throughout Arabia today is fine black gauze which filters the dust. It is a double layer to the chin and both the top layer and the bottom layer (which falls to the chest) are generally edged with some pretty trim. These veils are attached to a headband which leaves kohl-enhanced eyes visible. Originally ths style was made of coarse black silk and seen only in the Najd and the Eastern Province.

Top right: *Almond-shaped eye slits are created by joining the double veil to a headband,* **X**, *at three points: at the bridge of the nose and from the outer corners of the eyes to the edges of the mask. Ties are affixed at points* **A**, **B**, *and* **C**.
Below right: *The batula mask worn in all of the eastern regions, is made of black coarse silk or cotton. Sticks inserted at points* * *stiffen the mask.* **A** *and* **B** *denote tie positions. The centre protrusion is formed from a stitched-down pleat.*
Below, far left: *Asir masks usually feature beadwork. Red, yellow, green, blue and*

white beads match embroidery and cover the white calico-backed black basecloth. Gold, silver coins, pearl buttons, cowrie shells and braid are popularly added.
Below left: *Soft cotton with woven silver and white braid form this Hijazi mask. A stitched-down box pleat supports silver coins.*
Below right: *Hijazi masks are usually red with silver and white braid, silver coins and pendants of stranded silver on twisted cotton.*
Below, far right: *An unusual Hijazi mask trimmed with zip fastener teeth and bells.*

misfa, taraha, habaya and other names is universally worn today, bought ready-made with beaded, embroidered, braided or tasselled ends which by their weight help keep it in place. One end usually drapes down the back and one hangs in front.

A *burga* totally covers the face but leaves slits or openings for the eyes. Many soft veils cover the eyes. The mask was traditionally the preserve of the Bedouin and village women of Arabia, not the townswomen, although the latter did wear veils. The town veil that comes closest to the *burga* is commonly called the ''Meccan veil'' because it was a style peculiar to Meccan women in olden times. It is, in fact, also called *burga* (*burga milaaya* or *nigaab*) and commonly made from delicately embroidered light white gauze, stiffly starched. This style is unique in that the veil reaches the floor and sometimes further. The Meccan veil often reached elaborate ''heights'', not to mention incredible

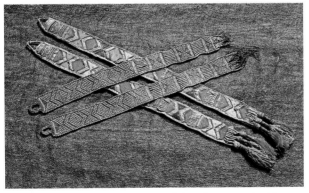

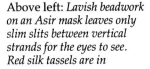
Above left: *Lavish beadwork on an Asir mask leaves only slim slits between vertical strands for the eyes to see. Red silk tassels are in*

dramatic contrast with the white beading.
Above: *Orange-coloured silk and Ottoman coins make up this elaborate Hijazi mask*

which also displays white and silver beadwork, bands of silver and white braid, mother-of-pearl buttons with silver beaded centres and a

band of fringed weaving, incorporating silver beads. Silver-coloured metal pendants finish off the leather thong warp strands. Black embroidery edges the main body of the mask and outlines the eye holes which are separated by seven strands of small glass beads.
Above: *Mask pendants take their colour from the weft threads. Warp threads are white cotton or fine leather thongs. Silver beads are sometimes stranded vertically. Red, black, yellow,*

pink and green embroidery with silver beads divide geometric patterns. These ''book-mark'' pendants are worn in matched pairs, one hanging each side of a mask. Loops at the top ends are threaded in the mask ties. The ends invariably display tassels with fringes weighted by tiny silver beads. Metal thread binds the heads of the tassels.

length and weight. Some were encrusted on both the front and back with silver metal thread embroidery and pearls. These, of course, were worn by the rich and kept by them for special occasions.

Very elaborate masks are also worn by the Bedouin and rural women in western Arabia, and it often takes tribeswomen up to six months to complete one. Most of them have pendant tassels which are made from materials bought in the *souq*. The Bedouin women and girls spend much of their spare time fashioning mask trimmings which are known as *taly*.

It has been said that the wealth of a Bedouin woman in western Arabia is in her mask because on this she has sewn silver coins. In fact, her jewellery is often worth more. However, the coins are often of high intrinsic value, especially if they are old – many of them being eighty percent pure silver. For the most part, white shirt buttons and metallic braid have replaced silver charms and coins on masks. In the past, the buttons were made from mother-of-pearl shell and these masks and various other headscarves look as though they might have come from a Pearly King's wardrobe in London.

In western Arabia, twin sections of woven, beaded, fringed and tasselled, and sometimes silver embellished strips (resembling book-marks) are sometimes worn each side of the mask in similar fashion to silver pendants, *ilagah*, which, in other parts of Arabia, are traditionally hooked into a head circlet and fall over the ears. The addition of the strips probably had significance in the past.

These days, tribeswomen leave masks behind when venturing outside their domain. They don instead, the simple black veil, *taraha*, as they still wish to present a modest appearance in public. The *burga* is worn less and less in favour of the more comfortable *taraha*, *mahanna* or *shayla*. The costliest examples are embroidered with silver. Many of these rectangular headscarves are plain cotton gauze while others are synthetic textiles.

The traditional headgear of the Hijazi townswoman is made up of three pieces, excluding the face veil. They are three geometric shapes. The first is a small triangle which is placed over the hair at the forehead – the thin straps at each side tie it in place. The second piece, a rectangle, is placed on the head over the triangle. Equally divided, it is wound around the parted tresses which fall down each side of the face and these are then fixed on the top of the head. The third piece is a square, one edge of which is placed on the forehead, while the long sides are looped up and folded on the top of the head.

Another traditional Arabian garment for women the *bukhnug* or *mukhnug* should correctly be classified as headgear because it efficiently covers the hair, head and shoulders. It is worn by unmarried girls. The *bukhnug* can be short or long, the longest example forming a train to trail behind. This additional length is worn draped over one arm when the wearer wishes to move about more freely, in the fashion of the extra-long version of the Meccan Veil. It is claimed as a Central Arabian garment although it is seen in Eastern Arabia, the Gulf lands and other parts of Greater Arabia.

Many Bedouin women wear an *osba*, a folded or

Above: *Heavy and ornate headcloths are worn by rural women in Western Arabia – some styles are sufficiently large as to serve as a mantle. Embellishment has been carried out on opposite sides in two corners of this large square headcloth. When it is folded unevenly diagonally, the appliqué and other decoration can be seen.*

Left: *Also from the Hijaz and Asir, come heavily decorated rectangular mantles with embellishment on opposite sides. This rectangular* gnaa *is placed on the head to fall equally down front and back before the crown is bunched, pinned and twisted, and the front length is tossed back over the head. See opposite page.*

padded scarf, underneath the outer headcovering. It is a thick circlet which serves to secure veils, scarves and hair ornaments. In some parts of Arabia a woman's long tresses are plaited and fixed on the top of the head and this forms a basis for headgear. The southern Arabian style of this headband is often merely wadded paper around which is stitched a piece of colourful brocade. This is said to be a Turkish circlet.

Another type of headband is made from a roll of stuffed leather decorated with silver beads. Attached are pendants of various lengths which display small white buttons, silver beads, tassels and other objects such as silver-plated thimbles. These and other leather and silver head circlets are common in the west coast regions. The pendant ornaments are reminiscent of silver *ilagah*.

Hair ornaments, *hilyat shaar*, often form an integral part of Arabian headgear and therefore

should be included with the other forms of head apparel. In some cases, the items are clearly jewellery, fashioned from metal and studded with semi-precious stones, as in the case of the *ilagah*. A certain type of Turkish brooch, made of gold and diamonds, becomes integral with Arabian headgear when used to top the traditional Hijazi *mihramah wa mudawwarah*. Similar brooches were once used on the bodice of the Hijazi townswoman's traditional bridal wear.

Various *hilyat shaar* are worn directly on the hair at the back of the head in traditional Arabia. One style of straw hat worn by the rural women of the Asir, incorporates criss-crossed silver chains attached to the back edge of the brim. This trimming looks exotic against black hair or the black scarf which is often worn under the hat.

It can be seen that Arabian women enjoy wearing hair ornaments in large modern cities even

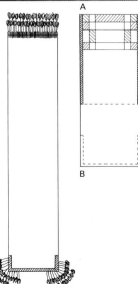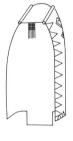

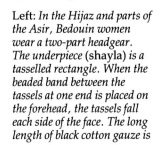

Left: *In the Hijaz and parts of the Asir, Bedouin women wear a two-part headgear. The underpiece (shayla) is a tasselled rectangle. When the beaded band between the tassels at one end is placed on the forehead, the tassels fall each side of the face. The long length of black cotton gauze is* twisted once about the waist and arranged to show the tassels of the other end at back mid-calf. A heavy black satin-finished cotton gnaa is the second part worn over the top as shown. The black and white drawings illustrate areas of embroidery – shading on one side and within dotted lines on the reverse. *Appliquéd squares, triangles and strip edging in various shades of red are combined* with yellow, green, black and orange embroidery and silver and white beading. The work is predominantly at one end and this is worn at hip level. Centre: *There are many styles of shayla and usually these rectangular scarves are no more that 150 centimetres long and not wound around the waist. Both ends are invariably weighted with decorative braid, beading or as depicted. This tasselled* braid is commercially produced. In the past, Bedouin women made their own silk tassels. Above: *Black and white drawings illustrate the basic design of hoods which are usually made of black cotton lined with unbleached calico. Appliqué is the predominant form of embellishment as a rule. Occasionally beadwork is favoured, especially in the Asir.*

Below: Striped sheets were once imported from Egypt to be worn as mantles. Jeddah women wore a blue/black silk mantle, and Meccan women chose grey. Today, Arabian women prefer the plain black cloak abaaya, *and it is worn draped from the centre crown.*

Before the introduction of this cloak, the sheet or milaaya, *was universal. Some women still cling to this fashion. There are various names and sizes for the many styles – the most frequent appellation is* milaaya *meaning sheet.*

today. On the second night of a Saudi Arabian princess's marriage (the traditional night for women to gather for the wedding celebration) hair ornamentation was lavish. Each lady whose head was uncovered wore some decorative hair pin, chain or clasp. Several of the most elegant wore strands of pearls plaited in their hair, glittering clips, or a sprinkling of dainty, sparkling pins.

On the western side of the Arabian Peninsula, from the Hijaz in the north to Yemen in the south, it is not uncommon to see rural women wearing palm-frond hats woven into a variety of attractive shapes. Distinctive styles can be found in each area

where palm weaving is a developed craft. They are usually worn over the rectangular cotton head-cloth. Peasant women in the southern region wear a wide-brimmed straw hat with an exceptionally high-pointed crown unlike any other in Arabia. They are remarkably Mexican in appearance.

The outer wrapper, the *abaaya* – the universally known Arabian woman's garment – forms part of the headgear, in that usually it is worn draped from the centre crown. The *abaaya* is so successful as an outer mantle that it has led many Westerners to believe that the ladies of Arabia always wear black. Closer observation will reveal that Arabian

Above: Metal-thread chain stitching enhances old hand-dyed silk, left, *in a curious set of motifs – an aircraft flies amongst fish, stars, crowns, crescents, palm trees and a sailing ship. The Indian printed cotton sheet,* centre, *is currently popular in southern regions. The striped version on the* right *is a Yemeni power-loom product.*

women not only enjoy colour but choose for their dresses vibrant and pretty hues in preference to sombre shades. The black *abaaya* is merely the outer layer donned when venturing out into the streets. Its colour is ideal because it "goes with anything".

The cloak is a very practical garment, too, as it is more comfortable to wear than a coat. It provides warmth when the weather is cool and conserves body moisture when it is hot.

Long before Islam, it was customary in the Middle East to wear an outer mantle for travel outside the home, and remarkably, this long-

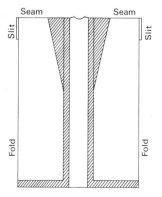

Prior to the plain black abaaya, women's black cloaks were embellished with gold, as shown left. The pattern was the same as the men's bisht, page 41, and this style is still popular. Damascus has devised a new style by shortening the textile lengths. It is decorated in a similar way to the old-fashioned version which was also produced in Syria.

51

Opposite page: *The basis for traditional Arabian costume is the* kaftan, *such as the example standing before the hand-painted, iron-trimmed door at Diraiyah, once the stronghold of the Amirs of the House of Saud. This Damascene version is worked with white silk and gold metal-thread* aghabani *– a style of Syrian embellishment that has been popular in Arabia since it was first evolved. The* kaftan *here is devoid of darts and zipper but it does have a banded collar. The original style was collarless.*
Left: *The* kaftan *is the most widely-known Oriental garment. Its classic lines took formal identity in Turkey long ago, and it has endured because simple elegance is combined with comfort and practicality. This cerise silk version is embroidered with gold and silver metal thread. The work is said to be Indian – commissioned for an Arabian lady – the motifs, however, are reminiscent of Turkish brocades. This exotic* kaftan *is framed in a doorway at Diraiyah, a Najdi town destroyed in 1818 by an army sent by the Ottoman Empire.*

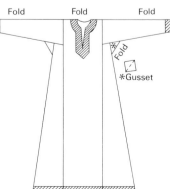

Fold   Fold   Fold

*Fold

*Gusset

Left: *The pattern employed by the Arabian Bedouin for the basic bodyshirt, or* kaftan, *is made up of segments in continuance of a custom resulting from narrow looms which limited the textile width. The commercially-cut* kaftan, *today, is fashioned more simply with fewer pieces. The Arabian pattern requires the front and back centre panel to be cut from a single length.*

established tradition has prevailed in the Arabian Peninsula up to modern times. Arabian women clutch the *abaaya* closely about them to cover their pretty gowns, and occasionally in a marketplace a lady can be seen gripping one edge with her teeth to maintain her modesty as she uses her hands to fetch a child or reach into her purse. The *abaaya* apparently superseded the *milaaya*, possibly long ago – a fashion adopted by townswomen from the Turks. The *milaaya*, a sheet, is worn identically.

There is very little difference between a man's and woman's version of the mantle apart from the name. For women today, the *abaaya* is invariably black, a colour said to have been introduced or consolidated by Islam as the perfect disguise for the attractive feminine garments underneath. It has to be remembered, however, that indigo was the usual Middle Eastern dye in the past, especially indigo blue. The poorest Bedouin could only afford to dip the textile once, thus making the finished product blue, but the best dyed cloth was dipped three times and even steeped in indigo, creating a base cloth of deep bluish-black. It is highly likely that the present-day black continues this age-old preference for the best.

The Arabian cloak, for both male and female, is roughly a double square, 150 centimetres in length and width, consisting of two lengths seamed together horizontally at approximately the hip line. There are no side seams – the textile is wrapped around the body and the selvedges sewn together on the shoulder line. Short slits about twenty-two centimetres long are cut for the hand holes. Sometimes these are tiny token openings. If the garment needs to be shortened, it is done at the hip seam.

Townswomen have led the fashion for wearing an *abaaya* instead of a *milaaya*. Many townswomen once wore a gold metal thread-embroidered black *abaaya*. Today the *abaaya* is usually decorated with only black cord at the edges, along the shoulder line and around the wrist. The trim on the women's version is commonly black soutache and occasionally black lace. The textile quality varies greatly and one of the most expensive silk versions has the initials of a leading Paris fashion house woven into the cloth.

Throughout the Arabian Peninsula, wrappers, shawls, scarves, hoods and cloths are an important facet of a woman's life and many items form part of age-old rituals.

A bride-to-be in Hijazi towns traditionally wore a large red wrapper in a cocoon-like fashion for her pre-wedding henna party, *ghumra*, also known as henna night, *laylat al hinna*. Unable to see, she would be led by the *hareem* to the appointed position for the application of henna. This long length of soft red textile (usually embroidered) is most commonly called *milaaya* or *sharshaf*.

One of the most symbolic Bedouin cloths specially prepared by a Bedouin mother comes from rural western Arabia. It is the *sitara*, used in the *qataa al-sitara*, the public announcement of a forthcoming marriage. Without warning the mother tosses this red cloth over her daughter's head. As the girl noisily resists, the commotion invites female friends and neighbours who rush to enjoy the event. Then the married women help the mother hang the *sitara* to form a screen within the tent. The girl confines herself behind this divider, where she is visited by unmarried girls only until the wedding, a period of approximately one week.

All of these unmarried girls wear a large shawl known as *smaada* instead of the *abaaya*. The bride-to-be also wraps herself in a *smaada* during the engagement period as it is believed any exposure to the sun during this time might spoil her complexion. For at least a week after the wedding, she also wears a black shawl called a *mahabdy*. Another important occasion, usually about a week after the marriage – when the wedded couple

move to their new residence away from the girl's mother – the bride must be led as she is totally enveloped by a large shawl, the *sharshaf*. Traditionally, they are accompanied by her family on this journey. The *sharshaf* is also worn by women during prayer.

From the western side of the Arabian Peninsula, there are still elaborately decorated head scarves – many are large squares meant to be folded into triangles. The embellishment on one triangular half of the square is done on the reverse side to the other half so, when folded diagonally and unevenly, the point on the bottom half dips beneath the upper, allowing the decoration to show on both halves. Appliqué, white shirt buttons, cowrie shells, silver and sometimes white beadwork form geometric patterns on these head scarves and occasionally woven leather and silver beaded "horns", *magruna*, are added. Tassels as a trimming are particularly favoured. Various hoods, similarly decorated, are also worn by Bedouin women and girls of rural western Arabia.

Rural, Bedouin, and many townswomen on the Peninsula still wear a sheet as a mantle rather than a cloak. One short western Arabian version is richly embroidered or decorated – the various designs conveying the wearer's tribe. It is known as a *muzoon*. Others, slightly larger, are imported printed pieces resembling tablecloths while some are colourfully striped local weaves. In Mecca, some ladies wore grey outer wrappers in olden times.

Special cloths are ritually hung by the women in front of tribal tents. Pelly reported in 1865 that Najd Bedouins, with the exception of four tribes, Sibea, Anazah, Mutayr, and Shammar, had a ceremony in which a red cloth was hung at the door of a tent announcing a forthcoming circumcision and signalling an invitation to attend the celebration.

Throughout the Peninsula, Arabian women enjoy dressing-up. It is common amongst tribes for a bride to receive at least five new dresses as part of her dowry so that she may begin her new life well dressed. Her dowry clothing is expected to last at least one year. A town bride might have many more.

The names for the various traditional frocks worn in the past change with more frequency than does their superficial appearance yet analysis of these garments reveals them to be derived from a single style, the *kaftan*. One Arabic word for such a garment is *fustan*.

The original *kaftan* is a loose, long-sleeved, ankle-length tunic – quite dartless and devoid of zippers. The variations in generosity of cut are apparently keyed to geographic and climatic conditions. The usual high round necklines are generally collarless, with a slit front opening normally fastened by a button and loop. In the Najd, such a dress is known as a *dharaah* or *migta* and in the Eastern Province it is often called a *dishdasha*. The Hijazi townswoman's dress is known as a *zabun*. The *zabun* is different in that it does have a collar and sometimes has a full-length centre-front opening which allows shaping. It is undoubtedly of foreign origin as it in no way resembles other traditional Arabian ladies' dresses.

Right: With the restoration of the House of Saud, and the formation of the Kingdom of Saudi Arabia, traditional costume began to be more uniform for men throughout the Peninsula. For women, pride in the new era gave rise to a new garment – an opulent gown bearing the Kingdom's emblem of palm tree surmounting two crossed swords, symbolizing prosperity through justice. This "era" dress is a notable link in the chaim of Arabia's costume history. It is no longer fashionable. The garment is a basic kaftan to which a zip fastener has been added – the fact that this dress came into being in the "forties" explains the new-found closure and how a little more shaping than was customary could be achieved. Proud of their new Kingdom, women placed orders with their Indian embroiderers for lengths of royal purple, parrot green, cerise, peacock blue, buttercup yellow and pillar-box red. Conforming to the established lore for placement of embellishment, the Saud era dress embroidery and appliquéd gems fall predominantly within the bordered centre front and back panels, at the cuffs, hemline and neckline. The front panel generally holds the emblem – some versions carry the emblem, or a variation of it, on both front and back.

Left: *Traditional Arabian wedding dresses are cerise and invariably richly embellished. Since the introduction of the zip fastener, the basic* kaftan *acquired shaping, unlike the example here which skirts the body and falls in graceful lines from the shoulders. An elaborate gold-embroidered and sequined version of the* dharaah *such as this, is known as an* omasa. *The textile varies, as does the quality and quantity of gold work, depending on the family's wealth. This dress would be worn on the actual wedding day.*

Right: *Close-up view of machined embroidery on the sleeve cuffs of a silk* dharaah.

Far right: *It is usual for the* dharaah *embroidery to be confined to the cuffs as these are visible when worn under the wide-sleeved* thawb. *Such a* thawb *as this cerise silk chiffon would be worn by the bride on the second evening of the marriage celebration, when it is traditional for the women to have a party.*

The fullness of cut makes traditional Arabian gowns ideal maternity wear. This is beneficial as large families are desired in the Muslim world – children are regarded as bringing a blessing into the home.

Although the majority of dresses are ankle-length, some are purposely cut long at the back so that they trail. Royal garments were once cut longer at the back to indicate status. Generally beltless, some Bedouin dresses are a full metre longer than the wearer, and designed to be hitched by a belt. In the south, dresses are shorter, showing the *sirwaal* from approximately mid-calf.

The sleeves range from roomy to tapered, again according to provenance. Narrow sleeves are common in the western mountain areas of the Asir while enormous, open sleeves are common in the hot interior of the Najd and further north. Invariably, all kinds of sleeves in traditional Arabian

dresses join to an under-arm gusset from which side gores (panels) radiate to the hemline. Even when the gussets serve no useful purpose in a capacious gown, they are incorporated for decorative purposes. Under-arm gussets are often a special feature of Arabian women's garments and generally cut from contrasting cloth and embellished.

The Arabian woman's love of colour is expressed by her choice of dress textile. Dark colours are worn but generally reserved for elders. Whether deep or vivid, pale or dark, the base colour of the chosen textile is generally enlivened with contrasting coloured motifs – especially for party wear – and these often sparkle from the lurex content or the addition of metal thread work, beading and sequins. The traditional wedding dress colour is cerise; the *omasa* is an especially elaborate cherry-red gown with Indian gold embroidery and sequins over bodice and sleeves.

Bedouin embroidery, which used to be hand-done, continues to be lavishly employed using multiple colours. However, the quality is deteriorating as the years pass. The patterns once indicated a gown's region, tribe and sub-tribe in traditional Arabia but now the old designs are becoming obscured.

Some Bedouin dresses occasionally feature a small opening in the underarm seam and the edges of this opening are customarily decorated with embroidery. The same opening appears in various different tribal dresses. It has been said

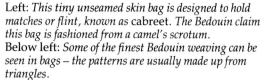

Below: *Traditionally, both men and women carried bags and each had a specific purpose. There were bags to hold incense, the Koran or verses, herbs, money, tea, coffee, dates and rice. Small or large, these bags were gaily decorated. This camel leather example has an indigo-dyed neckband, cotton appliqué, silver beads, silk tassels and a colourful band of weaving supporting a fringe. The three triangles are seen on Asir dresses.*

Left: *This tiny unseamed skin bag is designed to hold matches or flint, known as cabreet. The Bedouin claim this bag is fashioned from a camel's scrotum.*
Below left: *Some of the finest Bedouin weaving can be seen in bags – the patterns are usually made up from triangles.*
Below right: *In the traditional range of bags, some are not meant to be containers. According to custom, some small and elaborately embellished bags are designed to be placed over a pole outside the tent when a celebration is about to be held. This pole bag is claimed as one belonging to the Beni Salim tribe in the Hijaz. The bag displays white shirt buttons, cowrie shells, red cloth appliqué, stranded silver beads, coins and wool fringe. It is tribal custom in some parts of the Peninsula to hoist a woman's colourful garment outside the tent for the same purpose.*

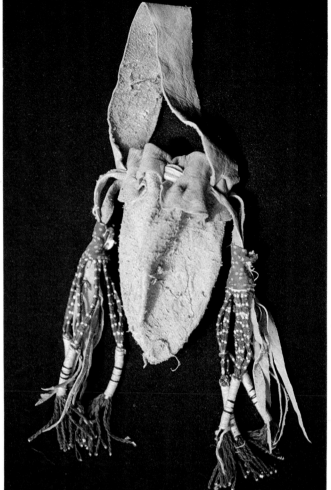

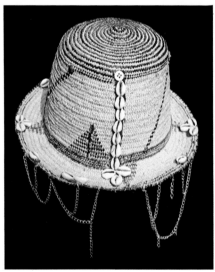

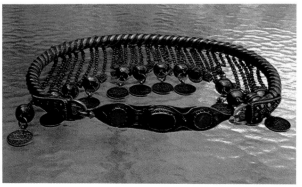

Far left: *Bedouin costume accessories may not extend to gloves, yet hats are fashionable. Palm frond hats for men and women are generally called* tafasha *in Arabia. This elaborate example has its own name,* mizalla, *in the Asir. Natural and brown-dyed fronds are dressed up with cowrie shells, white buttons, and laced and linked chains which are worn at the back by women. Chained back-of-head ornaments are a fashion for women of the Peninsula.*
Left: *Women's festive occasion waistbelts are still made by the silversmith. These heavy belts can be made from fine silver or low-grade – as required. The stones here are glass and the base metal belts have been dipped in silver.*
Bottom left: *Old belts are commonly fine silver and semi-precious stones are set. This rare belt matches a torque necklace, bracelets, and possibly anklets. The jewelled clasp is believed to be worn at the front.*

that they are for breast-feeding purposes. This theory is refuted, however, since milk stains did not appear on the old and soiled examples examined. Furthermore, the placement of the holes make breast feeding a near impossible feat. As the sleeves are always fitted, perhaps these holes are designed to ventilate.

Rural women often add a waistbelt, *hizam*, even though it is not part of the original costume. One style of southern long dress is worn with a belt. It is known as *tawb aswad* and fits a description given by Musil for a dress worn in the far north of the Peninsula.

Children

In the past, children of the Arabian Peninsula wore scaled-down versions of adult clothing, with the exception of headgear. Arabian Bedouin traditionally wind a piece of black cloth around the head of a newborn baby. This is replaced by a bonnet, *gub* or *kufiyyah*, when the child is about a month old.

The problem of headgear for children was cleverly handled in old Arabia. The need to protect a child's head from the strong Arabian sun was most important, and it was obvious that adult forms of head covering could not remain securely in place on toddlers, not known for their steady and sedate carriage. The snug-fitting *gub* with its secure fixture under the chin was therefore ideal.

In the northernmost regions of the Arabian Peninsula, the *gub* is traditionally black. The origin of this custom lies in the belief that it would make children less attractive and thereby avert the malevolent gaze of the jealous. The black *gub* was sometimes colourfully decorated. It was topped with a black tassel bound with silver and gold metal thread and the top half of the bonnet's crown was appliquéd with five coloured silk triangles. Gold braid is applied to divide these segments and gold trimming is repeated around the bonnet above the ear flaps where the chin strap is affixed. Children's bonnets were once made of cotton but in the south-west today the *gub* is fashioned from colourful synthetic brocades and jacquards.

When children reached the age of eight years, it was customary to replace the *gub* with a hood, *bukhnug* (also known as *mukhnug*) in the case of girls, and the *kufiyyah* or skullcap in the case of boys.

Little girls in traditional Arabia learned about caring for babies by helping their mothers. Baby-care was handled in a specific way. It was customary to keep babies wrapped in swaddling clothes until they reached three months of age – the arms placed by their sides or folded across the chest and bound there and legs tied close together at the knees and ankles. This is a very ancient custom. It is believed in many western countries today that a baby feels more secure when firmly wrapped for sleep – perhaps this theory is inherited and not new.

From the end of the third month to the end of the ninth, the child was swaddled only at night with strips of material wrapped two or three times around the full length of the body. Thereafter, tiny copies of adult clothing were usually worn.

Until very recently, Arabian baby clothes were made out of a gauze-like material which a husband ritually bought in the market as soon as his wife became pregnant. The practice of making baby clothes has all but ceased now because of the ready availability of imported items. This seems a pity because gauze is the ideal textile for a baby to wear in a hot climate; its light and absorbent properties make it eminently suitable.

At puberty costume customs change for Arabian boys and girls. They normally begin at this time to wear the headgear of an adult.

Below: *This drawing depicts the old style of boy's body-shirt, known as* mizolaj. *Egyptian unbleached calico is decorated with cotton tassels attached to the sleeve lappets.*

Below: *It is customary for children to wear scaled-down versions of adult clothing. Old pictures show town lads wearing embroidered brocade* bisht, thawb *and* sirwaal – *and older boys wore turbans also.*

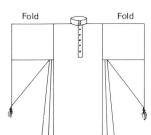

When a girl was considered to have reached womanhood in the olden days, she put on a veil, and childhood activities outside the home ceased for her. She began to learn how to run the home, improving upon the knowledge already gleaned about cooking, spinning, weaving and sewing. Boys would begin to emulate their elders and don the *ghoutra* which quite naturally would dislodge easily with rough juvenile play. It is easy to imagine a certain pride these young people gained when they accepted traditional adult headgear.

School uniforms and sports in modern Arabia are responsible for many changes in traditional children's wear. It is likely, however, that maturity will see young Arabians conform to the accepted adult style of dress. Change has been slower in the south. In the south-west, south and south-east, where men wear the traditional dagger, little boys may be seen still with broad belts buckled with fine silver. At puberty these children gain the right to wear a dagger in their belt.

Below: *The gub, or child's hood has several forms. All styles are snug-fitting and are secured under the chin. A firmly fitted hood is the best way to ensure a child's head is well-protected from the strong Arabian sun. The black satin-finished cotton example shown here is appliquéd with cerise, gold and green silk patches and gold braid. At puberty children begin to wear adult headgear. A boy usually wears a* kufiyyah *and the girl wears a* taraha *before that.*

Left: *Bedouin women still make children's hoods in many parts of Arabia. The textiles are anything from cotton to tinsel-threaded velvet as shown here. Seams are machine sewn but the finishing off is usually done by hand. Southern souqs display a wide variety of colourful textiles made up into "pixie" hoods. While a safety pin is supplied as a fastener for under the chin, the tailors have usually gone to a great deal of trouble to decorate by hand the band that circles the face.*

59

Undergarments

The comfort of Arabian clothing holds true especially for traditional undergarments. In a society where reclining and squatting are favoured ways of relaxing and traditional activities such as riding and weaving are strenuous, undergarments must not be restricting. Furthermore, it is necessary they be comfortable and adaptable in a decorous way to every movement, particularly for the prescribed Muslim prayer positions.

The main undergarment is a pair of long pants, or *sirwaal*. These understandably bear a close resemblance to ancient trousers as their history is long and unbroken. Their style evolved in much the same way as all other garments. Throughout history, invasions and migrations saw costume fashions influenced and enriched until each race wore a version of the basic garments that they considered suitable and desirable apparel. One important example is the narrow-legged garment worn throughout the world and known in the West as pants.

The origin of pants is traced back to the nomadic tribes of Central Asia and other east Asian regions. Their story goes back to the time when fur and leather were worn and weaving was unknown. Pants were worn then probably for warmth. Among the Asian nomads were the Huns, ancestors of the Turks and Mongols (together with the *kaftan*, long pants were a part of Turkish costume centuries ago). Arabian men wore a loincloth prior to the introduction of pants so it is likely that the fashion for wearing *sirwaal* gained popularity on the Peninsula with the rise of the Ottoman Empire. Bedouin and rural men in Arabia still wear the ancient loincloth under a *thawb* or *fouta*. In fact, peasant men at work often wear only the loincloth. There are also accounts of Bedouin in the past stripping to their loincloths for spear-throwing contests or to enter battle – no doubt to allow greater freedom of movement.

Because a connecting trade network spread the fashion for wearing pants, there is a similarity in cut to be seen in widely separated continents. Traditional long pants of Africa, Turkey, India and Arabia share a remarkable likeness because they all evolved from a fundamental pattern. All combine great comfort and practicality. Oriental pants are basically the same cut even today – the straight legs branch from a roomy top section and the secret of the style difference is in the crotch gusset.

Originally the textiles used to make pants were hand-woven and the width of the loom dictated the width of the waistline. The simple length of textile measured twice the length of the finished article. By removing a diamond-shaped section from the middle, shaped leg sections were formed and the diamond shape was turned and inserted between the legs to form an ample crotch gusset.

The distinctive appearance of Persian pants is created by having additional width of material gathered in at the waist and ankles. Turkish pants, which are extremely full, owe their unique shape to an enormous rectangular gusset that reaches from front waistline to back waistline. The simpler-looking African pants particularly rely upon an ample crotch gusset for freedom of movement as the legs are tapered to the ankles. Indian pants also have tapered legs but a wide panel, from the hipline to waistline, cleverly gathers the wide leg tops at the centre front and back, again creating an ample crotch.

Arabian *sirwaal* are generally made of cotton, the men's pants usually matching the white or cream *thawb* textile. Today this material often includes a percentage of synthetic fibre. The women's traditional *sirwaal* were often more colourful, and lace and frills might be added to the ankle bands. Townswomen wore silk and satin *sirwaal* as well as cotton. Arabian women mostly wear Western undergarments today.

Oriental pants are traditionally gathered at the waist with a drawstring although elastic is increasingly favoured. *Sirwaal* in olden times had a wide waistband through which was threaded the *dikka*

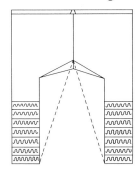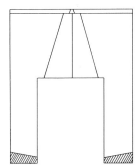

or sash. The ends of the *dikka* were often extravagantly embroidered. Sometimes ankle bands on *sirwaal* for both men and women were also elaborately embroidered. These pants were known as *sirwaal mashtaghal*.

The *dikka* is threaded with an attractive dressing aid called *midak*. This threader is sometimes brightly painted wood and sometimes ivory. One fine example of this needle is gold-capped carved ivory with a thirty-centimetre eye in the form of a chain. The cap and chain can be removed from the nineteen-centimetre *midak* to reveal another smaller eye through the end which is perhaps for threading fine cord.

Today Arab menfolk often wear a short version of the traditional *sirwaal* and do not generally wear the traditional-style undershirt, the *fanilla*. In the past this round-necked, short-sleeved vest was made of cotton or wool, once hand-woven. At present the popular vest for men is of the Western knitted cotton kind, either short-sleeved or sleeveless. In the past, the woman's vest was a high-collared, waist-length garment with sleeves to the elbow. This blouse, known as a *sidaireeya*, was usually made from fine, absorbent cotton. It served as brassiere and vest – and, in the Hijaz, worn under the V-necked *zabun* it formed a cravat. The Oriental pants and top set is recorded as being the model for the Western pyjama suit which reached Europe via India in the eighteenth century. They had long been considered ideal lounging and sleeping gear in the Orient.

Underdresses, or chemises, are also worn and these are virtually petticoats. Some are full-length with a blouse-like bodice and others are long half-slips. They are not worn by Bedouin women and appear to be a Turkish import.

Left: *Arabian* sirwaal *customarily feature embroidery at the ankle bands. This work can extend to mid-calf on the women's version, and it often matched the embellishment on the* kaftan. Sirwaal *in the past were sometimes made from unbleached cotton, calico, black cotton, silk or satin. It was not uncommon to have silk or satin embroidered leggings appliquéd over cotton* sirwaal. *The patterns shown here are but two variations of the straight legged, wide-seated long pants which are drawn in by a sash threaded through the waist band.*

Pilgrimage Garments

Below: *The embroidery on women's* sirwaal *often extended from the cuff edge to mid-calf. This work is visible in the south where dresses are shorter. Three versions here show,* left, *red, yellow and green stitchery divided by lavish white work;* centre, *satin leggings over calico pants display primitive but pretty machined embroidery in red, yellow, green and white, while on the* right, *fine gold and silver metal-thread handwork accents red and green.*

The fifth pillar of Islam, the *Haj*, or pilgrimage to Mecca, occurs in *Dhul Hijjah*, the twelfth month of the *Hejiri*, the Islamic year. Every Muslim hopes to complete the *Haj* at least once in his lifetime.

For both men and women within Arabia, pilgrimage clothing generally falls into two main groups: clothes for travelling and a costume for the four "holy days" in Mecca. For men, traditional *Haj* garments are mandatory during the holy days which begin on the evening of the ninth day of *Dhul Hijjah*. These are the robes of consecration which are usually donned after the major prescribed ablution, *ghusl*. The ninth of the month is the latest a pilgrim can enter this state of sanctity, *ihram* – a period in which the pilgrim divests himself of vain preoccupations and seeks forgive-ness, guidance and salvation from God. It is possible to enter the state of *ihram* before, providing the costume is not worn prior to the beginning of the month of *Shawwal*, approximately sixty days earlier.

For men *ihram* costume consists of two seamless white lengths of textile – one is wound skirt-fashion around the lower half of the body while the other is thrown loosely about the upper half of the body and over the shoulder. It resembles ancient Greek costume. A waistband formed from another piece of seamless white cloth, the *bugsha*, can also be worn to secure the lower section of the costume and hold money and papers.

It is recorded that many women in Arabia once wore a special costume for the Pilgrimage. It was green and consisted of *sirwaal* (long pants), *fustan* (a dress) and *thawb* (overdress). For travelling, the usual *abaaya* and *taraha* were worn. Indian and Pakistani Muslim men have a custom whereby they may don a green headcloth after completing the *Haj*. Perhaps there is some connection with the old custom of Arabian women wearing green *Haj* garments.

Today, women usually wear white garments during their stay in Mecca. While they complete the *Haj* with heads covered, women should not normally cover their faces on the holy days. Pilgrims do not wear scent or jewellery during these special days.

Some Bahraini women make seven special pairs of *sirwaal* for the journey – the upper part of these pants are cut out of floral coloured cotton and the gusset and legs are either green, black or purple satin. The leggings are embroidered with multi-coloured threads. They also make five new under-gowns, usually from a dark-coloured floral velvet or cotton and seven new muslin overgowns with broad open sleeves in bright colours. For travel-ling, these women wear a rectangular black tulle head scarf trimmed on three sides with blue glass beads. It is known as the *ghaswa*, and is held in place with thin cloth straps. A special outer mantle is also worn instead of the usual semi-circular cloak. It is the *daffa*, a black silk cloak, without hand slits and similar to the Turkish *charshaf* and the Persian *chador*. For the four holy days, they wear unembellished white. The *gawan*, an under-dress, is shorter than the usual one worn at home and has long, narrow sleeves. Under this, long white *sirwaal* can be seen. The face is unveiled but the head is covered by a white hood, the *bukhnug*, such as the one traditionally worn by unmarried girls.

While Muslim men normally cover their heads during prayer for the rest of the year, the opposite is the case during *Haj*. Their heads should be uncovered for the four special days. Part of the ritual ablution signifying the successful completion of *Haj*, is cutting the hair and trimming the nails. Many men shave their heads while others merely cut a few locks and women snip a small section from their hair.

The wearing of the *ihram* costume makes it impossible to distinguish rich from poor; the symbolic significance of this lies in the Islamic belief that all men are equal in the sight of God.

Above: *Slipper satin* sirwaal, *that once belonged to a Hijazi townswoman, show elaborately gold-worked anklets. These broad bands* have been padded to make them stiff. The rest of the costume cannot be found but it is likely that similar work decorated the *sidaireeya.* *The garments would be visible through a transparent* tawb.

Burial and Mourning Garments

After death, a Muslim body is washed by professional washers before it is clothed in a long, full-cut new white garment (males are washed by men and females by women).

There is no opening for the head in the burial garment. This lack of a neck opening in a new gown is a custom in the Middle East and conveys that the garment has never been worn. Customarily, a hole is torn for the head to pass through.

A dead female's forehead is bound with a white folded cloth, *osba*, such as Arabian women often wear when they are sick. Then a headcloth is placed over the head and sewn under the neck and down the front to resemble the *bukhnug* worn by young girls. Males are dressed with a white headcloth which is tied under the chin. Finally, a white shroud, *chifan*, *kafan* or *tsifan* is placed over the body.

Within the Arabian Peninsula, in times past, a woman in mourning dressed in green. Green, *akhdar*, had especially good connotations for Arabians in the past, and that is perhaps why the Saudi Arabian flag is green and why women chose to wear it for *Haj* and mourning. For instance, green stands for the palm trees and abundance springing forth from an oasis, offering refuge, sustenance and cooling shade. The colour green is frequently mentioned in the *Koran* in connection with these comforts on earth and in Paradise.

For those that have faith and do good works, according to the Koran, "... they shall be decked with bracelets of gold and arrayed in garments of fine green silk and rich brocade".

Footwear

Hidha is the Arabic word for shoe or sandal and *niaal* means open footwear such as a sandal. These words, however, are but a few applied to traditional Arabian footwear.

Amongst the variety of appellations is *zarabil*, which is used for a style of shoe that is believed to have originated in the Najd and is probably the forerunner of the Western slipper. *Zarabil* were either made from canvas or leather – either imported or local camel hide. For men, women and children, this basic three-piece shoe pattern was standard. The sole consists of several layers joined tightly together with small stitches that cover the entire section; this is hand-sewn to the two upper pieces, one returned over the front of the foot and the other curved behind the heel.

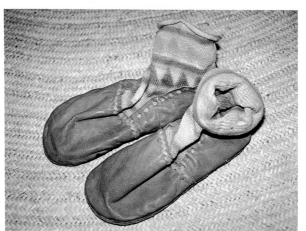

Above: Zarabil *made of camel hide illustrate the traditional Bedouin three-piece shoe pattern. The upper is formed from two pieces which have been decorated with red leather and a white* fabric. The third section, the sole, has, in this case, been made out of several layers of hide that have been stitched together with strips of leather. The work is rough but the shoes are long-lasting.

Left: *This version of the* zarabil *has a fourth section. The round-the-heel section has been extended upwards to meet the additional piece at front, and creates a turn-down cuff. There are descriptions of red and yellow Arabian shoes but these are the only ones so far available. The leather is very thick and hard and probably facilitated walking on the burning sand. This pair, however, have never been worn – they were found hanging in a corner of an old shop in the* souq.

Centre: *The fourth section of this boot is a knitted anklet resembling a sock top. The knitting is excellent – the tension even despite the fact that the stitch is jacquard. The yarn is cotton in orange, yellow, white, green and blue. The ancient amuletic shape, the triangle, is alternately inverted. Great skill is required to knit as well as this. The leather is soft and would be much easier to "break-in" than the pair above.*

Bottom: *Another style of Bedouin footwear displays knitted anklets. In this style, the knitted section is open and secured at the front or on the sides. This pair resembles old-fashioned Western button-up boots.* Hidha, zarabil *and* niaal *were once made by the Bedouin by hand from camel skin. Town* souqs *stocked shoes, too, and many of these were made from Egyptian leather. Records reveal that ready-made footwear was also imported from Egypt, some of which was red and yellow.*

One variation of this Arabian shoe includes a fourth section in the form of a knitted ankle piece. When sewn together, the finished product looks like a sock within a shoe. Knitting is said to have originated in southern Arabia and it is obvious from these old shoes that knitting was a perfected craft performed throughout the Peninsula, although there is little evidence of it today. Wilfred Thesiger writes of coarse black-hair socks worn by the southern Bedouin when traversing the sands of the Rub al Khali. Possibly they were knitted goat hair.

The most popular Arabian footwear, which persists into modern times because of the practicality in a hot climate, are *niaal*, sandals. The thonged style (which is the most favoured) is still made locally from camel hide and costs a small fortune. Again, they are said to have originated in the Najd, where they are known as *madaas* – this style is known as *hidha* in western regions. Woven palm-frond sandals of various kinds are generally called *zarabil*.

In 1761, the German explorer, Carsten Niebuhr, recorded that there were a limited number of sandal styles in Arabia. Charles Didier observed in the 1850s that Jeddah had over five sandal-makers and the styles varied greatly: "from province to province, some peculiar to certain classes."

According to Didier, Jeddah craftsmen also produced thick-soled wooden sandals with leather bindings. These were decorated with blue and silver inlays. They fit the description of silver-inlaid wooden sandals which were traditionally worn by Hijazi town brides in the past. Although these *gubgaab* were almost certainly of Turkish origin, they were part of traditional Arabian footwear – worn throughout the Peninsula and Bahrain in days gone by. Sometimes they were inlaid with mother-of-pearl while others were merely painted.

Didier claimed that there were no shoe-makers in Jeddah, and that local merchants sold imported Egyptian shoes. Also imported from Egypt at the time were red and yellow slippers, *jezma makshoofa*, popular with wealthy merchants and the ladies. It is recorded, too, that Egyptian leather was actually imported specifically for making shoes. One elderly Arabian lady recalls that one area in Mecca, Muddaa, was known for producing shoes in olden times.

One Meccan-made shoe, traditional for town ladies, was the two-part *khuf babooj*. This footwear consists of a boot-like soft leather sock called *khuf*, over which is worn a backless clog-like leather slipper. Both sections are lemon-coloured, *jild asfar*, *jild* meaning leather and *asfar* meaning yellow. There are also traditional Arabian Bedouin boots made from very thick *jild asfar*. The insides are red and visible because the ankle tops are folded over to form a wide band.

A visitor to Mecca long ago quaintly described the townswomen out walking as "penguin-like" because of their grey cloaks, long white veils and bright yellow feet. Gazelle skin, which was widely used throughout the Peninsula in the past, tans to a delicate lemon colour and it is possible that it, too, was used to make footwear in this popular hue.

H. R. P. Dickson recorded that the Bedouin women of the northern, central and eastern regions of Arabia wore black slippers. These would appear to be indigo-dyed canvas *zarabil*. He also mentions woollen top-boots worn by both men and women in winter. It is not known if these were fur-lined skin or knitted wool. The only available Bedouin boots are either unlined or partially knitted in various yarns. Many styles must have been abandoned long ago when they wore out. Arabian-made traditional footwear has been replaced by factory-produced shoes and sandals from India for the most part. Even in the past, India made shoes for Arabia. Ladies recall beautiful bridal shoes, some lavishly embellished to match the gown. They were without heels, made of velvet or leather and known as *kanader*. Such footwear also came from Bahrain.

Right: A cluster of niaal *in a town* souq *show a variety of geometric patterns woven from leather and plastic strips on the band of the upper. Most of these cow-hide sandals are imported from India and other places. The totally hand-made leather examples of the same style are made by local craftsmen but the prices are very high. A fine pair of camel-hide sandals costs hundreds of riyals and the most expensive are only partially finished awaiting a proper fitting on the purchaser. Indian-made cow-hide copies are very cheap and this import is responsible for a decline in the local cobbler's trade.*

Centre: Palm-frond footwear may not be as durable as hide but it is considerably more comfortable to wear in the hot and humid coastal regions. This particular style comes from the Hijaz. Medina, blessed with many fine date groves, has a thriving palm frond weaving industry and may have been responsible for these clever sandals.

Bottom: Wooden sandals are found now and again and suggest that they were once part of the range of Arabian footwear. They are not comfortable or easy to walk in, particularly on sand, and it would seem that they are more typical of town wear. Variations of this style were worn in Turkish bathhouses throughout the Ottoman Empire but insufficient water precluded such buildings on the Peninsula. It is likely that these shoes were adopted by well-to-do townspeople.

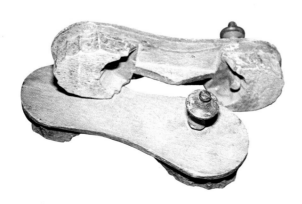

People of the Arabian Peninsula

The historic homeland of the Arab is Greater Arabia – the sock-shaped Peninsula with a north-eastward tilting toe. It is depicted on early maps as having no northern border but reaching well into Sinai, Jordan, Syria and Palestine in the west, and bounded by the Euphrates in the east. At no time in history could the exact size of Arabia be determined accurately because the inhospitable interior precluded surveying and the northern boundaries were continually re-interpreted.

The population figure also remains an estimation. The task of census is complicated because privacy in matters relating to the family is highly valued among Muslims. Moreover, many people lived a nomadic or semi-nomadic existence until the creation of the Kingdom of Saudi Arabia and the subsequent discovery of oil.

Since 1950, settlements have sprung up by the water-pumping stations along the northern Arabian pipeline. Additionally, with the development of the oil industry and the wealth it has introduced, new urban centres have been created, particularly in eastern Arabia. Then, of course, modernization has caused the old cities throughout the land to burgeon. In the next decade, the migration of nomads, semi-nomads and farmers to these towns and cities is expected to increase. The pipeline settlements are growing fast and the new agricultural communities will continue to draw pastoralists from remote regions.

Prior to these population movements, approximately half the inhabitants of Greater Arabia were nomadic or semi-nomadic, while the rest were almost equally divided between settled farmers and urban dwellers. The latter definition is difficult to assess because "urban" could be construed as including trade or administration orientated people living in oasis centres in such rural settings as Hofuf and Qasim. Whatever exact numbers could convey, it is sufficient to say that, until this century, the Arabian way of life changed little over thousands of years.

The reason the Arabian people retained their old life-styles is largely due to the relative isolation in which they lived, and that in turn was due to the nature of their land. Yet they were never totally cut off from external influence. Even in the heartland of Arabia, where Arab culture was considered purest by virtue of its remoteness, influence filtered in and left marks. The regional variations in culture and costume evolved over countless ages and are unquestionably the result of topographical differences and external influence. Trade was the doorway through which influence passed back and forth. New settlers over thousands of years have also lent a hand.

Although the indigenous people of Arabia share the belief of Islam, the populations of Mecca, Medina, Tayif and Jeddah are liberally sprinkled with citizens who are of non-Arabian origin. Throughout the Peninsula there are people who descended from settled pilgrims and their presence has added further to the ethnic individuality of their region.

Whatever an Arabian is today, he is inextricably bound to an ancient past. In both customs and costume, the people of Greater Arabia perpetuate facets with roots that go back into the clichéd mists of antiquity.

It is known that the land has been exploited by man for many thousands of years. An early linking of Arabia with the outside world occurred between 5000 and 3500 BC, when eastern Arabia traded with southern Mesopotamia.

Archaeological discoveries reveal many stone structures in northern, north-western and central regions of Arabia which are thought to be associated with early semi-settled populations in these areas (these were possibly the forbears of the Arabian nomads who are believed to have emerged at a later period in history). There are many gaps in the history of Arabia which only time and diligent research may fill. So far as a costume study is concerned, the chances of closing the gaps are great it is believed Arabians clung to their ancient traditions until early this century.

The present-day life-styles of the townspeople and those of the peasants and nomads seem, at first glance, to be totally unrelated. Closer inspection, however, reveals strong cultural links between them.

In the past, townspeople al hadur were mainly involved with trade. The peasants and Bedouin al badw supported themselves with agriculture and herding. Even now that the motor car has brought an end to Bedouin prosperity based on camel breeding, the nomad's economic independence relies upon herding just as it did in biblical times.

The Arabian nomad was much less dependent upon the towns in the past although there was always an inter-relationship in times of drought. Yet in traditional Arabia – the legendary land of long ago – the indigenous people lived in a way which was much less divided than it is now and urban culture therefore reflected tribal customs. Arabian poetry illustrates the shared values of the heroic society in which they lived. Age-old ways had a greater chance of persisting in the desert, of course, because urban society was subject to continual subtle change because of its greater exposure to outside influence.

Old villages perhaps best reflect the traditional life which, in fact, still exists elsewhere albeit camouflaged by recent economic growth. Whether large or small, these villages share a number of features which illustrate the important aspects of an Arab's world.

The mosque is the central feature in an old village or town and the number of mosques depends upon the population. Traditionally, the Muslim elementary school is encompassed within the mosque's walls. The other important site is the souq, the central market place where periodic markets are held. The souq also serves as a gathering place for special occasions and is frequently the camping ground for travellers and visiting nomads. There are also one or more coffee houses where men spend hours exchanging news. Along the narrow meandering lanes, which radiate out from a town souq, small single or clustered shops can be found between tall houses that are built tightly packed to promote cool temperatures indoors. Here and there women can be seen purchasing their needs and more often than not bargaining with the shopkeeper. This is a highly ritualized activity, enjoyed by buyer and seller

A special map, right, *has been devised to assist the reader comprehend the tribal locations of long ago in relation to the topography of the Arabian Peninsula. The three deserts, from north to south, are the Nafud, the Dahna, and the Rub al Khali, or Empty Quarter. Throughout the sandy interior, garments were larger than those worn in the surrounding regions. The modern designation for the Najd (central region), and the Asir (south-western region), have been drawn but no northern border has been included for the Hijaz, Northern region, and the Eastern Province, because tribal grounds extend beyond the present-day limits. Costume traditions consequently also over-reached the modern boundaries. The eastern section groups the Arabian Gulf lands. The southern section takes in all those lands which seem logically grouped for a costume study. Ideally, a more detailed costume survey should be made – one that covers every major tribe and this would divide the present delineation further.*

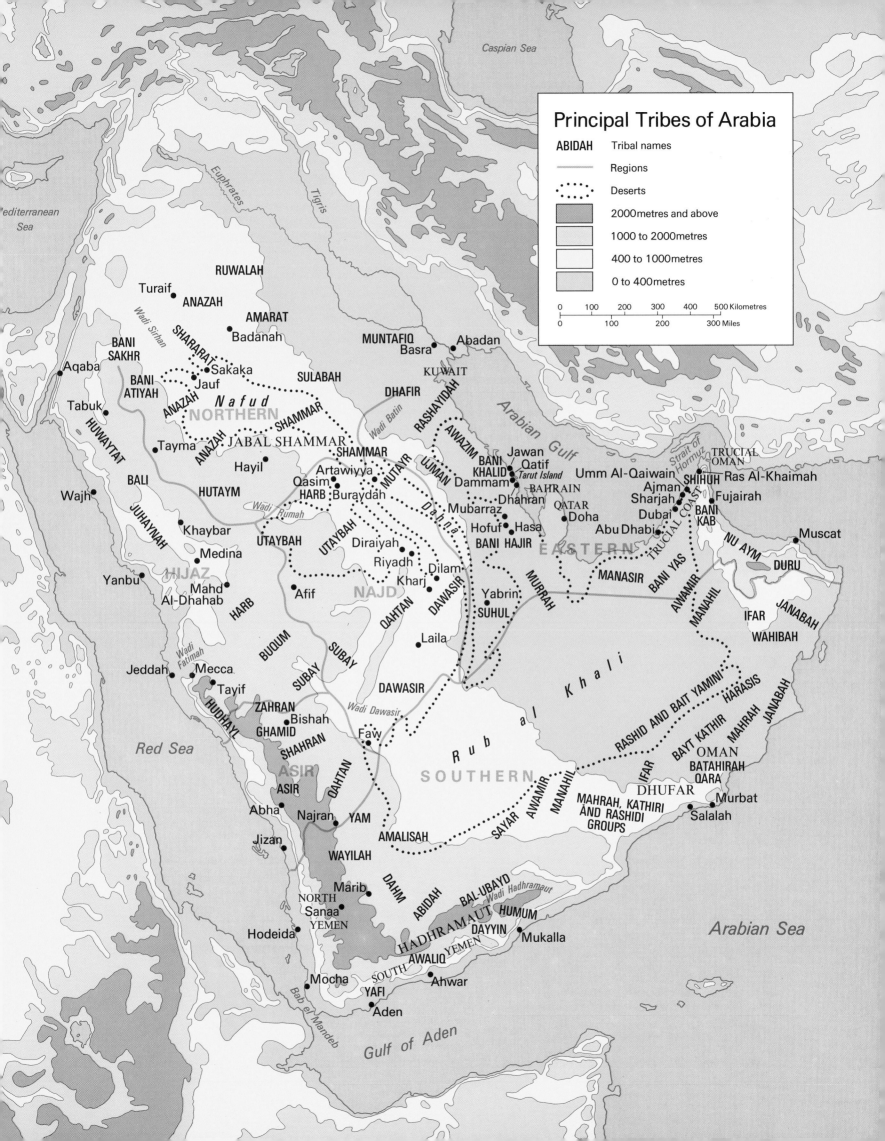

Principal Tribes of Arabia

ABIDAH   Tribal names

—— Regions

········ Deserts

2000metres and above

1000 to 2000metres

400 to 1000metres

0 to 400metres

| 0 | 100 | 200 | 300 | 400 | 500 Kilometres |
| 0 | 100 | 200 | 300 Miles |

Mediterranean Sea

Caspian Sea

Euphrates

Tigris

Wadi Sirhan

RUWALAH

Turaif
ANAZAH

AMARAT
Badanah

MUNTAFIQ
Basra
Abadan

Aqaba

BANI SAKHR

SHARARAT
Sakaka
Jauf

BANI ATIYAH

ANAZAH

KUWAIT

DHAFIR

Wadi Batin

Arabian Gulf

Strait of Hormuz

TRUCIAL OMAN

Tabuk

HUWAYTAT

Nafud
NORTHERN

Tayma
ANAZAH
JABAL SHAMMAR

SHAMMAR

SHAMMAR

RASHAYIDAH

AWAZIM

Jawan
BANI KHALID
Qatif
Tarut Island
Dammam
Dhahran

BAHRAIN

Umm Al-Qaiwain
Ajman
Sharjah
Dubai
Abu Dhabi

SHIHUH
Ras Al-Khaimah
Fujairah
BANI KAB

Muscat

BALI

Wajh

JUHAYNAH

Hayil

HUTAYM

Artawiyya
Qasim
HARB Buraydah

MUTAYR
UJMAN

Mubarraz

QATAR
Doha

Hofuf Hasa
BANI HAJIR

EASTERN

TRUCIAL COAST

NU AYM

DURU

Khaybar

Medina

Wadi Rumah

UTAYBAH

Diraiyah
Riyadh

UTAYBAH

Kharj
Dilam

Dahna

DAWASIR

Yabrin

MANASIR
BANI YAS
AWAMIR

MANAHIL

IFAR

JANABAH

Yanbu

HIJAZ

Mahd
Al-Dhahab

HARB

Afif

NAJD

QAHTAN

Laila

SUHUL
MURRAH

WAHIBAH

Wadi Fatimah

Jeddah

Mecca
Tayif

BUQUM

SUBAY
SUBAY

SUBAY

DAWASIR

Rub al Khali

HUDHAYL
ZAHRAN
Bishah

GHAMID

Faw

Wadi Dawasir

DAWASIR

AWAMIR
MANAHIL

RASHID AND BAIT YAMINI

HARASIS

BAYT KATHIR
MAHRAH

JANABAH

Red Sea

SHAHRAN

QAHTAN

ASIR
ASIR

Abha

Najran
YAM

SOUTHERN

SAYAR
AWAMIR
MANAHIL

IFAR

OMAN
BATAHIRAH
QARA

DHUFAR

Murbat
Salalah

MAHRAH, KATHIRI AND RASHIDI GROUPS

Jizan

WAYILAH

AMALISAH

DAHM

Marib

NORTH
Sanaa
YEMEN

Hodeida

ABIDAH

BAL-UBAYD
Wadi Hadhramaut
HUMUM

HADHRAMAUT

DAYYIN
YEMEN

Mukalla

Arabian Sea

Mocha

YAFI

SOUTH

AWALIQ

Ahwar

Aden

Bab el Mandeb

Gulf of Aden

alike. Superimposed on the scene are children who scamper about, in and out of dimly lit doorways. Although village houses are also commonly grouped, sometimes a more dispersed arrangement prevails and family houses, each with adjacent orchards and fields, are all enclosed by a mud wall. While mountain and hill villages took advantage of natural defences, towns and villages in open plains were generally surrounded by strong walls with defensive towers at intervals.

For the Arab (whether a member of town or village society or from a nomadic tribe), poetry, formal prose and oratory, have long been esteemed as the highest of the arts. There is a special attraction therein for the nomad whose life is essentially spartan. The skilful use of language alone is valued, especially in the heart of Arabia.

Traditionally, the Bedouin poet is the repository of tribal history and spokesman for his tribe. Often a warrior himself in days of old, a poet strives to express in his work the ideals of manliness, gallantry, bravery, loyalty, independence of spirit and generosity. Oral folk literature comprises proverbs and stories also. The narrative of professional story-tellers, whose recitations are particularly popular, are in great demand during *Ramadan*, the Muslim holy month of fasting. These men provide and perpetuate a wealth of pious, earthy or epic oral literature which has been passed on for countless generations. Much of the poetry also contains genealogies to accompany tribal history.

Vocal and instrumental music is part of the poetic tradition. Musical expression on an informal folk level comprises repetitive bars and intricate beats, sometimes played simply with a coffee-grinding mortar *hawan* and pestle *yed al hawan*. The most famous Arabian musical instrument is the *oud* (similar to a guitar). It is the standard Arabian instrument belonging to the family of short lutes and is used for solo instrumental music or to accompany a singer. Another well-known Arabian instrument is the *rababa*, a one-stringed fiddle which is commonly accompanied by a flute (*nay*), a fiddle (*jozay*), a zither-like *ganoun*, a long lute (*buzuk*), a tamourine (*daff*) and a goblet-shaped drum, the *darabukkah*. The ability to improvise on a melody constitutes one of the standards by which a performer is judged.

Although associated with these folk arts, dancing is not generally a group activity. There are a few exceptions such as the sword dance which is still performed by the menfolk on special occasions. Women, however, do frequently dance amongst themselves, informally grouping or taking turns in pairs or singly for the entertainment of their party. The exceptional circumstances which provide an opportunity for group dancing occur on such festive occasions as religious holidays, circumcisions and weddings.

Kinship was the primary organizing principle in traditional Arabia, with the patrilineal extended family composed of related lineages tracing descent from a common ancestor. These extended families formed the basic social and economic units which constituted relatively independent groups. They sometimes consisted of thousands of members while others contained only a few lineages.

Many tribes have always been sedentary, especially in southern Arabia where the land is not barren and there is therefore no need to travel far to find pasture. In parts of Arabia, enormous multi-storied houses served to keep town and village lineages together.

Marriages are generally arranged within the kin group by the parents on behalf of the young people. Arabs tend to marry early. Traditionally, a girl (*bint*) wed prior to her sixteenth birthday and the boy (*walad*) before he reached his eighteenth. The prospective husband makes the bridal payment to the father (*aab*) of the girl before the marriage is consumated. This token is often paid in kind rather than in cash. Customarily, a payment is mostly used for the purchase of the bride's clothing, articles for the new home, livestock (if rural), jewellery and other investments for her future security. A woman's jewellery is her personal treasure, to be kept or sold as she desires. In olden days, it was stored (together with household linen, clothing and other personal items) in the *sundouq hashab*, the great cedar dowry chest known as a "Medina" or "Kuwaiti" chest – the essential piece of furniture presented at the time of the marriage.

Even in the remotest regions, physical beauty and a pleasant disposition are sought in a bride. Family prestige is also considered, as a proper social status and satisfactory material circumstances are regarded as an essential foundation for a successful marriage. It is believed that affection should grow out of a marriage, not precede it. It is most important that the bride be a virgin before marriage and a faithful wife afterwards. Disgrace and dishonour would fall upon her family otherwise.

The marriage is regarded as a civil contract and the ceremony is presided over by a respected member of the community or a tribal *sheikh*. In town and desert, the marriage celebration frequently occurs in two stages, one at the home of the girl's family and one at the bridegroom's dwelling where the couple often go to live. Sometimes they will live close by. In taking her place as a member of the community, the girl brings honour to her family yet the parting is tinged with sadness.

During the ceremony, an Arabian bride, *arousah*, is seated in an elevated place in order that her bridal clothes, jewellery and appearance may be observed and applauded by all present. Music, dancing, singing and feasting are part of the celebration at the bride's home, and when friends and relatives of the bridegroom, *arease*, have escorted her to her new abode, more feasting generally follows.

Although such marriages are normally entered into with the expectation that they will last for the lifetime of the partners, it is not imperative that they should be preserved under all circumstances. There is no disgrace for a Muslim in divorce and many adults have two or three marriages in their lifetime. Most marriages are monogamous but some men do have two or more wives at one time. A man is allowed four under Islamic law as long as he observes the Koranic injunction that he treat his wives equally.

Nominally, the husband makes decisions regarding the family, including the marriage arrangements, but generally only after discussions with the family. Activities within the home, however, are under the authority of the wife. She has responsibility for children, daughters-in-law, servants, and to some extent the men themselves, when it comes to the organization of household routines.

For all practical purposes, women's activities are confined to the home even in the desert. If a woman goes out in public, usually she is chaperoned by a servant or male member of the family. It is not unusual, however, for a group of women from one or more families to sally forth unattended to go visiting or shopping. They are, in this case, chaperones for each other.

Large families are desired since it is believed that children bring a blessing to a Muslim home. A common felicitation is "May you have many children". Special value is placed on sons in the Arab home as it is said they will add to the reputation of the family, whereas daughters will "build someone else's house". At the birth of a son, a mother may change her name to incorporate that of her boy. For example, she might henceforth be known as *umm Abdullah*, "mother of Abdullah", attesting to the importance attached to the birth of a boy. Despite this special pride in sons, great affection is felt for and shown to daughters.

Arabian children, from the time they are able, are expected to help their parents. Little girls take care of their younger brothers and sisters and perform other household tasks while boys after the age of eight or thereabouts keep company with their fathers in performing outdoor tasks. Young people of both sexes are expected to look after their elders.

The extended family system has traditionally handled the problems of the needy, the aged and ill, the handicapped and divorced and the widowed and orphaned. All of these victims in adverse circumstances are cared for by the more fortunate members of the family. Any individual in need of economic aid or protection is expected to turn to his kinsmen.

The emergence of Islam in the seventh century, while not fundamentally altering the traditional pattern, superimposed a concept of broader responsibility. Muslims accept inequalities of talent and wealth as ordained by God, and they insist on the moral obligations of the rich and more fortunate members of the community to assist and support the poor.

To understand the people of the Arabian Peninsula, it is essential to know something about their religion. Islam means "submission" – submission to the will of God – and a Muslim is enjoined to uphold the "five pillars" of the Islamic religion while putting himself totally into the hands of his maker.

The *Shahadah* is the first of the five tenets, and is the testimony and pronouncement of the words "There is no god but God (Allah) and Muhammed is His Prophet". Prayers, *Salah*, constitute the second tenet and this is often said to be the backbone of Islam. The first prayer is at dawn, the second at high noon, the third in the afternoon, the fourth at sunset and the fifth at night. The formalized prayer consists of a sequence of obeisances made first from a standing position and then from a kneeling one.

Fasting, *Siyam*, which means complete abstention from food and drink from sunrise until sunset during the month of *Ramadan*, is the third tenet of the Islamic religion. *Zakat*, almsgiving to those who deserve it, represents the fourth pillar, while the pilgrimage, *Haj*, is the fifth. Every physically and financially able adult Muslim should make the *Haj* to Mecca at least once in his or her lifetime.

In an Arabian household, the day begins with the first prayer. Then, after a light breakfast, girls and women attend to household work and meal preparation while men and boys work outside the home. In the desert, care of camels is of vital importance and receives priority. Well-to-do townswomen *al hidiriyyat* direct their servants and the gentlemen *al hudran* depart for business.

Women's tasks in the past included spinning, dyeing of yarn, and weaving, as well as tailoring and embroidery. Although the artisan classes generally performed crafts such as leather work and silver-smithing, many tribesmen were skilled themselves and produced shoes, bags, garments and camel trappings. They were also able to mend a coffee pot. Townsmen were usually occupied with trade and their sons were drawn into the business at an early age.

Because of the extended family social system, meal time often resembles a banquet. But, while the townspeople enjoy meat, fruit and honey-drenched pastries regularly, the diet of the nomad usually consists of dates, rice (sometimes wheat) and milk products from goats and camels. For the Bedouin, meat is a luxury, eaten only on special occasions such as religious holidays or when a visitor arrives – at which time an animal is slaughtered. Sometimes there is a welcome change in diet when wild game is available. Fresh fruit and vegetables are available to Bedouin only when they visit villages of settled cultivators but, despite a meagre and relatively low-nutritional diet, they are reputed to have considerable physical endurance.

Unlike the townspeople who eat mid-day, desert dwellers do not usually return home to eat during the day. Instead, they generally carry a small pouch of dates. Their largest meal of the day is in the evening. In both desert and town, the evening meal is a family affair unless there are guests who are not close relatives. In such cases, the men are generally served apart from the women and children.

Before this evening meal, there is a long social time. Women who have leisure time will have spent the early part of the day visiting friends, but, irrespective of how wives spend time in the late afternoon, they are expected to be home to greet their husbands when they return. The food, which might have taken a woman the greater part of the day to prepare, is served quite late and any friends who are present depart shortly after it is eaten.

Whether nomadic or sedentary, an Arab's legendary characteristics of courtesy and hospitality, rooted so deeply in the customs and traditions of centuries, remain rigidly upheld.

Regional Styles

In times past, outward signs of provenance and social hierarchy figured prominently in the lives of the people of the Arabian Peninsula. Then, early this century, superficial equality in their traditional costume began as oil revenue poured into Arabia. Now, distinctive regional apparel, that used to serve as an indication of social standing or tribal affiliation, is worn only by those living in remote areas, and by the very old.

For the men of Arabia, there now exists a modern traditional costume but as yet nothing that could be termed a "costume" has taken shape for the women. As the women still conform to a completely cover-up mode of dress, it is likely that this custom alone will continue to represent Arabian women's traditional dress.

The transformations Arabian costume has undergone in this century involve the same processes of evolvement that transformed the ancient, simple Middle Eastern body-shirt into the classic *kaftan*. Just as the *kaftan* grew into distinctly different regional costumes because of the environment and separate spheres of influence, changing lifestyles and new foreign influence continue to make changes.

Most agree that it is about thirty years since hand-sewn garments were worn. Some traditional styles have perhaps been lost since. From about the 1930s, examples of Arabian handwork have worn out and been discarded, sometimes miles from their place of origin. Ten years ago, a traditional dress of the Asir province was found in Dammam, on the opposite side of Arabia, approximately 2,179 kilometres away. Such finds, while welcome, sometimes make it difficult to ascertain a garment's provenance. Nevertheless, an attempt is being made to catalogue the traditional costume of each tribe and sub-tribe, in the hope that this cultural aspect of a disappearing desert civilization's heritage may be preserved.

Arabia has a long history of regionalism and tribal autonomy. Decades of separate rulers resulted in social and cultural gaps between the various regions and chasms existed between the ways of townspeople and rural folk. Each town in the past, like each great tribe, carefully kept its separate identity. The result is manifested in the variations in colourful costumes.

The Peninsula comprises several landscapes and climatic zones which create natural geographic sub-divisions within its six main regions. These regions are Northern, Eastern (sometimes called Hasa), Western (the Hijaz), the South-west (or Asir), Southern, and Central Arabia (known as the Najd). Sub-divisions within each region often show clear cultural differences that once reflected superficially on their costumes, but, for the sake of clear presentation, the six major divisions seem to be the most efficient method for general classification.

Hasa, Kuwait, Qatar, Bahrain, the United Arab Emirates, Trucial Oman and the Muscat coastal region have been grouped together and added to the section on Eastern Arabia because their history and geography are intertwined. The Yemens, Oman and the Empty Quarter are grouped because a similarity of costumes and customs is evident throughout these southern areas.

Najd

The Najd, or "highland", is a flat plateau spreading over the central part of the Arabian Peninsula. It sits in geographical isolation and in the past was inaccessible because it is flanked to the west by the mountains of the Hijaz, while the other three sides are bordered by a desert wilderness.

Stark landscapes with occasional springs and wells paint a picture of most of the Central Arabian region. The weather is excessively dry and the rainfall is low; yet, the town which lies in the heart of the Najd is called Riyadh, meaning "the gardens".

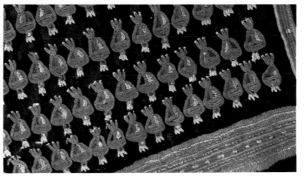

Left: These two pictures provide a close-up view of embroidery motifs traditional for the Central Arabian women's thawb. Far left, old lanterns or pomegranates are sometimes used to cover the back shoulder section which is plain black on the example in the photograph on the opposite page. The second motif seems to be a palm tree and appears in the sleeve panels, each side of the plain black centre-front panel. Slight embellishment variations are usual.

Left: A further example of the red, cerise, green and gold hand-done embroidery on the traditional black cotton Najdi thawb. These colours are echoed in the bold silk patches appliquéd to both front and back. The number of silk patches and the amount of embroidery varies but the placement is kept strictly to a format.

Opposite page: The Najdi Bedouin women's traditional thawb is a unique black garment made from fine linen, soft cotton, or lightweight wool. It is derived from the kaftan, yet it appears to be fashioned from two large squares. The slit neckline is buttoned. The thawb is worn as an overgarment as a rule although records reveal such a gown was once worn by itself in the hot interior of Arabia. The kaftan probably grew to this size because loose garments are cool to wear – this style is wonderfully comfortable yet graceful in line. It allows free movement and air circulation – an ideal maternity dress. This spectacular gown brings to mind romantic tales of Arabian desert life long ago.

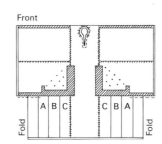

Gusset

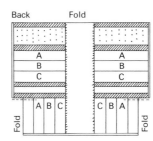

Left: This pattern shows patch and embroidery order. A = orange, B = green, and C = Cerise. Dots denote embroidery motifs and shaded areas are embroidered.

Dotted lines are embroidered seams. The back and front full-length centre panels are cut from a single length to approximately the width of the shoulders. The sleeves are so enlarged that they appear as squares attached to the centre panel. The side panel "gores" grew accordingly and are separated from the sleeves by an overgrown gusset of gaudy material.

Riyadh, 600 metres above sea level, is located at the point where Wadi Hanifa meets its tributaries Wadi Aysan and Wadi Batha. In modern times, it has been a dry area, relying upon ancient sources of water which lie far underground. Once Riyadh and nearby Diraiyah were part of a vast oasis of date palm trees and other vegetation – hence the name. The area was then lush enough to sustain life through the intense heat of summer. Through the centuries, as the heat of summer encroached, the Bedouin from the arid outlying areas habitually made their way to the protection of the great oasis to replenish saddle bags and refresh their spirit.

Historians believe that as early as the sixth century BC this oasis was settled. The numerous springs and extensive date palm groves made it an ideal spot for agriculture. This fact accounts for why townspeople of the Najd have always far outnumbered the nomadic people.

Riyadh is today the capital of the Kingdom of Saudi Arabia. At the turn of the century, it was merely one of a cluster of small hamlets along the Wadi Hanifa – an area once walled in by mud brick and encompassing several small oasis hamlets including Diraiyah.

Diraiyah is the most important historical site in the Najd. It was settled in the fifteenth century and became the first Saudi Arabian state capital in the middle of the eighteenth. Although Central Arabia has never been technically conquered or settled by foreigners, Diraiyah was destroyed in 1818 by an Egyptian army sent by the Ottoman Empire. It revived in the nineteenth century and is today a burgeoning modern town.

In total contrast to the surrounding regions, the Najd, by virtue of its inhospitable terrain, has had little outside influence in the past. Consequently, for thousands of years, artistic expression was a mere evolution of ancient forms, virtually uninterrupted and unadulterated.

Central Arabia's inaccessibility and aridity deterred all but the most intrepid explorers. This led many scholars to call the Najd "true Arabia" and thus the most fascinating province for them. Lady Anne Blunt called it "the Cradle of the Arab race".

The people of the Najd descend from a mixed group of northern and southern stock. The remoteness of their land has resulted in a purity of race, matched nowhere else on the Peninsula. This gives rise to the claim that they are the aristocrats of the Arab race.

Najdis have a reputation for being pious and conservative. They inherited strong ideals – and great traditions of hospitality and generosity were fostered and have blossomed because a simple lifestyle in the harshness of a desert existence bred a kind and friendly disposition.

Today's landscape is dotted with ruins of mud houses and old town walls reinforced with towers. Many fine beige-coloured dwellings are being preserved. Crenellated edges of the flat rooftops and windows are freshly picked out with vivid white, and the carved wooden doors, hatches and window shutters are repainted in traditional multi-coloured geometric patterns. These homes are made of unfired clay bricks with roof structures made of mud and tamarisk wood beams supported by mud pillars. These are often painted with

colourful patterns to match the doors, shutters and ceilings.

Occasions for celebration were eagerly awaited in olden times by both men and women in Central Arabia. Music and singing, sword dances and desert banquets with burning incense and sprinkled rosewater gave levity to a life that was otherwise hard. The men enjoyed the chase, using falcons and *salukis* while riding the legendary and beautiful Arab horses. Camel and horse races were also an important part of Najdi life.

The people of the Najd particularly enjoy eloquence in both conversation and poetry and this accounts for the fact that much of the finest Arab verse was composed in this region. Poems depict the life and ideals of traditional society, which involve honour, manliness and fortitude.

On every special occasion, gay new clothes would be worn. Traditional garments, like other forms of artistic expression in the Najd, show a unique flavour, accountable to their relatively untarnished evolution. The traditional costume of old Najd is particularly flamboyant in cut and colour, almost as if in defiance of its stark mono-

Above: Traditional festive finery in the Najd requires the addition of a sheer "overthrow" to basic costume. Most of these are transparent thawbs, *designed to be worn over a* fustan, *or* dharrah, *conforming to the Arabian custom of wearing layered clothing. In olden times, ladies often wore matched sets of* sirwaal, dharrah *and* thawb, *and the textile and embellishment revealed their station. This style is often called a "wedding" dress because all the ladies wear them to a marriage celebration. A bride would wear a cerise-coloured version. Most of the black tulle versions are made in Pakistan and India and are now totally machine-made. The yoke returns over the back.*

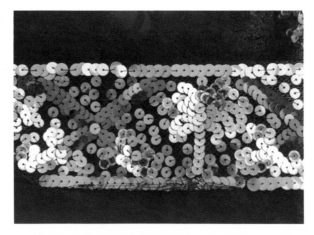

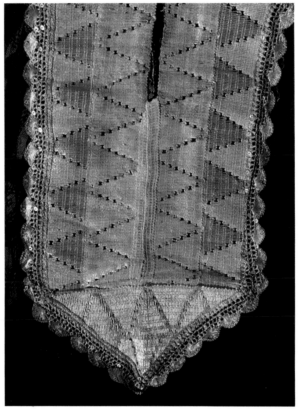

Left top: This thawb's *wide sleeves have a broad band of embellishment, usually clustered sequins featuring crossed swords, palm trees, crowns, crescents or stars. These cuffs are stitched on inside-out in order to show uppermost when the sleeves are folded back to either rest upon the shoulders or cross each other on the top of the head, forming an elegant head covering. The largest of these garments is made from approximately 35 metres of tulle (one bolt) and the back hem trails magnificently. This train is hitched over the forearms when necessary. Women in Istanbul used a ribbon to fasten up similar trains when they intended to walk. The motifs on the black tulle are often unique – see* Textiles.

Left: A close-up view of the gold and silver metal-thread yoke – this broad braid continues over the shoulders to fall down the back. The width and length of the braid varies. Its edges are crocheted with gold metal thread and sequins are added as a rule. The decorative yoke is customary but by no means obligatory – it would seem to be a matter of wealth. The under-arm gussets are a spectacular addition to an otherwise sedate gown. This pattern segment is always cut from a brilliantly coloured textile.

chromatic setting. It is in this region that the most exotic examples of traditional Arabian costumes, exhibiting the fabled loose and flowing quality, could be seen in olden times.

Najdi women's traditional costume conforms to a basic formula that is shared by all the Peninsula regions. It can be seen that all costumes provide total coverage and follow the layered format which conserves body moisture, while the "cover up" element protects the body against the strong sun. Where Najdi dress differs from the costume styles of other regions is in shape, and this would seem to be directly related to the region's climate. In the Najd, the basic *kaftan* grew into a capacious garment, obviously adapted to cope with the dryness and excessively high temperatures, bringing to mind the comfort provided by tent dwellings. The body of the garment is spacious and does not cling, and the sleeves are enormous, catching the slightest breeze.

The women's *thawb* is made from fine linen, cotton, wool, silk, a sheer textile or tulle. The most common colour is black, but the garments are enlivened by a combination of appliquéd silk

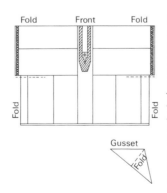

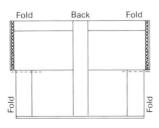

Left: The front and back view of the pattern for the gown shown on the opposite page. The * denotes the opening for the head which has a slit fastened by a turquoise and gold button. The under-arm gussets, drawn separately, are inserted at the dotted line. It has been enlarged proportionately to the dimensions of this enormous kaftan. *The centre panel, front and back, are a single length. The textile length runs at right angles for the upper sleeve section which folds over the shoulder-line. The sleeve bottom sections, front and back are also at right angles to the centre panels. There are two panels, with the textile length vertical, at each side of the*

centre panels, front and back, and the outside panel at the back continues for a short distance around the front to join up with the gusset and front panels. Because the neckline is set as shown, the back hem of the gown automatically trails and the under-arm gusset fans out to display this splash of colour. It is a most disconcerting task for anyone to fold such a dress as this if they have not studied the pattern, and it is wise to do it correctly. All thawbs *are best folded by making the hemline even first. Then the opposite end, above the neckline, is made even. By drawing up and laying flat the gusset, the gown can be seen as a square or rectangle and folded easily.*

Below: *These drawings
illustrate the pattern used for
many Najdi silk thawbs for
women. Lines delineate the
pattern segments. Silk
patches are often inlaid rather*

*than applied as they would be
on the cotton version.*
** denotes the neckline which
invariably carries embroidery
which may be extensive and
cover the bodice. Some rare*

*examples exhibit embroidery
and sequins over the entire
front panel, yet the hemline is
never embellished. The gusset
is drawn separately.*

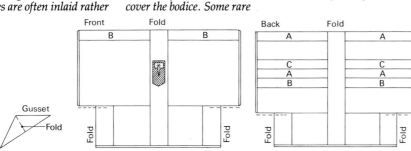

Above: *Machine-sewn gold
metal-thread aghabani work
and gold sequins decorate this
rare royal purple silk gown. It
is called* tawb magassab, *an
elaborate overdress. The
under-arm gussets are
patterned brocade,
embroidered and sequined.
The edges are braided. It was
found in Jeddah and once had
a matching body-shirt and
sheer tawb overthrow,
Possibly there were matching
sirwaal originally, too. It is
claimed as Najdi and the clue
is the gold and turquoise
neckline button – a type
traditional to the central
region. The style is, in any
case, pure Najdi. Well-to-do
women customarily wore silk
and chiffon thawbs instead of
black cotton.*

patches in cerise, green and orange and by vivid and intricate embroidery or sequins. The well-to-do wear the silk versions. For special occasions, extra layers of either tulle or sheer textiles with sequins are worn. Many of these garments were made in India for the ladies of the Najd.

The black tulle versions of these Najdi *thawbs* generally feature a decorative yoke which continues over the shoulders and falls down the back, resembling ecclesiastical vestments. This piece of embellishment is made of two-tone gold metal thread, woven and crotcheted, with a sprinkling of gold sequins at the crotcheted edging.

The addition of the metal-thread yoke and the ten centimetre wide sequined braid on each sleeve cuff serves to create a most exotic garment. Rare examples have embroidered cuffs. This particular "overthrow" *thawb* is commonly called a "wedding" dress because every lady attending a Najdi wedding celebration traditionally wore one.

It is a unique stylistic format which arose in the Najd; while the voluminous *thawb* was originally worn for the practical reason of survival, these stoic women chose to make these garments hand-

somely distinctive. In contrast to the western woman who changes her mode of dress each time the clothing industry dictates, the Arabian woman of the past wished to perpetuate an accepted cultural style. Tradition was so important that she imitated as closely as possible not only the textile but also the embellishment placement and mediums.

The female body-shirt known as *dharaah*, *migta* and other names, is a *kaftan* with embroidery often only on the sleeves. The Bedouin cotton version has silk patches and generally a townswoman's version is silk. It is worn ankle-length so the embroidered ankle bands of the *sirwaal* are not visible. They are generally less elaborate than western Arabian pants, although they sometimes match the dress and form an essential part of the traditional Najdi costume. Over the dress and *sirwaal*, a woman in the past wore a *thawb*, the enormous flowing garment previously described. This served every practical purpose but also gave the wearer an opportunity to display her Arabness in a positive use of bold colour and grand style.

The everyday black *thawb* of Central Arabia is generally made of fine Egyptian linen or cotton, but in the past it was apparently sometimes handwoven from local sheep's wool.

Najdi embroidery motifs are fascinating and stay within the prescribed design boundaries although there are visible variances in execution. Stylized palm trees predominate. Another common motif, perhaps the second most popular design, resembles the lamp once used in ancient Arabia. These lamps are still found in the antique shops of the south.

Each gown is fastened at the centre-front neck slit with a silver, gold or brass button which is usually studded with a turquoise or blue stone. Massed silver balls are commonly sewn to the sleeve cuffs of the Bedouin *kaftan*.

Najdi *thawbs* generally serve as a third layer, although an early explorer in Arabia recorded that the poor Bedouin woman wore it as a single item. Charles Doughty, travelling in Arabia in the nineteenth century, took particular note of the women's traditional costume of Qasim, just north of Riyadh. In particular, he remarked on the "sidelong, large sleeves" of the garment. He wrote that the women wore "a strange fashion of clothing in that the sleeves in Qasim are wonderfully wide, that if an arm be raised the gown hangs open to the knee. One must go therefore heedful of the garment, holding the sleeves gathered under the arms". He is obviously describing the garment still found in Central Arabia today.

A poor Bedouin woman would use extra funds to purchase an outer mantle rather than a *migta* or *sirwaal*. The *abaaya* has the additional advantages of protection from the elements and, since it is a mantle, it maintains the prescribed Muslim etiquette for modesty and provides freedom to venture out of the home. The cloak could also serve as a sheet when taking a rest.

Also in pursuance of a modest appearance, Najdi women wear the *burga*. The Central Arabian version is made from a soft, loose-woven cotton or silk, constructed in two layers from the eye-slits down. These layers are joined between the eyes at the bridge of the nose, and at each side of the head to a forehead band which is tied about the head. The top layer usually ends at the chin with a fringe or some other pretty decoration, and the bottom layer falls to the chest. This face veil was also worn in Eastern Arabia in the past and is now seen throughout the Arabian Peninsula, replacing many of the stiff masks. Najdi Bedouin women once wore the *litham*. Today, they wear a square or rectangle of soft, porous, stretchy black material; the top of this section rests on the top of the forehead and the ends are generally tied behind the head. The bottom of the veil falls below the chin-line to any length according to preference. Sides are wrapped back around the head. The *taraha*, the second part of the headgear, is a rectangular scarf that can be placed over the head to fall about the shoulders although some women wrap it about the head more securely. The *abaaya* is placed over the *taraha*, draping from the centre of the crown, although some Riyadh women wear it on their shoulders. Many modern Najdi women wear a silky length of black textile, *habaya*, with end decorations of silver or beading. This is wrapped around the head and under the chin, one end falling down the front and the other down the back.

Men of the Najd have always enjoyed fine clothing, according to early records. In 1865, Lewis Pelly, visiting Riyadh described the *Imam* at that time as a tastefully yet richly dressed gentleman. His headdress consisted of a green cashmere shawl twisted up into a turban and worn over a skullcap. The *Imam*'s servant, in contrast, wore what Pelly described as a "sober Riyadh costume" which he is recorded as having exchanged for one of bright colours once on his journey out of town. According to Pelly, this change of garments "transformed him so that he took on the appearance of a man of some consequence". Pelly's observation confirms the power of apparel. Strict Islamic teaching of that period in the central region of Arabia enjoined men to dress decorously whatever their circumstances. It is interesting to read of the difference in appearance between the religious leader and his flashy servant.

Pelly also noted that people of the Najd bought their mantles from Hofuf, then a flourishing trade centre in eastern Arabia. Hofuf provided much of its manufactured items for the Central Arabian market. It was from this town also that Najdi men bought most of their arms – the rest coming from Damascus, Najran and Basra at that time.

In olden days, unbleached calico *thawbs* were worn by the ordinary menfolk of the Najd. This textile has since been replaced by white cotton, generally with a small percentage of synthetic fibre. The new traditional *thawb* has a slimmer cut than of yore, and ordinary shirt sleeves. Some elegant modern *thawbs* seen in the Najd are made of silk with matching corded and braided necklines and cuffs, similar to Egyptian and Damascene *kaftans*.

In the past the body-shirt worn by men in the Najd was known as a *merodan*. It was again a basic *kaftan* but featured enormously wide sleeves, the under-arm seams forming a point which dipped to the hemline of the garment. The *merodan* ceased to

be fashionable everyday wear in the 1940s with the advent of civil servants in the new ministries; a more serviceable sleeve was in order. The old style *merodan* is today reserved for special occasions.

Najdi men, today, generally wear an immaculate white *thawb*, a crisp-looking red and white chequered *shmagh* (headcloth) or *goutra* (white headcloth) over the *kuffiyyah* (skullcap). This headgear is topped by a double black woollen rope, the *igaal*.

Over the *thawb*, the *bisht* is worn, with the invariable gold edging on a black, brown, beige or honey-coloured textile which ranges from camel hair, wool and cotton to synthetics. In winter a Najdi man may be seen wearing the *farwah*, the sheepskin-lined cloak which is generally a black-braided navy-blue and black garment. The *bisht* is more usual for a townsman, however, and the finest camel hair versions can be warm enough. On cool evenings at events such as the sword dance, he may wear a *kaftan*-cut short, gold-embroidered *furmilaaya*. In the past, there were also full-length, front-opening coats for Najdi men – possibly styles inherited from Turkey.

Above: high, parched rocks, usually stark against the background of a lush palm grove, are momentarily enlivened by this georgeous thawb. The bland deserts of Arabia were once alive with the vivid spectacle that was traditional Arabian costume. This robe is pure silk chiffon and the gold and silver metal-thread work is precious and to a high standard. The basic pattern is claimed to be Najdi, but this gold-embellished, sheer silk interpretation is now considered to belong to the eastern regions of the Arabian Peninsula. All edges – neckline, sleeve and hem – have been embroidered and the entire front panel and under-arm gussets are elaborately worked.

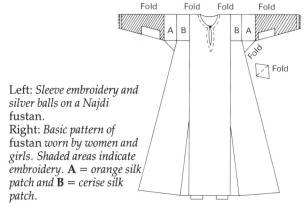

Left: *Sleeve embroidery and silver balls on a Najdi fustan.*
Right: *Basic pattern of fustan worn by women and girls. Shaded areas indicate embroidery.* **A** = *orange silk patch and* **B** = *cerise silk patch.*

Above: *Married women generally wear a* thawb *over a* fustan *such as these. This tribal dress is generally blue or green and sometimes ruby red – commonly a floral cloth today. Needlework as good as this no longer done by the*

Bedouin *and the sleeves of old gowns are detached and used again on machine-sewn* fustans. *The rectangular unembroidered section on the sleeve is overlaid with a patch from the textile of the new* fustan. *The silk patches are*

always cerise and orange and worn in these same positions. Their presence once again confirms the importance of these colours as part of traditional Najdi costume. Turquoise-set silver buttons close the slit neckline.

Northern Region

The northern frontier of present-day Saudi Arabia borders with Jordan, Iraq and Kuwait, from west to east. Jordanian costumes clearly show the influence of the Hijaz, western Arabia, and this is not surprising because it is geographically an extension of the Arabian Peninsula. Kuwait in the east, is also historically and geographically bound to the Arabian Peninsula and shows the influence of Hasa, or eastern Arabia. Iraqi costumes, at least those worn south of the Euphrates River, show similarities to northern Arabian garments. One of the larger Arabian tribes, the Rwalla, traverse a *dirah* (traditional tribal ground) spanning a vast area that crosses the Saudi Arabian northern border. The Rwalla are notable for being the only Arabian tribe that used a true tribal banner, known as the *markab*. It is a glorified and richly decorated version of camel litter, commonly called *maksar* or *ghabeet*.

The Northern Region comprises the Great Nafud Desert, the Aja and Salma mountains of Jabal Shammar in the south, and lava flows in the north. The climate is harsh, with extreme heat and a paucity of rain. Temperatures in excess of 120° Fahrenheit are not uncommon.

The area north of the Nafud Desert, which is geographically part of the Syrian Desert, is an upland plateau with a dark-coloured rock and gravel surface. There are numerous wadis, the most significant being Wadi Sirhan – a large basin set in the surrounding plateau. Sparse grass and steppe vegetation provide pasture for the herds of the nomadic and semi-nomadic northerners. For thousands of years, this region has been the home of the stoic people who early developed a life-style suitable for desert living.

From the earliest known times, a sharp distinction existed between the way of life of the Bedouin and the townspeople of Arabia. In the past, the principal towns in the Northern Region were Jauf and Hayil. In particular, Hayil, set at the southern edge of the Great Nafud, has long held a fascination for adventurers and explorers. It was considered by them to be "true Arabia" and part of the "heartland" like the Najd. For the indigenous people, Hayil was a stronghold of Arabian traditions. Modern Hayil is often described as the metropolis of Jabal Shammar, the vast northern highland rising to 2,000 metres above sea level. On the opposite side of the desert, in the north, lie the most important oases in the region, Jawf and Sakaka. These centres served the ancient caravans which traversed Wadi Sirhan.

A great deal is known about the colourful period when the ancient trade routes were active, but, until quite recently, there was no evidence of the pre-historic heritage of Northern Arabia. It is now confirmed that the Northern Region of the Arabian Peninsula contained one of the earliest known Stone Age settlements about 150,000 years ago, situated along the northern boundary of the Great Nafud Desert. There is also evidence of later Stone Age settlements around Hayil, Wadi Sirhan and elsewhere which match sites throughout Arabia, dating about 30,000 years ago. Although there are enormous gaps in the knowledge about these settlements, they do confirm that the region was extensively populated from the earliest times.

Settled life, domestication and agriculture cannot be accurately defined as yet, but the evidence suggests that by 7000 BC, partially settled communities subsisting on herding were under way. Permanent stone structures in Northern Arabia of the mid-fourth millennium BC have been construed as evidence that these settlers were the forebears of the mobile Arabian Bedouins who are believed to have appeared much later in history. These nomads knew in their earliest history how to spin wool and hair from sheep and goats to make tents.

The finest example of rock art in Arabia, found at Jubba, eighty kilometres north-west of Hayil in the Great Nafud, depicts adorned humans alongside long-horned bovids. It is also likely that sheep were kept at this time, between 6000 and 3000 BC, and spinning and weaving were known.

There is little available evidence as yet of developed crafts in the Northern Region but there is enough to suggest that garments were tailored by the Bedouin in the mid-nineteenth century. According to Georg August Wallin, the Rwalla and Shammar tribes looked to Hayil for their textiles and clothes. The Rwalla, a large and powerful confederation of tribes, still live a life steeped in traditions which were so well reported by Alois Musil, another early explorer in Arabia. Musil carefully documented the various pieces of Rwalla costume. While the names of the garments differ from those used in other parts of Arabia, the descriptions confirm that the clothes are basically the same. Only the superficial appearance changes within the provinces from tribe to tribe.

For the men, Alois Musil lists a body-shirt, an overgarment, belt, "kerchief", headband and cloak. The cloak is made from a striped textile. In winter these northern men wear a sheepskin version with sleeves. He writes that many men were barefoot. Others wound textiles around their feet or wore camel-hide sandals. There are also records of a rough leather shoe worn by northern Bedouin.

Carlo Guarmani, sent by Napoleon the Third in 1864, met with the ruler of Jabal Shammar. The *sheikh*'s chief officials, slaves and servants were sitting about him in a semi-circle and, according to Guarmani, all were well dressed in fine black cloaks with red or blue cloth coats heavily embroidered with gold. The description of the coats fit those which have been made for centuries in Damascus for Arabian men. The prince and all of his followers also wore scimitars in silver scabbards, writes Carlo Guarmani.

The same gentleman writes enthusiastically of the Hayil women. He claims that "for purity of line, they rivaled the most graceful creations of Canova" with their "long glossy hair oiled with an odourless pomade composed of finely powdered palm bark and clarified fat obtained from sheep's tails".

On her visit to Hayil in the late nineteenth century, Lady Anne Blunt confessed that she found it hard to describe the gowns of the well-to-do women, other than to remark on their "splendid shapelessness" and observe that they were cut like the *abaaya* but closed up the front. She supposed they had to be pulled over the head. The description fits the Central Arabian *thawb* which was also typical female costume as far north as Hayil.

Lady Blunt felt that the women enjoyed the occasion of a visitor as it gave them a chance to display their silks and jewels. Great pains were taken then: "their toilet is a most elaborate one with *kohl* and fresh paint, and it takes a long time – carmine used on lips and cheeks; eyes with borders blacked with *kohl* . . .", dressed in "rich gold brocades", Lady Blunt found the *hareem* women "pretty, agreeable and dignified".

According to Lady Anne, poor Bedouin women wore dark blue or black "woollen stuff" bordered with a very narrow red edge like a cord or binding which, she said, "looks well". In Hayil, no belt or fastenings were worn at the waist which is also the case directly south in the Najd. In both areas the weather is extremely hot and waistbelts would not be comfortable. Such facts confirm the theory that temperature, terrain and topography have helped to shape ethnic costume.

Lady Anne Blunt wrote of a gorgeous gown of crimson and gold, and of magnificent materials of gold interwoven with silk. She describes a lady of Hayil wearing "a mass of gold chains around her neck, studded with turquoise and pearls". The images are vivid and dramatic. The jewellery described is identical to that worn in the Najd. Both regions share costume and jewellery styles similar to those of Iraq and Afghanistan.

The wife of a *sheikh* who received Lady Blunt, wore her hair in four long plaits which were "plastered with some reddish stuff". It was quite likely henna. On the top of her head, "placed forward to the edge of her forehead", the lady wore a small gold plate-like ornament of about four inches in diameter. It was studded with turquoise and fastened back with gold and pearl chains to another ornament resembling a lappet – also of gold and turquoise. This was hooked on behind the head and attached to flaps which fell each side of the head and neck, ending in long strings of pearls with bell-shaped gold and pearl tassels. "The pearls were irregular shapes and unsorted as to size and quality". Coral beads were also mentioned.

Another piece of jewellery described is a nose-ring "larger than worn in Baghdad or elsewhere, measuring one half to two inches across, worn in the left nostril, consisting of a thin circle of gold with a knot of gold and turquoise attached by a chain to the cap or lappet before described". These ornaments were taken out and left dangling when the wearer wished to eat or drink. It appeared to Lady Anne Blunt that the diameter size of the nose-ring denoted the rank of the wearer as she saw only smaller rings worn by inferiors. (It could, of course, have been a matter of wealth.) The Bedouin had far less jewellery but they are described as having "bright laughing faces" with "teeth like pearls".

It was the custom at that time in the Northern Region to dress the children's heads in black, with the intention of making them less captivating in the hope that this would avert the malignant gaze of the jealous (known throughout the world as "the evil eye"). There is no other mention of children's costume.

The menfolk apparently enjoyed rich and colourful textiles. The Blunts were met at Hayil by "some twenty well-dressed men" – the sons of *sheikhs*. "In their midst stood a magnificent old man, clothed in scarlet". His costume consisted of several layers of brocaded Indian silk – the garments topped by a black cloak interwoven with gold. He wore at least three "kefiyahs" (referring to headcloths), one over the other – "of a kind made in Baghdad". His *igaal* was also described as "the Baghdad type" which Lady Blunt had hitherto supposed was only worn by women. (She was referring to a circlet common to the women of central Iraq.) This is interesting, as the head circlet was "bound up with silk and gold thread and set high on the forehead so as to look like a crown". It would seem to be the golden *igaal gassab* once worn by *sheikhs*, *amirs* and royalty. Today it is available to everyone and it is worn sometimes for celebrations.

To complete his costume, the *Amir* of Hayil wore several golden-hilted daggers and a handsome golden-hilted sword, ornamented with turquoise and rubies. Most probably the latter stones were garnets. Turquoise and garnets (real and fake) are common to traditional northern Arabian jewellery. The workmanship, it was discovered, was done in Hayil and exhibited a very high standard according to Anne Blunt and her husband, Wilfred Scawen Blunt.

The *amir*'s immediate attendants, though less splendid, were also magnificently clothed and each soldier at the palace wore a brown cloak and a blue or red "kefiyeh" (the name of the Arabian skullcap which is often applied to a headcloth in some Middle Eastern countries). Their swords were silver-hilted. Overall, appearance in northern Arabian towns at that time was one of vivid colour.

For her personal use, Lady Anne Blunt found the turban was the most practical headgear of all. She observed that it was equally good in hot and cold weather and in both wind and rain. "It protects the head from a blow as effectively as a helmet; it can be torn up to staunch wounds; it can be used as a rope or a girdle; and above all it is a pillow", she added. The latter attributes give some insight into the Blunts' adventures.

She did add as an afterthought that a turban was "the badge of the *fellah*" (peasant farmer) in the Northern Region, and did not command respect. Turkish officials in the area at the time wore the red high-crowned skullcap, the *fez*, while the Bedouin fastened their headcloths with the *igaal* which was made of camel's hair rope according to some records. It seems more likely that generally *igaals* would be made from black sheep's wool or goats' hair as they are tougher fibres.

In 1913–14, the noted Arabist Gertrude Bell, followed such famous explorers as the Italian Carlo Guarmani, the Austrian Baron Nolde and the Englishman Charles Montague Doughty, to cross Wadi Sirhan, east of the region later called Transjordan, to reach the Great Nafud Desert. Miss Bell took the path which leads west of Jauf, a desert township that was the traditional home of the Shaalan family, the hereditary *amirs* of the Anazah tribal confederations and paramount *sheikhs* of the Rwalla. In 1913, however, it was occupied by the Rashids. Gertrude Bell also crossed the Huwaytat tribal territory and called on *Sheikh* Auda's *hareem*. At that time, no European man, with the exception of a Turk, had seen Hayil for more than ten years, and no woman for more than thirty. When she arrived, Hayil was a busy trading centre in regular communication with the outside world. The men wore "silks" and the women of Hayil were all "closely veiled".

According to Colonel Dickson, northern tribal women did not wear the *burga*, or mask, but wore

instead the *milfa*, a semi-transparent black scarf drawn over the lower features of the face. Women of the Bani Sakr, Huwaytat, and Bani Atiyah tribes in the north, did not cover their faces at all in the past. It seems the custom of veiling was more prevalent in the towns.

Alois Musil took careful note of traditional costume of the Rwalla Bedouin women. Apparently they habitually wore a *magruna* on their heads, which he describes as a large dark headscarf folded to a triangle. Wealthy women wore a headscarf called *sumbar*. On top was worn a headband called *sitfa*. Their cloaks were plain-coloured and worn draped from the top of the head. These mantles were called *mezwi*.

The Bedouin dark blue dress for women was called the *baarim*. Over this they wore the *tawb aswad*, a blackish gown with broad sleeves ending in a long lappet. This high-necked garment was one metre longer than the wearer and hitched up by a belt to free the ankles. The woman sewed the dress herself out of approximately six metres of textile, usually cotton. Although the Rwalla ladies

Left: The embroidery on this tribal dress is subtle against its ruby-coloured background, yet it is also outstanding. The finest work can be found on this style – particularly on the under-arm gussets where they merge with the bodice embroidery. The work is unique also in that there are perhaps four botanical motifs amongst the geometric. See Embroidery. The lined upper section of the bodice to the bustline is stiff with this work and a double skirt falls softly from bust level. It is the only Arabian dress to have a double skirt. Brilliant originality is displayed in the extension of the under layer at hem and sleeve cuff to show appliqué and embroidery. The silver bells at the cuff edge are usually attached to the shorter outer layer.

Right: The shaded areas on this drawing denote areas of embroidery.

have "milk-brotherhood" with the nomads there. As a baby, he had been wet-nursed by an Anazah tribeswoman of the Misrab section of the great Rwalla tribe. This tribe's domain spreads over the northern and eastern regions of the Arabian Peninsula.

According to Dickson, warm friendliness is manifested amongst Eastern Province tribes in the form of generous hospitality to a passing stranger. Even if the head of the household is away when an important cavalcade passes by, the lady of the tent may correctly attract the riders' attention and invite them to eat. To signal them she will hang her colourful holiday garments on a pole stuck in the ground in front of the tent. This custom is apparently an established Bedouin signal in Arabia for inviting a stranger to come and partake should no menfolk be able to ride forward with an invitation. For a passer-by to approach otherwise would be an infringement of privacy.

Dickson recalls the days of tribal hostilities. "In times of war the traditional sanctity of the Arab woman was proven," he writes: "It is she, if the tribe has to be rallied, who uncovers her face, lets down her hair, and spiritedly mounts the decorated tribal litter to encourage the young and old men to victory".

His records reveal that traditional clothing for men in eastern Arabia consisted of either the *thawb shillahat* – the old style, wide-sleeved body-shirt, known also as *merodan* – or the *dishdasha* – the narrow-sleeved version commonly called a *thawb*. The *zibun* was considered to be a superior kind of *dishdasha* and opened down the front from top to bottom with one side folding over the other in dressing-gown fashion. The *zibun* is held in place by two pairs of little strings, one inside and one outside. This garment was common to other parts of Arabia in olden times, too, and was known by various names. Underneath were worn loose-fitting, narrow-ankled *sirwaal*. Overgarments consisted of the *damir* – a black jacket embroidered with gold, and a cloak.

Dickson's books are full of delightful impressions and early this century eastern Arabia was obviously a very colourful province. He recounts scenes of massed decorated tribal litters on the move. The *maksar* is the common type used by various tribes. There are other styles of camel litters with different names. All are made from pomegranate wood purchased in the markets. It is a timber that can be bent easily into the required hoop shapes. The women make them and they are variously decorated with gazelle skins, cowrie shells, brightly-coloured curtains and trappings. On the march, rich colourful silks and wools drape the frame – the more brilliant the colour the better, for this will attract attention and give prestige to the owner.

Costumes in the past were also colourful and important. Colonel Dickson noted that gifts of men's cloaks, strips of silk for men's outer garments and coloured cloth for women were offered when a prince or important *sheikh* visited another of like status. The *sheikh*, in order to prove himself "father of his people" and so as not to appear miserly, would not only keep an open house, but would send regular presents of frocks and material

over the head to form an elegant hood. It is known as the *thawb nashal*. The style of dress is claimed to be originally Central Arabian. The Najdi sheer versions of the women's traditional *thawb* are quite often made in India, and it would seem that the pattern found favour along the route. Strengthening this theory is the fact that the *thawb nashal* shares the same bassic pattern with the age-old cotton *thawb* of the Najd which was hand-made in Central Arabia. Being a capacious cut, it is logical that a style such as this would evolve in the hot interior. This gown is made today in Pakistan, India, Kuwait and Bahrain.

The other woman's traditional garment still popular today – and shared between the Najd and the east – is a hooded cloak known as *mukhnug* or *bukhnug*. This is also made in India and Pakistan, and worn by unmarried girls.

Colonel H. R. P. Dickson, British political agent in Kuwait from the twenties, casts interesting light on traditional Arabian costume. He had wonderful opportunities to study the Eastern Province Bedouin in particular because he could claim to

for dresses to the wives of the less fortunate members of his tribe. Also, for the special *Eid* following *Ramadan*, it was the custom for husbands and masters to dole out *kiswa* (textiles for new clothes) to their wives, dear ones and servants.

George Forster Sadleir who journeyed across Arabia in 1819, noted in his diary that a *sheikh* of the Beni Khalid tribe wore many layers of clothing. "The under-robe was of gold tissue while the top layer was a thick scarlet cloth robe". He wore a costly shawl on his head. Lewis Pelly, visiting Al Hasa in 1865, remarked on the popularity of silk as a garment textile – at a time when silk was said to be regarded as undesirable for men's wear. The women's holiday garments, worn under black *abaayas* outside the home, are described as "brilliant green, cerise, crimson, scarlet, purple and blue". Little girls were decked out in a lot of jewellery over gaily coloured frocks. Small boys also wore new clothes. Most wore the traditional black slippers while others were barefoot. These black slippers were most likely made of canvas, fashioned from three segments, and dyed with indigo. The wealthy had high-heeled shoes.

Burgas, face masks, and *abaayas*, cloaks, were discarded by women for dancing in the desert since the menfolk remained at a decorous distance. The young women, dressed in their spectacular *thawbs* and "long flowing undergarments" and holding a small cane, would coyly cover the lower part of the face with one hand, or hold a piece of sleeve in front of the mouth and begin to dance. This description of the garments is close to that of the traditional costume of Hijazi townswomen.

The *bisht* described by Pelly was made of finely woven sheep's wool or camel's hair, fashioned from two pieces. The texture of the cloth varied from superfine to coarse, "according to the weaver's skill". Around the neck and down the front, gold embroidery ended with a couple of gold tassels on both sides. Colours varied in shades of brown and black. In Dickson's book, a drawing shows a coat, *farwah*, worn by *sheikhs* and the rich Bedouin. It resembles the *bisht* but sleeves are added. This *farwah* is made of predominantly black and blue cloth with additional scarlet, green, mauve or maroon pieces, the sections trimmed with pale yellow and black braid and lined with black or white lambskin – preferably the former.

The common headgear, according to Sadleir, was a headcloth and circlet only (the skullcap is not mentioned). "In the days of tribal raiding, every Bedouin went to battle with his 'kuffiyyah' wound tightly across his face and the ends tucked into the *igaal* on the top of his head. This hid all but his eyes".

The traditional dagger was the *khusa* in this region and in the north, and it was kept in a scabbard known as *jiffar al khusa*. There is also a miniature knife for hunting, known as *huardhi*. The *khusa* is attached to the inside of the belt and the *huardhi* is attached inside the bandolier.

From Colonel Dickson's descriptions, it appears that the unbleached calico body-shirts were cut very full. He speaks of "voluminous folds". This conforms to the styles worn in other Arabian Peninsula territories in the past.

The small bags, made of sheep's wool and

camel's leather for carrying money or small quantities of dates and other items, were known as *mizuda*. Bedouin also carried camel sticks, the *asa* or *bakura*.

When the weather turned cold, between mid-November and mid-February, both Bedouin men and women wore "woollen top-boots", Dickson writes.

The range of traditional clothes for Bedouin men and women was similar. Women's *dishdashas*, which could be cotton, flannelette or silk, were always colourful. The sleeves of the women's *thawbs* must have been of the wide deep lappet kind in olden times, for Dickson remarks that they were bound behind the ladies' necks to free their arms when they set off to collect *arfaj* – the tough brushwood root used for fuel in the Middle East. Wealthy townswomen also possessed a *zibun* – a long front-opening coat.

Sirwaal were basically cut the same for both men and women. The over-garment was a black cotton *thawb*. The *abaaya*, made from black wool edged with black silk, was worn by every Bedouin

Above: *Handsome red and black in curving panels swirl with the wind despite heavy metal-thread machined embroidery. The colours do not seem garish against the warm hues of the desert. This thawb is an unusual interpretation – such gowns are commonly a vivid colour but rarely are two colours combined. The machined embroidery is particularly well-done in this instance and is probably Indian. Modern Indian versions are poor replicas.*

woman outside her tent if men were in the vicinity. On special occasions this was substituted with another version embroidered and edged with gold.

Traditional headgear for rural women in the Eastern Province was the *umm raugella*, a black cotton rectangle consisting of four segments. This was worn over the hair and hanging down over the neck of the *thawb*. Townswomen added the *milfa*, a straight piece of transparent black cotton cloth drawn over the lower part of the face. Tribal women traditionally wore a *burga*, which Colonel Dickson found "very becoming" as it "shows off the eyes to great advantage".

One Eastern Province version of the *burga* is long and falls to the chest with almond-shaped slits left for the eyes; it is formed in two tiers from the eye-slits down. The top layer ends at the chin with the lower layer reaching to the chest. This is often made from *jezz*, coarse silk. The Ajman tribal women, on the other hand, wore a shorter mask common also to the Murrah and Manasir tribes, as did the Trucial Coast tribes and those living on the island of Faylayka off Kuwait. This short mask is usually made from a black mercerized cotton or shiny coarse silk into which a tiny stick is sewn down the centre from forehead to chin. The protrusion gives a strange beak-like appearance to the wearer. This style of *burga* is known as *batula*. It is kept in place by cords bound around the head and neck in three places. In the past the women made their own clothes including the mask.

Young girls don a gold embellished black *bukhnug* on festive occasions. This hood fits tightly under the chin. It is a rectangle of cloth (usually tulle), folded in half to form a narrower rectangle. This is partially sewn up at one end beginning at the selvedges, thereby leaving an opening for the face that is edged with gold embroidery or gold braid which continues down the seam at centre-front from under the chin. Sometimes sequins are added.

Throughout history, because of steady outside influence, coastal life-style differed greatly from that of the eastern Arabian nomads. From around the fifth century AD, north-east Arabia came under Persian influence. In fact, costume on the coast reflects the influence of various cultures, whereas the garments worn inland are akin to those seen throughout the other desert regions of Greater Arabia.

The Gulf States, Trucial Oman and the Muscat Coastal Region

Along the eastern coastline of the Arabian Peninsula, from north-west to south-east lie Kuwait, Bahrain, Qatar, the United Arab Emirates comprising Abu Dhabi, Dubai, Sharjah, Ajman, Umm Al-Qaiwain, Ras Al-Khaimah and Fujairah. All these countries, and Trucial Oman and the Muscat coastal region, were subject to British influence which lasted for over one hundred years until 1968 when the Federation of Arab Emirates was formed.

There were also other outside influences at work throughout the Gulf area, mainly since the early thirties and the discovery of oil. Oil was found on Bahrain in 1932, Kuwait in 1938, Qatar in 1939,

Abu Dhabi in 1960, Dubai in 1966 and Sharjah in 1974. The latter three member countries of the United Arab Emirates (formed in 1972) were the only Trucial States to have oil in viable quantities, while oil has been the chief source of revenue for Muscat since the 1950s.

Furthest north, located in the north-western corner of the Arabian Gulf, lies Kuwait. It is bounded on the east by the Gulf, on the north and west by Iraq and on the south and south-west by the Kingdom of Saudi Arabia. Included in its territory are a number of offshore islands, the largest of which is Bubiyan. Of these islands, only Faylaykah at the mouth of Kuwait Bay is inhabited. This island, which is the site of an ancient Greek temple built by Alexander's men, is believed to have been a centre of civilization in antiquity.

The country's only prominent geographic feature is Kuwait Bay, which indents its shoreline for nearly half of the total length. It provides natural protection for the port of Kuwait. Most of the land is a waterless, gravelly desert with one small oasis at Al Jahrah at the western end of Kuwait Bay. There are a few wells in the coastal villages but no permanent streams. Only a few wadis fill with winter rain. The intense humidity suffered throughout the Gulf area is somewhat less severe in Kuwait. Sand and dust storms are frequent in summer and are blown down from Iraq by the *shamaal*, a strong north-east wind. In the past, even in a year of good rainfall, Kuwait suffered an acute and chronic shortage of water.

Historically, Kuwait is important. There is evidence that before man migrated to the European geographic area, traders from the western coast of the Gulf were enriching the first civilizations of the Fertile Crescent, both commercially and culturally. In the ninth century AD, Gulf traders were travelling back and forth to China and exchanging ideas and goods with the great civilizations of the time. Arabs and Persians interacted across the Gulf quite freely.

Because of the sweeping changes brought about by oil revenue, much of traditional costume has been swept away. Surprisingly, the general shape of garments has changed little. It is mainly the textiles that have changed, and, in the case of men's clothes, bright colours are no longer worn.

Colonel Dickson records 1935 as the year when town ladies ceased to wear some items of traditional Arabian clothing. His wife, Violet, was in constant company with these ladies and had intimate knowledge of their garments. It is recorded that the *sirwaal* were replaced by *saujar*, or short knickers. Colonel Dickson believed the word was a corruption of the English word "soldier", referring to the short pants worn by British soldiers in the Middle East at that time. Clothing was otherwise similar to that worn in other Arabian territories in the past. In fact, the garments worn today in Kuwait are practically the same as those worn within the Kingdom of Saudi Arabia. The men's *bisht* presents the exception.

In Kuwait, men wear an additional section of gold braid on the *bisht*. This takes the form of a horizontal bar on each side at the front. These bars are attached to the end of the gold braid around the neckline at the point where the tassels connect.

In the past *bisht* was generally reserved for the *Sheikhs* of Kuwait.

Southward lies Bahrain which comprises an archipelago of thirty-three islands but with a total land area of only about 660 square kilometres. The main island accounts for approximately one-third of the total and it lies at the entrance of the Gulf of Bahrain, an inlet of the Arabian Gulf between the coast of Saudi Arabia and the Qatar Peninsula. For centuries this position has given Bahrain regional importance.

Only four islands are of significant size. They are Bahrain, Sitrah, Umm Nasan and Al Muharraq. The others are little more than exposed rock and sand bar. Most of the main island is desert with outcroppings of limestone. Manama, the capital, is located on the north-eastern tip of the island of Bahrain where the main port, Mina Salman is also located. A causeway links the islands of Bahrain and Al Muharraq, and the island of Sitrah is joined to Bahrain by a bridge. North of Sitrah is An Nabi Salih where freshwater springs irrigate date groves. North-west of Bahrain is the rocky islet of Jiddah which serves as a prison settlement.

The weather is only pleasant from October to April and the *qaws*, a dry south-west wind, frequently blows sand clouds across the barren end of the island of Bahrain towards Manama.

Bahrain is the site of the lost civilization of Dilmun (circa 4000 to 2000 BC) which also included 400 kilometres of the eastern coast of Arabia from present-day Kuwait to Bahrain and extended ninety-six kilometres inland to the oasis of Hofuf. Dilmun was the trading link between the civilizations of the Indus Valley and those of Mesopotamia and the Mesopotamians regarded Dilmun as a holy place and its people were considered blessed.

Dilmun's commercial power began to decline in 1800 BC, perhaps as a result of the invasion and devastation of the Indus Valley civilization which disrupted trade in the region for several centuries. In the period that followed, piracy flourished. By the end of the third century BC, trade revived slightly but in 228 AD, Sassanian Persia took Bcontrol of the area until routed by the Arabs in the seventh century.

Farming and fishing supported most of the people of Bahrain before oil was found. Natural resources consisted of dates and pearls. Bahrain sits in one of the richest natural pearl beds in the world and pearl traders in the Arabian Gulf amassed great wealth and merchants traded in woollens, rare woods, ivory, copper and gold.

Gulf pearls have been prized since remote antiquity. They were popularly worn by the Arabian people and formed an important part of ancient trade treasure. When the first Japanese cultured pearls reached the markets in the 1930s, prices of natural pearls dropped, resulting in the collapse of Bahrain's pearling industry. Other aspects of traditional life continued for a time.

Weaving is still performed in some villages of Bahrain. In coastal areas sailors weave sail-cloth in the winter. *Awzar*, the simple garments worn by the villagers are also locally woven, using imported cotton. These are sari-like skirts probably of Indian influence. Because of eastern Arabia's cultural ties with Persia and India, values and customs are reflected.

The woman's traditional costume of Bahrain consists of four pieces. The undergown, *diraa gawan*, a waisted, scooped-neck, short-puffed-sleeve garment made today from every imaginable colourful material. The *diraa gawan*, too, is more closely related to Persian and Turkish costume than to Arabian. Underneath are equally colourful *sirwaal* with embroidered leggings. Over the *gawan* is worn a floral *thawb*, similarly cut to the Hijazi woman's *tawb* which is somewhat smaller than the Najd *thawb*. Outside the home, many women still wear the traditional Bahraini cloak – a semi-circular mantle such as was commonly worn in Persia, Iran and parts of India. For the most part, Bahraini ladies now favour the black *abaaya* seen throughout Arabia today.

Eid holidays on the islands are particularly colourful still today because of the bright clothes worn. Even little boys wear new white *thawbs* and bright-coloured artificial silk embroidered caps. Little girls dress like their mothers in gold-decorated and gold-sequined sheer *thawbs* of many colours.

Although Bahraini brides wear long white Western gowns today, traditionally many wore the *thawb nashal* and a lot of gold jewellery. Hair ornaments of twenty-one carat gold, sometimes forming a cap, are an important part of traditional Bahraini woman's costume, especially for a bride. These head ornaments are remarkably similar to Indian trinkets and it would seem likely that this Bahraini fashion came from there.

After Dilmun's commercial decline, seafarers and merchants turned their attention to Dhofar (the southern region adjoining South Yemen in present-day Oman) as Dhofar was a producer of the finest frankincense and myrrh. Thereafter in the Gulf, Gerrha (which is believed to be located somewhere opposite Bahrain and perhaps tucked into the northern neck of the Peninsula of mainland Qatar) became the most important commercial centre of that time.

The best "fisheyes", or pearls, listed on ancient Mesopotamian import documents came from just south of Bahrain, between the tip of Qatar and Sharjah, suggesting that pearling was a thriving local industry there many thousands of years ago. Qatar is a peninsula jutting out 160 kilometres northwards from the eastern Saudi Arabian mainland, varying in breadth from fifty-six to eighty kilometres. It separates the Arabian Gulf from the Gulf of Bahrain. Qatar's land is largely flat desert covered with sand and pebbles and broken occasionally with limestone outcroppings. There are low cliffs and hills on the western coast. In the south, sand dunes and salt flats predominate. Doha is its capital and the main population centre of this tiny desolate land.

The greatest social, political and cultural event for the inhabitants of the Gulf was their conversion to Islam late in the seventh century. Their "golden age" of shipping began in the eighth century with the establishment of the Abbasid Caliphate in Baghdad (750–1258). The Gulf was favoured in that Baghdad lay due north.

The intrepid sailors of the area went as far as

Below: It can be seen that the thawb nashal of the Eastern regions is similar to thawbs worn by women in other parts of Arabia. It is cut a little narrower than the Central Arabian thawb and the under-arm gusset is smaller. The sequin-sprinkled embroidery falls within the shaded areas which are at all edges and over all joins. Most of the work is confined to the centre-front panel which is a single length for the back and front. Because of the neck opening placement, the back hem trails but less so when it is worn in the traditional Eastern Arabian fashion with one wide sleeve drawn up over the head to form a hood. The amount of embellishment varies from gown to gown and sometimes the flimsiest thawb nashal is extremely heavy by virtue of the amount of metal-thread and sequins.

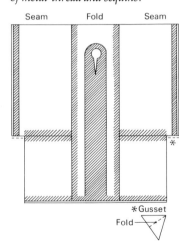

Above: Tailors on Bahrain embroider the thawb nashal in separate panels before the gown is made up. They move the textile deftly under the machine needles to skilfully accomplish the curvilinear arabesque designs. Sometimes representational motifs of flowers and birds are added. Finishing touches accent pattern segments, such as panels and gussets, which are embroidered after the garment is made up. The Arabian custom of drawing attention to the under-arm gusset is most evident on the thawb nashal and suggests its Central Arabian origin. This gown is currently popular.

Through the centuries, traders have entered the Arabian Gulf to bring fabulous textiles to desert hareems. These three gowns have come from India. They are exactly the same style but the basecloth is different in each case. The metal-thread and silk embroidery also differs. This thawb nashal *can be cut from marquisette, chiffon, georgette, organza, nylon and the sheerest silk. It is invariably semi-transparent. Although the gown is said to be of Najdi origin, it is the traditional costume of women in the Gulf lands.*

noted that *kaftans* were worn over loincloths. At Bai, Thesiger noted that some tribal women wore the black visor-like stiff mask. He writes that one of the women wore white, and "this was most unusual".

South and west of Abu Dhabi, the vast rolling sand dunes merge into the Empty Quarter of Saudi Arabia. Large sections of the coastline are salt marshes that extend for miles inland but, from the Gulf of Oman coastline, the terrain is sharply different. The Western Hajar Mountains which rise in places to 2,500 metres above sea level, run down close to the shoreline in many places.

The salt marsh sweeps east then north across Dubai and the territories of Ajman, Fujairah, Ras Al-Khaimah, Sharjah, Umm Al-Qaiwain, to reach the Musandam Peninsula which is today controlled by Oman. It overlooks the Strait of Hormuz, a narrow passage separating Arabia from Hormuz on the Persian coast. Hormuz was for a time the foremost trading centre in the world. In fact, the Arabs and Persians of the ancient world shared a saying: "If the world were a ring, Hormuz would be its jewel".

Trucial Oman and the Muscat coastal region share many geographic and historical similarities with the previously discussed Gulf lands. Trucial Oman refers to an area bordering the seven Emirates – the Musandam Peninsula on the Strait of Hormuz which links the Arabian Gulf and the Gulf of Oman. Muscat is the name of Oman's capital city but it also once referred to the north-eastern Muscat coastal strip of present-day Oman. Oman is the broader term used to describe all areas governed by the Sultanate of Oman, including Inner Oman and Dhofar which fall naturally into the Southern Region in relation to traditional costume.

Ras Al-Khaimah, Fujairah and the eastern part of Sharjah, are hilly and mountainous, topographically distinct from Abu Dhabi and Dubai which together account for more than eighty-seven percent of the territory. All share a hot climate, dry in most areas but unpleasantly humid near the coast. During the late summer, the humid wind, *sharqi*, makes the coastal regions stifling.

To the casual observer, the U.A.E. is today devoid of obvious traditional features and seems to have been integrated into a modern-looking land. It is true that change has been swifter here than in any other part of Arabia but profound cultural values have not been completely lost. Approximately seventy different tribes have now been identified in the U.A.E. and these are believed to have ancient connections with tribes from the northern Euphrates River.

It is only in the remote interior today that nomads can be found wearing traditional garments. These are, not surprisingly, parallel in style to garments worn in other parts of Arabia. The differences are superficial, a fact which assists tribal identification. In addition, as in other remote regions of Arabia, a Bedouin's broad belt and dagger are the most prized items of his traditional attire.

China in incredibly flimsy craft, following the monsoon winds yearly between the major centres of medieval civilizations. Numerous small islands, reefs and shifting sand bars combine with strong tides and occasional windstorms to menace navigation even in the region of the Emirates.

South across the neck of the Qatar Peninsula, lies the largest Gulf Emirate, Abu Dhabi. Despite a long coastline, it has no natural harbour and relied, as did the other five Emirates, upon neighbouring Dubai which has a large natural port.

When Wilfred Thesiger visited Shakhbut, the ruler of Abu Dhabi, and his close relatives in the 1940s, they were dressed in "Saudi fashion", wearing long white *thawbs*, gold-embroidered cloaks, and white headcloths which fell around their faces and were held in place with black woollen head-ropes. The ruler's dagger was ornamented with gold. His black beard was carefully trimmed. The servant wore a shirt dyed yellow with saffron, and Thesiger noted that such shirts were also worn by others. The common headcloth was brown and worn bound about the head. He

Hijaz

The Hijaz, or Western Arabia, is a land of great variety. Its vast dry deserts contrast sharply with the cultivated areas. At the highest point in the Hijaz, over 1,800 metres above sea level, stands Tayif, the summer place for rich townspeople and a stronghold of traditions. It is around Tayif that many of Arabia's finest examples of handicrafts are still found and the area, for centuries, has provided abundant fruit for the towns and roses from which Arabia's legendary rosewater is distilled.

To the south-west toward the coast, lies the Tihama, or lowland area of the Hijaz. Here, as in the Asir, descendants of Africans have merged into the Arabian population, welding their colourful crafts to those of traditional Arabia. The influence of adjacent Africa is also strongly evident in the thatched dwellings along the Red Sea littoral. Yet is is Indians in Jeddah who predominate with regard to foreign blood. They came originally as traders – mostly from Bombay.

Jeddah has always been the commercial centre, and immigrants seeking work have come towards this port for centuries from other parts of the Peninsula as well as from outside. Early reports record that the merchants of Jeddah dealt in French textiles, Indian cashmere, locally made footwear, locally indigo-dyed Egyptian cotton, pilgrim's garb made of Indian cambric, Turkish dresses, Egyptian wool cloaks and cotton *milaayas*.

The word *Hijaz* means "barrier", referring to the great escarpment that runs from north to south forming a natural corridor. This was the path used by ancient frankincense and myrrh traders from the south. Along this trade route, towns such as Mecca, Medina, Kheybar, Tayma and Tabuk served as resting places for merchants. Both Mecca and Medina were particularly blessed with abundant wells, so caravan routes linking China and West Africa met there.

The Hijaz, which has been a major travel area since the earliest times, continued through history to be strategically important because of its prime location. As the homeland of the holy cities, Mecca and Medina, it was an important province of the Ottoman Empire for centuries. Foreigners were particularly attracted to the coastline, so these population centres were continually subject to outside influence.

Mecca is an ancient city and an early trading centre close to the Red Sea coastline. Long before oil was discovered, bringing Saudi Arabia into world focus, Mecca was a household word in the West. Even ordinary people, who were not the least bit scholarly, associated Mecca with a special personal goal or a place that they held sacred. In the long history of Arabia, Mecca has always been special but never more than it is today. As the birthplace of the Prophet Muhammed, Mecca is a venerated shrine, and therefore represents the place of pilgrimage for Muslims throughout the modern world.

Even in pre-Islamic times, Mecca was a centre where pilgrims gathered, but since the Dawn of Islam, believers from widely separated parts of the Islamic World have visited there, sometimes re-

Above: *The Red Sea resembles molten gold at sunset and dramatically silhouettes a typical Bedouin dress of the Hijaz, western Arabia. This basic shape displays several differences in full light although these fall into well-defined embellishment areas. The colour of sleeve godet and shoulder patch are but two features that vary. It is thought that the variations had significance in the past. In traditional Arabia, it would have been immediately apparent to which tribe a woman belonged because of the superficial appearance of her dress. This particular dress is decorated with fine appliqué over patches rather than embroidery.*

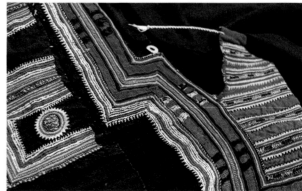

Above: *A close-up view of the black cotton dress, top, shows embroidered red cotton appliqué on the shoulder-line and one side of the slit neckline. This horizontal slit appears at both sides and there are button and tie closures. The embroidery is neatly executed in parallel lines – the patterns and thread colours identical in many examples of this style found in the Hijaz. The dress pattern segments appear to have been embroidered before construction.*

Left: *Three variations of the broad hem band on a Bedouin dress from rural Hijaz show similarities. The needlework is limited to the appliqué of fine strips of white cloth and continuous rows of triangles overlaying red and blue patches. The sleeve cuffs are also worked in this fashion. The variations may be a social indicator within one tribe, or a sub-tribal identification.*

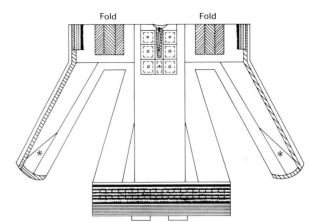

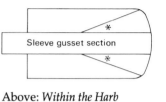

Above: *Within the Harb tribe there are many embellishment variations on women's dresses but the basic shape is constant. Western dress design concepts are shape, line, form, pattern, texture and colour. Usually only a specialist is conscious of these basic principles so it is a visual surprise to find this style answering so many fashion requirements. It is a pity that most examples found today are well-worn and often torn. The sleeve length varies along the shoulder fold – measuring sometimes approximately 35 centimetres. The longest is approximately 55 centimetres. Under-arm gussets are rectangular when separate. Quite often the rectangle is extended to form the under-arm segment of the sleeve lappet. Sleeve gore colour and sleeve patches also exhibit differences. Patches return over the shoulder for an equal distance and are placed in "drop-shoulder" position. Some examples have additional narrower patches appliquéd on the shoulders and running parallel each side of the rectangular yoke.*
Above left: *The relentless sun offers little protection for the nomadic woman. Her dress therefore covers most of her body – the long sleeve lappets also serve to cover her hands modestly during prayer. She has decorated her black tribal dress with splashes of red, white and blue, and added buttons and beads to delicate embroidery in stoic defiance of a harsh desert existence.*

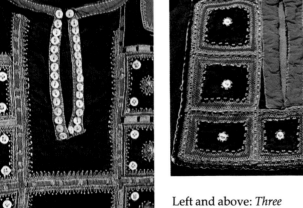

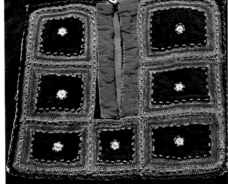

Left and above: *Three variations in yoke decoration on black satin-finished cotton dresses. These are worn by women of the Harb tribe whose area encompasses Jeddah, Mecca and Medina, and sweeps east then north across the land. This style is* worn in the Hijaz and claimed by the Beni Salim sub-tribe. The bodice decoration on these dresses falls within a square or rectangle which is divided by the centrally-slit neck opening. The intricate embroidery is usually red and white with touches of yellow, and the red cotton appliqué, white shirt buttons and tiny silver beads are a common addition. The yoke in the centre has been cut from an old garment to be re-used on this newer one. The stitches are very fine and even.

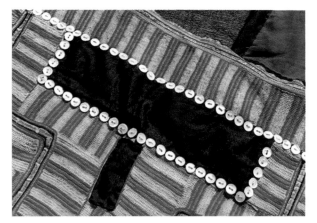

Left: *The neckline and shoulders of Hijazi rural dresses, are often heavy with embroidery – the work is commonly overlaid with white shirt buttons – the oldest examples display real mother-of-pearl buttons suggesting perhaps that the original appliqué was pearl shell.*

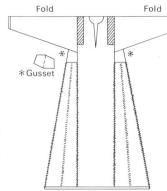

Left: *The thawb al Hijaz is a style worn by settled, semi-settled and nomadic women. It is the same pattern as the Asir dress. The appliquéd shoulder bars are usually larger and worn further down the sleeve in the Hijaz. Narrow patches such as these are features on Najdi fustans.*

maining in the area after completing the *Haj*. These settlers have brought with them the benefits of their skills which have been absorbed into the Hijazi way of life. Thus, apart from its spiritual character, Mecca is also a flourishing cosmopolitan city, active and prosperous. The influence of these immigrants spread to surrounding areas and the end result is a region rich with ethnic diversity.

It can be seen that, since antiquity, the Hijaz has been the most cosmopolitan region in Arabia; yet, being a largely rural region, there are still pockets of land where tribes cling to their traditional ways and live much as they did centuries ago. In these areas, outside influence can be detected by observing individual design elements of costume.

Considering the tapestry of influence in the settled areas of the Hijaz, it is not surprising that incredibly beautiful traditional costumes are found there, particularly in Mecca where the women's garments are unique.

Old etchings of Hijazi scenes show women wearing large turbans on their heads, fitted dresses and large shawls knotted about their hips. Women are also pictured with scarves draped around the chinline and tied on top of the turban. Turbaned women out walking have long braids falling down their backs from beneath their headgear. Also strolling in the same vicinity are closely veiled women with only their eyes visible. Slippers peep from beneath the all-encompassing cloak which even hides their hands. The turbaned ladies also wear a cloak but their hands and faces can be seen. At a distance bare-breasted women wear short skirts; yet another clutches a wrapper about her body – and her face is uncovered. The latter women may be slaves.

Many shoes in these olden times were apparently backless like the modern "scuff". Others were the conventional slipper shape without fastenings of any kind. The male body-shirts in these old etchings are depicted full-cut with wide sleeves and uneven hemlines. Over their shoulders, men carry large shawls. Many men are turbaned. Other men wear the two-piece *Haj* garments. The men's cloak has normal-length sleeves while the body-shirt underneath has wide sleeves much longer than the arm and consequently, they protrude beyond those of the cloak.

A group scene shows men in short skirts and short-sleeved vests worn with a cloth waistband. Each woman in this picture wears a long veil from the eyes downward – the head is covered with a shawl and a cloak envelopes the clothes. Men of

this era smoke long pipes and carry daggers, swords and lances when on horseback. Women carry fans.

An old photograph said to have been taken in the Hijaz shows a man leaning on a staff and carrying what looks like a club. His thick coarse clothing suggests that he is a Bedouin. Many other old Hijazi photographs show men wearing crossed bandoliers and waist belts – all of which fasten weapons securely to their bodies. This, of course, was necessary as they rode camels and horses.

Layered clothing is the common feature of all traditional Middle Eastern costume. It is the unifying factor in all provinces of the Arabian Peninsula, although superficially the traditional costumes often differ greatly from region to region and between rural areas and the towns. For instance, the traditional costume worn by the townswomen of the Hijaz, concentrates a great deal of attention on the embellishment of the *sidaireeya* (under blouse) and *sirwaal* (long pants) as these are designed to be seen when worn with only the sheer *tawb*, also known as *kirta*. The neckline and most of the yoke of the *sidaireeya* are meant to be visible also when worn under the V-necked *zabun* (traditional frock of the townswomen).

The Hijazi *tawb* is cut identically to the Najdi *thawb* although the former is of smaller proportions. This gauze over-garment can be any colour and is generally designed to match or contrast attractively with the *sidaireeya* and *sirwaal*. On special occasions *tawb* neckbands may be embellished to match the work on the *sidaireeya* and *sirwaal*.

The *sidaireeya* is traditionally made of fine, pure cotton – either muslin, voile or organdie – often eyeletted and embroidered. It is a high-collared, waist-length bodice with elbow-length sleeves and takes the place of brassiere, vest and scarf when worn with the V-necked *zabun*. The "mandarin" collar and sleeve edges are generally frilled or edged with embroidery. The front opening is buttoned high on the neck with removable buttons called *zarayer dhahab*. These are a set of seven cuff-link-type buttons attached to a chain. The top button is usually fixed but the other five slide on the chain.

As a rule, *zarayer dhahab* (gold buttons) are fashioned from gold, sometimes plain and sometimes shaped and occasionally set with diamonds. Sometimes only the first four buttons are shaped (star, crescent or heart, etc), leaving the last two or

Right: *This style of Hijazi Bedouin dress allows a lady to sit "tailor fashion" modestly and comfortably. The garment falls flatteringly from the shoulders, taking up flare from side gores that radiate out from under the arms to reach the broad hem band. This hem strip is decorative and practical – the skirt hangs and "moves" well and does not fly away in a breeze. The cut allows free movement and air circulation – and makes an excellent maternity dress. It is both Kurdish in form and "Elizabethan" in appearance. Kirtles in Iraq have similar sleeves – the ends are knotted behind the back for working. The bodice decoration here is confined to bars of parallel red embroidery and the slit neckline opening is off-centre in this style. A variation of this dress has a neckline slit opening horizontally on the shoulder-line.*

Right: *This dress bodice has red cotton appliqué at the yoke, overlaid with black, white and yellow needlework. The sleeve patches are usually blue – or, as they are in this case, fine blue and white checkered cloth. The sleeves vary from elbow length to wrist length. Except for the bodice, the embroidery on this style is mostly vertical whereas other dresses of identical cut have predominantly horizontal embellishment. The high collar is too small to close and possibly the buttons and ties are meant to be purely decorative. The many subtle and obvious differences in this style of Hijazi Bedouin dress may have once served to distinguish sections of the great Harb tribe.*

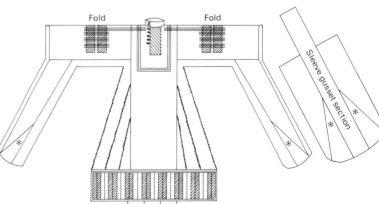

Above: *The cut of this garment looks intricate because there are many overlaid patches and these are traversed by lines of embroidery. It is, in fact, a simple kaftan with a broad hem band. The straight sleeves have a spectacular under-arm gusset which extends from the top of the side gores, joining to the under edges of the sleeve and taking in further segments of cloth to create deep lappets. Straight lines of embroidery stress the design in true Arabian fashion.*

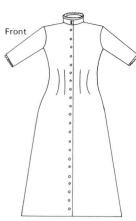

Front

Right: Diamond brooches such as these were worn on dress bodices and headgear.

Left: The sidaireeya *is a blouse customarily made from semi-transparent cotton and once took the place of brassière, vest and cravat when worn with the V-necked* zabun. *Silk and satin versions were reserved for special occasions. Correctly, the Hijazi* sidaireeya *is closed at centre-front with seven chain-threaded buttons (known as* zarayer dhahab) *that resemble cuff-links. They can be removed as required.*

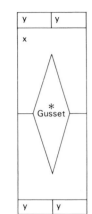

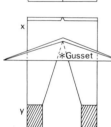

Left: Sirwaal, Arabic long pants, are roomy about the seat because of the ample crotch gusset. Legs narrow to the ankle or higher. The waistline is drawn in by a sash known as dikka, *threaded with a* midak, *a pencil-like "needle". The* dikka *was often an elaborate item and the ends were usually finely worked. In the past, it was common for* sirwaal *ankle-bands to be embroidered for both men and women. The textile is usually a solid cotton but women also wore silk and satin* sirwaal. ** denotes the diamond-shaped crotch gusset segment which is rotated and then stitched to the inside leg seams.*

ally with a rolled collar set in a V-neck, but sometimes the collar is high and frilled like the *sidaireeya*. The latter style is known as the "princess cut". It is a darted form-fitting dress with no join at the waist. The sleeves are elbow-length. The V-necked version has long sleeves with buttoned cuffs, and the dress closes down the front with buttons. The *zabun* is made in many textiles and in many colours. It is quite unlike other traditional Arabian garments and would appear to be of Turkish origin.

In olden times in the Hijaz, ladies' footwear in the towns was called *khuf babooj*. This style was red and yellow (see **Footwear**). Records show that red and yellow slippers were also worn in Jeddah by all the ladies as well as the well-to-do merchants. Red leather is still used to trim skin items in western Arabia. Descriptions from all over the Peninsula of gazelle skin items, as variously yellow, lemon, and cream, raise the possibility that these slippers may have been fashioned from gazelle hide.

In the towns, brides were presented with platform-soled, silver-inlaid wooden shoes which are identical to Turkish bridal shoes, a style of footwear derived from the Turkish bath-house wooden sandals. These high shoes are held fast by a strap upper. Wooden shoes of this style, known as *gubgaab*, are commonly inlaid with mother-of-pearl and other mediums also.

Although there was always a vast difference in life-styles between the Bedouin women and townswomen, both were similarly respectful of custom. In olden times, before air-conditioning, rich townspeople lived in mansions, using benches and cushions placed about cool tiled courtyards with playing fountains. Indoors they often had beautiful imported furniture and oriental carpets. Wealthy Bedouin had fine rugs, too, but these were spread on the sand under the protection of great hand-loomed tents. Despite this contrast in life-styles, both townswomen and Bedouin women veiled to go out of doors because it is a custom fostered by their shared Islamic faith.

The traditional headgear of Hijazi townswomen is *mihramah wa mudawwarah*. It is made up of three pieces. The first is a triangle, the *shambar*; the second is a rectangle, the *mihramah*; and the third is a square, the *mudawwarah*. The first piece, the *shambar*, is a small gauze-lined triangular scarf with a tie on two points. This covers the front hairline. The *mihramah*, a rectangular scarf, is then placed on the head with equal parts left on each side of

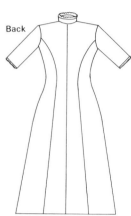

Back

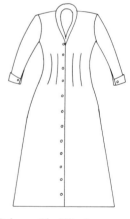

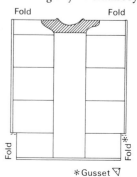

Below: The Hijazi townswoman's traditional overgarment is the tawb. *It is a semi-transparent capacious gown, usually made of cotton gauze. The shaded area of the yoke depicts a double thickness which is sometimes lavishly worked with gold, silver and pearls or more simply embroidered to match* sirwaal *anklebands and the edges of the* sidaireeya.

three plain as they are not seen when the *zabun* is worn. These chained blouse buttons are sometimes made of silver.

Sirwaal are the usual Arabian loose pants with an ample crotch gusset, and narrow legs. However, Hijazi townswomen's *sirwaal* often feature very heavy and exotic metal thread decoration from calf to ankle. A sash known as *dikka*, threaded through the waistband, draws in these wide pants and this, too, is often elaborate silk with richly embroidered ends. There is a type of *dikka* peculiar to rural and Bedouin women in the Hijaz, which is attached to a long front under-apron. No examples are available but Hijazi women describe a garment that is similar to one worn in rural Levant.

Sirwaal are commonly silk or satin for townswomen, and cotton is worn by rural and Bedouin women. Embroidery is common to ankle bands and on the ends of the *dikka* even for cotton versions. The *sidaireeya* is also made in rich textiles such as satin, and the outer edges are sometimes banded with wide, elaborate embroidery, encrusted with sequins and pearls. Hijazi townswomen traditionally wore a chemise known as *shalha*; this could be full-length or half and was worn under the *zibun*. Such garments were a Turkish influence.

The *zabun* is a floor-length shaped *kaftan* gener-

Left: *The top and centre drawings illustrate the front and back of the "princess-cut" zabun – the high frilled neckline opening for the full length down centre front. This style is often made in voile, muslin or organdie which has been self-embroidered. The bottom drawing depicts the more usual V-necked, rolled collar version of the zabun which is made in any solid textile.*

Right: *At the bottom of an old Jeddah garden, amidst lush green foliage, an Arabian lady appears as a fragile fairy in diaphanous garments of a bygone age. She is wearing the Hijazi townswoman's traditional costume of tawb over sidaireeya, sirwaal and zabun. The creamy-coloured satin sirwaal match the delicately embroidered voile sidaireeya and the eyeletted organdie zabun. This "princess-cut" zabun usually has elbow-length sleeves with lace or frilled cuff edging to match that which decorates a high neckline. The tawb is unembellished rust-coloured gauze, in tasteful contrast to the layers visible underneath. The costume is completed with the* mihramah wa mudawwarah *headgear with its elaborate* oiya *edging and diamond brooch. The central flower quivers on its spring stem. Less elaborate versions of this traditional headgear were also worn. These garments are more delicate-looking than those worn in other parts of Arabia but a similarity can be seen in the sirwaal and tawb. Overgarments from east, west and central regions are basically the same, varying only superficially. This tawb features unnecessary under-arm gussets, barely larger than postage stamps.*
The Hijazi tawb is different in that it often represents the second layer rather than the third or fourth – when it is worn without the zabun. The neck closure is also unique – the wide slit-shoulder neckline is closed with two loops at the back which fit over two silver ball buttons at the front – one each side of the neck.

91

the face to entwine with the equally divided tresses. Care is taken to see that the embroidered edges and ends show. The braids are then fastened securely to the top of the head with pins. The third and final piece, the large square *mudawwarah* is then placed on the head with one edge to the forehead. It is then deftly doubled up on each side of the face and folded back over the head, making sure that the embroidered edging frames the face. Usually, the edges of all three pieces are decorated with the traditional Hijaz edging, *oiya*, sometimes very elaborately (*see* **Embroidery**). The everyday *mihramah wa mudawwarah* is made of fine cotton voile, often printed with pale yellow and violet-coloured floral motifs. The edging is correspondingly delicate.

On special occasions, elaborate diamond-studded brooches are often set at the very top of the *mihramah wa mudawwarah*. These brooches are usually large floral arrangements and peculiar in that the central flower is often set on a spring so that it trembles when the wearer moves. Such brooches were also worn on a cushion-like yoke placed on a bride's bodice. A nineteenth-century Meccan bride was reported as spectacular "with her headdress looking like an entire jeweller's shop full of brooches and her dress covered with silk pads studded with countless ornaments".

A report written in 1885 makes mention of the Meccan women's penchant for new dresses and jewellery, and of how they made excuses in order to acquire them. It describes the gold embroidery on their trousers, confirming that Meccan women then, as they did earlier this century, wore sheer *thawbs* over richly embroidered pants suits.

In days gone by, when leaving the home, Hijazi townswomen used to don the *burga milaaya* (sometimes called the "Meccan veil"). It was a long, stiffly starched white gauze or fine linen veil which often reached the hemline. It is called *nigaab* in classical Arabic. The veil was held in place by its ties after securing the *shambar*. When thrown back over the head (as was the custom when visiting in the home of other ladies) this style of *burga* resembled the traditional Dutch woman's cap. The *nigaab* differs in that it was sometimes heavy with crusty embellishment. This appeared on both sides in order to look attractive when turned back. A great deal of Hijazi townswomen's traditional clothing was gorgeously exotic bringing to mind the court life in Baghdad and Topkapi rather than anything truly of the Arabian Peninsula.

Together with the *burga milaaya*, many Hijazi townswomen once wore a heavy silk taffeta mantle made in Indonesia. This expensive version was actually a sheet of navy-striped, black "weighted" silk. It had a medallion of velvet embroidered with silver metal thread and sprouting silver ball buttons each side of the neck. Cream-striped braid edging about the head section ended with silver tasselled ties which were more decorative than useful as the cloak was worn clutched to the body. Meccan women habitually wore a grey-coloured mantle. The clothes worn under these sombre cloaks were usually in bright contrast, although not as elaborate as festive finery.

The wedding is, without a doubt, the most elaborate celebration for the Hijazi people and the womenfolk are especially happy because it presents an opportunity for them to wear their best. In the past, a town bride's relatives and neighbours customarily joined together to produce enough pretty garments to last her for at least a year. Just as soon as the engagement was announced, the ladies would gather at the bride's house, offering their skills in sewing and embroidery. Long hours were spent sewing and embroidering as every item was hand-made. The work extended to specially made handkerchiefs designed to hold nuptial sweets. These were sewn by the women of the bridegroom's family.

Gifts, particularly those decorated with silver, symbolic of the dowry, were traditionally carried through the town to the bride's home in formal procession. The central attraction was a pair of wooden slippers inlaid with silver and these were ceremoniously carried on a cushion. After the procession arrived, the women displayed the trousseau and had a small evening feast.

An evening wedding celebration, *farah*, takes place on an appointed date, and puts the seal upon the marriage contract in the eyes of God and the community. In olden times, the festivities could last as much as three weeks and the bride might change her costume many times. On the wedding night, *dukhlah*, the bride wears the traditional colour which is cherry red, or cerise. She may have changed from white, to blue or pink beforehand. The cerise dress is usually embroidered Indian silk with an overlaid padded yoke to take the weight of the many pearls and diamond brooches. Some families rent the dress and jewellery to present the bride to her groom in her best possible light.

The women of the bridegroom's family customarily wear elaborate dresses, although still the same pattern is employed. The gowns of this *hareem*, the *nassasseen*, were traditionally white with the neckline and side panels colourfully embroidered and encrusted with metal-thread work and sometimes gems and sequins. It is not done in an attempt to outdo the bride but rather to convey that she is entering a good family.

A special woman, *mashta*, is usually on hand at a wedding to assist the guests to arrange the *mihramah wa mudawwarah* headgear and to help the bride.

Despite the fact that Bedouin women lack the luxuries available to town Arabs, nomadic ladies pay constant attention to appearance, dressing their hair and applying makeup. In rural areas of the Hijaz, women also wear the absorbent white cotton blouse-like undergarment, the *sidaireeya* and it is often skilfully embroidered. The rural and nomadic dresses, however, differ from those worn by the town women in that they are loose, full-cut *kaftans*, often with wide sleeves – the under-arm seam reaching to the calf or hemline. These dresses are predominantly black with colourful appliqué and geometric patterned embroidery which is exquisitely fine. For decoration, one version relies heavily on appliqué that resembles *mola* work at a glance.

It is recorded that some Hijazi tribeswomen wear plain black silk dresses. Apart from their various shawls, colourfulness comes from the brilliance of their masks which mostly combine vivid red with the glitter of silver plus white for a crisp accent.

An unmarried girl wears a simple full-length *kaftan* which is sometimes embroidered. The elaborate tribal costume is prepared in time for her wedding. In remote areas of the Hijaz, it is said that tribal women still weave their dress textiles by hand but most stitch them on a sewing-machine today. The chosen textiles vary more and more and, in some cases, floral or striped cotton is used as appliqué.

Red is still the predominant colour for appliqué and would seem to be the original choice. Blue is also popular. It is employed as a sleeve cuff trimming and for sleeve godets, the decorative triangular inserts which create a flared effect. There are sometimes blue patches on dresses too. Perhaps the tradition of employing red and blue appliqué is in some way connected with the custom of using blue and red stones in Arabian jewellery. In many parts of the Middle East, in times past, red and blue were believed to have prophylactic properties.

At Bani Sharfa, in the foothills of the Sarawat mountain range adjoining the Hijaz coastal lowlands (Tihamat Ash Sham) the womenfolk collectively present a very colourful appearance. Married women wear blue dresses while unmarried girls wear red. Both red and blue dresses are identically cut *kaftans* with a uniform geometric embroidery pattern. These women wear masses of silver jewellery – the many necklaces obscure to a great extent the delicate embroidery patterns at bodice and wrist. Hemlines are not generally embroidered. Although various coloured threads are used, the Bani Sharfa traditional costume is mostly embellished with silver metal thread. The decoration on their unique headgear is silver also. A silver decorated headcloth is tied under the chin and holds in place a silver encrusted "cushion" which is perched on top of the head.

In the Hijaz, headgear of the semi-settled, nomadic and village women conforms to traditional basic requirements while it is outwardly highly individual. There is the soft rectangular scarf and the heavy solid cotton rectangular shawl. A few styles are square-shaped. It is generally a rectangular-shaped garment most probably because a length of material is a convenient beginning, having two selvedges, leaving only two other edges to be hemmed. The soft rectangular scarf is draped behind the head from the left shoulder to the right, then pulled across the lower part of the face, over the left shoulder and around the back, to be securely tucked in on the right side of the face. This is worn when outside the home as a replacement for the stiff mask, *burga*.

The most elaborate women's masks are from western Arabia, particularly those worn by the various Harb and Utaybah tribes. *Burga* are made of leather or cotton textiles, both red and black, and variously embellished with red paint, coins, shells, metalwork, beads, tassels and appliquéd cloth. Openings or slits are left for the eyes to see through. In these tribes, according to Professor Katakura, the *burga* may be handed down peacefully from mother to daughter, but if a dispute arises, the mask is sold at the *souq al-badw*.

The decorative *burga* appendages with tasselled ends, and the "book-mark"-style pendants which hang each side are made by the women from special materials purchased at the *souq*. Sometimes, the masks take as long as six months to complete. The workmanship is often very skilled as Bedouin girls are taught how to make masks from childhood.

The shape of the various masks and the placement patterns of the coins served once to distinguish the women of different tribes and sub-tribes. Those from Wadi Fatimah, between Jeddah and Mecca, are very elaborate. The Utaybah women wear short, coin-decorated masks while, close to Jummum, women wear stiff leather masks much larger than their faces. The latter *burga* is painted in bright colours and gives a frightening appearance, although the women are friendly. The tradition of wearing such masks may lie in an old belief that women could ward off unwelcome intruders if their menfolk were away. Masks differ in length and decoration to convey status also. Unmarried girls cover only the nose and the lower part of the face in some Hijazi regions. The girls decorate these short masks with embroidery and coins in a similar fashion to the married women who wear full-face masks.

The longest tribal mask in the west belongs to a sub-section of the Harb tribe who live in Wadi Fatimah. This leather *burga* reaches nearly to the waist, and is painted with red powder found locally in the mountains. The edges are decorated with silver. Further embellishment relies on gold and silver coins. The number varies according to the woman's wealth. The wealth of a Bedouin woman in the Hijaz is said to have been in her mask which often carried coins of high intrinsic value, such as the various large trade dollars which were worth almost their weight. A short *burga* is typical of the Saleem sub-tribe, in the Staara Valley, east of Harbiya, and the Kolace, Gadeed and Asfan tribes which again form part of the larger Harb tribe. Tribeswomen today leave their masks behind when they travel outside their domain, but to present a modest appearance in the town, they wear the more simple black veil, *taraha*. The *burga* is worn less and less.

The traditional cloak, worn draped from the centre of the crown of the head when venturing forth, also varied considerably in the outlying areas of the Hijaz. One such garment is the *mouswan*, which reaches almost to the knees. It is a large rectangular- or square-shaped piece of thick black material which is hand-embroidered with motifs indicating the wearer's tribe. The work is sometimes in silver, continuing in a wide band from the centre of the forehead down the back to the hemline. The *mouswan* is reserved for festive occasions when it is part of a dancer's costume. Women of the Al Jedaan tribe wear it with a long, leather, red-painted mask. Another style is the *muzoon*, a heavy black short mantle which is traditionally embroidered with gold. Again each tribe to which it is peculiar has a specific design for the embroidery.

The *sharshaf* (literally "sheet"), exclusive to married women, is also an outer garment. It is generally of lighter material than the *milaaya*, and

Below: *At Bani Sharfa, a village located in the Hijazi foothills of the Tihamat Ash Sham (lowlands of the Sarawat mountain range) married women wear blue gowns and unmarried girls wear red. The embroidery patterns on these traditional dresses are similar. The work on the machine-seamed blue silk taffeta example here is carried out in gold and silver metal-thread and the work is*

commonly a large shawl of some sheer textile. The *smaada*, although much longer, is worn by unmarried Bedouin girls who have reached puberty. Often a tail end of the garment is left to trail along behind and a girl dressed in *smaada* resembles a cocoon.

Women's ethnic garment styles seen in remote recesses of the Hijaz have a long history, but elderly ladies in these areas confirm that the outward appearance of these dresses has changed a great deal from the originals. They still display many individual tribal characteristics but inter-tribal influence has been at work, altering true traditional designs.

For men's costume, the changes have been more

was twice as high as the modern *kufiyyah*. When the skullcap was richly embroidered it was known as *kufiyyah magassabeh*. The *imma* was completed by winding the *ghabana* around the *kufiyyah belladi* until it resembled an enormous turban.

A garment worn as an alternative to the body-shirt still today, is the *fouta* – a length of striped, checkered or floral textile. This is wound around the waist and pleated at front to form a skirt. It can be seen in the rural areas of the Hijaz and is popularly worn by townsmen when at home. With this a short-sleeved shirt known as the *fanilla* is customary. In days gone by the *fouta* and *fanilla* were seen in the towns, worn by men and boys.

Although a belt is not part of a townsmen's costume today, in the past all well-dressed men of the Hijaz wore a waistbelt. It was commonly a fine cotton cloth formed from a large square shawl, known as a *bugsha* and its soft folds made excellent pockets for keeping money and other objects such as the *sikeena*, a small sheathed knife. It was a sensible waist garment in that cotton would be considerably more comfortable than a stiff leather belt in the extremely hot and humid weather.

The traditional jacket which is sometimes worn under the mantle in the Hijaz is similar to a Western tuxedo or dinner jacket. It is called a *cote* – undoubtedly a loan word.

Men of the Hijaz used to consider themselves smartly dressed only when carrying a *shoona*. This was a straight stick made of acacia wood or similar timber and was generally richly ornamented.

In the Hijaz, Western footwear was already in use in the early nineteenth century, although photographs show that traditional Arabian foot-wear was still popular, obviously as it was more suited to the hot climate. In rural areas, the *fallahat* and *fallaheen* often went barefoot, although they wore sandals made of sheep or camel leather for long walks. Bedouin, too, were often barefoot.

In the past, there were apparently external differences in male costume amongst the Bedouin of the Hijaz. The basic body-shirt, *fanilla* and *fouta* were universal, but subtle differences, even in hairstyle, served to indicate to which tribe or sub-tribe a man belonged. The large-sleeved full-skirted traditional body-shirt was known in the Hijaz as the *woniya*; the long pointed sleeves of this robe were customarily knotted together behind the neck when they were likely to restrict movement, just as Bedouin women do when wearing such cumbersome sleeves.

The Bedouin and peasants in the Hijaz habitu-ally wear belts on whatever they wear. The wide leather belt, *hizam*, or textile waistband, *bugsha*, are very practical aspects of their costume still as they carry knives and a dagger, plus money and other useful items. A shepherd continues to wear his headdress in the coiled turban fashion, while most settled, semi-settled and nomadic men in the Hijaz wear the three-part headdress common through-out Saudi Arabia, consisting of the skullcap, *kufiyyah*, headcloth, *ghoutra* (sometimes called *ihram* in this region) and the headcord circlet, *igaal* (usually called *shattafa*). When leaving the home, Hijazi men correctly wear the outer robe which is known as *mishlah*.

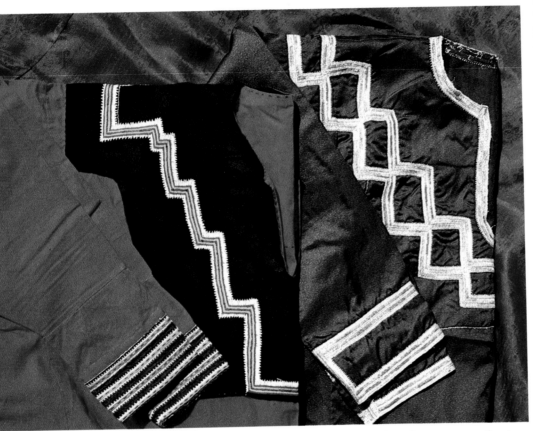

incredibly fine. The geometric pattern, repeated on the red hand-sewn cotton example is worked in white, yellow, red, green and orange. The same coloured threads are used on the cuffs. There is no decoration on the hemline of the blue dress but a surprisingly attractive broad saffron yellow band with black "adidas" stripes decorates the hemline of the red dress. Those who have visited this remote village make no mention of yellow bands to edge the dresses of the unmarried. It is possible that this band was added to lengthen a girl's dress.

sweeping. In about the last forty years, the tra-ditional garments worn by the men of Arabia have become uniform throughout most of the Penin-sula. In the early fifties, new government officials chose to wear a slimmer *kaftan* with more service-able sleeves than they had worn previously. Prior to this national adjustment to costume, there were differences to be seen between Hijazi menswear and that worn in other parts of Arabia.

The headcloth changes name in the Hijaz; in Medina it is known as *shaal*, while in Mecca, Jeddah and Tayif, it is called *ihram*. The *ghabana* was a traditional headcloth of Hijazi townsmen, especially popular in Mecca. It was a square and larger than the modern headcloth, and usually made of a creamy-coloured fine textile with self-coloured embroidery, sometimes incorporating gold thread into the motifs. This work was known as *cassab*. Many *ghabana* were imported from Damascus, Syria.

The traditional complete Hijazi townsmen's headgear was called *imma*. It consisted of a stif-fened white cotton skullcap, *kufiyyah belladi*, which

Left: *Hastening lady in lengthening shadows above the ruined hilltop village of Al Jamal. The remnants of the Al Jamal tribe remain to till the soil in the wadi beneath. Throughout the southern Hijaz highland area (which is in fact the start of the Sarawat mountain chain of the Asir) women wear black dresses embroidered with colourful silk chain stitching such as the gown depicted here. As in the case of Hijazi Bedouin gowns, the front yoke panel is a rectangle. The similarity ends there as Hijazi sleeves are huge while Asir Province sleeves are slim-fitting.*

Asir

Asir means "difficult region", and refers to south-west Arabia where the terrain comprises high peaks, deep terraced valleys, plateaus over 1,200 metres high and coastal lowland. Because of this topographical diversity, the region's costumes have various shapes and these are also worn over the designated borders of the Asir. The geographic characteristics of the Asir reach into the Hijaz region in the north to include Tayif and dip into Yemen in the south to include Najran (by virtue of the Sarawat Mountain range which runs parallel to the Red Sea coastline). Therefore, it is sensible to extend the study of Asir regional costume to these limits. Tayif in the north and Najran in the south have long been important trading centres for the people of the Asir and ready-made traditional garments are made in both places.

From the northernmost point of the Sarawat Mountains, the Asir slopes gently down to the Rub al Khali in the east. To the west lies the Tihama, a lowland strip of sandy plain and scrubby valleys, bordered on one side by the mountains and on the other by the Red Sea. The population of the Tihama is both settled and nomadic, and costume is superficially highly individual from group to group and invariably colourful. In the far south, set in a sandy desert, lies the oasis of Najran, where Bedouin from outlying areas come for provisions. Najran is typified by mud and straw dwellings, date palms and excellent grapes. Temperatures throughout the Tihama and the oasis are generally high.

In the highlands the weather is cool even in summer and there is plentiful rain. It is an agricultural region, active in trade also. Asir produce, which includes vegetables, fruit, cereal grains, fodder and sesame oil, is regularly sent north to the port of Jeddah in the Hijaz. Tayif has been the most important trading centre for the populace of the Asir for as long as anyone can remember, but Abha, also in the highlands, is the provincial capital.

Because the Asir was not easily accessible in the

Above: *Although machined, the embroidery on this dress is closely worked in parallel lines and beautifully done, especially around the broad hem bands. The chain stitching is carried out before the gown is sewn up and finishing touches are sewn over the seams when the dress is almost finished. Beadwork is never included. This style is becoming quite rare and the tailors are reluctant to put too much work into the dresses they produce today, unless for a princely sum.*

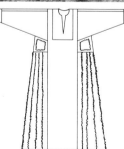

Above: *This Asir style is known as* milbas *and claimed to be an accurate drawing of an authentic Bedouin dress. This is likely as a male counterpart exists that is old and also verified. Chain stitching dividing the side gores vertically, appears to multiply these four panels. Thread colours are red, green and yellow on a base of black mercerized cotton.*

past, it was partially isolated from the rest of Arabia, giving rise to great individuality of costume and customs. As this region is subject to monsoon rains, its highlands display meadows of wild flowers as well as the ancient contours of cultivated terraces, giving rise to the title "garden province". The coastal communities rely upon fish for their subsistence; the rich fishing grounds allowing a thriving industry with markets centred in Jizan on the coast and Sabya further inland.

Housing varies from area to area. Conical straw thatched huts show a definite African influence also evidenced in some local costumes. The "iced ginger-bread" style of architecture, known as "Babylonian" in Yemen, can be seen in the Asir too. Some traditional costumes correspondingly reflect the styles of neighbouring Yemen. There are also stone houses, colour-washed mud dwellings and majestic two- to seven-storied houses with downward-slanting drainage slates set into the mortar between mud strips – the architectural style considered most typical of the Asir. Internally, houses in the Asir are gay with designs painted

by women. Some add imported enamel wall plaques. The people of the Asir enjoy colour, as confirmed by their flamboyant use of it.

Men's *thawbs* are still worn in the traditional full-cut style, tailored in blue, green or white. Arabian men in rural areas of the Asir Province and as far north as Tayif, once wore unbleached calico. Today this is replaced by cotton containing a small percentage of synthetic fibre. Unlike the *thawb* worn by Arab men in any other part of the Peninsula, the Asir version is sometimes machine-embroidered with straight lines of coloured chain-stitch, also seen on women's garments. This sparse decoration is confined to the wrists and forearms, side panels, and neck as a mock yoke. Men also wear gaily-coloured and embroidered headcloths wound turban fashion, although some are beginning to adopt the universal *shmagh*, the red and white checkered headcloth.

Today, women make dresses of the traditional *kaftan* shape from multi-coloured imported textiles and they are generally just as richly embroidered as they were when home-dyed solid-coloured base cloths were used.

In her book, *Saudi Arabia – Past and Present*, Shirley Kay mentions "close-waisted" dresses with embroidered bodices on a black base textile with blue stripes worn by the Bedouin women in the valleys around Tayif. It is possible these were home-spun and dyed with indigo because some cloth in neighbouring Yemen fits this description. The most prevalent traditional female garment of the Asir (both the old hand-made and the newer machine-tailored and embroidered version) is a straight-sleeved, shaped *kaftan* and not "close-waisted". Waisted dresses are a modern innovation.

Traditional regional or tribal dresses are first worn when a girl reaches maturity; at a time when she more than likely marries. Very often, no special dress was reserved for a bride; in most cases everyone present wore their best tribal dress. The tailors of Tayif produce their individual interpretations of the traditional dress of the Asir Province, from either a base cloth of satin-finished cotton, black satin, black velvet or bright coloured velvets. These are now called Tayifi wedding dresses. The original textile was shiny black indigo-dyed cotton.

This basic *kaftan* is of a slimmer shape than most Arabian dresses but can be slipped over the head easily. Undoubtedly the cut is directly associated with a cooler climate, as looser fitting garments prevail in all other regions. Although sometimes a belt is added, waistlines on old Arabian Bedouin dresses are never "nipped in". This is very practical as it facilitates movement, keeps the wearer cool and comfortable and provides ideal maternity wear.

Broad bands of hem embroidery often appear on one version of the Tayifi gown – and the number varies upwards from three. The weighted skirt hangs well, "moves" well, and does not fly away in a breeze.

The traditional Asir Province dress sometimes has so much embroidery, machine- or hand-stitched, that at a distance the base textile appears to be multi-coloured rather than black. Generally,

Right: *This drawing is said to be representative of the true Asir* mudandash. *It is still found in black satin, a natural progression from hand-dyed and beaten indigo cloth and shiny black mercerized cottons.*
Below: *Yoke decoration on Asir dresses varies greatly. Sometimes the deep peak dips well down the centre panel. Other times, the embroidery falls within a long or short rectangle. Lavish or sparse lines divide the side gores.*

Left: *Bold-coloured velvets make very pretty dresses when combined with the novel combinations of embroidery thread colours and patterns. Sometimes silver and gold metal-thread work is added. The tailors of Tayif sought inspiration from early styles and have developed a range of colourful velvets to please the local Bedouin women and delight Western visitors. The original dresses were black cotton. Black satin and black velvet followed and remain the most stunning of the tailors' creations. It is unfortunate, however, that the interpretations of traditional styles have obscured the originals to a great extent.*

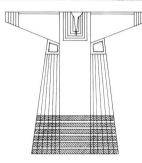

Above: *This illustrates a machine-made black satin Asir dress claimed as worn by the Bani Malik tribe, and a style worn in the Tihama. Yellow and red embroidery threads predominate – white and green are used to a lesser extent. Hemline bands vary in number from two to ten. It is a heavy dress probably originating in the highlands.*

97

the bodice, hem and cuffs are embroidered, but the predominant areas of decoration are traditionally the side gores, and this characteristic embroidery placement assists in attributing provenance even when a dress is a modern derivation featuring the Saudi emblem.

Today the embroidery is stitched by a sewing machine but, even so, the needle must be expertly guided by the machinist. The parallel straight lines on the Tayifi dress require a keen eye and a steady hand. The workmanship is often superb although the finish of the garment is sometimes poor. Quite naturally, this depends on the ability of the tailor just as it does when the garment is hand-made by a Bedouin woman.

The earliest available example of the totally hand-made Asir dress is black cotton backed with white calico. Red cotton is appliquéd in three places: in rectangles within the side gore decorations, in three triangles attached above the front hem border, and in strips one over each shoulder. These are edged with embroidery and accented with white seed beading (beading is an African influence and identifies a dress as coming from one of the west coast regions). White and silver seed beadwork adds a crisp-looking outline to the coloured thread work and continues down the sleeves from the shoulders and circles the cuffs. (The white beads are an especially African influence as silver is the traditional embellishment in the Arabian regions further removed from the west coast.) Beading is also used to create a yoke effect – white bead designs are filled in with silver-coloured beads. A matching area is repeated on the back and this is often additionally overlaid by indigo-red coloured satin outlined with blue and yellow embroidery. Such shoulder patches are supposed to protect a dress from the stains of hair oil.

In the *souq* of Aba Saud, the principal town of the Najran oasis, the most common textile used to make the Bedouin women's *kaftan* is imported black satin-finished cotton. This popular tunic, *tawb aswad*, falls gracefully from the shoulders flaring to a wide hemline, assisted by inserted side gores plus godets. The gores radiate out from unembellished diamond-shaped underarm gussets. The godets fan out from knee level. The gussets are included for traditional purposes rather than function as the gown is loose-fitting. The matching *sirwaal* are usually lightly embroidered at the ankle bands. The sleeves flare to fullness well below the hands, with a long underarm seam which falls to mid-calf, creating a V-shaped point. These impractical sleeves are worn pinned up to the shoulders when freedom of hand movement is necessary.

Sparse red, yellow and white machined decoration is confined to the neckline, yoke and bodice which may have been more elaborate in the past. The waist is gathered in with a felt-lined leather belt decorated with red, green, yellow, blue and white metal eyelets. It is worn with a plain black cheesecloth scarf wound around the head – the face unveiled. Sometimes a broad-brimmed straw hat with a high pointed crown is perched on top. Both men and women wear broad and colourful leather belts which hold money and other items.

Sometimes the belt is formed from a section of twisted textile.

Women rarely veil in the south-west but men and women do cover their heads in most areas of the Asir. There are many kinds of headgear within the region including unusual heavily decorated cotton hoods and several styles of straw hats. The most common palm-straw hat for Asir peasant women is the Spanish-looking, broad-brimmed, high-pointed-crown style which gives the best protection when working in the fields. Both men and women may be seen wearing colourful lengths of cloth draped around the shoulders and falling down the back. The old Spanish touch is again seen in the colourfully striped and folded cotton blanket the men toss over one shoulder. It is possible that Spanish Muslims took these fashions to Mexico.

Some nomads who regularly visit Najran wear tall, black, brimless hats with flattish back-sloping crowns. These men are generally bare-chested, wearing only the *fouta*, a colourful plaid cloth wound around their hips to form a skirt. Over this is worn a broad belt which serves to hold the metre-long dagger which, they assure people, is merely for protection against wild animals.

Lots of ornamentation is worn with the colourful Asir costumes by both men and women. Rijal, a Tihama stone-built village, is famous for its goldsmithing, while Najran, at the southern tip of the mountain chain, traditionally produced chunky silver Bedouin jewellery. Ornaments of the south-west are often fashioned from a combination of leather and silver.

Head circlets, *asayib*, are worn by men and women. They are variously made of twine, copper wire-bound straw, copper wire, leather and silver, or plain silver. Some, worn like the *igaal*, are a padded roll of leather decorated with silver from which long tasselled pendants hang. In the highlands, some mountain women wear twisted red textile *asayib* with pendant objects. Some plainer circlets hold a colourful array of wild flowers and scented herbs.

Hair styles are distinctive in the Asir. Generally, men and women wear their hair long and flowing free. The *isaaba* is worn by some men to train their hair growth upwards while uncircumcised boys may be recognized in this area by a distinctive cock's comb hairdo.

In the Asir, it is not uncommon to see women with blue tattoo marks on their chins – yet another aspect of Arabian body ornament (*see* **Body Ornament**).

East of Dhahran-Al-Janub the women present a most attractive appearance in green dresses with yellow head scarves. Green was the colour traditionally worn by women making the pilgrimage to Mecca and the colour once considered correct for a newly widowed woman of Arabia. The original dyestuff is not known but it was probably available around Dhahran-Al-Janub accounting for the traditional dress colour. Locally produced cloth is popularly dyed a rich yellow with saffron in the Asir which explains the yellow scarves.

Bishah is an Asir town which conjures up romantic Arabian images. Charles Montague Doughty (1843–96) described the nineteenth-

Above: Mudandash *translates approximately as "very decorative" and is applied to this dress from the Asir. However, it is more often called the* soun. *The various highland styles are kaftans with straight sleeves. In the past, they were cut from indigo-dyed cotton, and later satin-finished cotton was adopted. Red cotton twill is overlaid according to tradition within three small triangles at the bottom of the centre-front panel directly above the hem border and in strips over the shoulders, as well as in three places within each side gore. The yoke is delineated as a rectangle with beadwork, and is often repeated at the back by an overlaid satin patch.*

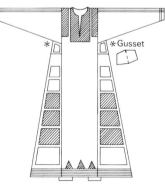

Left: *A close-up view of handwork on the western Arabian highland dresses shows predominantly yellow threads with red, orange and white for the most part. There are also touches of blue, green, mauve and purple. These dresses are totally hand-sewn from black cotton.*

Above: *Sleeves and bodices are always embellished in the western highlands. The cuffs shown here exhibit silver and white beadwork which links up with a broad band of similar work that extends from the shoulder-line down the sleeve.*

Above: *Shaded sections on this drawing illustrate appliqué and embroidery placement. The under-arm gusset shape for this style of Asir Province dress is different from gussets used in the surrounding regions. The men's version is the same shape but enlarged.*

century men of Bishah in a way that suggests they dress today much as they did in days gone by. He said they bound their "kerchiefs upon their foreheads – the worsted headband in great rolls as if it were a turban". These headcloths, he recorded, were from Iraq; today they are generally from India.

Souqs are just as important to the Bedouin as they are to settled and semi-settled Arabians, for it is there on market day that nomads come to trade with the villagers and townspeople. Markets are generally held once a week in Arabian towns and many take their name from the day of the week that they are held. Khamis Mushayt means Thursday Market, Ahad Rufaydah is Sunday of Rufaydah and Sabt Tanumah translates as the Saturday of Tanumah.

For centuries nomads and rural folk have made their way from the low coastal area of the Asir's Tihamah to the highlands for market days when the need arose. This narrow belt of land hemmed in by the Sarawat Mountain range is the home of tribes who still choose to wear traditional clothing. The garments are colourful and unique, displaying elaborate seed-bead work, appliquéd cowrie shells and white pearl-shell buttons (derived from pieces of mother-of-pearl). Silk tassels are also popular, just as they are in Najran across the mountain range. Red is the most common colour, especially to border black textiles. All the primary and secondary colours can be seen today too, confirming the Arabian penchant for vividly colourful garments.

Highland men and women of the Asir Province wear furs and natural-coloured skins decorated with hand-sewn red leather strips and red leather thongs. Some leather is also indigo stained, the various designs resembling tattoos. The fur side is worn inwards as it can become cold at night after the warmest day in the Asir and winter is surprisingly chilly. Mostly, the capes are made from sheep and goat skins and carry a small chain which fastens across the neck, at the front, from shoulder to shoulder. Another sheepskin garment similarly decorated with red leather embroidery is worn in the same way although it is merely a narrow panel worn down the centre of the back. It is claimed to be a woman's garment, designed to protect her back when carrying objects. As men share the work load, it is probably worn by them also. It resembles an African garment which had tribal significance in that the leader was the sole person with the right to wear it.

Jackets in rural Asir are logically heavier than those from the other regions of the Arabian Peninsula. The cooler mountain air makes it necessary to make thick garments from coarse woven sheep's wool. In Najran, and throughout the Asir, the Bedouin wear a capacious sleeveless jacket of coarse virgin wool dyed dark plum and orange. It is woven from thick yarn and embroidered with fine reddish-coloured wool. Even the cloak is lined with sheepskin for winter. Many consider the Asir as the region in which the lined mantle, the *farwah*, originated although it was also recorded in the Eastern Province long ago. It is often called a shepherd's cloak because the herd keeper could use it as a cosy bedroll during cold desert nights.

Southern Arabia

The southern part of Greater Arabia includes Saudi Arabia's most formidable desert, the Rub al-Khali, or Empty Quarter, and from west of east, the two Yemens: Yemen Arab Republic and the People's Democratic Republic of Yemen, and the Sultanate of Oman.

These lands form part of traditional Arabia, and basic differences between them and the Kingdom of Saudi Arabia were once minimal. All shared the same age-old environmental problems and in most areas there was a general scarcity of natural resources. Also, with the overwhelming majority of the population, in each state, being Arab – they enjoyed a common cultural heritage and the unifying religion of Islam. Economic patterns, too, showed little variation in the past. Coastal settlements served as centres for boat building and fishing while inland the inhabitants depended on animal husbandry, subsistence cultivation, spinning, weaving, dyeing, the preparation of skins and hides and other assorted handicrafts.

North Yemen (Y.A.R.) is divided into two distinct geographical areas: a flat coastal plain of sand dunes and scrub with jagged peaks rising to over 2,000 metres above sea level. Cradled in the mountains is a large central plain of rich volcanic soil. While the shore plains of the Tihama suffer a harsh desert climate, the arable mountain regions are temperate with abundant rain.

It is a pretty land of rocky hills and mountains surrounded by exquisitely terraced fields. There are groupings of fortress-like houses with thick mud walls, pierced by many small deep casement windows. A characteristic Yemeni window is outlined with decorative bands of whitewash and crowned with half-moon sections of stained-glass edged with white. Apart from this "iced gingerbread" or "Babylonian" architecture, there are mysterious and fascinating towns of dry stone masonry set high on rocky outcrops – and pockets throughout the land where thatched-roof mud dwellings cluster.

Sanaa, the capital, lies in the centre of the mountain plain. It is rivalled as a commercial capital by Tayiz which sits at the base of a spectacular rock peak, Jebel Sabur. The main North Yemen port, Hodeidah, once a small fishing village, is set at the edge of a particularly bleak and unattractive strip of land.

Yemen was already ancient in biblical times when it was known as "Arabia Felix". Because it produced the prized resins, frankincense and myrrh, caravans laden with gold, ivory, spices, silks and these aromatics radiated out from Yemen, linking Africa with China. Traders trekked north through Saba, biblical Sheba. Marib, the capital of ancient Sheba is now a ruin, but evidence of the great civilization remains. It was from Marib that the Queen of Sheba set out with her camels laden with spices, gold, precious stones and silk. All that is left of this fabled land is its beautiful scenery, captivating architecture, and the indefinably serenity which pervades Yemen as powerfully today as ancient historians said it did in the past.

The Yemens, because they lie in the south-west

corner of the Arabian Peninsula, command the Red Sea Straits of Bab-al-Mandab, the narrow gateway to Jeddah and the Suez Canal. Only thirty-three kilometres away on the opposite shore lies Ethiopia, Djibouti and Somalia. Yemen is geologically part of the African Continent from which it was separated billions of years ago. As Bab-al-Mandab admitted immigrants for centuries, it is not surprising that the coastal people of the Yemens appear to be linked culturally with the Africans. The thatched villages of the Arabian coastal plain resemble those in Africa, and handicrafts, in particular, display African influence.

The seaport, Aden, is the capital of South Yemen (the People's Democratic Republic of Yemen). It sits at the southern end of the Arabian plateau, an irregular segment of land comprising ancient granites partly covered by sedimentary limestones and sand and a narrow, flat coastal area. Further inland, the country is mountainous, reaching a height of approximately 1,800 metres in the west and tapering off to the east. The tableland is interspersed with arid valleys and *wadis*, the dry river beds.

To the east, located in the central part of the country and running parallel to the coast, lies the formidable Wadi Hadramaut – a name believed to suggest death is present. This narrow, mostly arid valley is surrounded by desolate hills and desert. It is a hostile region where temperatures are high, especially along the coast and droughts are common. Coastal humidity and interior dust storms afford little relief.

Archaeological investigations reveal that many of the first Arabian coastal settlements were found in the south. In the third millennium BC, the unique and highly desirable aromatic gum resins attracted foreigners to southern Arabia and settlements here became important trading ports. *Boukhor*, frankincense, and *morr*, myrrh, were the basis of an industry which was controlled by Mesopotamians and Egyptians for two thousand years. Evidence suggests, however, that by approximately 1400 BC, the Arabians had taken over and these people possessed skills known in Mesopotamia at that time.

Based on the two prized commodities, the southern Arabians developed a huge and complex commercial network comprising both land and sea routes. They became middlemen for trade with India and Africa and their markets in the north were the Mediterranean coastal cities and Mesopotamia and Egypt. Merchandise included pearls, spices, Chinese silk, slaves, monkeys, ivory, Ethiopian gold, and ostrich feathers.

Foreigners were envious of the riches which seemed to pour forth from Arabia Felix but this was not to last. By the fourth century AD, the commercial basis of southern Arabia began to weaken; the seeds of decay being sown in the first century when the Romans challenged Arabian trade monopoly. When the Greek and Roman merchant shippers learned the secrets of the monsoon winds, Arabian marine supremacy began to decline, and after Imperial Rome embraced Christianity, the core of Arabia's market dissolved. Furthermore, the foreign mariners, who now knew that many of the products were not of

Arabian origin, began to deal directly with the sources.

The south lay in commercial disorder and became prey to foreign invasions. The introduction of Islam in the seventh century provided not only a religious system for the societies of the south, but also a political and social structure as well. It was this fact, however, that eventually facilitated the Ottoman occupation of much of the Arabian Peninsula. Being Muslim, they quickly established their rule along the southern Arabian coasts, although the difficult terrain kept encroachment in check.

There is frequent reference in historical records to steady traffic of coffee ships departing from the south-western port of Mokka and it appears that Yemen was continually exploited by foreigners entering here. In the early 1600s Mokka was governed by a Greek renegade. It was then a great trading centre for tin, iron, lead, sword blades, and textiles. Many foreign commercial navies established trading colonies along the southern coastline, and in the nineteenth century, Britain

The tawb aswad *of the Najran Oasis, which flares from the shoulders to the hemline, is worn with a colourful black leather, felt-lined belt, studded with red, white, blue, yellow and green metal eyelets. The centre panels, front and back, are cut from a single length of textile on Arabian kaftans. These panels are generally embroidered prior to being sewn together.*

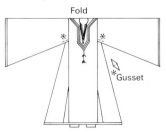

Fold

Gusset

101

created a colonial city at Aden.

Inland areas remained as they had been for centuries. Throughout its history, Yemen was under the power of various local *sheiks*. With the disintegration of the Ottoman Empire, at the end of World War One, Yemen gained independence. The subsequent trade with India brought a more insidious influence than the former obtrusive Turkish one. Although Yemeni costume has Turkish overtones, items of apparel worn in the south today are generally from India. There are still hand-crafted items but these are disappearing; this is particularly true of textiles. Most are imported today from Bombay, Japan and Korea.

In the early part of this century, a partition separated North Yemen from South when the British negotiated a border with the Ottoman Empire which had ruled since the sixteenth century.

Yemen is a poor country and primarily agricultural. Although it is a fertile land for the most part, it is prone to the destructive forces of hail and locusts. Traditional crops were grains and fodder, cotton, beans, vegetables and exotic tropical fruits and it was once famous for its coffee which was named Mokka after the port. Cotton is once again produced in exportable quantities but coffee production has declined in favour of the easier grown *gat* (of the toxic shrub, *Cathae edulis*), the high-priced mild narcotic that Yemenis like to chew. It is interesting to learn that locusts do not eat *gat*. Walnuts are also grown along with twenty-one varieties of grapes which are said to be among the best in the world. Of all the produce, sesame ranks as the most traditional crop because its paste and oil are staple foodstuffs.

Weaving was traditionally a craft carried out on a small scale and, until quite recently, handicrafts were the only real industries. Now, cotton ginning workshops and plants and commercial spinning and weaving mills have been set up with the aid of China. The clatter of power looms has silenced forever the gentle sounds of the handloom shuttle.

Since it was opened to the West about ten years ago, Yemen has been transformed from a proud, independent little country into one caught between two worlds where ancient traditions are mixed with modern values; and it has no oil. Yet, more than any other single factor, oil has indirectly been responsible for breaking down traditional life in the southern lands. The new Peninsula economy has attracted to Saudi Arabian cities not only Bedouin from the southern interior but settled people as well.

Although the adjectives "tribal" and "nomadic" are virtually synonymous today, the vast majority of tribesmen in the Yemens have always been sedentary cultivators. Approximately half the population is rural, with a small percentage nomadic and the rest urban. These people staunchly defend their ethnic identity; they are aware of their history and even their remotest past is preserved in folk traditions. It is noticeable, however, that the wind of change has been blowing through the land.

Foreign aid has seen once unchartered desert penetrated by roads which now span country where previously only camels could cross. Social mobility has increased and even remote tribesmen have become subject to new influence and aware of new ideas. Aden's indigenous people were the first to wear Western clothing because of British influence and now, only in the hinterlands are traditional garments worn.

There are records of explorers in olden times which give a colourful account of past southern costume. Carsten Niebuhr, sent by King Frederick the Fifth of Denmark in 1761, wrote an account of a journey on a small Omani coffee boat. The captain was wearing the *fouta*, a garment still popular today. The *Imam* of Sanaa, who received Niebuhr, is described as hospitable and wearing a bright green robe with gold lace on the breast. The outfit was topped by a great white turban. Pieter van den Broecke, who visited Mokka in 1620, described a previous Pasha at Sanaa as wearing a coat of gold brocade. The textiles described were imported luxuries.

Imported factory-produced textiles of such opulence are now available for all. Today, the men and women of Yemen can fully exploit their love of colour. In confirmation of this, each element of the women's costume is cut from a different piece of cloth. Velvets, satins and machine-embroidered and brocaded synthetics peek from beneath their cloaks and sheets. Men wear colourful headcloths and skirts.

Throughout Yemen today, women wear long-sleeved, full-skirted dresses reaching below the calf. Under these can be seen their embroidered *sirwaal*. The dress is dartless, zipless and loose, despite gathers at the waistline. There is also a popular three-piece outfit consisting of an un-pressed-pleated skirt (the pleats stitched down for approximately ten centimetres), an elbow-length sleeved bolero and a white "puffed-sleeved" chemise which doubles as a blouse and petticoat. The skirt and bolero are made in every conceivable colour and textile. A similar costume is worn in the Gulf lands and is attributable to Ottoman influence.

In the south, it is easier to study the transition of women's costume from the past to the present, as modernization arrived quite late in comparison with other parts of the Peninsula. Four clear stages can be seen. The first true traditional garment is well represented by one of Arabia's most interesting dresses. It comes from a place near the coastal town of Hodeidah, Bayt al Fakih, which means "house of the scholar". The dress is visually striking because natural-coloured braid and silver metal-thread braid are applied to a bluish-black indigo hand-dyed cotton basecloth. It commands admiration because of the incredible skill that is required to apply the unique kind of natural-coloured braidwork. Although needlework is involved, it cannot correctly be considered embroidery. It is, in fact, a complicated arrangement of quarter centimetre wide braid which has been skilfully twisted and tweaked as it was "couched", or "laid" onto the surface of the dress with fine stitches. This work is seen on several traditional southern *kaftans*.

The woven silver-coloured flat metallic wire and cotton braid displayed on the Bayt al Fakih dress is a popular form of embellishment seen on other items of apparel such as veils and masks from the Hijaz and the Asir. It is available in the market places. There is red and green embroidery between the silver braid around the neckline, cuffs and bars that are placed over the shoulders and in three places under the arms on each side of the bodice. This garment is slim fitting and, true to Arabian custom, attention is drawn to shape and form elements of design – in this case by the placement of the silver bars at the waistline. The hemline is edged with natural, silver, red, green, yellow and metallic gold braid. The dress is particularly interesting as it shows both the influence of the Asir neighbours directly north in the Sarawat mountain range by the addition of the shoulder bars and side panel decoration, as well as the influence of Oman by the concentration of embellishment within the centre-front panel.

The second stage in the story of Yemen's traditional female dress was caused by the sewing machine. Dresses continued to be cut from old patterns but the seams were machined. Embroidery was still hand-done for a time. Later, embroidery was machined or left off altogether in favour of pre-embroidered textiles.

Subsequently, a revitalized trade with India flooded the market and brought with it the third stage. Ready-made, wide-legged, machine-embroidered pantaloons found favour and replaced the traditional narrow-legged *sirwaal*; the face veil became a black silk rectangle with tie-dyed red and white "targets" all over (called *mogmud*); and the hand-woven mantle, *milaaya*, was replaced by an inexpensive red and blue printed tablecloth.

The fourth and present stage, now quickly overtaking the previous fashion, is the addition of an ankle-length black satin unpressed-pleated skirt, worn over the usual dress and trousers. This is accompanied by a black satin cape worn from centre crown to fall over the shoulders to the waistline. Attached to this short *abaaya* is a full-face veil of semi-transparent black material that is sometimes embroidered with gold at the edges. More usually, it is a double layer of plain black gauzy textile.

Face veils can number up to three in the south, including the first scarf which is wound around the lower and upper parts of the face. These are not generally worn in the home. If a visitor arrives, a woman dons the rectangular wrap-around headscarf which leaves her eyes visible. Amongst one most interesting Yemeni tribal confederation, the women never veil. The Hashid, who occupy some fifty villages north of Sanaa, also wear their hair very long. The men wear long beards and moustaches and often have waist-length hair. The women habitually cover their long hair with a scarf which is held in place by a twisted piece of textile or silver head circlet.

Kaftans are worn shorter in the Yemens than in the regions beyond its northern borders. The *sirwaal* embroidery is therefore visible from just beneath the calf. The original textile for dresses and trousers was cotton. Most old hand-made dresses are based on blackish-coloured cotton – the oldest being hand-dyed with indigo. The "right side" of the textile is the shiny side. In the case of the indigo-dyed cotton, the sheen is produced by beating the textile. This gloss is lost if the garment is washed or drycleaned and the true colours of the embroidery would also be lost if it came in contact with any form of liquid – such textiles are so steeped in dye, the excess would inevitably run.

From Al Bayda near the border of North and South Yemen, a "filled-in" type of Byzantine work uses red and yellow thread on a black background. The black cotton is almost completely covered with embroidery, and only the sleeves are plain. There is, however, fine red embroidery on the cuff edge. The same loose *kaftan* is worn at Maouit near Daida and once again the body of the garment is covered with similar hand-done embroidery which is mainly white thread with some red, yellow and green.

At Hojariyah, near Tayiz, the base cloth used is often black satin and occasionally machine-embroidered motifs are scattered across it. The embroidery, if any, is sparse today and machine-done. Although tight across the chest with a deep placketed neck slit, this *kaftan* skirt is cut wide, taking extra width from side gores. The most remarkable feature about the Hojariyah dress is the fact that the sleeves are a quarter of a metre longer than the arms on the shoulder line and dip to a V-shape on the underarm seam, the lappet reaching the ankles.

Another fascinating southern dress is from the Tihamat, the coastal lowland. It is again made from indigo hand-dyed imported cotton. The *kaftan* cut is plainly seen when the garment is lying flat, but when worn, the enormously wide straight sleeves, half again as long as the arm and the additional width of the body of the garment, disguises its basic pattern.

The centre panel seams, both front and back, are embroidered where they join the sleeves and side gores; otherwise it is only the front centre panel and side gores that are embellished. These are also extensively decorated with embroidery, brass chains, brass sequins and triangular pieces of mother-of-pearl shell affixed with red embroidery. (Pearl shell and cowrie shells are commonly employed to embellish garments in coastal areas). The traditional *sirwaal* for each of these dresses would correctly exhibit calf-length embroidery. In the past the knee to ankle section was narrow.

Between the cool mountainous regions where slim dresses with straight sleeves are worn and the neighbouring hot climate areas, dress styles often share design features. While a dress may have wide, flaring sleeves much longer than the arm and a voluminous skirt, the bodice, from shoulder-line to bustline, can be extremely tight-fitting. This is a characteristic of dresses in the western corner of the southern regions. To facilitate dressing, a deep centre-front slit is made at the neckline and a placket, formed from the basecloth or from colourful brocade, allows the wearer modesty. It is curious that the Tihamat gown of great proportions also has this deep-slit neck opening and backing placket when the garment is easily slipped over the head. It would seem that the tribe who wear this style are impressed by the innovation.

In the past, silver jewellery was worn profusely in the south according to Arabian custom. Red stones, and glass, or reddish-brown stones such as

Below: *Southern Arabian women's dress bodices are often firmly fitting and rely upon a deep slit centre-front neck opening to facilitate dressing. The textile is black cotton but the placket is lurex brocade. This Bayt al Fakih dress skirts the body from the bust downward. This kaftan does not have an under-arm gusset but the comfort comes as a result of three bars of decoration positioned just above the waistline in the side gores,* which draw in the garment. The slimmer, shorter dresses are seen as a result of a lifestyle where women work in the cultivated areas. The decoration consists of twisted and tweaked natural-coloured braid tacked to the base cloth. Also, silver-coloured metallic and white cotton braid divides red and green embroidery. Shading denotes embroidery.*

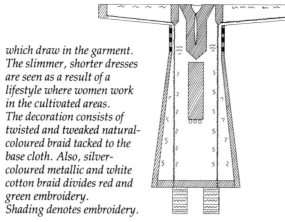

cornelian are commonly set in Southern Arabia – in contrast to the northern regions where turquoise is more prevalent. Coral is particularly coveted on the western side of the southern region, and its counterpart on the eastern side would seem to be amber. Today gold ornaments are favoured by the womenfolk.

On the westward side of Arabia's southern region lies the Sultanate of Oman. Until quite recently Oman ranked as one of the least known countries in the world. Hemmed in by sea on one side and the desert vastness of the Rub al-Khali on the other, it was left to develop in comparative isolation. The formidable Hajar mountain chain which forms a belt between the coast and the desert from the Musandam Promontory to the city of Sur, has also served to keep Oman relatively free from both cultural and military encroachment.

The Sultanate of Oman occupies the south-east corner of Arabia with a coastline that runs south along the Gulf of Oman and then west along the Arabian Sea. Its northernmost tip touches the Strait of Hormuz, the gateway to the Arabian Gulf. On the north, it is bordered by the Trucial Sheikhdoms; on the north-west and west by the Kingdom of Saudi Arabia; and on the south-west by the People's Democratic Republic of Yemen. Muscat, set in the Gulf of Oman coast, is the capital city.

Geographically, the land is divided by natural features into several distinct districts: the tip of the Musandam Peninsula, the Batinah Plain, the Muscat coastal area, Inner Oman, comprising the Jabal Akhdar or Green Mountain, the western foothills and the desert fringes, the Southern

Province of Dhofar, and the offshore island of Masirah. Virtually an island itself, Oman's contact with the outside world in the past was largely by sea.

The summer climate is one of the hottest in the world, reaching temperatures as high as 130 degrees Fahrenheit, and rainfall is generally insufficient except in Dhofar where there are perennial streams, small ponds and waterfalls. It is a land of great contrasts with modern towns and prehistoric sites, dusty villages and lush green countryside with more than 250 different botanical species and awe-inspiring black volcanic rock mountains and creamy gravel plains.

The cities of the Sultanate retain the character of old Arabia and likewise the towns are much as they have always been. Muscat is a walled city which grew up around a natural anchorage on the Gulf of Oman. It was perhaps the last city in the world where the population was locked within the walls at night; until earlier this century, anyone wishing to travel about at night was required by law to carry a lantern.

Although subject to foreign invasions from time to time, Oman generally maintained independence until 1507 when the Portuguese seized control of the coastline. After the Omanis defeated the Portuguese forces in 1650, they gained strength and independence once again. Their renaissance conquests in Africa included coastal Mogadiscio, Mombasa and Zanzibar, and thus Oman absorbed some African influence. Britain, too, by her advisory presence, has helped to shape modern Oman.

Ancient records from the Magan Civilization give accounts of substantial quantities of copper, silver, and coal in Oman, yet so far this century only clay for pottery and tile, marble for building and oil have been exploited. Fishing and farming have been the economic activities in the past. Cotton was also grown in small quantities. Traditional industries were the production of *samn* (clarified butter), dried fish, dates and lime. Weaving, goldsmithing, pottery-making and boat-building were the crafts practised but these are steadily declining. In a few pockets of Oman, women still make their dresses but, for the most part, weaving, spinning, dyeing, embroidery and hand-sewing have all but ceased.

Traditionally, women did the weaving. However, one old man could be seen recently weaving *wazaris* (loincloths) and special headcloths for women. The latter combined Indian cotton, silk and metallic threads bought in the Muscat *souq*. Prior to weaving the cotton threads, this patriarch dipped them in animal fat to control their fineness.

Local sheep's wool and goat and camel hair is also still woven, usually into saddle bags, blankets, and other donkey and camel accoutrements. Cloaks, traditionally, were woven locally in black, brown, white and red. Other colours are occasionally woven and yarn for these is invariably imported.

Although weaving is said to have been discouraged by the previous Sultan, steps have been taken recently to revive the craft amongst the womenfolk. Dyeing is still practised, at least in the Interior and Nizwa, the old capital of the Interior, is famous for its indigo dyeing.

In Oman, outside influence has always been vastly different for the people of the Interior to that for coastal dwellers, and this is reflected in the variances between the two groups' traditional costumes. The most obvious difference is colour. In the Interior, colours worn are more subdued and warm earthy hues such as beige, rust and blue-black prevail. This suggests that natural dyestuffs have been employed by the Bedouin.

Coastal folk now wear a variety of brightly coloured turbans and wrappers from Indonesia and India, and, although cotton prints predominate, polyester with its bright sheen, strong colours and bold patterns is strongly favoured. The latter textile comes from India, China and Japan. It is likely that coastal Omanis have worn imported textiles for centuries due to the fact that they have always been seafaring.

Women's headscarves are not so colourful as a rule. Many are plain black. Faces are generally unveiled and the *lihaf*, a thin gauze headcloth is wrapped around the head and shoulders and passed under the chin before being draped back

over the head. This headcloth is sufficiently long to hang down the back and be drawn around the body or trail.

The women on the coast and many nomadic women wear shortish *kaftans* over *sirwaal* with embroidered cuffs. A mantle is added to this outfit and is usually a mere sheet of colourful cloth draped from the top of the head and clutched about the body. In Dhofar, the traditional long dress has a trailing back hemline and is similar to the northern and Najrani *tawb aswad*, except that it is deep red and worn without a belt in most cases. The silk embroidery is black, white, green, orange and cerise and appears on the yoke and front panel – the satin stitch forming horizontal and diagonal patterns. *Sirwaal* are matching and a fez-shaped cap embellished with coins and other ornaments completes the costume.

One unusual traditional Omani style of women's *sirwaal* is made from small horizontal strips of cloth. Otherwise, they are the same as *sirwaal* throughout the Peninsula in that they are capacious and drawn in at the waist by a sash. The styles worn in the Interior are usually embroidered on the legs with black, white, green, orange and silver metal thread. Today, these decorative trouser cuffs can be bought separately in the markets. The average dress is embroidered around the neck, down the front panel, on the sleeve cuffs and at the hem. Zig-zagged machine stitching is currently popular.

In the village of Ibri, the women present a unique appearance, with long *kaftans*, long hair tied in a pony tail and an exotic golden halo-like circlet over a sombre black headcloth. Although silver is the traditional metal for jewellery in the south, young women now scorn it and prefer to wear a small amount of gold rather than the profusion of cumbersome silver ornaments of the past. However, traditional multiple-chain belts are worn over dark-blue *kaftans* and nose-rings are common. Toe-rings are also seen in the south.

In 1825, a southern Sultana posed for a drawing by one Mrs. Mignan. The likeness shows an elegant and rich-looking woman in a full-length, shaped, long-sleeved gown and coat. Her head is covered by a long shawl and her face from the eyes downward is veiled by some transparent textile. Her forehead, breast and arms are covered with jewellery. Mrs. Mignan also wrote a description of a princess in the Sultan's *hareem*. She was dressed in richly embroidered purple satin. On her face was a mask "which resembled a pair of broad-rimmed spectacles", made of some kind of stiff cloth, richly worked and spangled with gold. The princess also wore priceless jewels – an emerald the size of a pigeon's egg and pearls and diamonds covered her hands and feet.

In the olden days an Omani girl assumed a mask at puberty and thereafter not even her own mother saw her without it. The style of *burga*, seen then in most parts of Oman was normally blue-black, indigo-dyed and presented a beak-like appearance because of the stiffened centre rib which protruded between the eye openings for the length of the mask. Some Omani masks are soft textiles edged with beadwork and not unlike those worn in the Hijaz and Asir. Veils are rarely worn in central

105

Oman today but some Bedouin do still wear the stiffened *batula* mask also common to areas further north in the Eastern Province of Arabia. More usually, women living in the Interior cover the mouth and chin only. In the towns the black mantle is commonly worn over the veil and costume in public. It is called *chador* as it is in Turkey. As a rule along the coast, masks are worn although in the presence of a stranger a towns-woman sometimes pulls her headcloth or *chador* across the face instead. The hair net is a curious recent addition to traditional Omani headgear for women; black hair nets are now a popular way of keeping hair in place.

Many of the old ways passed on some time ago and costume customs would have been lost but for accounts by early travellers. In the late 1940s Wilfred Thesiger travelled extensively in remote parts of southern Arabia to learn about locusts and his subsequent book, *Arabian Sands*, gives descriptions of the appearance of Arabs he met between Salala and Mukalla. Most were from the Bait Kathir tribe and the Saar tribe. Some garments were dyed blue and dark blue with indigo (dark blue indigo-dyed cloth could be purchased in Mukalla). Thesiger noted that this cloth sometimes stained men's bodies and this could be seen as many were bare to the waist. They wore either a blue loincloth or a length of blue textile wrapped around the waist as a skirt – one tasselled end was worn thrown over the right shoulder. Some of the men wore the mid-calf length *kaftan* known as the *dishdasha*. The women wrapped their bodies completely in dark blue clothes although they were unveiled. Most men wore headcloths but some of the bare-chested men were also bare-headed. Many headcloths were embroidered. It was very uncommon to see men wearing the black woollen head-rope. A sub-tribe, the Bin Maarus, which Thesiger believed were part of the Saar Tribe, wore long white *dishdashas* with long pointed sleeves reaching the ground – the traditional garment for men in old Arabia. He records that they also wore headcloths with head-ropes "in the northern fashion". The Rashid, kinsmen of the Bait Kathir, both belonging to the greater Al Kathir tribe, dressed in long *kaftans* and headcloths. They wore their clothes with distinction, according to Thesiger, even when the garments were threadbare. This particular group took to dyeing their clothes a soft russet-brown with the juice of a desert shrub, the *abal*.

Thesiger found it advantageous to wear the time-tested Bedouin garments on his journeys and he added the back-supporting, many-stranded leather "cincture" around his loins under his clothes as they did. He also writes of knitted socks which Arabs wore in the southern desert during both winter and summer. These coarse black hair socks prevented their feet from cracking in the cold – a fact bemoaned by Thesiger who did not own such a pair of socks.

Circumcision initiates in the southern tribe Bait Khawar, he reports, traditionally wore short, tight-sleeved red jackets and baggy white drawers, tight at the ankle "similar to women's *sirwaal*". It was ceremonial dress as this was apparently the only time in their lives that they wore such pants.

Wilfred Thesiger writes that these boys were also ritualistically beautified for circumcision by having their skin stained. Their bodies were rubbed with butter and saffron until they shone. He himself was offered *wars*, this yellow anointing oil scented with amber, to rub into his face and beard at an evening parting. *Wars* is made from sesame oil and saffron. A similar anointing oil is common to the Wahiba and Daru tribes in the south, according to Thesiger.

Freya Stark, visiting the same area in 1935, described a young girl having her face "varnished" yellow by her relatives. This was the ritualistic first intimation that she had been promised in marriage. The dyestuff may also have been saffron or turmeric mixed with sesame oil or butter.

Apart from *kohl* for the eyes, it is common to see Omani women with yellow paste pressed into foreheads, chins and noses. This has the benefit of protecting the skin from the sun and cutting down glare reflected off the skin into the eyes. The paste is probably made from turmeric or saffron. Henna is also popularly used to decorate hands and feet.

Also in Southern Arabia, Thesiger saw some women in the Kidyut valley with their faces brightly painted. One had stained her face green and another had blue and green stripes painted down her nose and chin and across her cheeks. Mabel Bent, visiting the Hadramaut in 1893, described girls with their faces dyed "bright yellow with turmeric" over which they had painted black stripes, while their noses were red, and green spots dotted their cheeks. This makeup was apparently applied only for special occasions. It brings to mind some of the changes in Western women's make-up styles in recent years.

It is recorded that some southern tribesmen were given to anointing themselves with indigo. As indigo dye rubs off very easily, their hands and beards were also stained. When freshly done, it has an amazing metallic blue sheen, according to Wyman Bury, who visited the south in 1895. Wearing nothing but a loincloth and a dagger attached to a cartridge belt, these nineteenth-century Arabian warriors must have presented a fearsome sight. Bury describes the curving daggers as having hilts adorned with gold Byzantine coins and scabbards bulging with semi-precious stones. Every man also carried an old-fashioned firearm.

There are other records of tribesmen north-east of Aden who rub indigo into their bodies. Some claim it keeps out the cold, while others claim it keeps out the heat. There is the possibility that a layer of indigo does, in fact, act as an insulator. Many said they used it merely because their fathers did.

Group beauty culture in the form of henna-dyed palms, fingernails and toes is often practised by every member of a family. Tattooing is also popular. This has the added benefit, it is believed, of relieving pain in the joints when it is applied on the fingers.

Qara tribesmen pierce the right ear-lobe from which they hang a silver ring. Although nearly beardless, these men consider it unmanly to shave, and they traditionally wear their greased hair in long curly braids bound with a leather cord *mafif* wound seven times around the head.

In these three southern Arabian countries, traditional attire which was once regionally distinctive, is still undergoing radical change. It is said that totally hand-sewn and hand-embroidered garments ceased to be worn in most areas in the first half of this century. Machine-made versions which continue to exhibit traditional design features can still be found and they are often hand-embroidered; just occasionally a rare example of the "real thing" is discovered.

Men wear the *dishdasha*, or cotton body-shirt, in various colours. The *fouta* is also very popular, wound around the lower half of the body a couple of times and then the excess is pleated and tucked in at the waist. It is worn with the *fanilla* or a Western shirt plus a belt to hold a dagger. Belts are heavy, broad and strong, and often complex with a thick felt or cotton lining, pockets, woven metal-thread work and decorative silver pieces. In the hinterlands, men frequently wear only the *izar* with such a belt. Qara tribesmen, who wear the *fouta* with one end of the length of material thrown over the left shoulder, customarily wear a looped leather girdle and a leather shoulder strap bag slung under one arm.

In the olden days, a southern gentleman would not be considered well dressed without the large *khanjar* or *jambiyyah* tucked into a belt at the waist. These daggers were set in a curved sheath and worn over the stomach. Today, modern city men reserve them for ceremonial occasions when they are worn with a jacket.

The best blades are meticulously finished by hand to a mirror shine and signed in fine script with the names of the artisans who forged them. The metal medallion-studded hilts on Yemeni daggers are generally carved from horn as are many Omani versions. The sheaths and hilts display fine workmanship throughout the south but the styles vary. For instance, Omani khanjars are less curved than those from Yemen while Yemeni daggers are commonly set with cornelians, the reddish-brown variety of chalcedony found in the south.

Boys receive these ceremonial daggers at approximately the age of fourteen as a sign of having reached manhood. Omani boys wear silver buckles on their belts prior to this. Men continue to wear the dagger with great pride – traditionally, they are considered to be a symbol of fertility. In the south, the dagger can be seen in town and country alike although it no longer serves as a social indicator. Some men do not wear it at all, yet, in the past, the highest social group wore it to the right of the body; those of moderate rank wore the dagger in the middle; and those of the lowest rank, to the left. Today, it is rare to see it worn anywhere but in the middle of the body.

Men's headgear in Oman is much the same as in the Yemens. Skullcaps are often worn alone and vary greatly in colour and embroidery. Sometimes the headcloth is worn without the skullcap but combined or not, headcloths are generally wound into a turban. The most popular version is the imitation Kashmiri embroidered shawl which is available in many bright colours and white. Vivid cerise and orange are the two most commonly seen.

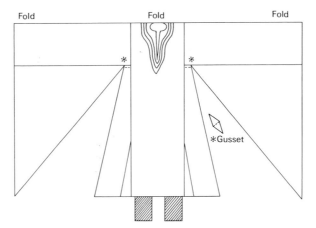

Left: *This garment is particularly attractive because the snug-fitting bodice contrasts well with sleeves that are a quarter metre longer than the arms. The centre-front neck opening is a deep slit backed by a placket to afford the wearer modesty. Dresses are worn shorter in the south and display the embroidered ankle bands on the* sirwaal. *The diamond-shaped under-arm gusset is usual but useless.*

Left: *Two incongruous strips of modern macadam now lie before the old worn wall of Sanaa and Bab al Yemen, the historic entrance to the old city. This two-lane highway symbolically crosses out the old life when women wore voluminous traditional costumes such as this one. Even in remote areas where this costume is still worn, the sewing machine joins the seams and adds a hasty touch of rough embroidery. This style is typical of Hojariyah to the south of Tayiz. The base textile is black satin which bears tiny pre-worked white flowers. Sparse red lines of chain stitch convey a mock yoke which dips deeply to a point at centre front. The chain stitched embroidery on the* sirwaal *is russet red, pale blue, green, cerise and silver metal-thread, and becomes a visual part of the costume as the dress is quite short.*

Men also wear a unique style of skullcap in Oman. It is made by the womenfolk and known as *gumma*. Repetitive designs are poked through stiffened cotton with thorns or pieces of wood whittled to a point – the resultant holes are edged with embroidery.

Far left: Kaftans *from Al Bayda near the border of North and South Yemen, are generally heavily embroidered all over except for the sleeve areas. The thread colours are red and yellow and there is a fine red embroidered line on the cuff edges of the black cotton.*

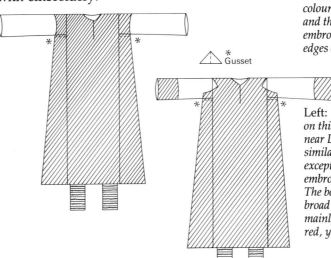

Left: *Embroidery placement on this dress from Maouit near Daida in North Yemen is similar to the Al Bayda dress except that the cuff embroidery is more extensive. The bodice work suggests a broad yoke-band. The work is mainly white and there is also red, yellow and green.*

Below: Hand-dyed indigo cotton from the southern Tihama features triangular segments of mother-of-pearl, triangular groupings of fine brass chain, brass ''sequins'' and red and white embroidery. The motifs may be palm trees. This bland interpretation of the kaftan is transformed by the unique embellishment. The enlarged straight sleeves with the broadened centre panel and the almost shape-less side gores and tiny useless under-arm gussets present an austere and grotesque garment turned stunning – the graphic and delicate detail is in perfect harmony with the blue-black background. Bright white and vivid red with touches of green amongst pearl and brass are unusually rich. This is a particularly fine example – the quality and quantity of decoration is a matter of wealth as well as skill. Most of the work falls within the centre-front panel and there are four decorated sections in each side gore.

The centre-front neck slit conforms to the extra depth with placket, typical of southern dresses, as is the length.

*Gusset

Body Ornament

Beauty Culture

A person's appearance is created just as much by body ornament as the manner in which he or she is dressed – a truth that can be applied to all cultures. Appearance generally serves as a social indicator.

There is evidence which confirms that, since man's earliest history, body ornamentation has held an important place in the everyday lives of both men and women. Although it is difficult to ascertain from rock art, both pictographs and petroglyphs, whether pre-historic body ornament is jewellery, paint, scarring or tattoo, it is certain that the underlying aims have been constant through the ages. From the time when man first observed how the seasons change the landscape, it must have been apparent that embellishment beautified. When he came to look upon the elements with awe and wonder and compare their power with the earth's beautiful treasures, he must have attributed magical significance to gem-stones and precious metals. Body ornament emerged as a method to protect as well as beautify.

On the Arabian Peninsula, ancient forms of

Above: Artist's impression of the Hijazi townswoman's sidaireeya *and* sirwaal. *This combination could have been finely embroidered white cotton or some exquisite silk satin with lavish embellishment to match the yoke and sleeve cuff edge of the* tawb.

body ornamentation exist still and traditional jewellery has changed little in thousands of years, despite the fact that it is generally melted down upon the death of its owner, or when it is sold in times of need.

Of all the ancient methods of ornamenting the body, scarring is the least practised on the Peninsula today. The only permanent marking still carried out, albeit to a lessening degree, is the tattoo. The most popular semi-permanent marks on the body are done with henna, and this is generally the preserve of women, today.

Henna

Staining the nails, skin and hair with henna (*hinna*) is by far the most favoured way of enhancing beauty throughout traditional Arabia. The practice is coming to an end as the old world passes from view and the new nation takes its place in the modern world and, quite likely, within the next twenty years, it will be a rare sight to see skin stained with henna in Arabia. It is interesting to see that the use of henna is now popular in the West, albeit as a hair dye and/or conditioner. This fact raises the possibility that the Peninsula too, will one day re-establish old henna customs.

Henna cosmetics are made from the sturdy Egyptian evergreen plant – a privet, *Lawsonia inermis*, whose shoots and leaves yield an extract which is mixed with *catechu*, an astringent substance obtained from various trees and shrubs. Arabians crush dried berries from this plant to obtain a red powder.

The dye gives a rich, russet-red polished look to the skin, and is considered to be cooling for palms of the hands and soles of the feet. Black henna (*saumer*) is reserved for the soles of the feet and hands while red henna (*hinna*) is used for the tips of the fingers and toes. Black henna is obtained by a second application over orange henna markings. This application involves another paste made from powdered lime, *nura*, and powdered crystal ammoniac, *shanadah*. The orange markings turn black at once and remain so for about twenty or thirty days.

According to Colonel H. R. P. Dickson, eastern and northern Arabian Bedouin girls used only red henna, which was reserved for the decoration of their hands, fingernails and toenails. They would apply henna three times in order to get the right shade – and occasionally four times if a very dark colour was required.

The process involves making a fairly liquid paste from powdered henna and water. This is applied very thickly and carefully with a wooden stick according to the desired pattern. It is allowed to dry quickly in front of a fire until the paste cracks and falls off, is picked off, or the decorated area is wrapped in cloth overnight to dry naturally. Any residue is washed off with clear water.

At times of *Eid*, or holiday connected with religious celebrations, entire Bedouin families have been known to decorate themselves with henna. In some parts of the Arab world, a bride has lacy patterns traced on the upper part of her body and feet with henna paste.

The application of henna often became ritualistic in the past. In rural areas, a special village woman, or professional woman, *mashta*, from outside the

Right: *Artist's impression of the* thawb nashal. *Although this gown is currently worn by women in every town of Arabia (due to imports from India), it is* considered the traditional dress of the Eastern Province and Gulf regions. The cut originated in the heartland of Arabia.

village, came to prepare a bride's face and body with cosmetics. She applied henna to the palms of the hands and instep of the feet. The latter application was repeated when the newly married girl stood for the first time before the entrance of her new home. It was a quaint wedding custom matching the Western one where the groom carries his bride across the threshold.

Townswomen in the Hijaz once had a custom whereby the bride was isolated from the guests by a special decorative curtain in order to have henna applied to her hands, feet and hair for the nuptials. On a night just before the wedding, the *hareem* gathered for the *laylat al hinna*, or Henna Night (the ritual was known as *ghumra*). Fresh henna, *hinna khadra*, was prepared for this occasion – the application symbolizing fertility and good fortune to the bride. Jeddah ladies recall a time when the bride-to-be, wrapped cocoon-like in an embroidered red cloth, was led blindfolded to the appointed place of application.

Although the use of henna was primarily a form of beauty culture, it was recognized as a method for hardening the surface of the skin and rendering the soles immune to cuts and scratches. Pearl fishers used henna on the palms of their hands in order to make them less likely to blister when rowing and hauling divers. Henna also acts as an astringent and a deodorizer and it is believed to have medicinal value also. The best henna is claimed to be Meccan and the next best is reputed to come from Basra, Iraq.

Kohl

Kohl (*kuhr*, *kuhl* or *kahal*) is a black substance used by the women of the Arabian Peninsula as eye-liner and eye-shadow, *mirwad*. Apart from making the eyes look brighter and larger and therefore more beautiful, kohl was once believed to have value as a protection against eye disease, a remedy for conjunctivitis and promoter of strong vision. It is commonly applied to the insides of the eyelids and is a method of controlling the sun's glare. Tribesmen use it, too.

In the far north-west of the Arabian Peninsula, in Jordan and in Syria, kohl is especially applied to the eyes of a woman who has just given birth. This has become ritualistic but there is no doubt that it is a fillip to the morale and therefore physically beneficial. Babies are also decorated with kohl.

Kohl is powdered antimony, a brittle metallic elementary body of bright bluish-white colour and flaky crystalline texture. The word "alcohol" is said to be derived from the Arabic *al-khul*, referring to the disinfecting qualities of this mineral.

Carbon from burned frankincense is often used as a kohl substitute to pencil a bride's eyebrows to make them meet. "Beetle brows" are considered to be very beautiful by some in the Arab world.

Rouge

Rouge (*zerkoun*), a fine red powder prepared from safflower (*Carthamus tinctorius*), was used to paint ladies' cheeks in traditional Arabia. It was worn by well-to-do brides, even in remote regions, and was also applied to the lips in olden times.

The Bedouin of Arabia are known to have used the red roots of the *Arnebia decumbens* (a plant of the *Boragnaceae* family) to make rouge.

Humra wa bawdra, rouge and powder, were part of a Hijazi townswoman's toilette in the olden days and possibly these were once made locally.

Ear-piercing and Nose-piercing

In Arabia, a girl usually has her ears pierced at birth and a Bedouin child may have them pierced in two or three places. Generally the holes are kept open with silk cords only until she is considered old enough to wear ear-rings.

Various tribal men on the Peninsula also have one or both ears pierced in order to suspend traditional silver ear-rings. Nomadic and rural women often have one nostril pierced to display an ornament – a custom popular throughout India. It is difficult to ascertain whether Arabia influenced India or vice versa. Most certainly the newly popular gold nose studs are Indian.

Lady Anne Blunt noted in the late nineteenth century that women of Hayil had the left nostril pierced to wear gold rings which were attached by chains to other head ornaments. Mrs. Mignan reported rings worn in the right nostril in Muscat. Thesiger recorded that southern tribesmen wore a ring in the right ear-lobe.

Tattoo

Tattoo, the practice of making permanent marks or designs upon the skin by puncturing and inserting a pigment or pigments, is practised by women in various parts of the Arabian Peninsula as a method of beautification. It is claimed that men never tattoo themselves merely for decoration.

The custom is said to have reached Arabia from Mesopotamia where tattooed designs were considered an enhancement thousands of years ago. It is still popular with Bedouin women in Iraq today. These Marsh Arab tribes developed the custom to a far greater extent than the Arabian Bedouin. In Iraq, marks sometimes cover the entire body whereas they are generally limited to the facial area in Arabia. In Najran, women can be seen with blue tattoo marks on their chins only. Colonel Dickson, speaking of north-eastern Arabia, believed the only tribe that disapproved of tattoos was the Ujman; for some unknown reason no Ujman woman would wear a tattoo.

The various patterns employed are attractive although invariably geometric. None thus far recorded involve representational art. Colonel Dickson inclined to the theory that the designs have been handed down from the ancient Sumerians and suggested the subject is large enough for a single study.

It is believed that carbon, taken from fire soot, is the chief medium used by the Arabian Bedouin to make tattoo marks. It is quite likely that indigo is also used as it is readily available in market places.

Cleaning the Teeth

Arabians traditionally used a piece of tree bark called *darum* to clean their teeth. It cleaned remarkably well and acted as a beauty aid by darkening the gums and lips. Still popular are small branches of the Arak tree known as *meswaak* sticks. With the constant rubbing, the end of the *meswaak* turns brush-like.

111

Hairdressing

Rarely is the natural hair colour of an Arab anything but black. The texture of the hair is not too fine and not too strong. An Arabian woman's hair generally looks beautiful because of these qualities and the fact that it is traditionally worn long and kept lustrous, yet few Western people have a chance to see this as it is considered a sign of modesty to cover the head when out-of-doors. Indoors, a married woman may allow her hair to fall free whereas an unmarried girl should not display her tresses once she has reached puberty.

An Arabian woman's hair is deliberately loosened for dancing, however. There are accounts of Bedouin women "loosing their hair and dancing with graceful movements of head, hair and body". Women of all ages let their hair down when performing the dance. The woman with the longest and richest tresses gets the chief praise. Elderly and many married women are known to refrain from dancing, yet, the most conservative old traditionalist may, in the momentum of a festive occasion, pull off her headgear to the beat of the *tar* and swing her loosened tresses to the right, then left, until she has reached the point that her long tresses can perform figure-eights behind her head. When the music stops, almost embarrassed, the lady coyly dons her headgear once again. Young girls also eagerly shed their scarves to free their beautiful long hair for the rhythmic Arabian dance. They are completely relaxed as no men are present. For women, hair has always been important as a means of expression in traditional Arabian dancing.

Traditionally, many Peninsula women braid their long uncut hair, interweaving a strip of gauze. Townswomen in the Hijaz used fine rectangles of exquisitely edged muslin. The braids were then fastened on top of the head and served the practical purpose of keeping the headdress in place, supplying an anchor for hair pendants. Plaited hair was also used this way.

Colonel Dickson writes that women of central, northern and eastern Arabia generally did their hair in nine plaits, divided as follows: two on either side of the face which showed down the side of the *burga*; six thinner ones at the back starting from the middle at the top of the head and one below, at the neck. These women redressed their hair weekly with *duhn*, or *dehen*, a local hair oil and applied afterwards henna paste or a mixture of herbs, *rashush*. Shammar and some Mutayr women used the dried leaves of *nifl*, a compound also known as *hangresse* (*Trigonella stellata*). Najdi townswomen used *moshart* instead of *henna*. It was a paste made from ground powder of dried flowers and leaves of *rayharn*, *misk* and *ward*.

A wooden comb, *misht*, was traditionally used by Bedouin women for hairdressing. Some townswomen used an ivory and gold *misht* and a brush. Many Arabian women claim that they owe their beautiful hair to drying it naturally out of doors.

Carlo Guarmani, visiting Hayil in 1864, observed that the women's glossy black hair was oiled with an odourless pomade composed of finely powdered palm bark and clarified fat obtained from sheep's tails. The dried and pounded leaves of the sidr tree are used as another common Bedouin hair wash, especially after applications of henna paste. Henna was applied primarily as a dressing to condition the hair although it was also used to colour the hair. As a dye, it produces a rich mahogany glow on black hair. *Moshart* imparts a brown colour.

In the 1880s, the English aristocrat, Lady Anne Blunt, visiting Arabia to buy thoroughbred Arab horses, described a lady of Hayil. She wrote of hair "plastered with some reddish stuff". Without a doubt it was henna, applied in much the same way as ancient Egyptian women wore perfumed wax on the tops of their heads. This form of conditioner was eminently suitable for a hot and harsh climate. In the past, men of the Arabian Peninsula frequently used henna on their hair. It is not uncommon still today to see a patriarch with his white beard stained orange with henna.

In remote parts of Arabia, men wear distinctive hairstyles which can denote the precise region from which they come. One southern tribe has a male fashion where the hair is worn long and braided into a leather thong that is worn as a circlet on top of the head. In central Arabia, tribesmen once wore long curls.

Traditionally the Arabian groom, as well as the bride, was ritually prepared for the wedding. In Hijazi towns, a groom was visited by a skilled barber and when the work was finished, his mother pressed a gold coin on the barber's forehead. Throughout the Peninsula today, men generally conform to a uniform style of hair cut – close to Western standards – although their hair is rarely visible because headgear is considered correct for out of doors. The exception occurs during the period of the *Haj*, when the head of a male pilgrim is uncovered.

A good Muslim is expected to complete the pilgrimage to Mecca at least once in his lifetime if possible, and, at this time, he traditionally cuts off some hair or shaves his head as part of the prescribed ablutions. Long-haired Bedouin, as a rule, cut off the ends of only two locks from the side plaits, *quran*. Both men and women usually roll these ends three times around the finger and cut off that much. The Bedouin man, but not the woman, also traditionally cuts off a small lock from his forehead.

Visitors to the Tihama, the coastal plain lying between the Red Sea and Arabia's western mountain chain, are immediately struck by the uncommon beauty of the people. It is beauty made up of their general appearance – the combination of bearing, garments and beauty culture. The men are often dressed in little more than loincloths while the women wear flowing, colourful embroidered *kaftans*. Both men and women wear their hair long, and it is the custom to crown themselves with a head circlet, *isaaba*, into which they affix scented herbs and pretty wild flowers. Annual circumcision festivals are held in these western lowlands and initiates of one tribe can be recognized by a curious cock's comb hairdo.

Pelly, visiting Najd in 1865, noted that young men wore long braids of hair at the back of the head. Some tied two of the side braids around the chin. The little girls, too, had braided hair, according to Pelly. In southern Arabia tribal men and

Left: *Artist's impression of the Najdi tulle* thawb. *The base textile ranges from plain tulle, through the many variations of patterned and appliquéd, to fine lace. It is invariably black and relies upon a yoke of gold and silver metal thread, and broad sleeve cuffs of colourful sequins or embroidery for relief.*

women commonly plait their long hair. Wilfred Thesiger vividly described one beautiful young girl drawing water from a well at Manwakh. ''Her hair was braided, except where it was cut in a fringe across her forehead, and the braids fell in a curtain of small plaits round her neck''. Thesiger noted that most southern men wore their hair long – sometimes plaited or curled.

In Arabia, a beard and moustache are considered a sign of virile masculinity. In some eastern Arabian coastal areas, men grow their beards very long, according to the tribal custom. A beard has a distinct religious value in the Islamic tradition as it is considered a sign of piety. In some tribes beards are never trimmed, whereas the Hijazi townsmen, say nineteenth-century travellers, took great pains to keep their beards neatly cut, however long. Records do show that there were four barber shops in Jeddah at the time. Their mustachios were cut closely and never allowed to hang over the lips, in direct contrast with the occupying Ottomans in the area, who wore thick, bushy mustachios.

Aromatics

In considering traditional Arabian appearance, it would be impossible not to make note of aromatics because they are integral to Arab toilette. Not only were the people of the Arabian Peninsula producers of the finest incense and attar in the ancient world, but they were, and still are, prodigious consumers.

It is immediately apparent when handling old Arabian garments that they are steeped in incense. Also lingering in the garments are other heady, sweet, penetrating, pungent scents.

Since time immemorial, both men and women on the Arabian Peninsula have wafted incense into their robes, and worn *itr* or *ittir* (attar) – the fragrance of a volatile essential oil obtained from petals and leaves of certain plants, trees and shrubs. It has also been a custom to sprinkle attar of roses, orange blossom or sandalwood on the head, neck, hands and feet of guests.

Ancient Egypt used to be the main consumer of frankincense and myrrh attar produced in southern Arabia, and from those times to the present day, the custom of anointing the body with aromatic oils, and soaking garments in attar has touched several other great civilizations. These small bulk, high value local commodities brought Arabians enormous wealth in the past and thus they were able to indulge their penchant for wearing exotic perfumes distilled from imported materials. Local perfumes were also popular and made from Tayifi flowers. Scent-making became an Arabian industry.

With the introduction of Islam in the seventh century, *taher*, the ritualistic cleansing of the body was established. Ceremonial cleansing at meal times was already an ingrained custom and at this time the Arabs' favourite scent of rosewater, *maaward*, would be used liberally. Other popular attars in Arabia are musk (*misk*), henna (*tamr hinna*), amber (*anbar*), jasmine (*yasamine*), lavender (*lawend*) and lemon grass (*zahr-laimoon*). The traditional Najdi scent for women was *dehen ood*, and *dehen wad* was worn by men. It was a mixture of *misk*, *anbar* and *khadi*, imported from India.

In the past, Arabian scents were extracted from natural sources. Now, synthetic materials are being introduced because authentic natural varieties are costly to produce. Despite this, Arab perfume-makers still pound their leaves and blossoms by hand in Mecca and Medina.

It is fascinating to discover that many of the methods for beautification in traditional Arabia had practical aspects to them and the use of these products began in the ancient world. The attar extract from the henna flower, for instance, is considered an excellent anti-perspirant.

Jewellery

In the nineteenth century, some Arabian tribesmen wore heavy jewellery (*jowaher*) just as they did thousands of years ago. Even today, in remote areas, some tribal men wear traditional ornaments that take the form of silver finger-rings and earrings – and leather head-circlets and belts decorated with silver. For the most part, however, a man's traditional body ornamentation is now confined to knives and swords in elaborate scabbards. These are usually fine silver or gold sometimes studded with gems. Bandoliers and belts were also commonly decorated with precious metals and from every belt there once hung a silver powder horn.

Arab women are inordinately fond of jewellery and, in the past, a town bride was customarily bedecked with it to impress the guests with her appearance – and perhaps convey that she belonged to a family of substance, although sometimes the jewellery was borrowed for the occasion. Jewellery remains a traditional wedding gift.

For the Bedouin woman, especially, jewellery represented personal fortune, a dowry (*mahr*), affording her security. The bulk of the jewellery she possessed came at the time of her marriage and remained her property until the day she died or until such time as she wished to dispose of it.

Mahr is a tradition in Arabia. Bedouin marriages, which are arranged similarly to those of town folk, are contrived by the parents on behalf of their children. The prospective husband may make a bridal payment, *mahr*, which can be paid in two halves to the father of a girl. The first part *muqaddam*, is paid at the time of the engagement or agreement, and the second part, *muakhkhar*, is a sum promised to the wife in case of divorce, or paid from his estate or by his family should he die before his wife. According to tradition the bride's father spends the money on household effects and jewellery as an investment for her future.

Traditional jewellery worn by nomadic, semi-settled and many settled women in the past, is mostly fashioned from silver and often has set stones – predominantly turquoise in the northern half of Arabia, and reddish-coloured stones in the south. The jewellery is bold in design, substantial in size and distinctly hand-crafted in appearance. It is always eye-catching and often exhibits praiseworthy skill, employing the techniques of annealing and hammering, embossing and repoussé, fusing and soldering, chasing and engraving, granulation, wire-making and wrought metalwork, chain-making and casting.

The characteristic features of Bedouin jewellery include chains, bells, coins, strands of irregular-sized, multi-coloured and silver beads, red and blue stones set in collets with fluted or beaded metal surrounds affixed in high-relief, snug-fitting bracelets with hinged openings and pinned fastenings, necklaces affixed with plaited hemp ties, and intricate meshed ornaments, often sewn to cloth backings. Multiple pendants and multi-stranded necklaces are also characteristic and diadems of similar construction are also worn. Head ornamentation is particularly favoured.

The materials employed are turquoise, garnet, carnelian, amber, coral, pearl, agate, glass, faience, silver, gold and brass. Most traditional Arabian jewellery is fashioned from silver – the fineness varying in order that every female member of tribal society may wear it. Some northern pieces are gold, and brass was used as a yellow metal substitute on occasions. The brass pieces are usually set with fake stones.

Since the introduction of Islam, jewellers have fashioned Koranic amulets that have been integrated into this ancient-style jewellery; it is not an orthodox Islamic tradition, however. Charm cases with origins in antiquity sometimes house verses of the *Koran* and circular pendants carry centrally set stones engraved with Koranic inscriptions. The ancient crescent-shaped component took on a new meaning, too, when it became the emblem of Islam. Carved figures from the second century BC, in a tomb discovered at Palmyra in Syria (an outpost of the ancient trade routes), show women wearing many necklaces at one time just as the

Above: *Artist's impression of a Bedouin woman from the Sarawat mountain regions. A dress such as this was once worn around Tayif. Although slim-fitting, the* kaftan *can easily slip over the head and the gentle shaping can enhance a fuller figure. Garments worn in the mountains are customarily more fitting than those worn in the interior of the Peninsula. Women from the western regions do not always veil – many wear hoods such as here and both dress and headgear are richly ornamented with appliqué, embroidery, beading and other embellishment.*

Bedouin do in Arabia today. Even then the most popular pendant was apparently the inverted crescent shape.

Jewellery is customarily worn in profusion by Arabian Bedouin women; they also wear pieces appliquéd to their clothes and in their hair for celebrations. On these festive occasions they add a belt fringed with bells. These can weigh as much as two kilos. It is usual for a Bedouin woman to wear all the silver she owns for parties. It weighs her down considerably but serves to give her prestige.

Although women are responsible for perpetuating jewellery styles by seeking traditional pieces, nomads do not make jewellery as a rule. The Arabian silversmith is usually born into the artisan class – his craft generally passed on to him by his father. They are, usually, settled or semi-settled folk concentrated in the oases and coastal towns, although silversmiths become nomadic if affiliated with a large tribe for whom they work exclusively. Despite the fact that they become part of the tribal

115

structure, such men are considered ignoble because they belong to the artisan class.

Silversmiths also made buttons in the past. In Central Arabia they were silver or gold and sometimes brass. These buttons are generally studded with turquoise or some other blue material. In the Hijaz, it was the fashion to wear seven buttons connected by a chain to affix the front opening of a woman's blouse. These buttons are usually gold, hence the name *zarayer dhahab* (gold buttons) but sometimes they are silver. Most *zarayer dhahab* (which are removable and similar to cuff-links) are in the shape of crescents, stars, hearts, etc, and many are studded with diamonds. Usually only the top four buttons are decorated because these are seen in the blouse front when worn under the traditional V-necked dress, the zabun.

It is interesting to learn that in the late nineteenth century, a Franco-Algerian professional photographer, Gervais-Courtellemont, had difficulty in purchasing jewellery in Mecca, although there was plenty of jewellery around. He writes that the procedure was complicated because all purchases had to be approved by the *sheikh* of the Goldsmiths' Guild. This gentleman weighed the article against an array of date stones and beans before setting the official price. Possibly the bean was the carob, the small Oriental bean remarkable

spot. It is believed these brooches are of Turkish origin.

Colourful beads have always been an important part of Arabian Peninsula jewellery. They can prove to be the most fascinating part of a necklace. While jewellery is consistently melted down and remade, many of these beads have been in continuous use for ages. It is therefore possible to find ancient and interesting beads incorporated into Arabian necklaces, although they may not be made of precious materials. Since the earliest times, glass and faience beads have been just as popular as semi-precious beads. Records show that, although fine Venetian glass beads were sometimes worn by Bedouin women during the mid-nineteenth century, amber necklaces were favoured. This is not surprising as amber was once a form of currency in many parts of the Islamic world. At this time black horn bracelets, Bombay agate beads, *reysh*, and Indian red wax beads were also worn. These latter items were originally destined for Abyssinia but found popularity with the Arabian Bedouin along the way.

All of these beads and many others have been used in *mesbaha*, or *subha*, the prayer-bead strands, often referred to in the West as "worry-beads". *Mesbaha* are universally popular with the menfolk throughout Arabia and therefore they must be

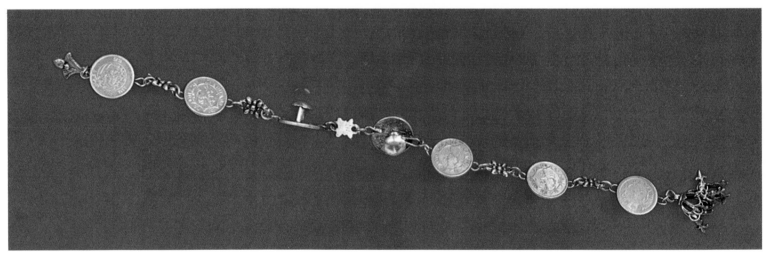

Above: Old silver coins have sometimes been used to create a set of linked studs for the Hijazi women's traditional blouse, the sidaireeya. *A shank has been attached to the back of each coin to form a stud. Such a set of buttons is not usually a rigid arrangement and the fleur-de-lis and edelweiss are an unexpected addition. There appears to be one flower missing.*

in its uniformity of size, and from which the basic gem-weighing carat (ct) is said to have been derived. It was particularly important that correct weight be established because the jewellery represented wealth and was used as a portable bank account and a negotiable asset.

Gervais-Courtellemont also described a Meccan ring (worn by pilgrims who completed the *Haj*) as being the equivalent of Western school colours, in that anyone wearing it must be entitled to do so. Such old rings are now rare. It is recorded that in 1885, a Meccan bride wore countless brooches on her headgear and dress bodice. These large, diamond set brooches are also rare today. They measure approximately fifteen centimetres in length and about eight centimetres in width, and often bristle with incongruous detail such as spears and other weaponry. The central motif is often a flower, and this is invariably mounted on a spring so it quivers when moved. Amongst the tiny set white stones there are usually a few coloured stones placed together in an unobtrusive

considered part of traditional costume. Prayer-beads have an obscure origin and it is not clear how they became an integral part of Arabian appearance. There is nothing in the Koran about them.

The custom of carrying a string of beads for the purposes of prayer is believed to have originated in Northern India or Persia and the fashion spread from there after Alexander the Great conquered the Persians and formed the vast Hellenic Empire. This would account for the existence of similar "worry-beads" appearing throughout Mediterranean countries.

As a rule there are thirty-three beads in *mesbaha*. These are sectioned in three groups of eleven beads by two spacer beads and one terminal bead which ends with a tassel. Sometimes there are thirty-three beads between each spacer, making a ninety-nine bead *mesbaha*, claimed by some to represent the ninety-nine attributes of God – and claimed by others to represent ninety-nine appellations for God.

Right: *Artist's impression of a Bedouin dress from the Hijaz. Appliquéd patches of red and blue cotton sometimes bear the stamp of "Two lions brand red twill" from "Prakash Cotton Mills, Bombay". Fine embroidery overlays patches.*

Below: *Superb examples of silver inlaid old black coral prayer beads and a red amber* mesbaha *have been restranded and perhaps the silver beads and tassels have been renewed. The fine patina on the beads indicates the use they have had.*

A devout Muslim methodically fingers each bead at prayer time, one at a time, intoning Koranic and extemporaneous phrases in praise of Allah or asking His forgiveness. He may say something different at each bead or repeat the same thing thirty-three times – or sometimes eleven times as it is a custom to change the adoration when a spacer is reached.

The rarest strands of prayer beads are made of *yusr*, a precious black coral found in the Red Sea. The best, which is a lustrous black and takes a fine polish, is located between Jeddah and Gonfode. Traditionally, the price of *yusr* beads was determined by size and the Jeddah bead-turners sold them in strands of one hundred. Most of Jeddah's black coral beads were destined for Malaya. Coral farming is no longer an industry in the Red Sea and old strands of *yusr* prayer beads, which are commonly inlaid with silver, are avidly sought by collectors.

Today, *mesbaha* are found incorporating all known gems and precious metals. The great skills of the finest jewellers now produce exquisite interpretations. Also, Muslim prayer-beads come from India and Pakistan, sometimes made from the scented *kalambac* or sandalwood. In Mecca, *mesbaha* are available in a wide variety of mediums, including colourful glass and plastic. Many pilgrims make a practice of purchasing a strand in Mecca as a gift for a friend at home.

117

Arts and Crafts

Violet Dickson, widow of the arabist and author H. R. P. Dickson, has resided in Kuwait since the 1930s. She observed some time ago that Arabian Bedouin women were spinning less and less, even for the tent, their most essential item. Instead they were buying tent strips from Syria. Although these were the same width, they were thinner and poorly woven so they leaked in the rain and needed to be patched.

Handicrafts have been generally waning for a long while on the Arabian Peninsula. It is possible the decline began during the days of the Ottoman Empire when there was heavy taxation. Certainly crafts were performed less after oil was discovered in the Eastern Province in the 1930s. Oil revenue brought the motor vehicle and imported textiles were thereafter more easily obtained. Thus sounded the death knell for hand-loomed cloth. Gowns are no longer tailored from hand-woven textiles

look – a visual impression that was both vigorous and colourful.

In some parts of Arabia, yarn is still spun and dyed, and weaving is still performed, though rarely is the product meant for garments. Occasionally, one can find old dresses that have been made out of hand-loomed textiles that may have been woven on the Arabian Peninsula. The hand-woven items still crafted are tent and camel accoutrements, but there are signs of modernization throughout the Peninsula which present a threat to their future production. There is presently sufficient interest in indigenous weaving to revive old skills, even if the end products are no longer traditional, functional items.

Traditionally, some kinds of work were considered dishonourable for certain Arabs. Among these activities were ironmongering, carrying and making salt, burning lime or charcoal and skinning

Below: *Until very recently the Bedouin wove only for their immediate needs. Very occasionally, an excess of yarn or spare tent strips would be sold or exchanged for their needs. Even now, traditional items are made for use by the Bedouin, and a Westerner must seek these pieces in the town market place. However, the tourist industry has begun, and Bedouin weaving is now being applied to boutique items. It may be difficult to discern the genuine from fake unless a serious study is made soon.*

and rarely today do Arabian women make their dresses by hand. The arrival of the sewing machine caused them to stop hand-sewing. The increased pace of life has also seen machined embroidery replace needlepoint. One can only speculate about the quality of craftwork produced on the Arabian Peninsula long ago. The oldest examples show a remarkable difference from their counterparts made today.

Evidence suggests that the costumes of the Arabian Peninsula were usually produced from a combination of locally produced and imported materials. The earliest textiles used were wool, cotton and silk. Wool and some cotton were processed in Arabia; silk was imported. Great quantities of cotton yardage were imported and dyed locally. The result was a distinctive Arabian

Above: *There is little doubt that this motif is a palm tree. It appears on many items found in the Hijaz, and it is said to be typical of one section of the great Harb tribe whose diyarat stretches across three Arabian regions. Most embroidery motifs traditional to Greater Arabia are geometric. The subjects that are representational are most usually stylized botanical ones.*

Left: *A camel litter or howdah gave the Bedouin woman ample opportunity to show how well she could weave. After the tent, a woman would weave colourful camel accoutrements which included saddle bags and draperies. All are traditionally hung with fringes and tassels which must have looked marvellous when swaying in rhythm with the camel's graceful gait.*

animals and curing the skins. Despite this, there were leather crafts performed on the Arabian Peninsula which exhibited great skill, and, as one might expect, the items manufactured were among the essentials of the nomad. While some nomads were skilled, generally settled Bedouin performed crafts.

More than one hundred years ago, the inhabitants of Jauf in Northern Arabia depended wholly upon trade with the Bedouin, in contrast with most other parts of Arabia, where this situation was reversed. Jauf's local merchandise included various kinds of woollen mats, tent-cloths, packsacks and a thick and strong woollen version of the Arabian cloak. The Jauf weavers were famous and these mantles were in demand far and wide. Their arid terrain would seem to be responsible for the development of handicrafts.

Western Arabia has traditionally seen a greater variety of handicrafts, so it is fortunate that a Social Development Centre has been formed there to preserve and encourage skills. In Wadi Fatimah in the Hijaz, the crafts of pottery, weaving, and jewellery-making are regularly displayed.

A chief craft of women in Wadi Fatimah, writes Motoko Katakura, is making *taly*, colourful appendages for decorating headgear. Many young rural girls in western Arabia are still taught to make *taly* and to sew and embroider men's and women's garments. They also learn to weave palm fronds into fans and carpets, to weave wool and hair tent strips and sew them together, to make reclining cushions, sleeping mats and decorative pot holders, and to make elaborate tribal masks – although the latter skill is not emphasized any more because masks are worn less and less.

In a modern, affluent world handicrafts have an established place, albeit as a leisure activity. It is to be expected that most Arabians will cease to

Left: *Saddle bags are eagerly sought by Western visitors to the Arabain Peninsula. They are, of course, a most useful item as well as decorative. It is remarkable that Bedouin women strove to make the camel draperies so elaborate when they had also to cope with the harshness of a desert existence – the example here must have taken many hours to accomplish.*

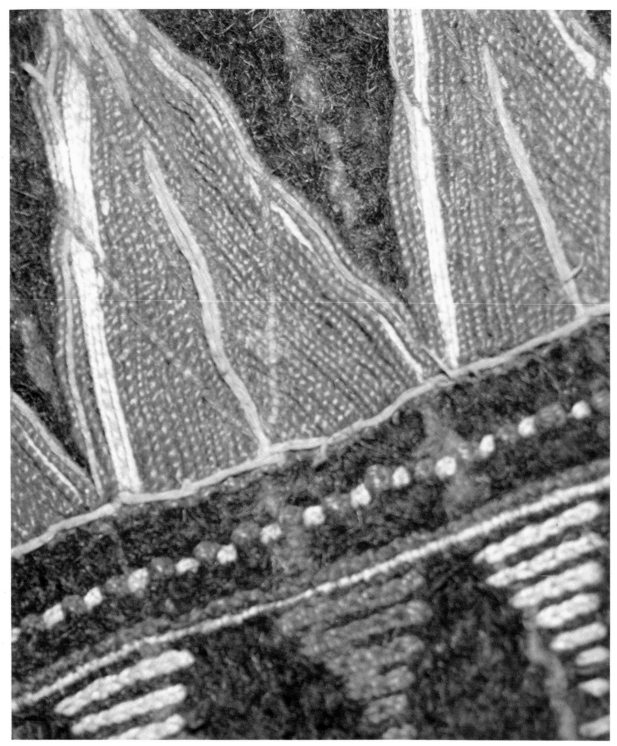

Left: *Weaving was once a highly developed craft on the Arabian Peninsula. It was probably developed because wool and hair were the most suitable and available mediums for making a nomad's home in a barren land. Western Arabian work is particularly skilled and colourful. Geometric shapes and designs formed from single and double triangles are characteristic. The subtle shades shown here are unusually sombre for the Asir highland region where this jacket is worn. The coarse wool oversewn with embroidery make it an extremely heavy garment.*

perform craft work because it is no longer a necessity. This theory is compounded by the fact that many are now preoccupied with new-found interests. Ultimately there will be a revival of the crafts. During the period of evolution, it is desirable that Arabians should at least have the opportunity to visually participate in this passing aspect of their heritage.

The crafts of pottery-making and sculpture have little to do with costume, except that they are forms of artistic expression which give an insight into the background of traditional Arabia where appearance is an integral part of the life-style. A brief outline of each craft is therefore included.

According to Georg August Wallin, who travelled in Arabia in the mid-nineteenth century, stone cutting was a traditional craft, the artisans of

Jauf being renowned for their stone mortars and various other utensils. These were similar to the sculpted antiquities unearthed in that area and found with very ancient coins and other artifacts. Latterly, replicas of these fine stone pieces have been made of clay. This change has taken place throughout the Peninsula.

Modern Arabia may not be known for the production of ceramics, yet it was the ancient Arab traders who took the manufacturing processes of painting ceramics to Spain, where the craft became world-renowned.

It has been determined from shards found on the Arabian Peninsula that pottery has been crafted there for thousands of years – its origin lost in the mists of time. The art of producing practical and well-designed pieces may have reached

Arabia in ancient times from other lands although it is just as likely that the various Middle Eastern water carriers and containers took shape in Arabia itself, where wells were often the only source of drinking water. Both storage urns and water vessels in Arabia are ideally formed for their purposes. They are tall, elegant-looking and narrow-necked, to permit minimum evaporation in extreme heat and facilitate transportation upon the shoulder. Because of the design the container holds the maximum possible quantity with no spillage.

There is a limited variety of suitable wood on the Peninsula for building and crafts. The Sidr tree is only suitable for fencing animal pens or for making the *mishaab*, or camel stick. The palms supply various materials for crafts but the date tree is too valuable as a food producer to consider cutting it down for lumber. The tamarisk is therefore exploited to the fullest extent. Arabs once used tamarisk wood for beams and pillars in their mud dwellings as well as for camel litter frames, wooden bowls of all sizes, the *shedaad* riding saddle and the *misama* pack saddle. These saddles were always made by men.

Jidda, or tamarisk wood bowls, are customarily studded with brass nails, silver or highly polished lead. Riding-saddle frames are similarly studded. In many parts of Arabia, tamarisk doors, shutters, beams and pillars are painted in traditional patterns with red, yellow and blue natural paints. This colour wears off easily, leaving an attractive mellowed effect soon after being painted.

For the most part, wooden items and timber used by carpenters were imported from Africa and India. The most popular timber for doors and shutters and *hareem* panels is teak because it withstands both wind and salty breezes. Hardwood chests (both dowry and "pearling" varieties) are generally imported ready-made from India.

In northern and eastern Arabia, a Bedouin woman traditionally spent a great deal of time making a *maksar* – the camel litter in which she would ride when her tribe decided to move on. Some are very elaborate and the various types have different names. Traditionally each tribe had its own style, but all shared an array of brilliant colours, designed to attract attention and thereby give prestige to the owner.

The frame of the *maksar* was made from pomegranate and tamarisk wood bought in the towns. The woman would bind these together and then cover the frame with gazelle skins. She would also decorate the front and rear pommels sometimes with cowrie shells, scarlet cloth and mirrored pieces. On the move, the *maksar* is draped with colourful woollen and cotton materials and together with their infants the women are thus sheltered from the sun and protected from the gaze of men. Within the litter, women carry their personal possessions in a treasure box, the *sahhara*. The contents include jewellery, trinkets, dyes, tea, sugar, saffron, coffee, cardamom and beauty aids.

Women also make the *habara*, a child's hammock, and the *mizbah*, a child's portable cradle which some mothers sling across their backs. The baby ends up tucked under the arm and is thus kept warm. The *habara*, *mizbah* and the *haudh*

(water trough), have frames made of pomegranate wood which is ideally suited as it bends easily into shape.

The production and decoration of armour was once a highly developed craft and some tribes became known for their blades. Many swords and daggers brought from other lands were decorated in Arabia by weapon jewellers. Royalty and the well-to-do had their names or Koranic phrases inscribed with artistic calligraphy by these skilled metalworkers; the name of the craftsman and date of manufacture were also etched. When firearms were introduced in the late eighteenth century, metalsmiths began to decorate these also. The craft became an independent art.

Metal craftsmen are generally settled folk. In the towns and villages throughout Arabia, they can be seen making *dillaat*, brass and copper coffee pots. The extra large examples are usually ornaments. The smiths are constantly called upon to repair the copper, brass and iron utensils they make and sometimes the task is a small one, involving a mere replacement of the chain which joins the *mahmas* (coffee roaster) to its iron twin, the *yed al mahmas* (coffee stirrer). These are sometimes very ornate with gleaming inlaid brass.

Leather and sheepskin garments are part of the traditional range of Arabian costume. Most of

Below: *Tiny silver beads are popularly stranded on cotton and leather thongs to fringe Bedouin garments. This old shawl has faded to achieve a mellow beauty, its threadbare condition weighted down by the lavish silver beading and fine embroidery. Items such as this can be purchased in the Jeddah souq where traders have discovered the Western penchant for handcrafted items – no matter how old and damaged they might be.*

these come from the western mountainous regions of the Hijaz, Asir and Yemen where the weather is often cool. The universally popular shepherd's great coat, *farwah* (virtually a *bisht* with sleeves attached), is also lined with sheep's wool, but this is often made outside the Peninsula. The Asir Arabs seem to have a preference for cloaks rather than sleeved garments. The reason for this cannot be that they are quicker to make because these cloaks are elaborately embroidered. The decoration is usually applied red leather and red leather thong stitchery.

Both Bedouin men and women of the Peninsula made leather goods, usually for their own use or for that of their immediate family. In the past, large tribes often had their own affiliated artisan-class to make leather goods which included hand-

121

bags, belts, head circlets and bracelets, often decorated with silver, beads and shells. Leather goods could also be purchased in the towns.

Bedouin women made leather bags for storage too, decorating them with painted patterns resembling tattoos, colourful weaving, beading with silver and coloured "seed" beads and appliquéd textile and tassels. Often, the scalloped neckbands were indigo-dyed to contrast attractively with the natural-coloured leather thong which was threaded through for closure.

The *aibah* is a leather saddlebag made for storing dates and the *daabah*, made of camel skin, stores fat or dates. The most elaborate and admired saddlebags are made in Al Hasa and Kuwait in the east. According to Dickson, "if they are well made, they must be three *shibr* and one *chaf* in width" – that is, three hand spans plus the distance between extended thumb and forefinger.

Leather and woven camel accoutrements *miraka* and *dawara*, are traditionally decorated with long pendant woollen cords and tassels. The pendants of the *mizawal* (women's saddlebag) are half as long as those on the *khurj* (men's saddlebags). Western and Najd *dawara* are also embroidered. Baby gazelle skin is used to make the *jeraab*, a small fringed bag for carrying coffee when a man is travelling alone. Pale yellow gazelle skin has a

variety of uses and some tribes once kept it solely for garments.

There are various other leather goods which form part of the traditional range of Bedouin gear: an all-leather horse-riding saddle, the *oukk*, a sheepskin used for storing clarified butter, the *madhara*, for the same purpose but made from lamb skin, the *girba*, a skin water-container made out of whole sheep's or goat's skin, *rawi*, *thilaithi* or

Above: Leather crafts are still practised on the Peninsula. This picture illustrates the usual red leather and white strip embroidery typical of the various styles of cloaks and coats worn in the Hijaz and Asir. Red leather as a trim is also worn in North Yemen. This item is a great sheepskin cloak from the Hijaz. Goatskin is also tanned.

Above: Fine embroidery on thin goatskin accompany appliquéd red cotton, painting, weaving and beadwork to embellish this apron. It is possibly designed for the chest of a horse or camel, although there are records of a style of leather apron worn by the Bedouin.

Left: Designs painted with indigo resemble tattoo on this Asir Province cloak.

minun, camel-skin water-containers, and *dalu*, small leather buckets used for drawing water from wells.

A purse and belt fashioned from leather were unearthed at Faw and it is ascertained that they belong to the period between the first and third centuries AD, suggesting that the craft was established on the Arabian Peninsula at that time. There is, however, the possibility that the items were imported by the Greeks and Romans who had penetrated the vicinity at that time.

Knitting is an ancient method for constructing a textile, as is knotting, netting, braiding, plaiting and weaving. Centuries ago sailors carried the techniques to all points around the known world. The Bedouin shoe, *zarabil*, with the knitted anklet, shows the intricacies of a technique commonly known in the West as jacquard. This complicated technique involves interweaving one or more threads of additional colours to create designs. It is also known as "Fairisle" because this Scottish Island is now famous for knitted garments of this type. The islanders received their knowledge centuries ago from shipwrecked sailors from Muslim lands who are believed to have taken it from southern Arabia.

On most of the available examples of Peninsular knitting, cotton yarn has been used, and the most decorative have plain bands of different colours and triangular-shaped "jacquard" patterns. The triangle was a familiar craft motif in Arabia and once had amuletic connotations – in ancient times it was considered powerfully prophylactic.

The weaving of dried palm fronds is another skilled craft, especially in the regions along the western coastline. Palm craft industries occur at places where there are oases, such as Medina which is particularly blessed with fine palm groves.

Rural men of the Hijaz make rope, *habl*, and brooms, *jarid al nakhil*, from palm branches. Hats, generally called *tafash*, worn by farmers and peasants, are made in several distinctive shapes in various parts of Arabia. The style defines the wearer's *dirah*, or tribal area. Rural women use palm leaves to weave *fraash* (also known as *khasaf* and *hasir*) matting, *znabeel*, palm-frond baskets and *sufra*, large palm-frond table mats. Men in Wadi Fatimah of western Arabia make *hasir*, matting, and weave *marwaha*, flag-shaped fans out of palm fronds.

Coconut fibre is used instead of palm fibre in the south to make pads for use under camel saddles. Also, in the south-west and south, the Bedouin crush the leaves of the *suf*, a species of Palmetto tree which grows in small thickets, to obtain fibre for plaiting into rope.

In the Arabian Gulf the palm tree was exploited in the past as a source of material for crafts. Ribs of palm branches were used to make *hadhra*, a kind of fish trap and a small boat the *huwairiyah* which held one adult and two children. This boat is constructed from date stems tied tightly together with date palm fibre.

While it is accepted that the various Arabian life-styles have remained constant through the centuries, the inherent nature of many early crafted items has not allowed the modern world to learn much about them. Pottery shards and gold jewellery present the exceptions. Textiles and other garment materials perish easily. Recent Saudi excavations, however, have brought forth enlightening information. At Faw, evidence of early weaving has been unearthed. Faw, situated in south-western Arabia, was an important staging post for caravans to the Arabian Gulf and flourished from the fourth century BC until shortly before Islam.

Palm-frond crafts abound wherever there are plenty of palms in the western regions of the Arabian Peninsula. The most attractive and useful items are hats – each style conveying to which region it belongs. This facet of Arabian costume alone could provide an interesting study. The medium is rarely woven entirely in its natural colour and the patterns created with the dyed material are tasteful and attractive. Baskets, mats, fans, tablemats and sandals are still woven.

In the Eastern regions, the palm was also once exploited. Palm fronds woven into hats offer excellent protection from the sun. The style shown at the top is said to be worn by fishermen at Bait Wella, a town near Yanbu. The central hat and basket are from Jizan. The style shown at the bottom is the most commonly seen although the crown does vary in height. It is common to the Tihama of the Asir Province but also found in most town souqs today.

Textiles

Weaving textiles dates back to antiquity. It is not known exactly when man began to weave but there are cave pictures from about 5000 BC, which show primitive looms. This great craft is basically a technique of working together two sets of elements at more or less right angles. The process is made easier by stretching one set on a frame called a loom. This first set of threads, the warp, is held by tension between two end rods, and the interlacing cross-threads are the weft – together they form a textile.

The word "textile" comes from *textere*, to weave, although it also refers to fabric which is knitted, looped, knotted, or otherwise interlaced. Textile is the most appropriate description for the material used in the making of traditional Arabian costumes, as the word specifically refers to woven fibres, which are the basis of these garments.

Fibres for weaving can be animal, vegetable or man-made. In the case of traditional garments of the past, most locally woven textiles were animal fibre. Cotton was mostly imported, usually already in yardage, although small amounts of home-grown cotton were woven for local consumption.

In surrounding countries, various other materials are used to make garments. In Africa barkcloth is common and in other Middle Eastern lands felt is manufactured. In the past, felt garments were worn in Arabia as part of traditional costume, but there is no record of it having been made on the Peninsula or used by local tailors. Weaving, on the other hand, was and still is done on the Peninsula, although the craft is diminishing.

The women of Arabia once spun, dyed and wove textiles for clothing. Weaving was among the domestic skills expected of an Arabian wife long ago. The textiles she produced were generally for her immediate use and solely for her family, although occasionally tent strips were sold, just as any surplus of *souf*, sheep's wool or goat hair, and *wabar* camel hair was usually sold.

Very few ancient textiles survive – some which do, owe their existence to the protection of tombs. The Egyptian tombs in particular had conditions very favourable for the safe-keeping of textiles. They were cool and dark with an even temperature and humidity – and the air was unpolluted. Some of the burial garments unearthed from tombs disintegrated when exposed to outside conditions. So far, few textile remains have been discovered in Arabia, although a stone spindle of the Ubaid Period, 4300–3500 BC, was discovered in the Eastern Province, linking the southern Mesopotamian Ubaid civilization with Arabia, and confirming that weaving was practised on the Arabian Peninsula in very ancient times.

The first use of textiles for clothing no doubt occurred when man first learnt to weave. This would seem to be borne out by the fact that the earliest costumes consisted of one or more lengths of cloth draped around the body. Early garments relied on strategic knotting; proper tailoring (wherein cloth was torn and sewn to fit the body) came much later.

Protection against the elements was probably the primary reason for clothing. Perhaps the desire for modesty followed. Archaeological evidence suggests that apart from technical ingenuity, early man applied artistic skill to produce his textiles. There are wall paintings and decorations on pottery which show that everyday clothes in ancient Babylonia were decorated with coloured patterns. Balls of coloured wools, dating back to 2000 BC, were found in Egyptian tombs.

Particular colours, decorative embellishments and certain shapes may have had prestige value in ancient times just as they do in some primitive lands today. Certain clothes in such societies generally distinguish the wearer as having wealth or status. Yet it is always possible for a relatively poor man to own one costly garment that is reserved for special occasions.

Garments in history have often had a political or ritual significance. Tribes and members of sub-tribes could be distinguished by garments of different styles and with individual embellishment. The colours of materials and embellishments were also often amuletic or otherwise significant. In the Middle East, blue was worn to guard against the Evil Eye and, in Africa, red is is associated with success, for instance.

Textiles have always been a marketable com-

Above: *Appliquéd velvet palm trees cover the ground textile – a fine black tulle. This particular garment is of spectacular proportions and possibly used up the entire bolt of custom-made fabric.*

Above: *Gold floss silk on cerise silk marquisette forms the under-arm gusset of a Najdi woman's thawb. Scimitars float between a sea of foliage, palm trees and crescent and star motifs.*

Left: *A wreath cups an emblem of crossed swords and crossed flags surmounted by a palm tree. These textiles are said to be Indian.*

modity, subject to extensive trade. In Africa some cloths were woven specifically for use as currency. At one time in Sierra Leone, cloths of a particular size could be used for paying court fines. They have also formed part of treasure and during the Middle Ages, European hand-made textiles headed the list of valuables in wills and inventories. Today collectors eagerly seek home-spun Bedouin dresses.

For spinning, Bedouin women and children pull wool from sheep, hair from goats and occasionally hair from camels, and collect pieces caught by shrubs where animals have rubbed or scratched.

Spinning (the general term for any assemblage of fibres which has been made into a continuous strand suitable for weaving) transforms raw fibres into yarn. Today, Arabian spindles, *maghzal* or *mubrah*, are usually housed in the women's portion of the tent where womenfolk spin camel's hair or sheep's wool. Bedouin women throughout Arabia also spin as they walk while tending sheep in the desert – their spindles forever whirring, whether on the march or on camel back.

It is a strangely stirring sight to see a Bedouin woman spinning and weaving – initially producing yarn from rough sheep's wool and goat hair and later weaving it into *gumaash* on a primitive loom. Perhaps it is this creation of the textile and its subsequent basic application as a body covering which evokes profound admiration for home-spun textiles. And, it has novelty value in this modern mechanized world.

Sheep's wool is the most common fibre used in Arabian weaving although tents made from goat hair are considered superior in that they are stronger, thicker and more durable. Sometimes sheep's wool and goat hair are mixed to make tents. Camel hair is rarely used.

Wool is divided into two categories – "harder" longer fibres that are kept for spinning warp yarn and "softer", shorter, crinkly fibres that make up the weft yarn. Before spinning, the wool is washed in clear water if possible and left for three days. During this time the wool will increase in volume due to its inherent qualities. Then, with two long-toothed combs, warp wool is drawn, one raking from the other until sufficient wool is combed to make a spindle-shaped sausage. This process is repeated. The resulting sausages are steamed prior to mounting them one by one on a distaff or stick. The drawing out process of spinning follows, producing a continuous strand from distaff to spindle.

Weft yarn is not combed but carded – a process consisting of scraping with two spiked "bats". This produces a pad of fibres on each card. These are divided in half and the four pieces joined to form a ribbon. After the process has been repeated many times, the long ribbon is spun into continuous weft yarn. Wool fibres are usually dyed before being woven.

According to Shirley Kay, local natural dyes were used in the past, although they were confined to yellows, reds and browns. On the other hand, Nabila Bassam, a patron of Bedouin weaving, believes that dyes were always imported. Investigation reveals that Bedouin women did make dyestuffs from local products and also

purchased imported natural and chemical dyes from the Bedouin markets. Imported dyes were more costly than those produced locally and, therefore, were probably used sparingly.

In the south of Arabia, the juice of a desert shrub, the *abal*, was employed to obtain a soft russet-brown colour, once favoured by the Bedouin for their garments. This is *Calligonum comosum* of the *Polygonaceae* family. Saffron was popularly used as a dye in the past in the eastern regions and cotton is still dyed to a rich yellow with saffron in the south-west. Saffron comes from *Crocus sativus*, which does not grow in Arabia. It is found in Mediterranean regions and exported in powdered form.

Various plants that grow in Arabia are known to provide dyes. From the Madder family, *Rubiaceae*, to which the coffee plant belongs, many members provide a red dye. *Gallium* and *Papaver* (a poppy) both provide red dye and grow on the Arabian Peninsula. It is likely that the Bedouin exploited these fully in the past, for it is well known they make good use of most locally grown herbs and plants.

The most extensively used dye in traditional Arabia was indigo. It is obtained from several plants of the *Genus indigofera*. *Indigofera tinctoria* now called *Indigofera articulata* grows in central

Below: Royal purple marquisette, laced with gold metal thread or floss silk forming dazzling motifs, is commonly employed as an under-arm gusset for the Najdi tulle thawb worn by women. Other popular colours are cerise and parrot green. An oasis and crossed swords alternate with garlands of flowers and enormous rosettes. Ottoman brocades were well-known for rosettes. The 16th century was the golden age of Turkish textiles and large motifs such as these were popular then.

Left: The crescent and star are occasionally seen alone as a motif on textiles produced for the Central Arabian black tulle thawb.

Arabia, and possibly in other places throughout the Peninsula. Imported Indian and African indigo dye balls are, however, readily available in Bedouin market places. Indigo is regarded as giving the most permanent dye for both red and blue colours. Red is obtained from indigo by slow oxidation in an acid medium, and blue by rapid oxidation in an alkaline medium. Although the process of reduction and deoxidation of a glucoside, called indican, are recorded to have originated in India, it was also known to the ancient Egyptians. Mummies dating back to before 5000 BC, were wound in fabrics that had been dyed with indigo. Ideally, indigo is made from fresh green leaves. The plant's leaves are first pounded in a mortar and the resulting pulp is formed into balls which are dried in the sun for two or three days during which time the fermentation process begins. The alkaline medium is obtained from the ash of burned green wood or bought in the markets. Soaked in water, the potash produces a liquid which not only draws off indigo blue from the dye balls but serves as a mordant for fixing the colour. The alkaline fluid is left to rest three days before use. The number of indigo balls used determines the strength of colour. The dye keeps for only five days, but ideally each dipping is done in a new dye mixture.

The yarn or textile being dyed will be dipped three or four times for approximately two minutes. The article is then dried in the sun. At first it is a green colour but this deepens to blue quite rapidly. The finished cloth was customarily beaten and, as it was steeped in dye, a metallic sheen would emerge on the beaten surface. This side is used as the "right" side of a finished garment, although the gloss is lost when the textile is washed. The textile is so laden with indigo that merely touching the shiny surface will turn the tips of the fingers blue. It is interesting to see that Bedouin women in Arabia today, who still wear traditional dress, select a satin-finished black cotton textile that closely resembles the beaten indigo cloth of the past.

Many natural and synthetic dyes have for centuries come to Arabia from India: blue and blue/black from *Indigofera articulata*; red from the Madder family of plants (*Rubiaceae*) – especially the member *Rubia tinctorum*; yellow from Wild Rhubarb or Chursta; green could be made in Arabia by treating copper filings with milk; red, pink and reddish-violet from *Cochineal* and *Indigo fera*. In the past many dyes also came from Africa. Most of these dyes were not colour-fast.

Both India and Africa once used only natural products for creating their many colours. It is recorded that in India, at the time of the Mughals, over three hundred beautiful and colour-fast colours were in use by the shawl makers of Kashmir. By the beginning of the nineteenth century the number had dwindled to sixty-four, but now that synthetic dyes have taken over, offering a wide range of hues, tints and shades, the number of dyes available is once more in the hundreds. These brilliant colours, although of doubtful permanence, are much easier to use.

It is recorded that in the mid-nineteenth century, dyeing cloth was an important local trade in Jeddah, and indigo was the most commonly employed dyestuff, accounting for historical reference to Arabian Bedouin dresses as dark blue or blue-black. Dyes and dyestuffs have been known to the Arabs for centuries. In fact, analine (the critical ingredient in textile dyeing) was introduced to Europe by Arab merchants.

Technically, yarn for dyeing should be mordanted first of all. Mordant is the agent used to fix colour. Afterwards the dye is applied. Mordanting, however, is not generally carried out by the Bedouin and is not in fact always necessary, because some dyestuffs such as indigo serve to some extent to fix colour by themselves, as explained previously.

Much yarn woven in Arabia is untreated by dyestuffs. This is perhaps why weaving is considered the most traditional Arabian craft. It is an essential skill needed to build a home suitable for nomadic life in inhospitable lands where wool is the most readily available natural building resource.

The great hand-loomed Bedouin tents, *khaima*, or *bayt al shaar*, are generally woven from the hair and wool of *ghanam*, goats and sheep. A combination produces a black-brown colour. Goat hair alone is the most popular because it is thicker, more durable and is a handsome jet-black. It is

Below: Saffron is used as a dyestuff in Arabia. In Yemen, commercial mills now produce bold-coloured printed textiles such as this scarf. The rich saffron yellow is popular with the local people who favour colours close to those that are traditional.

here that the Bedouin weaver's craft shows the most endurance. These heavy tents are constructed from relatively narrow strips known as *filjan* which are approximately sixty-eight centimetres wide – the width of the loom determined by a comfortable arm's span for the weaver. It is interesting that the tents which are always made by the womenfolk actually belong to them, and they take responsibility for erecting and dismantling them.

Women sit on the ground to weave as this is the most comfortable and advantageous position. It is heavy work to operate a Bedouin hand-loom, known as *mattarih* or *nattu* – and the finished product depends on physical strength as well as skill. The *mattarih* consists of a few bars of wood which nomadic women easily and cleverly dismantle. They take only the essential parts on treks. Once set up, the loom is long and narrow. The weaver attaches the warp threads to two end rods, each tied to an end beam pegged down to the ground. Between the beams, the warp threads are gathered over a central rod, the heddle, which is held up above the threads by being lodged on stones or other objects. The shed stick is inserted between the threads on one side and a wooden beater on the other.

The weft yarn is wound around a stick spool which acts as a *misha*, shuttle. This is passed between the raised threads and the weaver presses each row of wool into place with the rod *natha* – and using a *middrah*, a pick made of gazelle horn.

Bedouin women also weave *khidre*, carpets and other tent strips such as the back curtain section, *ruwag*, and the *gata* which curtains off the *hareem* (from the root *haram*, meaning "sacred" or "set apart" and, by extension, the room where women live).

Beautiful tribal patterns are often woven into these dividing curtains. The *ruwag*, back curtain, is generally plain brown or black if the Bedouin is poor, while the tents of the rich display handsome black and white *ruwag*. The *gata* is made in sections with one end section specially decorated with tasselled edging. If the tent opening is altered to catch the breeze or shut out blowing sand, the end sections are also reversed to display the decoration to the new tent front.

Other woven items include *idl*, women's camel bags, and *mizuda* for men, as well as other camel trappings. Rope is also made from *ghanam* wool and hair. Sailors along the eastern coastline once wove sail cloth in winter. Throughout the Gulf area many villagers and townspeople still weave textiles from imported cotton for clothing.

When a Bedouin woman could afford it, imported textiles were used to make garments for the family. This was often simple, unbleached calico which she would dye herself. Charles Doughty, the intrepid English explorer of the nineteenth century wrote that he was once invited to be a salesman in Kheybar – at the summer market – "to sit at a stall of mantles and kerchiefs, to measure out cubits of calico for the silver of the poor Bedouin". Although not all Bedouin dressed in coarse calico, Doughty recorded that it was their custom "to venture forth in their worst clothing for fear of forays". Undoubtedly, therefore, calico had a good market in the past.

Black satin-finished cotton has now replaced dyed calico for the average Bedouin woman's dress textile. Men, instead of unbleached calico, generally wear white cotton with a percentage of synthetic fibre. Occasionally satin replaces the satin-finished cotton and sometimes velvet is used. The textile was customarily black although, today, bright colours are also common.

Since multi-coloured textiles became easy to obtain, dark-coloured textiles have generally been reserved for elderly women, except, of course, in areas where black is still the traditional base cloth. In such cases it can be seen that the wearer is either poor or she holds the belief that black is correct and still the best foil for the colourful traditional embellishment.

Solid textiles of a good weight are worn by nomadic and semi-nomadic Bedouin women. Obviously this is because they are not transparent in sunlight; nor do they cling readily or fly up with the slightest breeze. Also, a well-chosen textile offers the most protection against the elements, especially if the woman cannot afford many layers of clothing.

Today, the textiles used to make Middle Eastern garments are generally factory-woven. Amongst the hand-made range of the past and these commercially produced fabrics, is felt. Felt has been made by Middle Eastern nomads in the past for mats mostly, but it has also been used for garments. Felt is still a popular medium in Iran and ready-made garments from there and Syria have been worn throughout Arabia for centuries. King Abd-al Aziz Ibn Saud, the founder of the Kingdom of Saudi Arabia, often wore imported felt waistcoats, jackets and coats – and garments tailored from imported weaves.

Orientals specialized from the earliest times in fabulous weaves for which men braved a multitude of hazards to acquire. Along the trade routes from east to west, travelled textiles with exotic patterns both woven and embroidered. These included closely woven muslin which was sometimes printed, interwoven silk and gold textiles,

Below: Locally produced and imported cotton are woven commercially in Yemen. The careless, splashy printing and dyeing processes result in attractive scarves with primitive appeal.

brocades, pure silks, satins, velvets and richly embroidered fine wools. Many of these found their way into Arabia but never have they been in greater demand than now, although most are produced on power looms today.

As beautiful as modern power-loomed textiles might be, they do not compare with the original hand-spun and hand-woven art fabrics which were so laboriously made, literally inch by inch. The weaver infused a little of himself into his creation which meant, of course, that each finished product was like no other. Tailored extravagantly in central Arabian styles, these early works of art must have been breathtaking.

One very colourful sheer textile, once produced by the master weavers of India, is commonly used as the chief decoration on one traditional woman's *thawb* from central Arabia. Enormous underarm gussets, cut in colour and textile to contrast with the body of the garment, are made from a version of *jamdani*, a traditional Indian figured muslin. Of all the Indian art textiles of Dacca (in present-day Bangladesh), the most important and prized heirlooms of the past are the *jamdani*. Such floss silks are invariably made in bright hues such as blue, purple, scarlet, cerise and green, with gold sometimes embroidered into the textile during the weaving process. The most famous *jamdani* designs consist of large motifs such as rosettes.

Lengths of pretty cloth, *kiswah*, remain a popular gift in Arabia today. In ancient times, visiting royalty and tribal chiefs gave costly textiles to each other along with priceless gems and other treasure. Sophisticated fashion centres such as Damascus and Baghdad had the opportunity to trade their tailors' expertise.

In the past, typical Damascene brocades featured small motifs which were rich with gold thread. Ordinary Syrian and Arabian folk could not afford these so they chose striped cloth instead, because, although attractive, stripes are simpler to produce and therefore cheaper.

Townspeople throughout the Arabian Peninsula have for centuries been able to choose from a wide range of textiles – each type available in many qualities. Whether rich or poor, settled Arabians could select almost any colour and pattern and visually, there could be a superficial equality to garments if only for a brief time – the cheaper materials having a relatively short life.

Rows of textile merchants' booths in *souqs* today are a spectacle of vivid colour and glitter. Even in the more sophisticated Arabian shopping areas, the merchandise is revealing in that it conveys the customers' taste for rich-looking materials, many of which are "re-embroidered" and studded with sequins, imitation pearls and diamentes.

Arabia's history is entwined with the early evolution of the textile trade. It was Arab traders who first took the secrets of cotton cultivation from India to North Africa and Spain. Several textiles used in the West today take their names from Middle Eastern places. For example muslin is derived from Mosul (Iraq) and damask from Damascus (Syria).

For special occasions, Arabian women for centuries have selected the most transparent textiles available. These *thawbs* which have a floating quality are worn as "throw-over" garments – a top layer. This unique clothing concept follows the traditional, practical Arabian layering format. It adds to this an imaginative and clever design facet that allows rich embellishment to be visible on two layers. It also creates an alluring appearance for the wearer.

Tulle is popular, especially traditional black which looks particularly handsome with the addition of a gold and silver woven yoke and sequined cuff trim. Within the sheer range, festive finery is also created in marquisette, georgette, organza and silk. Chiffon, in either pure silk or synthetic, is a favourite with the rich. In fact, silk of all weights was considered a highly desirable textile among the women of traditional Arabia. Certainly it is the most costly. Georg August Wallin writes that strict

Islamic teaching in the mid-nineteenth century, enjoined men not to wear a textile with more than one-half silk when praying. In fact, silk has been considered an unsuitable cloth for men in the past and women were once constrained to wear it only on special occasions.

Sheer cotton textiles are big sellers on the Arabian Peninsula. Gauze and muslin had a great market as they were traditionally used for baby clothes and face veils. Gauze forms a major part of the traditional costume of Hijazi townswomen, as does muslin. Both are excellent materials for Arabian garments as they are light, absorbent, launder easily and dry quickly. Muslin was also used to back some textiles which were to be embroidered and beaded.

Seventeenth-century records show that the average East Indian sea cargoes included enormous amounts of fine cotton cloth, cotton thread, "Tessel" thread for high-quality tapestries, brocade or very rare gold-thread cloths, chintz, Japanese dresses, Bengal silk, Persian light silk and indigo. These commodities regularly passed along the Red Sea route.

Records of Jeddah imports in the mid-nineteenth century reveal that usually at least half the value of the merchandise was in textiles. Arab vessels also brought ready-made dresses, felts,

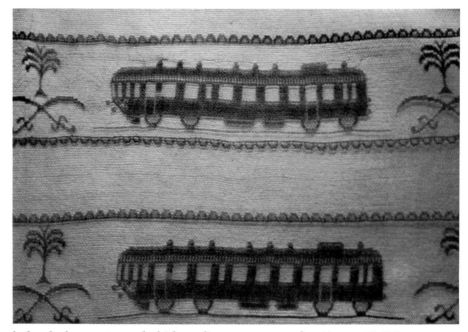

haberdashery, tanned hides, linen, raw and refined cotton cloths, silk, satin, printed cloths, gold drapes, gold thread, hemp fabrics and cotton seeds. Jeddah exports included veils, indigo, madder, henna, date-palm cordage and canvas. Indian percale, *rhassab*, came from both Calcutta and Bombay while silk and brocaded muslin was shipped in from Calcutta, along with common Indian cloths. Variegated headcloths of silk and cotton reached Jeddah from Basrah while imitation Kashmiri shawls came from Persia. Yemen sent canvas and rope in *agave* fibres as well as the fibre itself. Commerce summaries of nineteenth-century Jeddah show that export merchandise predominantly included *milaaya* (cotton mantles for women), textiles, shawls of muslin brocaded with silk and smuggled Kashmiri shawls. Threads for prayer

Above: *Of all the strange textile motifs used for Arabian women's gowns, this is perhaps the most curious. At this point, no one has an explanation for why a railway carriage should appear interspersed with the Saudi Arabian emblem which is cupped by a wreath. It may have been designed to commemorate the Hijaz railway or the tulle may have been requested for "a dress with a train" as indeed was its fate. See details of tulle thawb, Najd.*

beads were also exported.

Most of Jeddah's merchandise was shipped to Suez and sold in Cairo from where it found its way to the Mediterranean. Incoming goods were sold in the Hijaz. Sometimes Egypt paid in silver plus sequins. Large quantities were destined for India. Many of these sparkling gold appliqués were intended for the decoration of textiles and garments that would be worn by Arabian women.

The textiles used to make Arabian women's festive occasion *thawbs* are often quite remarkable. Curious motifs may often be seen on them. Many textile manufacturers around the world agree to supply individual motifs if the order is no less than one bolt of cloth (approximately thirty-five metres). The average black tulle *thawb* is made from almost that much yardage, so it is likely that the unique motifs are a result of Arabian women placing special orders.

One Najd tulle *thawb* displays a repeated black velvet palm tree motif. Another features an open wreath, cupping the Saudi emblem. Another is interesting in that it combines the emblem with the crescent and star. Often the latter motif appears alone. By far the most intriguing pattern is one where the Saudi emblem is alternated with a railway carriage. Perhaps the manufacturers of the textile were requested to add a train in commem-

oration of the Hijaz Railway. It is also possible that the yardage was required for a dress with a train (the trailing back hemline style) which, of course, it was.

The enormous underarm gussets which have become an important design element in traditional ladies' costume, are yet another place where astonishing motifs may be found. These gussets are invariably cut from a textile contrasting in both colour and texture and usually the motifs are worked in gold metallic thread. The most odd organza gussets show gold swords with flowers; the most interesting has stars and crescents plus the Saudi emblem, and the most amusing incorporates aeroplanes with a mixture of palm trees, swords and flowers. This chubby aeroplane appears regularly as a motif on Arabian gowns and is

Above: Embellished sleeve edging on a Najdi tulle thawb *is usually sequined. This rare example is embroidered – the motifs are crossed swords and an intriguing aeroplane.*

variously interpreted by the weaver or embroiderer as a bi-plane, a double-decker passenger plane and something similar to the Sunderland flying boat. Possibly the latter is accurate as this passenger-mail aircraft stopped at Dubai and Basra en route to the Far East in the forties and may have been seen.

Logically, the desire for individual textile motifs would seem to spring from the earliest times when traditional dresses were totally hand-made. Arabian women would embroider their gowns with motifs that symbolized things that were important to them in their immediate world.

Top: Textile motifs seen on Arabian women's dresses are full of surprises. It appears that the makers developed patterns strictly for the Arabian market. Gold floss silk and metal-thread form curious motifs such as oases, single palms, crossed swords, crowns, crescents, stars and national emblems. This picture shows a bi-plane that captured the imagination of weavers and embroiderers in both India and the Arabian Peninsula. See also page 50.

Tailoring

In the ancient world, human beings did not wear properly sewn or cut garments but merely wrapped hand-woven textiles around their bodies, or knotted them securely in place. In the earliest times animal skins were worn in much the same way. In fact, decorative fringes on some early textile garments have been hypothesized as an indication that the original styles were fashioned from skins – the fringes created to resemble fur. There is little doubt that fur was the first medium used for garments but it is unlikely that early weavers would consider hemming an untailored garment.

Ancient Arabian emigrants to Egypt wore loin-cloths, a fashion shared with Egypt, Mediterranean countries and the Levant at that time. Cloaks were also amongst the earliest forms of body covering and they perhaps persisted in Arabia to modern times because they were eminently suited to the land and life-styles. The custom of tying the mantle and sleeve lappet ends in a knot is very ancient and still exists on the Peninsula. Many Arabian rural cloaks are traditionally affixed across the neck by a chain attached at each shoulder; this fashion echoes ancient Rome.

Shirts with holes for arms are said to have come westward only after Egypt had close contact with Asia, and other tailored garments are supposed to have appeared then also. It is known that early Persians wore gowns with long, pointed sleeves and Assyrians wore headcloths wrapped like turbans and knee-length tunics with skin cloaks. Early Greeks wore a costume which consisted of unsewn pieces of textile. This was also customary in Babylonian antiquity, in Africa and in India – and in Arabia today.

It is not known at what point garments began to be sewn together on the Arabian Peninsula. Future archaeological excavations may reveal the complete history of Arabian tailoring. So far, only fragments of cloth and needles have been unearthed. Amongst other micro-artifacts, one copper needle, *ibra*, has been found at Tarut island in the Arabian Gulf. Tarut artifacts belong to both the Hellenic period and earlier in the third millennium BC. It is possible the needle came from the older civilization of Dilmun when it commanded the sea trade of the Gulf. Tarut was a trade centre for Dilmun, especially important because of the land routes which radiated westward from that point. At Faw in south-west Najd, excavations have brought forth a number of bronze, brass and iron needles as well as decoratively woven cloth. These items belong to a period between the first and third centuries AD.

Below: *Attention is drawn to the design features of an Arabian dress. The most obvious segment as a rule, is the under-arm gusset which sometimes measures one square inch in a garment that does not require such a component.*

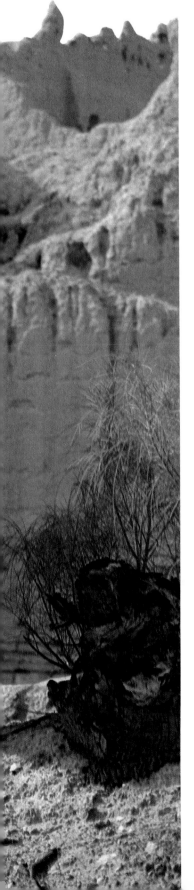

This Najdi tulle **thawb** *is an overgrown* **kaftan** *where the under-arm gusset has been enlarged many times to match the rest of the garment's pattern pieces. Furthermore, it is a vivid-coloured, gold-embroidered marquisette.*

Traditional Arabian hand-seaming is strong as it involves sewing at least twice – once to join the two sections together, and the second to tuck in the raw edges. Basically it is a technique similar to flat seaming, also known as flatfell, except that it is done inside out. The raw edges are placed together with one layer protruding slightly (as in grading) and both raw edges and stitches appear on the inside of the garment. The two parts are joined with backstitch. The second row of stitching is oversewing, carried out on the inside of the garment after the raw edges are turned in, the protruding layer folded over and under the lower layer. No attempt is made to disguise the back of this oversewing which runs parallel with the seam on the right side of the garment; on the contrary – it seems to be an embellishment. Sometimes a third decorative row of colourful silk oversewing is worked on the right side. This creates a ridge along the seam. Necklines are faced and hemmed as a rule and hems are turned up and hemmed.

In 1854, according to Charles Didier, there were four tailors in Jeddah proper, and there were many others in surrounding districts. One of the four within the city was the court tailor who exercised authority and influence over the other three. Although all four men catered to the citizens, garments were mostly hand-sewn in the home by the womenfolk.

It is said that an Arab girl's practical education began when she was taught how to make traditional garments. For a town girl in olden times, wielding scissors, *mugass*, was as important as spinning and weaving were to her desert sisters. The nimble fingers of mothers in town and country passed tailoring skills on to daughters and styles worn by their ancestors were adhered to zealously.

An Arab bride once took an active part in sewing and embroidering her trousseau and customarily displayed her handiwork on the eve of the wedding for the inspection of the bridegroom's friends and relations. New clothes are an important part of a tribal girl's dowry, which otherwise consists of jewellery and household effects.

Colonel Dickson writes that women who lived in the remote desert regions made most of their own clothes. "They possess no scissors or thread (*khaid*) but tear up the cloth using their teeth, and then sew with thread taken out of the cloth". When making a *thawb* or *kaftan*, the tailor measured the height of the subject with the material. This length was doubled. Other measurements were taken from the nose to the fingertips with an outstretched arm using the yardage. Small measurements were marked on the material by repeating a *shibr* and *chaf*.

Imported needles and thread have long been available to most Arabian women which explains why so many became adept at fine needlework. For centuries, Arabian townswomen received such things as scissors and thimbles from Europe through the port of Jeddah and tailoring aids from other lands through eastern ports.

While tailoring used to be a woman's preserve on the Arabian Peninsula, foreign men, mostly from Pakistan, have now set up shops throughout the land and taken over. Many women still make their own garments and those for their immediate families, but hand-sewing is rarely practised today. The sewing machine has even found its way into Bedouin tents, and camels really have something to groan about now under this additional burden.

Despite the advent of the sewing machine, traditional cut persists. Once a tribe established its style of dress, a strong sense of traditionalism saw womenfolk repeat the pattern. The loom width, initially limiting the textile width, necessitated panelling – an approach to construction surely perpetuated by custom. This theory is borne out by the fact that this design facet persisted when wider textiles were readily available.

All ethnic costumes on the Arabian Peninsula are multi-panelled garments. The most intriguing, so far as tailoring is concerned, comes from the heartland, the Najd. There in central Arabia, the women developed a style from the basic *kaftan* to suit their specific needs – just as the great hand-loomed Bedouin tents were designed to insulate, give shade and catch a breeze, so do these enormous Najdi *thawbs*. Strangely, this style of dress still features an underarm gusset (an essential part of a slim-fitting *kaftan*) but in the voluminous, billowing gowns, a gusset serves no useful function. It would appear that the tailors kept the design element because it was an established part of the original *kaftan*. They merely enlarged this pattern segment in proportion to the other magnified component parts. The result is a unique and spectacular garment.

It could be said that, as a design element, the underarm gusset is the most predominant feature of the central Arabian traditional women's *thawb*. It is invariably cut from cloth contrasting in both colour and textile to the base textile and is generally embellished with braid, embroidery, or sequins – and sometimes the gusset exhibits all three mediums together. Even in the other regions of Greater Arabia, the underarm gusset is notable – either for size or embellishment, or both.

Embroidery

Embroidery, *mugassab*, is ornamental stitchery usually worked with a hand-held pointed needle with a thread through its eye (the hole at one end) on a ground (base) material. Embroidery is a creative, expressive craft with intellectual demands similar to those of painting. It is considered to be one step from drawing. The Romans described it as "painting with a needle". Psychologists believe it is therapeutic. Both men and women throughout history have earned their livelihood at needlework. In relatively recent times men and women have engaged in needlework as an art form rather than as a utilitarian necessity.

The art of needlework must be as old as civilization itself. The simplest form was born when stout grasses or gut were threaded through holes in pelts. The holes would have been poked with a splinter of bone or a thorn. It is a craft whereby colour and design can be introduced into the home, and in most countries, it is traditionally recognized as a woman's preserve. For a woman with many children, in olden times, embroidery was a life-line, offering respite from dull household tasks. Beyond that, it was an expression of the innate human yearning for beauty and a triumph of the human spirit.

It is unlikely that the nomadic women of old Arabia were consciously aware of any of these facts and doubtful that the townswomen gave it thought, for needlework in traditional Arabia was an activity so deeply embedded in day-to-day life that it was carried out as automatically as cooking. In the olden days, Arab women took pride in this accomplishment because it afforded them enjoyment as well as great personal satisfaction. Their daughters were taught the rudiments of embroidery at an early age, and took an active part in embellishing their own bridal trousseaux.

Almost all Arabian garments in the past were embroidered by hand. Restrained self-coloured embroidery was worked on menswear and underwear for both sexes. Townswomen often embroidered outer garments with gold and silver while nomadic women and villagers used brightly coloured threads. More recently, since the introduction of the Cornely sewing machine, machined embroidery embellishes the clothing of Peninsula people.

The overall effect of Arabian embroidery is rich yet harmonious and the selection of coloured threads ornamenting old costumes confirm the Arab taste for polychromatic decoration. Embroidered women's costumes are basically composed of strong textiles which lend themselves well to this vividly-hued embellishment. The Bedouin's unique combinations of predominantly primary colours with some secondary colours are particularly lively and attractive, especially so because they are generally used against a blackish ground cloth.

The extensive plain surfaces of Arabia's traditional outer garments allow embroiderers excellent opportunities to show their skill. Yet, despite the fact that there are flat panels available at front and back, the whole lengths of the sleeves, as well

as necklines, wrists and hem, it can be seen that, traditionally, the various territorial regions of the Peninsula show different placement emphasis, unique to each area. In fact, one dress from the north restricts embroidery to the bodice and sleeves. This can be seen also on some dresses in neighbouring Najd. In the south of the Peninsula, although all edges might be worked, generally only the front centre panel is embroidered heavily. Eastern regions always feature the neckline, hemline and sleeve cuffs – and any additional work falls predominantly within the centre panel at the front. In the Hijaz, the yoke and hemline are particularly heavy with decoration. Costumes of the Asir Province show the influence of both their northern and southern neighbours.

Although it can be seen that each region within Arabia has its own recognizable embroidery patterns, these vary to some extent between tribes. It is believed that even within tribes there were once distinguishing sub-tribal variations in costume embellishment. Each was a time-honoured traditional pattern that differed only in quality of execution, and the interpretation of unwritten rules for colour combination and colour placement.

Embroidery motifs are generally geometrical throughout the Arabian Peninsula, although additional stylized botanical motifs do appear on women's garments and to a minor extent in other crafted items of the northern, western and central regions of Arabia. Patterns were usually purely geometrical on menswear.

Embroidery on men's garments, which was often quite lavish in the past, is now usually limited to the neckline of the outer mantle and to one style of ceremonial jacket. Occasionally *sirwaal* ankle bands are still embroidered. The only other embellishment presently favoured on menswear is a self-coloured soutache which is sometimes employed to enhance the simple body-shirt, the *thawb*.

As embroidery on traditional Arabian costumes generally appears around the neckline and wrist edges and sometimes at the hemline and along the seams, it has been hypothesized that it might be mere practical reinforcement. While this is possible, it is not confirmed by an examination of other traditional, crafted items. For example, there appears to be a clear correlation between embroidery traditions and those pertaining to the decoration

Opposite: Ottoman occupation of the Arabian Peninsula ended with the rise of the House of Saud. Left behind were traces of Turkish influence upon costume embellishment. The Turkish pants suit of plum-coloured silk is embellished with sarma and gold braid. Cardboard shapes have been bound with gold metal-thread and then couched to the surface. The jacket is the time-honoured kaftan cut and the pants conform to the basic principles for Middle Eastern pants – straight legs join to an ample crotch gusset for comfort while sitting "tailor" fashion. The Turkish version is much fuller than that worn on the Peninsula.

Left: A close-up of a delicate use of sarma which is enhanced with vines, flowers and leaves and sprinkled with gold sequins.

on jewellery. The geometric shapes used for the ornaments are invariably enriched by various jewellery-making techniques, especially three-dimensional granulation and filigree. All techniques are habitually employed as an accent around the outer edges of the metal shapes where no reinforcement is needed. In traditional Arabian jewellery, embellished patterns never cross a shape – they always confirm it. It would seem to bear out the theory that it is the design of Arabian costumes that is being reinforced, not the edges or seams.

It is interesting to ponder why shape and form elements of dress pattern segments were originally accented with embroidery. Tradition dictates the present Arabian embroidery placement and the custom is undoubtedly one handed down through countless centuries. In the ancient world, superstitious people had all garment openings embroidered in the belief that this would keep out evil spirits; perhaps there was once a belief concerning seams in garments also.

Richly embroidered garments which are often worked with gold and silver metal thread, sometimes precious, are referred to as *mugassab*, or *mushtaghal*, meaning "embroidered", "worked" or "gussied-up". Such clothes are mostly worn at celebrations. Old Arabian everyday costumes are often elaborately worked, too, but with cotton and silk threads. Embroidery threads and fine needles have been available to Arabian townswomen for centuries which accounts for the development of fine needlepoint. The quality varies, of course, from hand to hand. There is often an enormous discrepancy in skill between the embroidery and the sewing on a Bedouin garment. This indicates, perhaps, that the work has been carried out by two different people. Possibly one or more members of a family or tribe does the embroidery for their group while each wearer stitches her own dress together.

There are no records of market tailors in the past producing embroidered sections and panels for dresses, as they sometimes do now and as was often the case in other Middle Eastern countries. But, there are references to Arabian townspeople seeking the services of an embroiderer for wedding garments. It is also recorded that Bedouin women customarily sell off a surplus of homespun yarn and woven items, raising the question of whether some tribal women, skilled in embroidery, sell their work.

Attractive multi-coloured, hand embroidery showing great skill used to be carried out in central Arabia and in the south, but the work from the west, west-central and north-western parts of the Peninsula is superior. This is possibly the result of being close to the relatively sophisticated Hijazi cities of Mecca, Medina and Jeddah.

While all Arabian embroidery is beautiful, the finest examples of Bedouin needlepoint come from Northern Arabia, close to the Central and Western Arabia. This close-worked, multi-coloured embellishment – against a ruby-coloured base cloth – takes on the warm look of tapestry (the deep red colour may be an imitation of Indigo red). It is on this traditional gown that the neatest and most skilled Arabian needlepoint is consistently seen.

The work is especially clever on the underarm gussets which exhibit such exquisite workmanship that they often rival the legendary Victorian samplers. It is strange that such work appears in a place which cannot be seen when the gown is worn.

Needlework also reaches a high level of achievement in the Beni Salim tribe of Western Arabia. These mountain agriculturalists, who live between Tayif and Medina, embellish dresses and camel trappings alike with distinctive designs, enhancing their handiwork further with colourful pendants made up of woven strips and tassels incorporating tiny silver beads.

The stitches used by Bedouin women living in remote regions present some surprises. Many are remarkably similar to traditional Western and

Above: The tailors of Tayif have evolved the traditional dress of the Asir Province with the aid of the Cornely sewing machine. Long before reaching the Street of Tailors in the souq, the hum of their collective machines can be heard. Multi-coloured silk threads predominate – gold and silver metal thread is used and may have been a most recent innovation. The original dress was black cotton, and black still proves to be the best foil for the colourful stitchery.

In the middle of the 19th century, American inventors developed the sewing machine, perhaps based on one made in London in the previous century. The first domestic sewing machine was marketed by Singer in New York shortly afterwards. Machines that could produce embroidery followed quickly in Europe and America. Hand needlework declined as a result. To take its place, machine embroidery became a creative activity both commercially and at home. Possibly the first sewing machines to reach Arabia arrived in the homes of the rich in the Hijaz as a result of being closely linked to the sophisticated Ottoman Empire. These early machines were hand-operated and the treadle type was available, according to the discarded models to be found in the Riyadh antiques souq.

Indian embroidery stitches, although the Arab versions are more sophisticated. How women living in remote pockets of Arabia came to use certain stitches is a rich subject for conjecture. Tribal women probably perpetuate ancient work and it is unlikely they had contact with India. It is possible the stitches went to India with Islam – or even earlier by way of Arabs who traded with India long before Islam. The transfer could have happened later, long after Islam had reached into India, when the Mughal rulers (who were Muslims) ran huge embroidery *karkhanas*, or workshops. This was a time when indigenous designs were influenced by Persian and Islamic art. During this period, rich drapings for tents and pavilions were made, as well as resplendent garments for the Mughals. Thus far, only intricately woven cloth has been unearthed in Arabia by archaeologists. In time, the full embroidery story may be unravelled.

Arabian embroidery is generally characterized by a close-worked open chain stitch. It is used in straight lines or concentric rows to create and fill in motifs. Open chain stitch is the most prevalent traditional stitch and it can be seen on most old gowns. The standard chain stitch appears to have taken its place as it is worked on the more recently embroidered ethnic dresses, whether hand-done or machined. Chain stitch is a continuous line of interlocking stitches which can be of several kinds. It has a long history world-wide, and fragments of ancient chain-stitched textiles have reached the modern world from central Asia. It is recorded as being popular with the Copts of Egypt and with Islamic embroiderers (outside the Arabian Peninsula) by the tenth century. Open chain stitch is generally considered a variation of the simple chain stitch. It seems more likely, based on the evidence supplied by traditional Arabian garments, that chain stitch derived from open chain stitch. Chain stitch is worked beyond the northern borders of Saudi Arabia although cross stitch is more prevalent. It is possible that cross stitch (which is not worked on the Peninsula) took over from chain stitch in these regions.

Both forms of chain stitch are probably the most commonly employed stitches because they lend themselves best to abstract designs. Anyone who has ever done any embroidery will marvel at the regularity of some Arabian chain stitching and wonder how it could be achieved solely by hand. In fact, sometimes it may have been aided by a tambour hook, a tool similar to a cobbler's awl whereby the fabric is held taut and the thread is introduced from below and hooked through. This produces a perfect line. It is obvious, however, that Bedouin embroidery stitches have been achieved with the aid of a needle only.

Arabian women through the ages have also used other embroidery stitches, albeit to a lesser degree, these are usually reserved for design and motif borders and to fill in an area on the base cloth. Under the heading of knots and loops come two stitches commonly employed. One is the buttonhole stitch, and the other is similar to Cretan stitch, long-arm feather stitch, as well as ladder stitch. Several stitches used by Bedouin embroiderers have no exact counterparts in Western embroid-

ery. For example, Bedouin stitch *waahid* is the name given in this book to the aforementioned stitch which is very similar to ladder stitch although the ladder "steps" are interlocked as in Cretan stitch. Both sides of this stitch have "buttonhole edging". Bedouin stitch *ithnayn* is the stitch similar to both the Cretan and long-arm feather stitch, without the looped edges. Bedouin stitch *talata* refers to an open chain stitch which is threaded with two strands of another colour. *Arbaa* is threaded fly stitch. (*See* **Embroidery Stitches**.)

Cretan stitch and buttonhole stitch have an obscure origin and it has been said they evolved originally in the Middle East. These stitches may have reached the Peninsula from outside but it is unlikely. Considering the inaccessibility of tribes who use these stitches, it would seem more likely that Arabia was responsible for influencing the outside world of embroiderers.

There are stitches such as Bedouin stitch *ithnayn* which are so closely worked as to resemble satin stitch. Satin stitch in its simplest form is used in the south of the Peninsula. There are various kinds of satin stitch, again seen in early Coptic work.

Of the less exciting stitches employed by the Bedouin of Arabia, stem stitch is the most dramatically used. On one western Arabian tribal dress, closely worked rows of fine red stem stitch convert an otherwise drab dress into one that is spectacular. Blanket stitch, a type of open buttonhole stitch, is used less adventurously but edges many necklines and sleeves and gives the strength of a binding. The simple back stitch is commonly used within borders and becomes an attractive addition as it is invariably a crisp-looking white or pale yellow amongst heavy colours on a dark background. Oversewing also takes on some glamour from the colours in which it is worked. Vivid parrot green and cerise oversewing often decorates cuffs and neckline edges and finishes off seams. The simplest stitch of all is dotting or seeding. Like back stitch, it is worked in white or pale yellow and gives the finished garments a handsome appearance, confirming the embroiderer's intention of producing an artistic piece of work.

The stitch which stands out most is fly stitch. It is similarly executed in some cases to single fern stitches or single feather stitches. When it is worked in continuous lines, fly stitch *arbaa* is invariably a divider between bands of designs where two contrasting strands are threaded into the stitches. Such dividers are known as *dawwam* in Palestine. Wave or chevron stitches are employed to produce a zigzag effect. Worked singly, they create highlights. The fly stitch and highlight stitches are usually white cotton thread and the threaded strands are generally a dark-coloured silk. Most Bedouin threads are cotton, though silk is used now and again for highlighting.

The zigzag back stitch is often so finely and evenly executed that it baffles experienced embroiderers despite the simplicity of the stitch. An Arab lady tells a tale about olden times when young girls who did all the fine embroidery were married off as soon as their patience failed. This is an appealing story but unlikely as this work requires years of experience.

Herringbone stitch is generally close worked or

135

double worked and creates a border for embroidered areas, known as *dayer* in Palestinian Arabic. It is also used in its simplest form as the base for a lace design made up of three rows of stitches. Again, it makes a frame for embroidered areas.

The most exciting bit of embroidery is undoubtedly the small "pinnacle" set in each of seven squares on one style of Hijazi dress yoke. The nearest thing in embroidery books is the spider's web, a tiny wheel. Most Bedouin pinnacles incorporate metal thread which is spiralled around and down as it is interwoven with the pre-formed cotton spokes. Similar work is seen in Afghanistan in the form of medallions which are appliquéd to costumes.

Hemming, or felling, appears on all hand-made Arabian dresses, either to turn up hemlines or to finish off sleeves and necklines which have been faced. Oversewing, which is similar, is seen wherever there is appliqué. This technique is also employed to anchor silk threads and in this case the complete work is termed "couching" or "laid work". Generally, however, couching in Arabia is integral to open chain stitch or fly stitch which hold the additional threads firmly to the ground cloth.

Machined embroidery is popular today and the stitches are either straight, zigzag or chain.

In the Hijaz, the embroidery frame known as *minsaj*, or *tara*, was used by townswomen to work small sections of a garment at one time. These women also made a beautiful edging called *oiya*. It is similar to tatting and crotchet but is worked with a needle. *Oiya* is primarily a trim for various scarves and headcloths. Hijazi town embroidery, and Meccan work in particular, is often opulent. Although unlike anything found in the heart of traditional Arabia, this lavish work has a part in the story of Arabian costume. (Oiya is a Turkish word and this work is said to have originated in Turkey.)

Borders on Hijazi ladies' traditional garments have wide bands encrusted with precious gold and silver metal strip and thread work. Coiling stems and leaves support flowers oversewn with pearls, gemstones, diamantés and sequins made of precious metal. Metal-thread embroidery remains popular with Arabian women in all regions today. It is an exacting art, requiring great skill. Consequently, few women can satisfy themselves with their own efforts so they have it done for them in India. India for centuries provided the Peninsula market with metal-thread embroidered lengths of textiles, as well as ready-made metal-thread embroidered gowns.

It is interesting to learn that Indian embroiderers are generally Muslims and that their craft has been handed down to them through the centuries. In recent years, a more delicate style of machined metal-thread embroidery has been carried out in Bahrain by Pakistani Muslim embroiderers. Identical machined work also comes from Kuwait. Although the garments glitter still, the metal thread is rarely precious today.

Gold and silver embroidery is perhaps the oldest form of needlecraft. Fragments of gold embroidered cloth date from the fourth century BC. There are various kinds of metal-thread work

using different mediums. The most exquisite old Arabian examples, that often incorporate several metal-thread techniques, come from the Hijaz. One excellent illustration is a Meccan veil known as a *burga* – the word generally applied to a stiffened face mask. The usual Meccan *burga* is lightweight and made from starched, fine, white gauze. The metal-encrusted version is extremely heavy by virtue of the three-dimensional motifs which appear on both the right and wrong sides. The embellishment design is predominantly floral with birds entwined in leafy vines – the whole is overlaid with pearls.

By far the most important piece of embroidery produced within the Arabian Peninsula today is the Holy *Kiswa*, a specially woven black drapery which covers the *Kaaba*. Each year, in time for the

Above: *Ladies'* thawbs *are sometimes rich with machined embroidery. The centre panel here is totally covered with gold and silver metal-thread and turquoise silk embroidery. The work is overlaid with gold sequins. Motifs are generally geometric or floral arabesques and occasionally birds, such as this peacock, are added. The gown was made and embroidered in India.*

Haj, a new covering is made for the cube-shaped holy shrine which houses the sacred black stone. This lies in the centre of the inner court of the Great Mosque at Mecca. Throughout the year, a team of embroiderers work in gold and silver metal thread on black velvet, producing verses of the *Koran* in calligraphy which is surrounded by foliate *arabesque* designs. The embroidery technique employed is commonly known as *sarma*. It is a type of satin stitch whereby the precious metal remains on the surface of the ground cloth. *Sarma* is common to both Syrian and Ottoman embroidery. For years this *Kiswa* was a gift from Egypt, presented annually.

A less monumental piece, size-wise, is a most unusual hand-made *kaftan* for a lady which exhibits both machined and hand-done, metal-thread embroidery. The construction of the garment and the seam stitchery is pure Arabian although the textile was originally an imported machine-embroidered length of black silk. The work looks Damascene although silk lengths are similarly embroidered in India for the Arabian market. Usually embroidered textiles other than silk came from Damascus to Arabia.

The remarkable aspect of the black silk dress is the additional metal thread, hand embroidery, commonly known as *badla*. It appears to have been done after the gown was made up. Obviously an expert has done the work because the *badla* is perfect both inside and out, despite the fact that the embroiderer chose a demanding floral motif rather than a simple geometric pattern.

Badla is an embellishment technique whereby flat strips of metal take the place of needle and thread. The wire, used as the needle itself, is merely poked through the textile. The cloth is easily pierced and the wire is broken by twisting it. Great skill is required to keep this wire faultlessly flat on both sides. This is extremely difficult to manage even for geometric patterns and almost impossible to do without crimping the metal when representational art is involved.

Arabian embroidery patterns follow geometric lines for the most part and, when floral patterns are used, they are stylized. The patterns reflect the influence of *arabesque* – the Islamic form of decoration wherein interlaced patterns are formed, based either on pure geometric relations with a variety of angular movements, or on endlessly flowing curvilinears – sometimes displaying leaves, flowers and animals.

The influences embroiderers worked under were manifold and included fable, myth, legend, religion, climate and landscape, fauna and flora and more. The modern world can only ponder how it came about that the various tribes of internal Arabia adopted certain embroidery designs to distinguish themselves from those used by other tribes. The custom is echoed in the coats of arms worn by European knights in olden times, when the men in suits of armour could be recognized by the decorated textile slips worn over their shields.

Amongst the older, hand-embroidered garments, the motifs include palm trees, various plant-like shapes and a curious design which appears to represent a type of lantern once used in Arabia – or a pomegranate. On machine-embroidered dresses, the most common non-geometric design is floral and the peacock appears quite often. Those dresses bearing peacocks were made in India and Pakistan. The wild common male peafowl, the peacock, is native to India and Ceylon where they were traditionally kept as ornamental birds. While the female is a drab grey, the male of the species has long and colourful tail feathers which it vaingloriously displays by fanning them out. The "peacock throne" originally referred to the former throne of the Kings of Delhi. It was adorned with a representation of the peacock's tail fully extended and was studded with precious stones. The "peacock-eye" refers to the ocellus on a peacock's feather, sometimes considered to be good luck as it resembles the evil-eye charm allegedly imbued with the power to ward off the malignant gaze of the jealous. In spite of the connotations, peacocks are simply a beautiful subject from which to create motifs, be their tails open or closed. Peacocks are a popular addition to private gardens in Arabia today and equally enjoyed when embroidered on garments. *Arabesque* motifs, combining creepers with birds, found particular favour in the Hijaz amongst the wealthy merchant classes. The birds were usually parrots and peacocks, represented in *arabesque*'s stylized form amongst foliage. More recently, naturalistic representations of birds have emerged.

Throughout the centuries, embroidered lengths of textiles came to Arabia from many lands. The most beautiful cloth embroidered for Arabia is said to be a shroud made by Indians for the tomb of the Prophet Muhammed. India specialized in embroideries for the Arabian market from the earliest days when trade between the two countries was first active. It was probably then that motifs were especially developed. Because Indian embroiderers were usually Muslim and some of their work was destined for Arabia, motifs saluting Islam became fashionable, so much so that Indian women of all faiths began to consider them traditional for their country.

With the advent of the Kingdom of Saudi Arabia and the formation of the Emirates, India began to produce pre-embroidered and otherwise embellished dress-lengths and ready-made *kaftans* featuring the countries' emblems in gold and silver metallic threads.

Gold and silver metal-thread embroidery which dazzled the Indian courts of the past, enjoyed a revival half a century ago in India. Although this work is of ancient lineage and quite likely had Arabian patronage centuries ago, it seems likely that the Indian form of metal-thread embroidery seen in Arabia today became especially popular on the Peninsula at the time of its rebirth in India.

The manufacture of gold and silver wire and thread used for embroidery has always been a minor Indian industry, supplying itself and Arabia for decades until a cheap Japanese alternative became available. The Indian version is a remarkable one. It is created from a bar of silver, measuring about forty-five centimetres long and roughly two centimetres thick. This is completely wrapped with pure gold leaf and then heated in a furnace sufficiently to fuse the gold to the silver bar; the thicker the gold leaf applied, the richer the red-gold colour of the final product. The gold-covered bar is then beaten and pulled through a steel draw-plate with increasingly smaller holes until it is as thin as a human hair and measuring miles in length. The tensile capacity of the gold is such that no matter how fine the wire is drawn, the gold surface always remains. The resultant wire is then flattened by gentle hammering on a small anvil, and is finally wound around thread. Hence, it appears thicker than it really is. The dextrous and rapid hand process of winding the gold onto a silk or cotton core is a skill in itself. The final result is a strong and flexible thread. These characteristics are essential in thread to be used for weaving and embroidery.

Syrian gold-embroidered textiles were also popularly worn by Arabians in the past. Of the embroideries imported, two are noteworthy. In fact, Damascus is famous today for one, and that is *aghabani*. The other, *sarma*, is uncommon now. It is a very ancient form of embellishment indeed, possibly going back two millennia. In the National Museum in Damascus there is the reconstructed tomb of Yarhai of the second century BC, brought from the Valley of Tombs, Palmyra, northern Syria and stone relief figures in this crypt appear to be wearing clothes similar to Graeco-Roman ones. These are elaborately draped plain textiles under a mantle with richly embroidered edges whose motifs resemble both the floral and geometric motifs in Damascene *sarma*.

Sarma is a sort of padded satin-stitch, but the threads do not penetrate the textile on which it appears. It was generally made with precious gold and silver metal thread, the motifs created by winding metal around shapes which were tacked down to the garment surface by means of other threads.

Throughout the Middle East, in the days when Turkish bath houses were in use (in areas where water was available) *sarma* embroidered *bikshas* were very popular. The *biksha* is a clothes sachet, designed to hold a change of underclothes, bathrobe and other personal items. *Bikshas* were often embroidered with personalized designs which matched the embroidery on towel, face cloth, bathrobe and underwear. On these the *sarma* embroiderers could have full rein. Rich or poor carried a *biksha*. Actually, the rich usually walked before a servant who carried it.

The second style of embroidery worn by Arabians – and for which Syria is today famous – is the *aghabani* of Damascus. This is now machine-made and said to have been so for almost a century. *Aghabani* is couched work in a curvilinear form exhibiting strong floral patterns, in both abstract and representational styles. It is popularly worked with thick silk thread or metal-thread cord, the latter creating opulent-looking garments when applied to vivid-hued felts and sumptuous velvets.

There are approximately forty different styles of Bedouin dress today in Syria and as many different variations for embroidery patterns – the motifs and their placement indicating exactly the region from which the wearer has come. In Sarakeb near Aleppo, the motifs are mainly geometric. Closer to the border, they are generally floral. The stitches

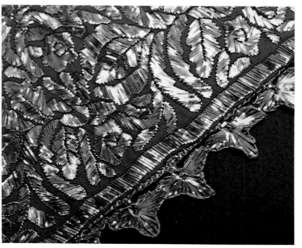

Above: *Hijazi townswomen's traditional costume bears little resemblance to that of other regions due to Ottoman influence. Elaborate gold work graced the gowns of the rich, echoing the opulence of Topkapi. The golden tree above may have been made in India where variations of the "tree of life" were popularly embroidered for export. Gold "purl" and "pearl purl" work, show short and long lengths of coiled precious metal, couched to the surface, combined with gold sequins.* Left: *Lavish* badla *work*.

over at the back. Shawls and scarves embellished in this fashion were worn in the past by well-to-do Arabian women. The lengths of light feathery-looking tulle become remarkably heavy and spectacular with this glistening silver decoration. This strip metal-thread embellishment technique was commonly employed in decorating clothing of the rich during the heyday of the Ottoman Empire. It is likely the technique originated in Turkey and spread to other Muslim lands, for there is more evidence of its use in traditional Turkey than anywhere else in the Middle East.

The splendid garments worn by well-to-do Turks in the past were, of course, a mere echo of those worn within Topkapi. In this palace city, opulence was a way-of-life, and velvets, brocades and silks graced the sultan, his family and favourites, setting the style for the world outside its walls. As bold and beautiful motifs gave way to small and dainty designs, so did the patterns change throughout the Ottoman Empire. No doubt Arabian townspeople's garment textiles reflected these changes.

Bindali, which means a thousand shoots, has always been a fashionable textile decoration in Turkey, and this style would seem to have had influence on Hijazi town embroidery. It can be executed boldly or delicately. As its name suggests, *bindali* is a curvilinear floral motif based on the Islamic art form *arabesque*. It is worked in an identical fashion to Syrian *sarma* which is, again, a technique that probably originated in Turkey. *Bindali* is usually worked in gold metal thread. Shapes are wound with metal until they are totally covered before being arranged on the surface of the textile where they are tacked down. Sometimes real gold sequins are lightly scattered on *bindali* – an Oriental embellishment technique for enhancing outer wear.

Ready-made Persian embroidered garments were worn by Arabians in the past and it is possible that these and Persian presence within the Arabian Peninsula had some influence upon indigenous embroiderers – at least in the towns. There is a remarkable similarity between the embroidery designs of Khorasan and Zai Hedan (the border area between Persia and Afghanistan), and that from Damascus. In both cases, a tracery of predominantly floral motifs is couched – the technique whereby thread or cord is held to the surface by means of other threads. This method of textile decoration is ancient, introduced originally to display metal-thread work on the surface only, because the metal employed was precious. It is, of course, easier to make a metal-thread motif separate from the garment.

Other garments that came from Persia to Arabia were decorated with *abhla bharat*, or *shisha* embellishment, a textile ornamentation technique involving the affixing of tiny circular mirrors, glass, mica or mylar. The circular shiny object is attached to the ground fabric with long straight stitches forming a circumferential net. This is oversewn with either Cretan stitch, buttonhole wheel stitch or *shisha* stitch. In India, both Gujarat and Rajasthan are famous for *abhla bharat* which derives from the fourth century BC, when garments of the rich were embellished with precious stones. *Shisha* is

Left: *Syrian* sarma *and Turkish* bindali *are similar types of textile embellishment. Both resemble satin stitch and are commonly worked with gold metal-thread on velvet. This old kaftan-cut royal purple Turkish jacket suggests some of the opulence that the Ottoman Empire introduced into the Arabian Peninsula. Townswomen, particularly in the Hijaz, adopted Turkish forms of embroidery such as this and* oiya, *a more delicate form of work used primarily for trimming. The photograph was taken amongst the ruins of Diraiyah where some houses have been constantly habitable and others are being restored.*

are tiny, and cross-stitch predominates. This is said to derive from the influence of mosaics accounting for why it is not worked in Arabia – there being no mosaics on the Peninsula. Old Druse hand-embroidery is the closest in appearance to modern Damascene *aghabani* and a resemblance can also be seen in work from Hama, Zedal, Ghabe and Djebel, as well as from around central Syria. Quite likely the influence of these Syrian regional styles of embroidery gave rise to *aghabani*.

The other form of embellishment (found in Syrian antique shops and private homes), which appears now and again on the Arabian Peninsula, is metal strip work similar to *badla* and it does not require a needle either. A short strip of flat silver wire is poked through two holes in the tulle base cloth to achieve a design. The ends are clamped also worked today in Pakistan, Bangladesh, India, Iraq and Afghanistan – by Muslim embroiderers.

It is particularly interesting that the four stitches commonly used by the Persian Gashgoy tribe, between Shiraz and Isfahan, are identical to those employed by certain tribes of Arabian Bedouin. There is no available explanation for this. The stitches may have originated in Arabia but perhaps an ancient Persian embroidery instructress found her way to Arabia. Perhaps, better still, Arabian *hareems* at some dim and distant time in the past included one or more Persian brides. The stitches

tinctive *qabbeh*. The original work resembles Greek, Turkish and Persian embroidery which in turn descends from the gold work of the Byzantine Empire of a thousand years ago.

The couched floral designs of Bethlehem embroidery contrast greatly with the geometric cross-stitched motifs worked in surrounding Palestinian areas. To some extent, both styles and, in fact, all forms of Middle Eastern embroidery eventually fell under the influence of *arabesque*, the art form which evolved to greatness in the Muslim Golden Age when the Islamic capital was Baghdad.

Below: *An exquisite old headcloth or shawl in creamy chiffon exhibits gold work in a scattered floral motif and around the edges as part of a trim. The flower and its leafy stem have been created with the* badla *technique whereby flat metal wire has been poked through the textile.* See Embroidery.

in question are Cretan stitch, buttonhole stitch, chain stitch and satin stitch.

It is fascinating to see that the square, front-bodice panels of western Arabian Bedouin dresses are as ornate and perhaps as significant as the similar *qabbeh* bodice panels of Palestinian traditional dresses. In Palestine dress embroidery is specifically designed to be worn on the square, front-bodice panel, the *qabbeh*. Bethlehem for centuries produced special embroidery known as *Bethlehem Couching* or *tahriri*. Young girls were sometimes sent to Bethlehem to learn this fine art. Naturally, when they returned home, young ladies would modify the designs to their own tastes and those of their villages and in this way regional styles developed. As the designs evolved, certain villages became recognized for their dis-

In the modern world of plastic arts, *arabesque* means a decoration in colour or bas-relief with fancifully entwining leafs, scrollwork, etc. It is a term that was originally applied to Arabic and Moorish ornamental architecture. In music, it is used to describe work that is conjectured to be decoratively expressive rather than emotionally so. In ballet, a dancer's certain position and posture denote an *arabesque*. The word is derived from the Italian *arabesco* which means Arab. The Italians were deeply inspired by Oriental artistic themes during the Renaissance and used their designs extensively. As far back as the fifteenth century, they had coined this word and introduced the Arabesque style of art to the Western world. Now it is often applied to any form of art that is richly decorative and consistent in pattern.

The trim comprises rows of gold metal-thread interwoven with orange cotton which has been taken further than the braid edge and twisted to form a fringe that is anchored with pendant gold sequins.

140

Other Embellishments

Embellishment of outer clothing in Greater Arabia throughout the ages has involved several mediums other than embroidery, especially in the regions along the west coast. A type of twisted braidwork, beadwork and the affixing of silver balls and shiny objects are employed as well as appliquéd patches – the latter method of decoration is by far the most popular.

The Arabian woman's love of colour has always

karat gold jewellery. There were many women present who wore locally tailored dresses. For the most part, these were fashioned from re-embroidered laces embellished with sequins and diamentes or pre-embroidered dress-lengths, studded with glittering objects. The whole effect was one of fantasy.

Most locally made gowns were cut along the lines of the time-honoured *kaftan* which had very simple sleeve and neckline modifications. Modernization, with the introduction of the zip fastener, has given the classic gown a little more shape, as

Below: *Traditional tribal costume on the Arabian Peninsula is probably the most exciting of its kind because the styles have evolved in a long unbroken chain through centuries. African influence can be clearly seen on this section of a woman's hood – beads are popularly used for garment embellishment in all the Peninsula's western*

extended to glitter – from early times when mother-of-pearl was commonly used, to a later period when pure gold discs or sequins were stitched on. This penchant for applied glitter still exists today – attested by its predominance at a recent Saudi Arabian princess's wedding. Many hundreds of Arab women attended the celebration, wearing their best dresses. Some of the full-length, long-sleeved gowns had been created for the wearers by couturiers in Paris, Rome, London and New York. Complimenting jewellery had come from Cartier, Van Cleef and Arpels, Andrew Grima and Tiffany's. Enormous diamonds, emeralds and lesser stones glittered amongst a myriad of multi-coloured sequins and lavish beadwork. Servant girls wore textiles threaded with lurex and their bodies shone with twenty-one

this clever garment closure makes it possible to get into slim-fitting darted dresses. Despite its slimmer shape, it was still the chosen textile and embellishment which accounted for the wondrous differences in *kaftans* seen at the celebration. Some materials bore abstract motifs, either re-embroidered, beaded or sequined, while a few dresses were decorated with all three mediums. Silk flowers were another popular and pretty addition.

Surprisingly, out of the multitude, there were only two traditional dresses and one of these was a style that evolved in Arabia only this century. The twentieth-century gown was an elaborately decorated, silk *kaftan* embellished on the skirt, front and back, with the Saudi emblem. This particular version was notable because there were two extra palm trees on both front and back, one on each

regions and in neighbouring Africa. Silver seed beads are used for borders between predominantly white work where double triangles form the major part of the design. Hand-made silk tassels are suspended from stranded beads to trim most items.

side of the emblem. The older dress was a *thawb* of sheer stuff richly embroidered with gold metal thread and sequins.

The custom of affixing objects to clothes goes back into antiquity when primitives regarded such pieces as protective amulets. Stitching on sequins and coins, which came later, was a way of displaying wealth and status. Sequins were originally made of precious metal and viewed as a form of currency. While charms might ward off bad luck and promote good health, or strengthen natural senses and abilities, sequins brought practical security.

sequins. The Najd black tulle *thawb* for festive occasions has heavily sequined cuffs. These broad four centimetre bands exhibit motifs which include crowns, swords, palm trees, crescents and stars.

An equally attractive embellishment is mother-of-pearl, the iridescent lining of a group of shells which yield pearls. It is correctly known as *nacre*, although it is called *mop* by the jewellery trade and is the same substance as pearl. Arabian coastal regions commonly used nacre for embellishment on traditional gowns.

Nacre is deposited on the inside of the shell by the mantle of the mollusc. It is the same substance

Below: The Bedouin of Arabia had the opportunity to wear garments made in other Middle Eastern lands, even long ago when the souqs *relied upon camel trains to bring supplies. Invariably the chosen garments were colourful, no doubt the wearer sought to introduce more vivid hues to his monochromatic scene. This is a picture of* shisha *work on a* kaftan-*cut jacket that*

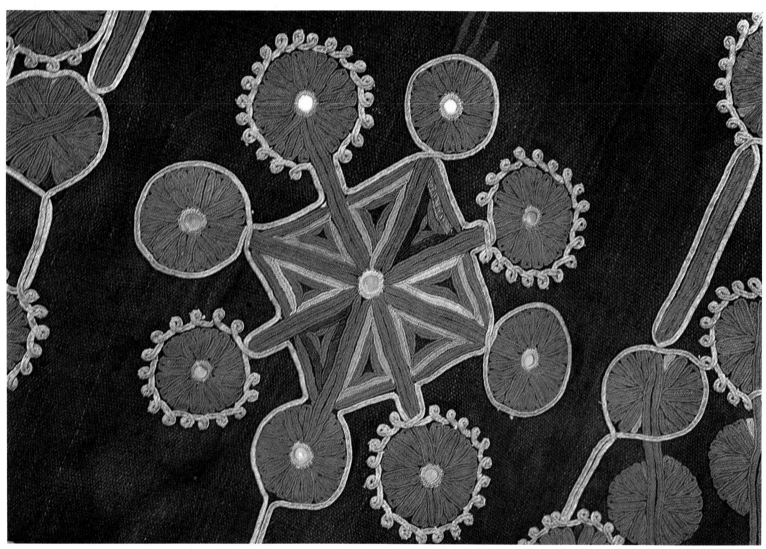

Old records of shipping transactions carried out in the port of Jeddah mention sequins as the currency used to settle a payment. There is also mention of a trader becoming very upset because he misplaced his bag of sequins. Obviously he was not irate over the loss of mere dress spangles, but rather this commercially-minded gentleman was distraught at the thought of lost gold. The word sequin is said to be derived from Arabic *sikka* meaning coinage die. In fact, the monetary sequin was, and many gold and fake dress sequins are still, imprinted with detail resembling coinage. In the past, precious metal-thread embroidery was often enhanced by the addition of gold sequins. Ottoman *bindali* work traditionally incorporated a light sprinkling to twinkle prettily when moved. Indian gold work makes a more lavish use of

as the mineral argonite found on land although nacre has an iridescent quality because the calcium carbonate, of which it is composed, has been laid down in minute ridges and gently undulating waves. Even when sawn into slabs or ground smooth, this iridescence remains as the new surface is still capable of reflecting light. Only prolonged exposure to bright sunlight will cause the surface to become "blind", or lose its iridescence.

Shell carving was a specialized art in the Middle East as early as the seventh millennium BC at Beidha (in present-day Jordan). Shell carvers clustered in groups of small workshops at this important trade route centre, creating a thriving industry from Red Sea shells. Nacre is not only glittering, but is extremely hard, making pearl shell an ideal form of embellishment. It was more readily avail-

once belonged to a tribal man. This kind of textile embellishment is not done in Arabia although it is common to several neighbouring countries. The work is hand-done and is no longer found for sale in the souqs. *Mass-produced machine-embroidered garments have long ago taken the place of handcrafted items.*

Hemming or felling

To secure the edge of a garment permanently in order to stop fraying, it is either necessary to turn under a small section of the textile to produce a hem, or to attach a strip of cloth to the edge in the form of a binding or facing. In either case, if it is to be secured by hand, the technique of hemming is required. The needle must pass into the main ground fabric and exit through that fabric as well as the turned up hem or attached strip. An oversewing stitch is employed. The hemming or felling method is also employed to secure appliqué and many other embroidery forms. The stitches should be diagonal parallels and look the same on both sides of a Bedouin dress.

Oversewing

Work from right to left. Take the needle over the edge and insert it diagonally through both edges, keeping the stitches near the edge.

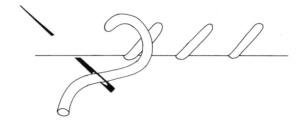

Couching or Laid Work

Lay a thread or threads along the line of the design and hold down with the left hand. Pins can also be used to secure threads in place. With a needle and thread make tiny oversewing stitches at right-angles over the laid thread or threads and through the fabric. Do not allow the laid thread to pucker. Take the ends of any laid threads through to the back of the work and fasten off.

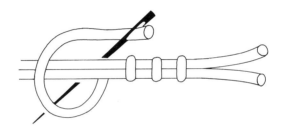

Machine embroidery

These illustrations show machine stitching, worked with even tension, as it appears on the front of an item.

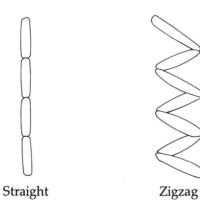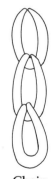

Straight   Zigzag   Chain
this type of stitch requires a hooked needle.

Appendix 2

Bedouin Dress Embroidery

Najdi (Central Arabian) Bedouin dress

Stitch	Placement	Use	Design	Motif	Thread colours
Open chain (wide and close)	Sleeve	To fill in sleeve	Continuous 4 mm wide parallel bands		Cerise, parrot green and red
Open chain		To create geometric patterns	Continuous band of geometric patterns		Predominantly red – also blue, black, green, cerise, gold and purple
		To create motif	Continuous band of motif	Stylized palm tree	Alternate red, gold and blue
		To outline motif			Cerise
		To create motif	Continuous band of motif	"X" motif	Red
		To fill in motif			Four cerise alternating with one blue
Bedouin *arbaa* (threaded fly)		Design border	Continuous vertical lines running parallel with other bands of stitches		Gold threaded with maroon
Herringbone		Base of edging for motif bands	"lace" edging		Red
Bedouin *khamsa* (Herringbone)		Outer edge of "lace"			
Back		To highlight embroidery	Straight line through shoulder-line "lace"		Gold
Seeding or dot		To highlight embroidery	Dots in centre of "X" motif and dots at tip of "lace"		Yellow

Najdi (Central Arabian) Bedouin thawb

Stitch	Placement	Use	Design	Motif	Thread colours
Open chain	Neckline	To confirm garment design and create designs and motifs	Straight lines and geometric patterns		Red
	Sleeve cuff on back of garment		Straight lines and geometric patterns – continuous design "X"		Red
	Garment joins		Straight lines and geometric patterns – continuous design "X"		Red with green and cerise
	Back shoulder panels		Repeated rows of motif	Lantern/pomegranate	Red plus yellow and cerise
	Front underarm sleeve panels		Repeated motif interspersed with another motif hemmed on each side by motif	Palm trees Flowers Minaret	Predominantly red plus yellow
	Shoulder line		Straight lines and geometric pattern made of continuous line of motif	stylized palm trees	Predominantly red plus cerise, yellow, blue and green
Bedouin *itnayn*	Neckline	Edging	Straight lines		Red
	Shoulder line	Divider	Straight lines		Red
	Front underarm sleeve panel	Half frame for minaret motif	Straight lines on two sides		Red
Oversewing	Neckline	Decorate and strengthen			Cerise and green
Bedouin *sabaa* (threaded blanket)	Sleeve cuff edges	Decorate and strengthen			Cerise threaded with red
Buttonhole	Within motifs	To fill in motifs		Lantern/pomegranate, palm tree, minaret	Cerise, green, blue and purple
Seeding or dot	Neckline and motifs	To highlight points		As above	Yellow
Bedouin *arbaa* (threaded fly)	Neckline				Yellow with cerise threads
Back	Down centre of borders	To highlight designs	Straight line through design "X"		Yellow
	Down centre of borders	to highlight border	Straight line through Bedouin *itnayn*		Yellow

Hijazi (Western Arabian) Bedouin dress: 1

Stitch	Placement	Use	Design	Motif	Thread colours
Stem	Yoke	To outline rectangle	Straight lines	Throughout garment, fine stem stitch is worked for the most part in three parallel lines that are grouped in bands containing units of one, two, three and four	Red
	Side gores	To accent and divide gore segments	Straight lines		
	Sleeves	To decorate appliquéd patches	Straight lines		
		To accent shoulder line and upper cuff	Straight lines		
	Hem border	To accent broad hem border	Straight lines		Red
		Vertical lines over appliquéd patches	Straight lines		Red
Chain	Yoke	To decorate appliquéd red patch	Straight lines		Black, white, yellow

Hijazi (Western Arabian) Bedouin Dress: 2

Stitch	Placement	Use	Design	Motif	Thread colours
Chain	Yoke	Border	Straight lines, circles and squares		Yellow, gold, red and black
Bedouin Pinnacle (Spider's Web)	Yoke	Centre-piece in each of seven squares		Pinnacle	Red with gold metal thread weaving
Wave	Yoke	Border	Straight lines to create "lace" look		White
		Border	Straight lines		Black, white and red
Bedouin *waahid* (open chain)	Yoke	Border			Predominantly red plus some black and green
Bedouin *arbaa* (threaded fly)	Yoke	Border	Straight lines		Black and white threaded with red
Bedouin *talata* (threaded open chain)	Yoke	Border	Straight lines		Red with white and black with white
Blanket	Neckline	Edging			White
Back	Upper section of sleeve cuff	To decorate appliqué	Straight and zigzag lines		White

Asir Province Bedouin dress

Stitch	Placement	Use	Design	Motif	Thread colours
Bedouin *itnayn* (Cretan)	Hemline band	Borders	Straight lines of alternately coloured sections		Red, brick red, royal blue, mauve, green
	Hemline band	Borders	Straight lines		Gold and white
	Bar above front hemline band	Borders	Straight lines		Gold
	Side gores	Outline	Straight lines of alternate colours		Red and gold
			Straight lines		Orange
	Side gores	Edging for red cotton appliquéd rectangles and dividers for horizontal rectangles	Straight lines		Gold and orange
					Orange
	Three bars above back hemline band	Borders	Straight lines Straight lines of alternate colours		Gold Red and gold
	Underarm gussets	Outline	Straight lines		Gold
	Shoulder bars	Outline	Straight lines		Brick red and gold
	Back bodice	Outline for back bodice appliquéd panel	Straight line		Gold
		Border for above	Straight line		Mauve
Bedouin *khamsa* (herringbone)	Bar above hemline band	End bars of zigzag border	Straight lines		Red
Back	Bar above hemline	To divide stitch above	Straight lines		White and gold
Chain	Hemline band	Borders	Straight lines		Brick red, white, red, green, mauve, gold
		Border	Lattice of zigzag in two directions		White
	Bar above front hemline band	Border	Zigzag		Red, gold, green
	Three bars above back hemline band	Border	Straight lines		White
	Side gores	Outline	Straight lines		White
Herringbone (double)	Bar above front hemline band	Outline and to edge appliquéd red triangles	Straight lines		Gold
Bedouin *sita* (herringbone)	Hemline	Edging			Red
Oversewing	Neckline	To strengthen			Orange

North Arabian Bedouin dress

Stitch	Placement	Use	Design	Motif	Thread colours
Open chain	Bodice and sleeves	To create and outline designs and motifs	Continuous square outline for palm tree motif which is alternately inverted		Green
				Palm tree filled in	Predominantly orange, others in red, green, purple. Some with white
			Curved zigzag lines in two directions as outline for cactus motif		Red and purple
				Cactus	Predominantly red, now and again purple
			Zigzag line to make triangle base for plant motif		Orange
				Plant	Orange, red, purple, green alternately
			Zigzag line to hold pendant bud motif on one side		Orange
				Bud	Orange, red, green, purple alternately
			Waving lines in two directions with buttonhole stitch filling in centre oval shapes		Orange
			Zigzag line in two directions with buttonhole stitch filling in triangles on one side		Orange
			Zigzag lines used horizontally to produce a band of geometric shapes filled in with buttonhole stitch filling		Orange, green and red
Buttonhole or close-worked blanket		To fill geometric shapes	See above		Predominantly red with either green or purple every third or fourth time
Seeding or dot	Bodice	To make central dot in diamonds formed by two zigzag lines			White

Back	Neckline	Border	Straight line		White
Open chain close-worked	Neckline and sleeves	Borders and dividers for designs	Continuous vertical lines		Orange and red
Bedouin *arbaa* (threaded fly)	Neckline, bodice and sleeves	Dividers for designs	Continuous vertical lines		White threaded with dark colours
Bedouin *khamsa* (herringbone)	Bodice	Border for embroidered areas	Continuous vertical lines		White
Bedouin *sita* (herringbone)	Neckline and protruding cuff lining edges	To strengthen	Continued around neckline and cuff lining edge		Green
Herringbone	Neckline	Base for "lace" edging to neckline embroidery	Straight line		Orange
Wave	Neckline	Middle of "lace" above	Close-worked straight line		Orange
		Pendants to "lace"	Open-worked straight line		Orange

South-Western Arabian Bedouin dress

Stitch	*Placement*	*Use*	*Design*	*Motif*	*Thread colours*
Chain	Yoke and bodice	To accent neckline and to decorate front panel of dress	Straight lines of different colours running parallel with each other		Red, gold, green and white
			Straight lines to create stylized inverted tree motif pendant from bodice embroidery	Tree	White

South Arabian Bedouin dress

Stitch	*Placement*	*Use*	*Design*	*Motif*	*Thread colours*
Chain	Yoke	To accent neckline	Straight lines and curved lines of different colours running parallel with each other		Red, gold, green and white

Appendix 3

Care of Textiles

There is presently a growing respect for the beauties of hand-craftsmanship, especially of fine old textiles, and perhaps this is because the tapestry of man's evolution can be seen in them. They are, in fact, a virtual history of civilization.

From the first, textiles were created to be used and therefore it is logical that they would eventually wear out. Yet, as they can be things of great beauty and historical interest, it is desirable that something should be known about their care to ensure preservation.

Scientists have discovered that even if textiles are protected from insects, the friction and soiling caused by normal use, and the strains of repeated cleaning, they remain under continuous attack from their environment. For instance, light fades the dyes and weakens the fibres; changing temperature and humidity make the threads work and twist as they absorb and give out moisture; and the destructive effects of dirt and chemicals in the air are also constantly at work. It is therefore surprising that textiles survive at all.

In order to assist those who own or are otherwise responsible for the care of old Arabian garments, the following information is a practical guide based on the advice of experts. Included are the basic principles for protective care, detailed instructions for the treatment of costumes or how to clean and repair them, as well as a guide indicating how to display, store and conserve them. The dangers and difficulties inherent in dealing with old, fragile and degraded materials and informative points about the problems which can arise, are also included.

Recognition of textile

Recognition of a textile is essential as the properties and characteristics of the fibres from which a textile is made will play a part in its reaction to the treatment it receives, whether restorative or environmental. By being fully conversant with the fibre's characteristics, the most suitable methods of cleaning and conservation can be followed.

Wool

Wool is by nature intended to keep warm and dry the animal on which it grows. It will, even when spun and woven into a textile, retain the ability to absorb up to one-third of its own weight in water without feeling damp to the touch. In fact, wool needs an atmosphere in which there is a certain degree of moisture if it is not to become hard, dry and brittle.

In their natural state, wool fibres are elastic and spring back after being stretched. Woollen material resists being pressed into sharp folds.

Wool does not burn very readily and this fact

may be used to identify it. In contact with a naked flame its fibres decompose, giving off a smell similar to feathers burning. When removed from a naked flame, the wool does not continue to burn and each fibre forms a black charred knob.

Wool tends to decompose under the action of strong sunlight and reacts unfavourably to heat. It will, however, store well in favourable conditions. Apart from sunlight and dry heat, wool is liable to be attacked by moths and mildew and, because of its cell structure, wool fibre shrinks and mats together if washed and rubbed in hot, soapy water. With care, wool will wash successfully. Reliable washing agents are available for wool and instructions should be followed carefully.

Silk

Silk is a natural thread which is spun by the silkworm into a cocoon. This "house" protects the worm in the pupae stage, from which it eventually emerges as a moth. Silk fibres are slightly less elastic than wool but they are long, smooth and fine. Because of their strength, silk fibres can be woven into a soft, luxurious material which drapes and hangs in beautiful folds.

If silk comes into contact with a flame it will burn, giving off a singed smell similar to burning hair or horn.

The gum-like sericin which holds the silk threads together in the cocoon is removed from the natural silk during manufacture. This loss may be replaced in various ways – sometimes it is done with metallic salts which produce "weighted" silk. The addition of these salts presents problems in the care of silk, especially if the amount of weighting is considerable, as is often the case in black silk or silk used in the making of fringes or tassels.

Sunlight and hot dry conditions cause silk (and especially weighted silk) to become dry and brittle. However, pure silk and good quality silk embroidery threads have longer-lasting qualities. These can also be washed, albeit carefully. Weighted silk can seldom be successfully washed. Overall, hand-dry-cleaning is recommended.

Linen

Linen is made from the stem fibres of the stalks of the flax plant which carry moisture from the roots through the plant to the leaves and flowers. Because of their inherent qualities, linen fibres retain the ability to attract and carry moisture along their length, even when woven into a textile.

Linen is always stronger when wet than when dry and therefore washes well. Although linen dry-cleans successfully, it is difficult to dye. Linen and cotton will shrink considerably the first time that they are washed so this must be kept in mind.

Cotton

Cotton fibres come from the seed heads, or bolls, of the cotton plant. As a textile, it has a greater resistance to heat than most others, and can be kept in storage for a long time without deterioration. Like linen, cotton is stronger when wet than when dry and humid conditions are favourable.

Sunlight causes cotton to gradually lose its strength, and it will cause white and natural coloured cotton to "yellow".

Cotton washes well, dry-cleans successfully, as it is fairly resistant to solvents. It dyes exceptionally well.

Man-made fibres

Man-made fibres such as rayon are either made from a material of natural origin such as cellulose or protein, or from simpler substances which produce synthetic fibres such as polyester and nylon.

Identification of man-made fibres is not easy and they are too numerous and varied to be coped with in this book. Suffice it to say that the safest course is hand-cleaning by experts. Advice should be sought to determine the characteristics of the fibres before choosing any action. It should be noted, however, that hand-dry-cleaning should be sought as a few synthetics do not respond well. Advice will be proferred if washing would be more suitable.

Some synthetics are more inflammable than others and some are stable and resistant to light, while others are adversely affected by heat. Being chemically inert, most will combine quite successfully with natural fibres.

Damage and deterioration

Apart from insects, the greatest enemy of all textiles is light – including visible and ultraviolet radiation in daylight and in fluorescent tube lighting. Deterioration of the structure of the fibres themselves and the fading of dyes, result from such exposure. Atmospheric pollution is also destructive to textiles because it cuts and erodes the fibres. Excessive dryness and heat are harmful, too, and so is dampness which can cause fibres to rot, and mould to grow. Chemical reactions from stains can also attack and weaken fibres and there is a constant threat from pests such as moths. Even the dyestuffs used on a textile can eventually cause its destruction.

Before the existence of chemical dyes, iron was used as a mordant to obtain dark colours, particularly black and brown. This led to rotting by oxidation. Modern starch dyes, created to be eye-catching, are also subject to deterioration if not kept clean, dry and in the dark. Any stains will work together with starch to attack and weaken the fibres of the textile.

Dyes of ancient times and of today (as well as from the period in between when natural dyes were being replaced by chemical dyes) have constantly threatened textiles. Analine dyes, discovered in the middle of the nineteenth century, were apt to fade and change on natural textiles but they have more affinity with man-made fibres.

Manufacturing processes and finishes can do long-term damage too. For instance, weighted silks which are stiff and rustle attractively, have been treated with metallic salts of either tin or iron. In time the silk will split and break where it is weakened along folds and hems. There are as many finishing processes for silks as there are for various other textiles and these dressings are generally harmful over a long period of time.

Combining materials can harm a textile. In the case of wool and silk, both require moisture to survive but silk will rot if damp, while wool will contain any destructive dampness.

Conservation

The future of privately owned Arabian garments is more uncertain than those properly housed in the controlled conditions of a museum.

All old costumes require some preventive maintenance to ensure their future well-being wherever they are kept. At best, an experienced textile conservator should be called to treat an old costume because irreparable harm can be done to a garment through inept attention, albeit well-meaning. Even some cleaning agents that give immediately spectacular results are likely to have long-term detrimental effects. This is where a trained conservator can assist. For example, London's Victoria and Albert Museum's Textile Department and Far Eastern or Indian departments offer appointments with appropriate experts who can advise upon the best course of action for individual pieces.

Caring for textiles, write Karen Finch and Greta Putnam, means having a responsible attitude towards them.

Display and protection

Although one likes to display beautiful and visually satisfying objects, it must be remembered that in the case of textiles exposure may be harmful. Because of this, the place chosen to display particularly sensitive textiles must be given careful consideration.

Privately displayed pieces must be kept far from direct light, whether natural or artificial and possibly have a well-placed source of artificial light. Incandescent lighting only should be used because fluorescent lamps emit damaging ultraviolet rays. The international unit of illumination is the lux, and inside a British house on a dull day one can measure approximately six hundred lux, while the recommended illumination for textiles is fifty.

Dimly lit hallways away from any form of heating is considered the best place for displaying textiles in the home. A constant temperature of thirteen to fourteen degrees Centigrade with a relative humidity of fifty to sixty percent is considered ideal. Special air-conditioned display cases are inconvenient for the average home but care should be taken to see that conditions are not drastically at variance with the recommendations.

Collections

Collections of textile objects present storage as well as display problems. The security of the collection is also to be considered. Good colour photographs and detailed descriptions are important and should be kept separately in a safe place. While a few pieces can be displayed, it is practical to store the bulk of a collection in ideal conditions with an index and labelling system to facilitate periodic examination.

Whether displayed or stored away, old costumes will be occasionally viewed but ideally they should never be worn or tried on. If displayed, they should be supported in such a way that no strain is imposed on any part of the fabric. Crumpled, acid-free tissue paper can be added as a padding to fill out the costume and prevent creasing. Any creasing of silk or wool will fall out and disappear if the costume is mounted on a dummy of the correct proportions. Ironing of any textile should be avoided and certainly never done unless the garment has been previously cleaned. The application of heat can seal in stains and any acid dust.

Ideally, a display showcase should have a cool and dry internal atmosphere away from the light and the case should be totally covered when not on show. Silica gel crystals offer protection against damp but care should be taken to remove the crystals when saturated.

Wearing old and beautiful clothing is a temptation that should be resisted because of the stress imposed on the textiles when dressing and undressing. When the wearer is not quite the right size for the garment this is especially true. Staining can also occur. Movement can cause further damage and sitting down in an old dress can cause its ruin.

The best way to display costumes on living models is to have copies made. The originals should be stored away safely. The other way is to make a film of the collection which can be shown time and again. Such a film would have to be meticulously done as film-making is a costly venture. However, one advantage would be that close-ups could show details of cut, material and stitching which would be both interesting and educational.

Storage

The state of preservation of many textiles retrieved from ancient tombs attests to the value of ideal storage. This requires an unpolluted area which is cool, dry, and dark, with a constant temperature and humidity and no disturbance. The burial chamber condition may not be possible in the average home so an alternative must be sought. The aim should be to provide adequate space (so as to prevent overcrowding) in a dark, cool and dry place with even temperature. The area should be clean and free from atmospheric pollution and the presence of moth eggs and other pests. Furthermore the textiles themselves must be clean.

Acid-free tissue paper, which is readily available, should be padded inside costumes and interleaved as they are folded. A list on top of a pile will facilitate identification, avoiding unnecessary disturbance of the other items. Never use adhesive tape or labels that may come in contact with the textiles.

Very long objects, such as belts, should be stored wound around a cardboard cylinder interleaved with acid-free tissue paper. Care should be taken to pad the cylinder with tissue in case the cardboard is not acid-free.

Large, flat items must obviously be folded. Any folds should be made loosely over thick rolls of acid-free tissue paper – otherwise the folded fibres will be weakened and eventually break. Stored textiles which are folded should be occasionally refolded in different places. Hats, bonnets and similar shaped pieces should be filled with crumpled acid-free tissue paper, while small flat items are best interleaved with tissue.

Garments are best stored on dummies of the correct size, providing they are also wearing the appropriate undergarments, and have washed calico or gingham overcoverings to prevent dust settling when not on view. Such dust covers should be left open at the bottom to allow air circulation. These bags should be large enough to avoid crushing the garments. Plastic or polythene bags are unsatisfactory as they can hold humidity and promote the growth of mildew. They also attract dust. Cellophane is not suitable either because it tears easily. If the garment does not fit the dummy exactly, then pads of tissue should be used. Undue sagging damages the textile over a period of time. A heavy skirt may need extra support which can be achieved by stitching several tapes to the inside top of the skirt. The other ends of the tapes can be attached to the dummy with safety pins. If they are made short enough, the tapes will allow the dummy to take some of the strain upon the bodice textile.

If dummies are not available, well-padded, cotton-filled, tissue-covered hangers should be used. Again, tapes can be used to take up the weight of a heavy skirt. Washed calico or gingham covers should also be provided. Crumpled acid-free tissue paper may then be added to round out the garments which should not be packed too closely together. Labels should be placed on the dust cover and not on the garment.

Beaded, sequined and heavily embroidered garments present the exception to the foregoing methods of storage. Their excessive weight can cause strain on the textiles if hung. As in the case of items cut "on the cross", they should be stored flat with ample acid-free tissue paper.

It is also wise to carefully examine the storage

area for anything hard, sharp or rough – and to line it with tissue. Moth balls or napthalene flakes first wrapped in tissue or muslin can be put into storage containers as an additional safeguard. Although moth-proofing preparations can be effective over a long period, the best safeguard is to examine stored garments on a regular basis.

Cleaning

As it is wisest to store textiles in their cleanest possible state in order to prevent harmful eroding of the fibres, the subject of cleaning must be considered.

Vacuum-cleaning is recommended as the easiest form of cleaning displayed garments and it is the least damaging to the textile. Garments on display should be surface cleaned in this way regularly. A nylon filtration fixture is placed over the hand-held nozzle of the vacuum cleaner for safe and careful cleaning. Nylon filtration fabric can also be bought in yardage to be placed over the entire textile during vacuum-cleaning. The nozzle of the cleaner should not actually touch the garment in case loose threads are drawn up by suction.

Brushing is less satisfactory because it is inefficient in that it merely moves the dust around. Also, no matter how carefully it is carried out, the textile may be damaged. In the case of cleaning raised work, a sable brush can be used to dislodge dust prior to vacuum-cleaning.

Spot cleaners and surface cleaning with any liquid are not recommended as even plain water can combine with the chemical content of dust, dirt and acids to damage the textile. Amateur chemical dry-cleaning should also be avoided. Firms which specialize in careful cleaning will give individual attention to special orders. However, since the responsibility lies primarily with the garment's owner, it is wise to seek a textile conservator's advice first, especially if the piece is of historic or artistic importance.

Conservation and restoration of costumes

Apart from cleaning, old costumes meant for display must look right. This often means that some restoration must be carried out. The success of the work lies in doing just enough and no more in order to maintain the artistic or historic importance. Conservation requires everything original on an object remain and nothing be added. Restoration suggests a degree of repair. Obviously, then, careful thought must be given to any proposed work. The actual treatment of each item will depend on its intended future. Conservation is sufficient for display only, while restoration will be required if the article is to be worn. However, if displayed pieces are badly damaged they may need some restoration if their deterioration is to be arrested.

It is sometimes necessary to unpick seams in order to get the garment flat for application of a supporting fabric. This involves a decision regarding the ethics of conservation. The original stitching and making up of a garment has a great deal of importance to those who study costume. Therefore, the minimum of unpicking should be carried out.

The material to be used as a support should be identical in colour to the original but lighter in weight and strong. Polyester fabrics are excellent because they are stable and resistant to light and humidity.

With the supporting material stretched on an embroidery frame, the various parts of the original garment can be laid over, pinned and couched with a fine needle and thread, using tiny stitches. They should be unobtrusive. This method of repair maintains the essential textile qualities of moving and draping. Very fine, thin, fragile textiles are best supported by fine net or silk, although the latter should be washed prior to being used in order to remove dressing.

Gold embellishment

Oriental gold work on textiles presents a challenge to a conservator and restorer, although it is patience rather than any complicated technique that is required.

Firstly, the lining (if any) should be removed but its position should be noted so that it may be replaced correctly. The design can generally be discerned from existing stitch holes. In this way the back of the embroidery is exposed for study. By observing undamaged areas, the same technique (which is usually couching) can be used to tack down the loose gold threads. To avoid time-consuming mistakes, it is recommended that the gold threads be pinned in place prior to couching.

If the textile seems fragile or has weak areas, a supporting washed light-weight cotton in a suitable colour should be applied over an embroidery frame under the section being repaired. Tension is important, both in the stitchery and between the base textile and supporting material.

Patching

Great care must be taken when patching. A closely matching textile is just as important as a fine needle, fine thread and small stitches. It is desirable to work slowly and carefully, inserting a needle between threads rather than actually piercing a thread.

Bibliography

Al-Farsy, Fouad Abdul-Salam, *Saudi Arabia – A Case Study in Development*, Stacey International, London, 1978

Aramco – Lebkicher, Roy; Rentz, George; Steineke, Max and other Aramco employees, *Aramco Handbook*, The Arabian American Oil Company, The Netherlands, 1960

Aramco – Lunde, Paul, Sabini, John A, *Aramco and its World*, The Arabian American Oil Company, Washington DC, 1980

Belgrave, James H. D, *Welcome to Bahrain*, The Augustan Press, Bahrain, 1968

Beresneva, L, *The Decorative and Applied Art of Turkmenia*, Aurora Art Publishers, Leningrad, 1976

Bibby, Geoffrey, *Looking for Dilmun*, Alfred Knopf Inc, New York, 1970

Bidwell, Robin, *Travellers in Arabia*, The Hamlyn Publishing Group, 1976

Binzagr, Safeya, *Saudi Arabia, An Artist's View of the Past*, Three Continents Publishers, Lausanne, 1980

Blunt, Anne, *The Bedouins of the Euphrates*, Volumes 1 and 2, John Murray, London, 1879

Blunt, Anne, *Pilgrimage to Nejd*, Volumes 1 and 2, John Murray, London, 1881

Burckhardt, Titus, *Art of Islam*, World of Islam Publishing Company, 1976

Burton, Richard, *The Gold Mines of Midian*, Falcon–Oleander, Cambridge, 1979

Butler, Winifred, *Needlework*, Pan Craft Books, London and Sydney, 1976

Cavallo, Adolph S, *Needlework*, The Smithsonian Institution, Washington, 1979

Dhamija, Jasleen, *Living Traditions of Iran's Crafts*, Vikas Publishing House, 1979

Dickson, H. R. P, *The Arab of the Desert*, George Allen and Unwin, London, 1951

Dickson, Violet, *Forty Years in Kuwait*, George Allen and Unwin, London, 1970

Doughty, Charles M, *Arabia Deserta*, Volumes 1 and 2, Philip Lee Warner, publisher to the Medici Society Limited, and Jonathan Cape, London and Boston, 1921

Fairservis, Walter A, Junior, *Costumes of the East*, Published in association with The American Museum of Natural History, Chatham Press Inc, Connecticut

Fikret, Altay, *Kaftanlar*, Topkapi Sarayi Muzesi, 3, Istanbul, 1979

Finch, Karen and Putnam, Greta, *Caring for Textiles*, Barry and Jenkins, London, 1977

Folkwear, Folkwear Ethnic Patterns, Forestville, California

Foreign Area Studies Group, *Area Handbook for Afghanistan*, The American University, Washington, 1973

Foreign Area Studies Group, *Area Handbook for Egypt*, The American University, Washington, 1976

Foreign Area Studies Group, *Iran – A Country Study Series*, The American University, Washington, 1978

Foreign Area Studies Group, *Area Handbook for the Peripheral States of the Arabian Peninsula*, The American University, Washington, 1971

Foreign Area Studies Group, *Area Handbook for the Persian Gulf States*, The American University, Washington, 1977

Foreign Area Studies Group, *Area Handbook for Saudi Arabia*, The American University, Washington, 1966

Foreign Area Studies Group, *Area Handbook for Saudi Arabia*, The American University, Washington, 1977

Foreign Area Studies Group, *Area Handbook for the Yemens*, The American University, Washington, 1977

Ghaleb, Mohammed Anam, *Government Organizations as a Barrier to Economic Development in Yemen*, University Bochom, 1979

Glover, June, *Silk – The World's Best Kept Secret*, The Lady Magazine, London, Jan. 1981

Gostelow, Mary, *The Coats Book of Embroidery*, David and Charles, Newton Abbot and London, 1978

Gostelow, Mary, *Traditional Designs, Techniques and Patterns from all over the World*, Marshall Cavendish, London, 1977

Guellouz, Ezzedine, *Pilgrimage to Mecca*, Directorate of Press, Kingdom of Saudi Arabia, 1979

Gunther, John, *Inside Africa*, Hamish Hamilton, London, 1955

Hansen, Henny Harald, *A Kurdish Woman's Life*, Nationalmuseet, Copenhagen, 1961

Hansen, Henny Harald, *A Bahraini Woman's Life*, Nationalmuseet, Copenhagen, 1961

Hawley, Ruth, *Omani Silver*, Longman Group, London, 1978

Hayes, John R, Editor, *The Genius of Arab Civilization – Source of Renaissance*, Original English edition by Mobil Middle East affiliates, MIT Press, Massachusetts, 1975

Hoberman, Barry, *Treasures of the North*, Aramco World Magazine, Sept/Oct, 1979

James, David, *Islamic Art – An Introduction*, The Hamlyn Publishing Group, 1974

Jenkins, Mary, *The China Trade*, Aramco World Magazine, Jul/Aug 1975

Katakura, Motoko, *Bedouin Village*, University of Tokyo Press, 1977

Kay, Shirley, *The Bedouin*, Douglas David and Charles, North Vancouver BC, 1978

Kay, Shirley, *Travels in Saudi Arabia*, edited by Rosalind Ingrams, 1979

Kay, Shirley and Basil, Malin, *Saudi Arabia Past and Present*, Namara Publications, London, 1979

Kemal, Cig, *Istambul*, Net Turizm ve Ticaret, Turkey

Khuri, Zahi, *Arabesque*, Ahlan Wahsahlan, Saudi Arabian Airlines, Issue No 1, Vol 2, Jan/Feb 1978

Khuri, Zahi, *Arabesque*, Arab Esk Europe Magazine, Nov/Dec 1980

King, Donald, *Imperial Ottoman Textiles*, Colnaghi, London

Konieczny, M. G, *Textiles of Baluchistan*, British Museum, 1979

Leslie, Angela, editor, *Dunhill Guide to Living and Working in Bahrain*, Tien Wah Press (Pte), Singapore, 1980

Masry, Abdullah H, editor, *Atlal – The Journal of Saudi Arabian Archaeology*, Vol 1, Department of Antiquities and Museums, Riyadh, 1977

Masry, Abdullah H, editor, *Atlal – The Journal of Saudi Arabian Archaeology*, Vol 2, Department of Antiquities and Museums, Riyadh, 1978

Masry, Abdullah H, editor, *Atlal – The Journal of Saudi Arabian Archaeology*, Vol 3, Department of Antiquities and Museums, Riyadh, 1979

McColl, Patricia, *Couture Arabesque*, Aramco World Magazine, Mar/Apr 1977

Menta, Rustam J, *Masterpieces of Indian Textiles*, Taraporevaia, India, 1970

Monroe, Elizabeth, *Philby of Arabia*, Faber and Faber, 1973

Mulhouse, *Bulgarian Embroideries*, Editions Th. de Dillmont, France, 1975

Musil, Alois, *The Manners and Customs of the Rwalla Bedouins*, American Geographical Society, Oriental Explorations and Studies, No 6, 1928

Nutting, Anthony, *Lawrence of Arabia*, Clarkson N. Potter Inc, New York, 1961

Pelly, Lewis, *Report on a Journey to Riyadh*, Oleander–Falcon, Cambridge, 1979

Pesce, Angelo, *Jiddah – Portrait of an Arabian City*, Falcon Press, Naples, 1974

Philipson, Norman W, *Creative Design for Fashion and Embroidery*, Studio Vista, London, 1976

Phillips, Wendell, *Oman*, Ministry of Information, Muscat, 1972

Phillips, Wendell, *Unknown Oman*, Librairie du Liban, 1971

Picton, John and Mack, John, *African Textiles*, British Museum, London, 1979–80

Ritchie, Carson, *Shell Carving – History and Techniques*, Yoseloff Limited, London, 1974

Rogers, Gay Ann, *Tribal Designs – Needlepoint*, John Murray, London, 1978

Sadleir, G. Forster, *A Journey across Arabia – 1819*, Falcon–Oleander, Cambridge, 1977

Salah, Nadha, *Costumes and Customs of the Arab World*, Said Salah, Al Khobar, 1980

Salah, Said, *Businessman's Guide to Arabian Gulf States*, The International Publications Agencies, Al Khobar, Saudi Arabia, 1978

Shihaab, Ali, Article: *The Arab Sword – Emblem of Chivalry*, The Supplement, Saudi Arabia, 17th Dec 1973

Simmons, Max, *Dyes and Dyeing*, Van Nostrand Reinhold, Australia, 1978

Stark, Freya, *The Southern Gates of Arabia*, John Murray, London, 1936

Stillman, Y. K, *Palestinian Costume and Jewellery*, Museum of New Mexico and the International Art Foundation, Santa Fe, USA, 1979

Sutton, Ann, *Work in Progress – Weaving*, The Crafts Council, London, 1979

Thesiger, Wilfred, *Arabian Sands*, Penguin Books, London, 1980

Thesiger, Wilfred, *The Marsh Arabs*, Longmans, Green and Co, London, 1964

Tibbets, G. R, *Arabia in Early Maps*, Falcon, Naples and Oleander, Cambridge, 1978

Tilke, Max, *Costume Patterns and Designs*, A. Zwemmer, London, 1956

Van Beek, Gus W, *The Rise and Fall of Arabia Felix*, Scientific American, Vol 221, No 6, Dec 1969, W. H. Freeman and Company, San Francisco

Vanderpool, Catherine, *Report from Yemen*, The Athenian, Greece, April, 1980

Wallin, Georg August, *Travels in Arabia, 1845–1848*, Falcon–Oleander, London, 1979

Waterfield, Gordon, *Sultans of Aden*, John Murray, London, 1968

Weir, Shelagh, *The Bedouin*, Museum of Mankind – UK World of Islam Publishing Company, London, 1976

Winstone, H. V. F, *Gertrude Bell*, Jonathan Cape Limited, London, 1974

Glossary of Arabic Words

Note: This glossary has been compiled with a view to aiding a non-Arabic speaking reader to correctly pronounce, as closely as possible, the transliterated words. The Arabic is colloquial and includes loan words from other languages. All words are subject to the many dialects used on the Arabian Peninsula. Authors have been accredited with their own spelling in many cases, while other words have been standardized by Dr. Muhammed Hasan Bakalla, Arabic linguist, University of Riyadh, Kingdom of Saudi Arabia.

Abbreviations
Syn: Synonymous
Sing: Singular
Pl: Plural

أب
Aab
father
والــــد

عبـــايـة
Abaaya
Cloak, mantle, wrapper worn by women
رداء خارجي تلبسه المرأة فوق ملابسها

ياجـة
Aga
Collar
ياقـــــه

عيبـــــه
Aibah
Leather saddlebag for storing dates
عدل خرج الدابة مصنوع من الجلد ويوضع به البلح

أخضـــر
Akhdar
The colour green
أخضـر اللــون

أمـــير
Amir
1 Prince
2 Tribal or regional chieftain
١ ـ أمير
٢ ـ شيخ القبيله أو شيخ المنطقه

عنـــبر
Anbar
Scent made from amber
عطر يصنع من العمبر

أربعة
Arbaa
The number four
العدد ٤

رقصة العرضة النجدية
Ardah
Ceremonial war dance performed by men with swords
رقصة تقليدية في الإحتفالات يقوم بها الرجال بالسيوف

عريس
Arease
Bridegroom
الرجل في ليلة زواجه

عرفـج
Arfaj
Tough desert brushwood root used for fuel
جذور نبات صحراوي يستخدم كوقود .

عروسه
Arousah
Bride
الفتاه في ليلة زواجها

عصا
Asa
Cane camel stick
عصا للجمل من الخيزران

عصايب
Asayib
See *igaal*
أربطه للرأس من الفضة أو من الجلد والفضة ، أو من القصب وأسلاك النحاس وغير ذلك ، يلبسه الرجال
والنساء . المفرد : عصابه .

أصفـر
Asfar
The colour yellow
اللون الأصفر

Awzar (sing. *wizr*)
Syn. with *fouta*. See *fouta*.

مرادف فوطة ـ أنظر فوطة ، مفرد : وزر

أوزار

Baakura (pl. *bawakeer*)
Hooked cane camel stick.

مرادف عصا ، عصا للجمل من الخيزران ، الجمع : بواكير

باكورا

Baalto
Similar to *zibun*. Arabian version of *qumbaz*.
See *qumbaz*

الإسم بالعربية القمباز، أنظر قمباز

بالطو

Baarim
Style of *kaftan*. Dark blue dress worn by women
(Musil)

مرادف فستان ، رداء أزرق داكن تلبسه النساء

باريم

Babooj
Clog-like leather slipper worn over *khuf*

شبشب جلدي يلبس فوق الخف

بابوج

Badw
Bedouin (*Badawi*: male – *Badawiya*: female)

البدو (بدوي : مذكر ـ بدوية : مؤنث)

بدو

Batula
Stiff face mask worn by women (Dickson)

حجاب كثيف للوجه تلبسه النساء

باتولا

Bayt al Shaar
Syn. with *khaima*. See *khaima*

مرادف : خيمة ، أنظر خيمة

بيت الشعر

Biksha
Clothes and toilet sachet. Textile envelope for
personal items

كيس تحفظ به الملابس وأدوات التجميل ، قطعة من القماش تستخدم لوضع الأشياء الشخصية

بكشا

Bint
Unmarried girl

بنت غير متزوجة

بنت

Bisht
Syn. with *mishlah*. Cloak or mantle worn by men.

مرادف مشلح ، عباءة يلبسها الرجال

بشت

Boukhor
Frankincense. Aromatic resin from tree (*Boswellia
carterii*), the major incense for burnt offerings and
funeral pyres in ancient times

مادة صمغيه من شجرة بوسويليا كاريترى ، تعطى رائحه جميله عند حرقها

بخور

Bugsha
Textile waistband worn by men and women

حزام من القماش يحيط بالخصر يلبسه الرجال والنساء

بوجشا

Bukhnug
1 Syn. with *mukhnug*. Hooded garment that covers
the shoulders and sometimes has a long trailing
end. Worn by unmarried girls
2 Head covering for dead women

١ ـ مرادف موخنج ، رداء يغطي الأكتاف وأحيانا يكون له طرف يمس الأرض ، تلبسه الفتيات
٢ ـ غطاء لرأس المرأة المتوفية

بوخنج

Burga
Stiff mask worn by women

حجاب سميك للوجه تلبسه النساء

برقع

Burga milaaya
Syn. with *nigaab*. Veil or mask, usually stiffened,
worn by women

مرادف : نقاب ، حجاب للوجه ، عادة يكون سميك ، تلبسه النساء

برقع ملايه

Burnous
Traditional long robe with hood worn in North
Africa

رداء طويل به قلنسوة لتغطية الرأس ، يلبس في شمال أفريقيا

برنس

Buzouk
Long lute

آلة نفخ موسيقية طويلة

بزق

Cabreet
Flint or match

ثقاب

كبريت

Chador
شــادور
Turkish mantle or cloak worn by women
مرادف عباية ، حجاب تركي تلبسه النساء

Chaf (kaff)
كـــف
Syn. with *fitir*. Distance between thumb and forefinger. A Bedouin measurement (Dickson)
المسافة بين الإبهام والسبابة وهو مقياس يستخدمه البدوي ، مرادف : فتر

Charchaf
شرشف
Persian mantle or cloak worn by women.
حجاب فارسي تلبسه النساء .

Charwal
شــروال
Turkish pantaloons worn by men and women
بنطلون تركي

Chifan (kafan)
كفن
Syn. with *tsifan*. White burial shroud
قماش أبيض يلف فيه المتوفى

Cote
كــوت
Hijazi jacket worn by men
جاكيت يلبسه الرجال

Daabah
دبــه
Camel skin container for storing fat or dates made by Najdi Bedouin men and women
كيس من جلد الجمل يحفظ فيه السمن أو البلح ، يصنعه البدوي والبدوية في نجد

Daff
دف
Tambourine
الــرق

Daffa
دفــا
Cloak without hand openings worn by women (Hansen)
عباية بدون فتحات للأيدي تلبسها النساء

Dallah (pl. *dallaat*)
دالـه
Brass and copper coffee pot
إبريق من البرونز أو النحاس للقهوة ، الجمع : دالات

Dalu
دلــو
Small leather bucket for drawing water from wells
سطل صغير من الجلد يستخدم في الحصول على الماء من البئر

Damir
دامـر
Jacket worn by men (Dickson)
جاكيت يلبسه الرجال

Darabukkah
دربكــة
Goblet-shaped drum
طبلــة

Darum
داروم
Tree bark used for cleaning teeth which imparts a reddish-brown colour to gums and lips (Dickson)
لحاء شجرة يستخدم لتنظيف الأسنان ولإعطاء لون بني محمر للثة والشفاه

Dawara
دوارة
Decorative leather or woven saddle bag
جلد مزخرف أو سرج الفرس من النسيج

Dawwam
دوام
Embroidery stripes which separate groups of floral designs on Palestinian women's dresses (Stillman)
شريط تطريز يفصل مجموعات من الرسومات تطرز على رداء المرأة الفلسطينية .

Dayer
دايـر
Embroidery borders on Palestinian women's dresses (Stillman)
جوانب التطريز على ثوب المرأة الفلسطينية

Dehen
دهــن
Hair oil derived from mixture of *misk*, *anbar* and *khadi*. Also known as *duhn* and imported from India and Pakistan
طيب ، يستورد من الهند والباكستان ، يستخدم في تمشيط الشعر ، يستخرج من زهور وأوراق نبات مطحونة (مسك وعمبر وخادي) .

Dehen ood
دهن العود
Scent for women
عطر للنساء

Dehen wad
دهن الواد
Scent for men
عطر للرجال

داره
قفطان طويل ضيق طويل الأكمام ، الجمع : دراري ، من الشالكي في الشتاء ، والشاش في الصيف ، عماسة ليوم الزفاف ، القفطان التقليدي للمرأة النجدية في المدن

Dharrah (pl. *dharaaree*)
Traditional *kaftan* for Najdi townswomen. Full-length dress with long slim-fitting sleeves made of *shalki* in winter and *shash* in summer (*omasa* is the elaborate version for wedding day)

ذو الحجة
الشهر الثاني عشر في السنة الهجرية

Dhul Hijjah
Twelfth month of the Islamic calendar (Hejiri)

دكــه
حزام للسروال للرجال وللنساء ، حزام للسروال الداخلي

Dikka
Sash or drawstring for *sirwaal* worn by men and women

ديره جوان
رداء طويل تلبسه النساء في البحرين

Diraa gawan
Long dress worn by women of Bahrain (Hansen)

ديــره
١ ـ منطقــة
٢ ـ منطقة الرعي للقبيلة البدوية ، الجمع : ذبارات

Dirah (pl. *diyarat*)
1 Area
2 Traditional grazing area for a nomadic tribe

دشداشــا
رداء قصير يلبسه الرجل والمرأة

Dishdasha
Ankle-length garment worn by men and women

دهن
دهن

Duhn
Syn. with *dehen*. See *dehen*

الدخلة
ليلة الزفاف

Duklah
Wedding night

عيد الأضحى
عيد التضحيه يبدأ في اليوم العاشر من شهر ذو الحجة

Eid al Adha
Feast of Sacrifice beginning on the 10th day of *Dhul Hijjah*

عيد الفطر
عيد يبدأ بعد نهاية شهر رمضان ، الإحتفال بإنهاء الصوم ، في بداية شهر شوال ويبدأ عند ظهور القمر .

Eid al Fitr
Feast held at the end of *Ramadan*, a festival of the breaking of the fast occurring on the 1st *Shawwal*, commencing with the sighting of the new moon.

عنتري
لباس داخلي تركي تلبسه النساء

Entari
Under-dress or chemise worn by Turkish women

فـلاح
مزارع ، الجمع : فلاحين

Fallah (pl. *fallaheen*)
Peasant/farmer

فلاحــة
مزارعة ، الجمع : فلاحات

Fallaha (pl. *fallahat*)
Peasant woman

فانلــه
قميص داخلي مستدير الرقبة وقصير الأكمام يلبسه الرجال

Fanilla (falina)
Short-sleeved, round-necked shirt worn by men

فـرح
الحدث السعيد ، الإحتفال بالزفاف الإسلامي وعقد الإتفاق أمام الله والأهل .

Farah
The happy event. A Muslim public wedding celebration sealing a marriage in the eyes of God and the community

فـــروه
معطف مبطن بجلد الغنم يلبسه الرجال

Farwah
Sheepskin-lined overcoat worn by men

فـز ، طربوش
غطاء للرأس تركي لونه أحمر، يلبسه الرجال

Fez
High-crowned red skullcap worn by Turkish men

فلجــان
حبال الخيمــة

Filjan
Woven strips for making Bedouin tents

فـتر
مرادف كف ، أنظر كف

Fitir
Syn. with *chaf*. See *chaf*

163

فوطـــة

قطعة قماش تلف حول الجزء الأسفل من الجسم ، يلبسه الرجال .

Fouta
Skirt formed from length of textile wound around lower half of the body, worn by men

فراش

١ ـ حصير مجدول من سعف النخيل

٢ ـ شرشف

Fraash
1 Palm frond woven mats
2 Bedding

فرملايه

مرادف صاعيه ، جاكيت بتطريز ذهبي يلبسها الرجال

Furmilaaya
Syn. with *saaya*. Jacket with gold embroidery, worn by men

فستان

قفطان تلبسه النساء ، يشبه داره

Fustan
Kaftan similar to *migta* and *dharaah*, worn by women (Katakura)

جلابيه

رداء مصري طويل

Gallabia
Full-length Egyptian robe

جانون

آلة موسيقية

Ganoun
Zither-like musical instrument

قــات

شجرة صغيرة تسمى كاتا اديولس ، لها خواص تخدير ضعيفة

Gat
Toxic shrub *Cathae edulis* with mild narcotic properties

قاطـع

ستارة في الخيمة

Gata
Decorative divider to separate *hareem* in Bedouin tent

جـــوان

رداء طويل تلبسه النساء في البحرين

Gawan
Long under-dress or chemise with narrow long sleeves, worn by women of Bahrain

غبانـه

قطعة قماش مربعة يضعها الرجال على الرأس في الحجاز

Ghabana
Large square headcloth worn by Hijazi men

غبيـط

هـودج الجمـل

Ghabeet
Type of camel litter or howdah

غنم

الماشيـة

Ghanam
Collective term for sheep and goats

غشـــوه

اللباس التقليدي في البحرين ، طويل وأكمامه طويلة تلبسه النساء

Ghaswa
Rectangular black tulle head scarf trimmed on three sides with blue glass beads worn by women of Bahrain (Hansen)

غـوطـره

غطاء للرأس يلبسه الرجال في نجد

Ghoutra
Headcloth worn by Najdi men

غمـره

حفلة للنساء تسبق الزواج ، وتعمل عندما تخضب العروس بالحناء

Ghumra
Pre-nuptial party for women when *henna* decorations are applied to the bride's skin

غســـل

الطهارة والوضوء

Ghusl
Prescribed Islamic major ablution

جبــه

شال أحمر به شريط أسود تلبسه نساء قبيلة روالـه

Gibbe (jibbe)
Red shawl with black strip worn by women of the Rwalla tribe (Musil)

قربــه

إناء للماء من الجلد

Girba
Skin water container

غنا

غطاء لرأس المرأه يلبس عادة مع شايله

Gnaa
Rectangular headcloth usually worn with *shayla* by women

Gub
جــب
قلنسوة أطفال تلبس في الشهر الأول من العمر
Child's hood or bonnet worn from one month of age

Gubgaab
جبجاب
صندل كعبه من الخشب
Thick-soled wooden sandals with fabric or leather strap upper, sometimes inlaid with mother-of-pearl or silver.
Bridal shoes worn by Hijazi townswomen

Gumaash
جماش
قماش ، نسيج
Woven cloth

Gumma
غمـا
قلنسوة مثقبة ومطرزة
Skullcap on which holes poked through the stiffened cotton with thorns or pieces of pointed wood and which are edged with embroidery

Habara
حباره
أرجوحـة الطفـل
Child's hammock (Dickson)

Habaya
حبايه
وشاح مستطيل تلبسه المرأة
Rectangular scarf worn by women

Habl (pl. *hubal*)
حبـل
حبل للربط ، الجمع : حبال
Rope

Hadhra
حادهره
مصيدة للسمك مصنوعة من سعف النخيل
Fish trap made from palm branch ribs

Hadith
حـديث
أقوال النبي محمد صلى الله عليه وسلم
Sayings of the Prophet Muhammed

Hadur
حضر
أهل المدن ، حضران : رجال المدن ، حضريات : نساء المدن
Townspeople (*hudran*: townsmen – *hidiriyyat*: townswomen)

Haggu
حـاجـو
حزام جلد مضفر يلبسه رجال القبائل
Plaited leather belt worn by tribesmen (Doughty)

Haik
حـايـك
رداء للرأس والأكتاف والصدر يلبسه الرجال
Seamless garment for the head, shoulders and chest, worn by men

Haj
حـج
أحد فرائض الإسلام الخمسة
The fifth of the five tenets of Islam – the pilgrimage to Mecca

Hajja
حـاجـه
المسلمة التي أدت فريضة الحج
A female Muslim who has completed the *Haj*

Hajji
حـاج
المسلم الذي أدى فريضة الحج
A male Muslim who has completed the *Haj*

Hangresse
هانجرسى
مرادف نفل : أوراق جافه من نبات ترايجونيلا ستيلاتا ، تستخدم في تصفيف الشعر.
Syn. with *nifl*. Dried leaves of *Trigonella stellata*, a herbal hair dressing (Dickson)

Haram
حـرام
مقدس
Sacred

Hareem
حـريم
الإناث في الأسرة والحجره التي تجلس فيها النساء
Women, thereby female members of the family and room where women sit

Hareer gazz
حرير جز
حرير نقي
Pure silk

Hasir
حصير
Palm frond matting
فراش مصنوع من سعف النخيل

Haudh
حوض
Water trough (Dickson)
حوض ماء

Hawan
هاون
Coffee grinding mortar of wood, iron or brass including *yed al hawan* or pestle
هاون طحن القهوة

Hejira
هجرة
Migration of the Prophet Muhammed
هجرة النبي محمد عليه الصلاة والسلام

Hejiri
هجري
The name of the Islamic calendar which dates from the time of the Prophet Muhammed's migration to Medina from Mecca in 622 AD. Derived from *Hejira*
التاريخ الهجري ويبدأ بتاريخ هجرة النبي محمد عليه الصلاة والسلام من مكة الى المدينة في عام ٦٢٢ ميلادي

Heremsy
حرمسى
Red, green, and gold silk panels on Palestinian women's dresses (Stillman)
قطعة قماش حريرية حمراء وخضراء وصفراء توضع فوق رداء المرأة

Hidha
هيدا
1 Syn. with *zarabil*. See *zarabil*
2 Thonged Hijazi sandal
١ – مرادف زرابيل جمع ، المفرد زربول
٢ – صندل يلبس في الحجاز

Hidiriyyat
حضريات
See *hadur*
أنظر حضر

Hijab
حجاب
1 Amuletic motif such as triangle or diamond shape composed of double triangles
2 Small silver charm
١ – تعويذة على شكل مثلث أو معين وتتكون من مثلثات مزدوجة .
٢ – تعويذه فضيه صغيره

Hilyat shaar
حلية شعر
Hair ornaments
مشابك للشعر

Hinna
حناء
Henna, shrub *Lawsonia inermis*. Flowers yield perfume (*tamr hinna*), leaves and berries yield extract and powder for hair conditioner and stain for skin
شجيرة لاوسونيا إنرمس ، الزهور تنتج عطر تمر حنا والأوراق والثمار تعطي صبغه للجلد وللشعر

Hinna khadra
حنا خضره
Freshly prepared henna paste
عجينة الحناء

Hizam
حزام
Waistbelt worn by men and women
ما يلف حول الخصر

Huardhi
حواردي
Small hunting knife (Dickson)
سكين صغير يستخدم في الصيد

Hudran
حضران
See *hadur*
أنظر حضر

Humra wa bawdra
حمره وبودره
Rouge and powder, cosmetics of Hijazi women
أحمر شفايف وبودره ، مواد تجميل للمرأة الحجازيه

Huwairiyah
حويريه
Boat made from date palm stems and fibres
قارب مصنوع من جذوع أشجار وألياف النخيل

Ibar (sing. *ibra*)
إبر
Sewing needles
إبر خياطة ، المفرد : إبره

Idl
عدل
Women's woven woollen camel bag for rice, flour, sugar etc. It hooks on to the saddle
حقيبة تستعملها المرأة في هودج الجمل

Igaal
Syn. with *shattafa*
1 Head circlet of cord, rope, or leather to hold headcloth in place. Usually a double coil bound with black wool worn by men
2 Leather circlet with pendants worn by women

عقـال
مرادف شطفا ١ ـ رباط للرأس مصنوع من الخيوط أو الجلد ، وعادة يكون مزدوج وملفوف بالصوف الأسود ويستخدم لتثبيت غطاء الرأس للرجال .
٢ ـ رباط من الجلد وله حلية متدليه تلبسه النساء

Igaal gassab
Head circlet bound with gold metallic thread except at four corners which are black wool, usually double, rarely four rungs, once worn by royal men

عقال قصب
عقال مذهب يلبسه الرجال

Ihram
1 *Haj* costume worn by men
2 Headcloth worn by men of Mecca, Jeddah and Tayif. Syn. with *shaal* (Medina), *ghoutra* (Najd)

إحرام
١ ـ ملابس الحج التي يلبسها الرجال .
٢ ـ غطاء للرأس في مكة المكرمه وجده والطائف ، مرادف شال في المدينه ، غوطره في نجد

Ilagah
Decorative pendants suspended from headgear worn by women

علاقه
دلاية للزينة مثبتة في غطاء الرأس تلبسها النساء

Imaamah
See *imma*

عمامه
انظر عمه

Imam
Islamic religious leader in prayer

إمـام
من يؤم المسلمين في الصلاة

Imma
Headcloth once worn over skullcap (Classical *imaamah*). A turban or long or large section of textile twisted and folded several times around the head worn by Hijazi townsmen

عمـه
(عمامه) غطاء للرأس فوق الطاقية في مدن الحجاز يلبسه الرجال ، قطعة من القماش تلف حول الرأس عدة مرات

Isaaba (pl. *asayib*)
Head circlet made of silver, leather and silver, reeds and copper wire, etc. worn by men and women

عصابه
رباط للرأس من الفضة أو من الجلد والفضة ، أو من القصب وأسلاك النحاس وغير ذلك يلبسه الرجال والنساء ، الجمع : عصايب

Islam
The Muslim religion, submission to the will of God.

إسـلام
الديانـة الاسـلامية

Itnayn
The number two

إثنـين
العدد ٢

Itr
Syn. with *ittir*, *attar*. Fragrance of a volatile essential oil obtained from petals and leaves of certain plants.

عطـر
زيت طيار ذو رائحة جميلة يحصل عليه من زهور وأوراق بعض النباتات

Izar
See *wazaris*

إزار
انظر وزاريث ـ عباية طويلة

Jambiyyah
Curved dagger usually kept in a sheath (*jeraab* or *ghemd*)

جمبيــه
خنجر مقوس يحفظ في جراب أو غمد

Jarid al nakhil
Palm branch brooms

جريـد النخـل
أغصان شجر النخيل

Jeraab
Small fringed bag for carrying coffee

جـراب
كيس يوضع به البن

Jezma Makshoofa
Slip-on shoe

حذاء مكشوف
حذاء بدون رباط

Jezz
Coarse textile

جـز
صوف خشن

167

جيـده
سلطانية من خشب الطرفـاء

Jidda
Tamarisk wood bowls, usually studded with brass nails or inlaid with silver or lead (Dickson)

جفـار الخوصـه
غمـد الخنجـر

Jiffar al khusa
Sheath for dagger (Dickson)

جلد
جلـد

Jild
Leather

جـواهر
مجـوهـرات

Jowaher
Jewellery

جوزاي
كمـان

Jozay
Fiddle

جبـه
رداء خارجي طويل مفتوح من الأمام يلبسه الرجال والنساء

Jubba
Long front-opening coat, earliest Islamic examples have wide, deep-pointed sleeves. Worn by men and women

الكعبـة
١ ـ الكعبة المشرفة ، أول بيت وضع للناس في مكة
٢ ـ مبنى مكعب الشكل يوجد به الحجر الأسود ، في مكه ، وهو قبلة المسلمين
٣ ـ شكل مكعب

Kaaba
1 First House of God. Koran
2 Cube-shaped stone building which contains the sacred black stone in Mecca to which a Muslim directs himself during prayer
3 Cube

كـاباك
زراير الثوب

Kabak
Cufflinks

قفطـان
رداء طويل يلبسه الرجل والمرأة

Kaftan
Full-length, shaped tunic originally without darts, collar or zipper worn by men and women

كحـل
مسحوق أسود من الأنتيمون يستخدم لتجميل العيون ، ولعلاج الجفون

Kahal
Syn. with *kuhr, kuhl* and *kohl*. A black eyelining substance made from powdered antimony, used for cosmetic purposes and as a remedy for conjunctivitis

كلمبـاك
خشب له رائحة عطره يحصل عليه من الهند وباكستان

Kalambac
Scented wood from India and Pakistan

كنادر
نعال عربي بدون كعب يستورد من الهند والبحرين مفرد : كنداره

Kanader (sing. *kindara*)
Shoes without heels imported from India and Bahrain. Velvet versions worn by brides

خـيط
خيط من النسيج للخياطه

Khait (khaid)
Thread for sewing, traditionally drawn from textile

خيمـة
مرادف : بيت الشعر ، مسكن البدوي مصنوع من الصوف والشعر

Khaima
Syn. with *bayt al shaar*. Blackish-brown hand-loomed Bedouin tent usually made from mixture of sheep's wool and goats' hair

خليفـة
حاكم إسلامي يحكم بالقرآن والسنة

Khalifa (caliph)
Islamic governor with the role of governing according to the *Koran* and *Hadith* (the sayings of the Prophet Muhammed)

الخـلافة
نظام الحكم في الاسلام

Khalifate (caliphate)
System of Islamic government

خمسـة
العدد ٥

Khamsa
The number five

خنجـر
سكين مقوس يوضع عادة في جراب أو غمد

Khanjar
Curved dagger usually kept in a sheath (*jeraab* or *ghemd*)

خصف
مرادف حصير

Khasaf
Syn. with *hasir*

خديوي
حاكم تركي في مصر

Khedive
Turkish ruler in Egypt

خدري
سجادة شغل يدوي

Khidre
Hand-woven rugs

خـف
شراب من الجلد الناعم

Khuf
Soft leather sock

خـرج
كيس يوضع على ظهر الدابة

Khurj
Men's saddle bags (double) which hang each side of saddle

خوصة
خنجـر

Khusa
Dagger kept in a sheath, *jiffar al khusa* (Dickson)

كنداره
أنظر كنادر

Kindara
See *kanader*

كيرتـه
مرادف : ثوب ، تلبسه النساء في الحجاز

Kirta
Syn. with *tawb*, worn by Hijazi women

كيرتـل
رداء كردي تلبسه النساء في أفغانستان

Kirtle
Long dress worn by Kurdish women of Afghanistan

كسـوة
١ ـ ملابس
٢ ـ أقمشة
٣ ـ قماش أسود مطرز بالذهب تغطى به الكعبة المشرفه ويستبدل سنويا

Kiswa
1 Textiles
2 Clothing
3 Gold embroidered black covering for the *Kaaba*. Traditionally replaced annually

القرآن الكريم
كتاب الله الذي أنزل على سيدنا محمد صلى الله عليه وسلم ، باللغة العربية

Koran (Quran)
Muslim book of the Islamic religion. The word of God as transmitted by the Angel Gabriel in Arabic to the Prophet Muhammed

كوفيـه
١ ـ مرادف : جب ، طاقيه يلبسها الأطفال
٢ ـ مرادف : طاقيه ، غطاء للرأس يلبسه الرجال والأولاد .

Kufiyyah
1 Syn. with *gub*, a bonnet worn by babies
2 Syn. with *taagiyyah*, a skullcap worn by men and boys

كوفيه بلدي
غطاء طويل للرأس كان يلبسه أهل الحجاز قديما

Kufiyyah Belladi
Tall skullcap worn under headcloth, *imma*, once worn by Hijazi townsmen

كوفيه بالقصب
غطاء للرأس مطرز بالقصب يلبسه الرجال والأولاد

Kufiyyah Mugassabeh
Richly embroidered skullcap worn by men and boys

لحـاف
دثار من القطن شـغـل يـدوي

Lahaf
Handwoven cotton blanket

لاونـد
عطر يصنع من زهور اللافندر

Lawend
Scent made from lavender flowers

ليلة الحنة
الليلة التي يحتفل فيها بوضع الحنة على العروس

Laylat al hinna
Henna night.
Women's evening when bride's skin is decorated with henna

169

Libas
لباس
Long cotton pants worn by men
سروال داخلي من القطن

Lihaf
لحـاف
Thin gauze veil sufficiently long to trail after being wound about the head and shoulders, worn by Omani women
حجاب من الشاش يغطي الرأس والأكتاف ثم يتدلى على الأرض ، تلبسه النساء في عمان

Litham
لثام
Headcloth drawn over the lower portion of the face worn by rural and nomadic women
غطاء للرأس يغطي الجزء الأسفل من الوجه ، تلبسه النساء القرويات والبدويات

Maadas
مداس
Thonged sandals
صندل

Maaward
ماء ورد
Rosewater
ماء به رائحة الورد

Madhara
مدهره
Lambskin for storing butter (Dickson)
جلد حمل يخزن فيه الزبدة

Mafif
مفيـف
Leather cord for binding the hair and circling the head seven times worn by men (Phillips)
شريط جلدي يلف حول الرأس سبع مرات ، يلبسه الرجال

Maghzal
مغزل
Syn. with *mubrah*. Spindle (Dickson)
مرادف : موبره ، إبرة خشبية لغزل الصوف

Magruna
مقـرونه
1 Large dark headscarf folded to a triangle worn by women of northern Arabia (Musil)
١ ــ منديل رأس للسيدات
2 Rolls of plaited and woven leather over packing core, decorated with silver beadwork and attached as two ''horns'' on headscarf. Worn by Bedouin women of the Hijaz
٢ ــ لفات من الجلد مزخرفة بالفضة تلبس فوق غطاء الرأس ، تلبسه النساء البدويات في الحجاز

Mahabdy
مهابدي
Shawl worn by newly-married rural girls of the Hijaz (Katakura)
شال تلبسه العروسة الجديدة

Mahanna
مهنـا
Similar to *taraha*, *shayla* etc. A semi-transparent, black rectangular headscarf with decorated ends worn by women
يشبه الطرحة ، شايله غطاء للرأس أسود نصف شفاف ، أطرافه مطرزة تلبسه النساء.

Mahmas
مَحمــص
Coffee bean roaster joined by chain to *yed al mahmas* or stirrer
يستخدم لتحميص البن وله يد .

Mahr
مهـر
Dowry
مبلغ من النقد يدفعه العريس الى،أهل العروس

Maksar
مكسـر
1 Plain camel hair cloak worn by men
١ ــ عباية مصنوعة من وبر الجمل يلبسها الرجال
2 Decorated camel litter made of pomegranate wood
٢ ــ هودج مزخرف ومصنوع من خشب الرمان

Markab
مركـب
1 Decorated tribal camel litter, or howdah (Musil)
١ ــ هودج الجمل
2 Tripod for cooking and coffee pots (Dickson)
٢ ــ مرجل ثلاثي القوائم

Marwaha
مروحـة
Flag-shaped palm-frond fans
مروحة من سعف النخيل تشبه العلم

Mashta
مشته
Professional woman who prepares bride with costume and cosmetics for the wedding
امرأة تجهز العروس باللبس والتجميل ليوم الزفاف

مطـارح
مرادف : ناتو، نول البدوي

Mattarih
Syn. with *nattu*. Bedouin handloom (Dickson)

ميرودان
مرادف : شلحات ، ونيا ـ رداء طويل واسع الأكمام يلبسه .الرجال

Merodan
Syn. with *shillahat*, *woniya*, etc. A full-length, capacious *kaftan* with large sleeves ending with deep-pointed lappets worn by men

مسـبحة
يستخدمها المسلم بعد الصلاة للإستغفار وذكر الله وتحتوي على ٣٣ أو ٩٩ حبة مقسمة إلى أقسام من ١١ حبة أو ٣٣ حبة ، يوجد بها عدد اثنين حبة فاصلة كبيرة وفي نهايتها مئذنة ، مرادف : سبحه

Mesbaha
Syn. with *subha*. Muslim prayer beads, sometimes referred to as "worry beads", strands of 33 or 99 beads in multiples of 11 or 33 divided by 2 spacer beads and 1 tasselled terminal bead

مسواك
أغصان صغيرة من شجر الأراك تستخدم في تنظيف الأسنان

Meswaak
Small branch of arak tree used for cleaning teeth

مزاوي
قفطان من الحرير تلبسه نساء قبيله رواله

Mezawi
Silk *kaftan* worn by women of the Rwalla tribe (Musil)

مزوي
مرادف عباية ، تلبسها النساء في قبيلة رواله

Mezwi
Syn. with *abaaya*. A cloak worn by women of the Rwalla tribe (Musil)

مدك
رباط رفيع من الخيوط يستخدم للسروال

Midak
Pencil-like sash threader for *sirwaal*

مدره
إبرة لنسج الخيوط

Middrah
Gazelle horn weaving pick (Dickson)

مجتـه
أنظر قفطان ، يلبسها الرجال والنساء

Migta
Type of kaftan. See *kaftan*

محرمه
قطعة قماش مستطيلة توضع على الرأس تلبسها النساء ، قطعة من محرمة ومدورة

Mihramah
Rectangular headcloth. Part of *mihramah wa mudawwarah*

محرمه ومدوره
غطاء رأس تقليدي تلبسه المرأة في الحجاز، على ثلاثة أشكال مثلث ومستطيل ومربع

Mihramah wa mudawwarah
Three-piece traditional headgear made up of triangle, rectangle and square scarves once worn by Hijazi townswomen

ملايـة
١ ـ قطعة قماش
٢ ـ عباية ملونة تلبسها النساء

Milaaya
1 Sheet
2 Colourful sheet-like mantle worn by women

ملبس
زي في منطقة عسير تلبسه النساء

Milbas
Style of Asir Province dress worn by women

ملفه
مشابه : أم الرجيلة ، طرحة ـ نسيج خفيف أسود يغطي الوجه أحيانا ، تلبسه النساء

Milfa
Similar to *umm raugella* and *taraha*.
Semi-transparent black scarf often drawn over the lower part of the face. Worn by women.

منسج
إطار التطريز

Minsaj
Embroidery frame

منون
قربة من جلد الجمل

Minun
Camel skin water container

ميراقة
جلد مطرز يوضع فوق الجمل

Miraka
Decorative leather apron for camel's chest used by sheikhs and leaders (Dickson)

مرواد
أداة لوضع الكحل في الجفون

Mirwad
Eyeliner

مسامه **Misama**
سرج الجمل من خشب شجرة الطرفاء Camel pack saddle made of tamarisk wood
(Dickson)

مصفه **Misfa**
قطعة قماش سوداء مستطيلة تضعها النساء في نجد على الوجه ، مرادف : طرحه Syn. with *taraha*. Najdi rectangular black headcloth worn by women

مسحه **Misha**
رأس المغزل Weaving shuttle (Dickson)

مسحاب **Mishaab**
عصاة للجمل من شجرة السدر Camel stick made from the Sidr tree (Dickson)

مشلح **Mishlah**
مرادف : بشت ، عباية يلبسها الرجال Syn. with *bisht*. Cloak or mantle worn by men

مشط **Misht**
مشط خشبي Comb

مسك **Misk**
رائحة ذكية Musk scent

مظله **Mizalla**
قبعة من سعف النخيل بها صدف أصفر وزراير بيضاء . Style of palm frond hat with cowrie shells and white buttons from the Asir.

مزوال **Mizawal**
حقيبة تستعملها البدوية في هودج الجمل Women's saddle bag. Two separate bags hang each side of the camel (Dickson)

مزبه **Mizbah**
مهد للطفل Child's portable cradle (Dickson)

مزلاج **Mizolaj**
مرادف ميرودان ، قميص للأولاد *Merodan* worn by boys

مزوده **Mizuda**
كيس صغير من الجلد والنسيج مزخرف لحمل الأغراض Small leather or woven bag decorated with beads, tassels, appliqué, etc, for storing and carrying coffee beans, dates, money, herbs, Koranic verses or a small version of the *Koran*

مجمود **Mogmud**
حجاب الوجه للمرأة في اليمن من الحرير الأسود مطرز بالأحمر والأبيض تلبسه النساء Style of face veil. Tie-dyed, Indian coarse black silk with repeated red and white ''target'' pattern worn by women of North Yemen

مر **Morr**
مادة صمغية من الأشجار، المادة الرئيسية في الأدوية ومستحضرات التجميل في الماضي Myrrh, an aromatic resin from tree (*Balsamodendron myrrha*). A major ingredient in medicaments and cosmetics in ancient times

مشارط **Moshart**
مخلوط من المسك والمورد والرياحين لونه بني محمر يوضع على الشعر Reddish-brown hair colouring and conditioning compound made from crushed, dried *misk*, *ward* and *rayheen* flowers and leaves from the Najd

موسوان **Mouswan**
عباية تلبسها النساء في الحفلات بالحجاز Cloak for festive occasions worn by Hijazi women

مؤخر **Muakhkhar**
جزء مؤجل من المهر يدفع فقط في حالة طلاق الزوجة Second part of dowry payment due only in case of divorce

مبره **Mubrah**
مرادف : مغزل Syn. with *maghzal*. Spindle (Dickson)

مدندش **Mudandash**
رداء في عسير تلبسه النساء
Style of Asir Province dress worn by women

مدوره **Mudawwarah**
غطاء رأس مربع ، جزء من محرمه ومدوره
Square headcloth. Part of *mihramah wa mudawwarah*

المفتي **Mufti**
أكبر مسئول ديني ، بدأ تعيينه في عهد العثمانيين في عام ١٥٣٩ م
Grand mufti of Islam, the highest religious authority, leading religious and legal official first appointed in 1539

مجـدم **Mugaddam**
جزء من المهر يدفع عند عقد القران
First part of dowry payment paid at the time of engagement

مجص **Mugass**
مقص
Scissors

مقصب **Mugassab**
مطـرز
Embroidery, embroidered

موخنج **Mukhnug**
مرادف : بوخنج
Syn. with *bukhnug*. See *bukhnug*

مشتغل **Mushtaghal**
مطرز
Embroidered

موزون **Muzoon**
عباية مطرزة تلبسها المرأة البدوية في الحجاز
Richly decorated sheet. A cloak or mantle worn by Hijazi tribal women

النصاصين **Nassasseen**
العريس في الحجاز
Bridegroom's family *hareem* of Hijazi townspeople

نطحه **Natha**
عود خشبي يستخدم لتضييق الخيوط
Flat wooden rod used in weaving for tightening threads (Dickson)

ناتـو **Nattu**
مرادف : مطارح ، نول البدوي
Syn. with *mattarih*. Bedouin handloom (Dickson)

نـاي **Nay**
آلة نفخ موسيقية
Flute

نعـال **Niaal**
صنادل ، المفرد : نعل
Sandals. Sing. *naal*

نفـل **Nifl**
مرادف : هانجرسي
Syn. with *hangresse*. See *hangresse* (Dickson)

نقـاب **Nigaab**
١ ـ الاسم بالعربيه لبرقع ، حجاب سميك
٢ ـ حجاب أبيض كانت تلبسه النساء في الحجاز
1 Classical Arabic for *burga*, a stiffened veil
2 Long white stiffened veil once worn by Hijazi townswomen

نـوره **Nura**
الجير
Powdered lime

أويـا **Oiya**
تطريز تقليدي لرداء المرأة في الحجاز
Traditional embroidered edging on Hijazi townswomen's garments. Turkish word for lace-making technique employing a needle

عماسـه **Omasa**
داره مطرزة بالذهب
Elaborate gold-embroidered *dharaah*. A *kaftan* of silk, velvet or nylon made in India, sometimes having matching *sirwaal* and *kindara*. Worn by Najdi women. Traditionally cerise for the bride

173

عصبه
Osba (pl. *asaayib*)
1 Head circlet made from scarf or section of textile folded to a width of four fingers, worn by men and women

١ ـ قطعة من القماش تطبق ليصبح عرضها أربعة أصابع ويلبسها الرجال والنساء على الرأس

٢ ـ قطعة قماش للرأس تلبسها النساء أثناء المرض

٣ ـ مرادف بوخنج وموخنج ، قطعة قماش بيضاء توضع على رأس المرأة المتوفية ، الجمع : عصايب
2 White cloth for the head worn by women when sick
3 Syn. with *bukhnug* and *mukhnug*. White cloth headbinding for dead female. The garment is torn and sewn as *bukhnug*

العـود
Oud
Standard Arabic musical instrument belonging to the family of short lutes, similar to a guitar, for solo instrumental music or to accompany a singer

آلة موسيقية عربية من درجات النغمة القصيرة مشابه للجيتار يستعمل بمفرده أو بمصاحبة المغني

أوكـه
Oukk (oukkah)
Sheepskin container for storing butter

قطعة من جلد الغنم توضع فيها الزبدة

كبــه
Qabbeh
Front bodice panel on one style of dress worn by Palestinian women

تطريز يوضع على صدر فستان المرأة الفلسطينية

قطع الستاره
Qataha al sitara
Ceremony announcing forthcoming Bedouin marriage performed by Hijazi women (Katakura)

حفلة دعوة بشأن الزواج المقبل تقوم بها النساء في الحجاز

قـوز
Qaws
Dry south-west wind bringing sand clouds in the Gulf region

ريح يهب من الجنوب الغربي في منطقة الخليج ، يحدث سحب من الرمال

قمبـاز
Qumbaz
Similar to *baalto* and *zibun*. Ankle-length front-opening outer garment closes right over left with ties inside and out, slits each side upwards from hemline and slits at underarm seams moving upwards from cuffs. Worn by Palestinian men and women (Stillman)

رداء طويل خارجي مفتوح يلبسه الرجال والنساء ، يشبه بالطو وزبون

كوران
Quran
Side plaits for the hair worn by Bedouin

ضفائر شعر تلبسها البدوية

ربابـه
Rabaaba
One-stringed fiddle

كمنجه لها وتر واحد

رمضـان
Ramadan
Ninth month of the *Hejiri* (holy month of fasting)

الشهر التاسع في السنة الهجرية ، شهر الصـوم

راشـوش
Rashush
Herbal hair dressing (Dickson)

مستحضر من الأعشاب للشعر

راوي
Rawi
Camel skin water container

قطعة جلد جمل يوضع فيها الماء

ريش
Reysh
Agate beads from Bombay

حبوب عقيق من بومباي

رواق
Ruwag
Decorative back curtain for Bedouin tent

ستارة خلفية في خيمة البدوي

صاعيه
Saaya
Syn. with *furmilaaya*. See *furmilaaya*

مرادف : فورماليه

سبعه
Sabaa
The number seven

العدد ٧

صحزه
Sahhara
Woman's treasure box

صندوق تضع فيه المرأة النقود

174

Saif
Sheathed sword

السيف
السيف

Salaah
The second of the five tenets of Islam – prayer

الصلاة
ذكر الله أحد أركان الاسلام

Saluki
Arabian hunting dog

السلوقي
كلب صيد

Samn
Clarified butter (*ghee*)

سمن
زبدة مكررة

Saujar
Short pants worn by women (Dickson)

سـوجار
بنطلون قصير تلبسه النساء

Saumer
"Black henna" achieved by an application of *nura* and *shanadah* over the first application of henna

سـومر
حناء سوداء تحضر بوضع النوره والشناده على الحناء

Sawm
The fourth of the five tenets of Islam – fasting from sunrise to sunset during *Ramadan*

الصـوم
الامتناع عن الأكل من شروق الشمس الى غروبها في شهر رمضان ، أحد أركان الاسلام

Shaal
Syn. with *ghoutra*. Worn by men of Medina

شال
مرادف غوطره ، يلبسه الرجال في المدينه

Shaash
Fine cloth for making Najdi women's summer-weight *kaftan*

شـاش
قماش خفيف تصنع منه قفطان المرأة النجديه في الصيف

Shahadah
The first of the five tenets of Islam – profession of Muslim faith: there is no god but God (Allah) and Muhammed is His prophet

الشهاده
شهادة أن لا إله إلا الله وأن محمدا رسول الله

Shalha
Underdress or chemise, full or half-length, worn by Hijazi townswomen

شلحـه
رداء داخلي قصير أو طويل تلبسه النساء في الحجاز

Shalki
Fine pure wool from India and Pakistan for making Najdi women's winter-weight *kaftan*

شـلقي
صوف من الهند أو باكستان تصنع منه القفطان الشتوي للمرأة النجديه

Shamaal
Strong north-east wind

شمال
رياح شمالية شرقيه شديده

Shambar
Triangular scarf with two tie cords. Part of *mihramah wa mudawwarah*

شـمبر
وشاح مثلث الشكل ، جزء من المحرمه والمدوره

Shanada
Powdered crystal ammoniac

الشنادة
نوع من البلـورات المعدنية

Shariah
Sacred law of Islam based on the *Koran*

شريعة
القوانين الاسلامية المعتمدة على القرآن الكريم

Sharqi
Humid wind in Arabian Gulf

شرقي
رياح رطبة في الخليج العربي

Sharshaf
1 Prayer shawl worn by women
2 Large shawl wrapper worn by women in rural Hijaz

شرشف
١ ـ شال تلبسه النساء أثناء الصلاة
٢ ـ شال تلبسه النساء في قرى الحجاز

Shattafa
Syn. with *igaal*. See *igaal*

شـطفا
مرادف عقال

Shatweh
شطاوح
Palestinian dowry hat decorated with coins and two pendant side ornaments (Stillman)
غطاء للرأس تستعمله المرأة الفلسطينية مزين بالعملة وبدلايتين

Shawwal
شوال
Tenth month of the Islamic *Hejiri* calendar
الشهر العاشر في السنة الهجريه

Shayla
شايله
Rectangular headscarf similar to *taraha* worn by women
مشابهة للطرحة تلبسها النساء على الرأس

Shedaad
شداد
Camel riding saddle made of tamarisk wood inlaid with lead or silver
سرج الجمل

Sheikh
شيخ
Respected gentleman, tribal leader, and religious scholar
رجل ذو مركز اجتماعي أو ديني

Sherif
شريف
Noble and glorious local governor and judge first appointed in 966 AD
حاكم من أصل عريق

Shibr
شبر
Span of the hand between thumb and little finger. A traditional Arabian measurement
المسافة بين الإبهام والاصبع الصغير ، مقياس يستعمله البدوي

Shillahat
شلحات
Syn. with *merodan* and *woniya* etc. See *merodan* (Dickson)
مرادف ميرودان ، ونيا ، انظر ميرودان

Shmagh
شماغ
Headcloth of the checkered red and white variety worn by men
غطاء للرأس ، أبيض وأحمر مربعات يلبسه الرجال

Shoon
الشون
Walking stick once carried by Hijazi townsmen
عصاة كان يستخدمها الرجال في الحجاز

Sidaireeya
صديريه
High-collared, elbow-length, narrow-sleeved blouse which serves as a brassière, vest and cravat
قميص له ياقه مرتفعه وأكمامه ضيقه وتصل إلى المرفق

Sikeena
سكينه
1 Knife
١ ــ سكينة
2 Small sheathed dagger
٢ ــ خنجر صغير

Sikka
سك
Coinage die
سك العملة

Sirwaal
سروال
Capacious long pants with sash to draw in waistline, worn by men and women
بنطلون طويل واسع يربط على الخصر تلبسه النساء والرجال

Sirwaal mushtaghal
سروال مشغول
Long pants with embroidered leggings
سروال مطرز

Sita
سته
The number six
العدد ٦

Sitara
ستاره
1 Special red cloth used in (*qataa al sitara*) Bedouin betrothal announcement ritual in the Hijaz
١ ــ فستان أحمر ترتديه العروس عند الخطوبه
2 Tent curtain behind which betrothed girl receives friends in rural Hijaz (Katakura)
٢ ــ ستاره في الخيمه

Sitfa
شطفه
Headband to hold *sumbar* in place among the Rwalla tribe (Musil)
عصابة للرأس تثبت الزمبار على الجبين

Siyaam
صيـام
Syn. with *sawm*. See *sawm*
مرادف : صوم

Smaada
صمـاده
1 Large shawl or wrapper worn by unmarried girls of rural Hijaz.
2 Coin-trimmed bonnet worn by women in Palestine
١ ـ عباية تلبسها الفتيات في قرى الحجاز
٢ ـ غطاء للرأس للمرأة الفلسطينية محلى بالعملات الذهبية أو الفضية

Souf
صوف
Sheep's wool and goats' hair
صوف الغنم وشعر الماعز

Soun
سـون
Style of Asir Province dress worn by women
رداء تقليدي في مرتفعات عسير تلبسه النساء

Souq
سـوق
Marketplace
مكان للبيع والشراء

Souq al-badw
سوق البدو
Bedouin marketplace
مكان البيع والشراء للبدوي

Subha
سـبحه
Syn. with *mesbaha*
مرادف مسبحة

Sufra
سـفرة
Palm-frond table mats
منضدة من سعف النخيل

Sumbar
زمبـار
Headscraf worn by well-to-do women of the Rwalla tribe (Musil)
وشاح للرأس تلبسه المرأة البدوية الثرية

Sundouq
صندوق
Container or box
خزانة كبيرة تحفظ بها الأشياء

Sundouq hashab
صندوق خشب
Wooden dowry chest, sometimes called a Kuwaiti or Medina chest
خزانة خشبية ، تحفظ به المجوهرات ، يسمى أحيانا خزانة كويتية أو مدينية

Sunnah
السـنه
Traditions and practice set by the Prophet Muhammed to be emulated
أقوال وأعمال النبي محمد عليه الصلاة والسلام

Swehi
سـويحي
Syn. with *hizam*. Woven broad red and black cotton and wool belt to *tawb aswad*, worn by women of the Rwalla tribe (Musil)
مرادف حزام ، شريط من القطن الأحمر والأسود ومن الصوف تلبسه النساء فوق الثوب الأسود

Taagiyyah
طاقيـه
Syn. with *kuffiyyah*. Worn by men and boys
مرادف كوفيه ، غطاء رأس يلبسه الرجال والأولاد

Tafash
طفاشـه
Woven palm-frond hats
قبعات مصنوعة من سعف النخيل

Taher
طاهـر
Muslim ritualistic cleansing for prayer
متوضأ إستعدادا للصلاة

Talata
تلاتـه
The number three
العدد ٣

Taly
طولي
Decorative appendages to headgear made by Bedouin women and girls of the Hijaz
دلايات لتزيين المصنوعات اليدوية ، تصنعها النساء والفتيات البدويات في الحجاز

Tamr hinna
تمرحنـا
Scent made from henna flowers. See *hinna*
عطر يصنع من زهور الحناء ، انظر حناء

Tar
طـار
Drum
طبـل

Tarah
Embroidery frame

طاره
اطار التطريز

Taraha
Rectangular black gauze scarf with beaded, embroidered, braided or tasselled ends. Similar to *umm raugella, milfa, misfa* etc. worn by women

طرحه
غطاء للرأس تلبسه النساء ، أسود اللون نصف شفاف ومطرز ، يشبه أم الرجيله

Tawb
Version of *thawb* worn by Hijazi townswomen

تـوب
مرادف : ثوب ، في الحجاز

Tawb aswad
Bluish-black voluminous dress with broad sleeves and deep-pointed lappets worn by women (Musil)

توب أسود
ثوب أسود تلبسه النساء

Thawb
1 Full-length, long-sleeved, high-necked garment cut similarly to a *kaftan* worn by men
2 Capacious overdress worn by women

ثوب
١ ــ رداء طويل ، طويل الأكمام ، له ياقة عالية مثل القفطان يلبسه الرجال
٢ ــ رداء خارجي شفاف تلبسه النساء

Thawb magassab
Festive occasion overgarment, richly embroidered, worn by women

ثوب مقصب
ثوب مطرز بالقصب تلبسه النساء في الحفلات

Thawb malak
Syn. with Bethany Dress or ''Queenly dress' worn by Palestinian women

ثوب الملاك
مرادف ثوب الملكة ، تلبسه النساء الفلسطينيات

Thawb nashal
Festive occasion sheet overgarment with gold metallic thread and gold sequins worn by women of the Eastern Province

ثوب نشال
رداء خارجي شفاف مشغول بخيوط الذهب والترتر الذهبي ، تلبسه النساء في المنطقة الشرقيه

Thawb shillahat
Syn. with *merodan*. See *merodan*

ثوب شلحات
مرادف ميرودان

Thilaithi
Camel-skin water container (Dickson)

ثيلثي
إناء للماء من جلد الجمل

Tsifan
Syn. with *chifan*. See *chifan*

تصفان
مرادف كفن ، انظر كفن

Umm
Mother

أم
الوالــدة

Ummah
A nation

أمـه
شـعب

Umm raugella
Rectangular black cotton scarf, similar to *taraha*, *milfa*, etc. worn by women

أم الرجله
وشاح أسود مشابه للطرحة

Uzrar (pl. *azarir*)
Shirt stud

زرار
زرار قميص ، الجمع : زراير

Waahid
The number one

واحد
العدد (١)

Wabar
Camel hair

وبـر
صوف الجمل

Walad
Boy

ولـد
ولـد

Wars
Annointing oil made from sesame oil or butter with tumeric or saffron

وريث
زيت مصنوع من السمسم أو الزبدة ويضاف اليه الزعفران

وزاريث

Wazaris (sing. *izar*)
Loincloths worn by men

المئزر ، يلبسه الرجال

ونيــا

Woniya
Syn. with *merodan* and *shillahat*. See *merodan*

مرادف : ميرودان وشلحات ، انظر ميرودان

ياجـه

Yaga
Collar

ياقة

ياسمين

Yasamine
Scent made from Jasmine flowers

عطر يصنع من زهور الياسمين

يشمك

Yashmak
Face veil worn by Muslim women of Turkey

حجاب الوجه تلبسه النساء التركيات المسلمات

يلك

Yelek
Turkish word for an ankle-length, fitted front-opening coat, with long, slim sleeves with slits as *qumbaz* from Palestine

الاسم التركي لرداء خارجي طويل ، يشبه قمباز

يســر

Yusr
Black coral from the Red Sea

مرجان أسود من البحر الأحمر

زابون

Zabun
Ankle-length, fitted front-opening dress once worn by townswomen of the Hijaz

رداء خارجي طويل مفتوح من الأمام كانت تلبسه النساء في الحجاز

زهر الليمون

Zahr-laimoon
Scent made from lemongrass flowers

عطر يصنع من زهور الليمون

زكـاة

Zakaat
The third of the five tenets of Islam – almsgiving – a religious tax contribution by the wealthy for the needy

أحد أركان الاسلام الخمسة وهي أن يقوم المسلم القادر بإعطاء نسبة من ماله الى الفقير المحتاج

زرابيــل

Zarabil (sing. *zarboul*)
1 Woven palm-frond sandals
2 Shoes
3 Three-piece pattern footwear – sole and two-part upper made of canvas or leather, worn by men and women

١ ـ صندل من سعف النخيل ، المفرد : زربول
٢ ـ حـذاء
٣ ـ شبشب مكون من نعل والوجه مكون من قطعتين من التيل أو الجلد

زراير دهب

Zarayer dhahab
Set of seven gold buttons threaded on chain whereby each button position is adjustable as it slides along. Worn cuff-link fashion on *sidaireeya*

زراير من الذهب عددها سبعة توضع على الصديرية

زركــون

Zerkoun
Rouge-red cosmetic powder obtained from various sources to colour the cheeks. A fine red powder prepared from safflower, *Carthamus tinctorius* and from roots of *Arnebia decumbens* a plant of the *Boragnaceae* family

بودرة حمراء توضع على وجنات المرأة ، تحضر من العصفر أو من نبات أرنيبيا دكمبنز من عائلة بوراجنيسي

زبــون

Zibun
Similar to *baalto* and *qumbaz* worn by men and women. See *Qumbaz*

رداء طويل مفتوح من الامام يلبسه الرجال يشبه بالطو وقمباز

زنابيــل

Znabeel (sing. *zaanbeel*)
Palm-frond baskets

سلة مصنوعة من سعف النخيل

زرار

Zorar (pl. *zarayer*)
Button

زرار (الجمع : زراير)

List of Technical Terms

عبل بوش : أنظر كاليجونم كوموسم .

Abal bush: See *Calligonum comosum*.

أبهل بهارات : مرادف : شيشه . أنظر شيشه .

Abhla bharat: Syn. with *shisha*. See *shisha*.

صبار : نبات يتبع عائلة أمريلديسي ، أوراقه بها أشواك .

Agave: Any of a genus of plants of the family *Amaryllidaceae* known for having spiny-margined leaves that can be used for their fibre.

أغاباني : غرزة الرهبان، تطريز روباني . طريقة تطريز تستخدم غرزة السلسلة لعمل تصاميم عربية على شكل أوراق النبات ، الخيوط العلوية من الحرير أو من المعدن أوكلاهما . الخيوط السفلى من القطن .

Aghabani: Syn. with monk stitching or *tatriz rubani*. An embroidery technique involving machined chain-stitched foliate *arabesque* designs. The surface threads are silk or metal-thread or both, and the thread underneath is cotton.

شبه : ملح معدني مكون من كبريتات البوتاسيوم والماغنسيوم يستخدم في دبغ الجلود وصناعة الورق والصباغة .

Alum: One of a series of double sulphates, a mineral salt (especially that of potassium and aluminium) used in leather tanning, paper making and as a mordant in dyeing.

فنون تطريزية : طريقة التطريز بالحشو، تسمى أيضا أبليكا .

Applied work: Embellishment technique whereby a medium is laid onto a base textile and secured with fine stitches. Also known as appliqué.

أبليك : طريقة التطريز بالحشو، أصل الكلمة بالفرنسية أبلكى (يضع) .

Appliqué: Embellishment technique whereby pieces of fabric or objects are affixed to a base fabric with stitches. The term is derived from the French verb *appliquer*, "to put on". Also known as applied work.

أرابيسك
طريقة الزخرفة الاسلامية وتعتمد على الأشكال الهندسية أو الخطوط المنحنية ، وأحيانا تحتوي على الأوراق والزهور والحيوانات .

Arabesque: Islamic style of decoration based on either pure geometric relations or endlessly flowing curvilinears, sometimes incorporating leaves, flowers and animals.

أرهي : مرادف : طمبور، أنظر طمبور .

Arhi: Syn. with *tambour*. See *tambour*.

أرنبيا ديكمبينس : نبات من عائلة بورجانسي ، يحصل من جذوره على بودره حمراء للروج .

Arnebia decumbens: Plant of the *Boragnacaea* family, the roots of which provide a red powder for rouge.

غرزة الظهر : أنظر، فصل التطريز .

Back stitch: See *Embroidery* chapter.

بدله : طريقة تطريز تستخدم الخيوط المعدنية من الذهب أو الفضة .

Badla: Embellishment technique employing flat metal wire. The wire pierces the cloth, making a needle unnecessary. Usually gold or silver.

بلازمودندرن مره : شجرة قصيرة الغصون تنتج مادة صمغية هي المر، وهو المكون الرئيسي لمواد التجميل في العصور القديمة .

Balsamodendron myrrha: Low spreading branched tree yielding aromatic resin, myrrh, major ingredient in medicaments and cosmetics in ancient times.

Bedouin seam: Similar to a flat seam or flat fell seam except that the finished side is reversed. The first row of sewing is backstitch and the second row is oversewing. Occasionally the finished right side of the garment is further embellished with a row of silk oversewing along this seam.

اللفقة البدوية : تشبه اللفقه المنبسطة وتختلف عنها في أن الطرف النهائي معكوس ، الصف الأول من الخياطة من غرزة الظهر ، أما الصف الثاني فهي خياطة من فوق ، وأحيانا يكون الجانب الأيمن من الرداء مطرز بخيوط الحرير من فوق فوق اللفقة .

Bedouin stitch arbaa: See *Embroidery* chapter.

الغرزة البدوية الرابعة : أنظر فصل التطريز .

Bedouin stitch itnayn: See *Embroidery* chapter.

الغرزة البدوية الثانية : أنظر فصل التطريز .

Bedouin stitch khamsa: See *Embroidery* chapter.

الغرزة البدوية الخامسة : أنظر فصل التطريز .

Bedouin stitch sabaa: See *Embroidery* chapter.

الغرزة البدوية السابعة : أنظر فصل التطريز .

Bedouin stitch sita: See *Embroidery* chapter.

الغرزة البدوية السادسة : أنظر فصل التطريز .

Bedouin stitch talata: See *Embroidery* chapter.

الغرزة البدوية الثالثة : أنظر فصل التطريز .

Bedouin stitch waahid: See *Embroidery* chapter.

الغرزة البدوية الأولى : أنظر فصل التطريز .

Bindali: Turkish style of embroidery which translates as "a thousand shoots", referring to the *arabesque* style floral and foliate motifs. It is elaborate work employing gold metal thread and sequins, and similar to Syrian *sarma*.

بندالي : الطريقة التركية في التطريز ، وتعني آلاف الأسهم إشارة إلى النظام العربي في الزخرفة الذي يحتوي على النبات والأوراق ، وهو عمل دقيق تستخدم خيوط الذهب والترتر ، ومشابه للصارما السورية .

Blanket stitch: See *Embroidery* chapter.

خرزة البطانية : أنظر فصل التطريز .

Bodice: Section of garment that covers upper half of the body.

الصدر : الجزء الأعلى من ثوب المرأة .

Bolt: Length of textile woven on a loom in one operation.

مقطع : قطعة من القماش تصنع على النول في عملية واحدة .

Boswellia carterii: Stiff low branched tree with red flowers yielding aromatic resin, frankincense, the major incense for burnt offerings and funeral pyres in ancient times.

بوسويليا كارتيري : شجره خشنه ذات أغصان منخفضة لها زهور حمراء تنتج مادة راتنجيه هي البخور، وهي العطر الأساسي في العصور القديمه ويعطي رائحة جميلة عند حرقه .

Brocade: *1* Textile of any weave or yarn enriched by a design which is formed by additional weft threads, often of metal, running back and forth across each motif only. It is woven on a jacquard loom.
2 Textile superficially resembling the above.

قماش مقصب أو مطرز : ١ ـ قماش به خيوط تطريز بعرض الثوب ، دائما تكون من المعدن داخل كل رسم ، وتنسج على نول جاكار .

٢ ـ قماش يشبه القماش المقصب أو المطرز .

Buttonhole stitch: See *Embroidery* chapter.

غرزة العروه : أنظر فصل التطريز .

Byzantine work: A style of embroidery employing satin stitch. Also known as *Oriental, Moorish, Milanese,* etc.

التطريز البيزنطي : نوع من التطريز تستخدم فيه غرزة الساتان ، وتعرف بالشرقيه ، المغربيه .

Calico: Plain unbleached or bleached coarse cotton textile.

شيت : قماش قطني مبيض أو غير مبيض .

Calligonum comosum: *Abal* bush, desert shrub of the *Polygonaceae* family, provides a soft russet-brown dye.

كاليجونم كوموسم : عبل بوش ، شجيره تنبت في الصحراء ، من عائلة بولجاناسي ، يحصل منه على صبغة لونها بني يميل إلى الوردي .

Cambric: Fine white linen originally made in Cambrai, northern France.

كامبرك : قماش أبيض ناعم يصنع في كامبرى بشمال فرنسا .

Carat (abbrev. ct.): *1* Measure for weighing gems and precious metals. Derived from the *carob* bean, an ancient measuring weight for gems and precious metals.
2 Sometimes used instead of *karat*. See *karat*.

قيراط : (١) وحدة موازين قديمة تستعمل في وزن الجواهر والمعادن الثمينة. يرجع أصل الكلمة إلى بذور الخروب . (٢) أنظر قيراط .

Carob: Evergreen Mediterranean tree, *Ceratonia siliqua*, bearing small edible seed pods with beans that are notable for uniformity of size.

خروب : شجرة دائمة الخضرة تنمو في مناطق البحر الأبيض المتوسط ، واسمها كيراتونيا سيليكوا ، تثمر قرون الخروب التي تؤكل ، وتتميز هذه القرون بأن البذور الموجودة في هذه القرون لها حجم واحد .

Carthamus tinctorius: *Safflower*, thistle-like plant, petals yield a red dye used in rouge, etc.

كارئمس تنكتوريس : القرطم ، نبات مثل الشوك يحصل منه على صبغة حمراء تستخدم في عمل الروج .

Cassab: Embroidery that is the same colour as the ground cloth. Syn. with *self-coloured* work. Sometimes gold metal-thread is added to *cassab*.

قصب : وهو نوع من التطريز لونه يشابه لون الفستان أحيانا تضاف خيوط الذهب إلى القصب .

Catechu: Astringent substance obtained from certain leaves which contain tannin.

كاتيكو : مادة قابضة يحصل عليها من أوراق نبات ، تحتوي على التانين الذي يستخدم في الدباغة .

Cathae edulis: Toxic shrub which yields *qat*, a mild narcotic.

كائا إيديولس : شجيرة سامة يحصل منها على القات وهو مخدر خفيف .

Chain stitch: See *Embroidery* chapter.

غرزة السلسلة : أنظر فصل التطريز .

Chevron: Bent bar of inverted V shape, sometimes used as an embroidery motif.

شيفرون : شكل الشارة العسكرية ، يستخدم في التطريز .

Chintz: Glazed, printed cotton textile, originally a painted or stained calico from India.

شنتز : شيت أو قماش قطني يحصل عليه أصلا من الهند .

Chursta: Plant yielding yellow dye, imported from India.

كورستا : نبات يحصل منه على صبغة صفراء يستورد من الهند .

Cochineal: Crimson-red pigment, carmine, obtained from the dried bodies of the female insect species *Dactlopius* found on desert succulents.

القرمز : صبغة قرمزيه حمراء ، كارمن يحصل عليها من أجسام أنثى حشرة داكتولوبيس بعد تجفيفها وهي تعيش في الصحراء .

Couching: Syn. with *Tahriri*. Embroidery technique whereby threads (usually gold or silver metal threads or floss silk) are affixed to the ground cloth by means of fine stitches at regular intervals. Also known as *laid work*.

كوشنج : طريقة تطريز تثبت فيها خيوط الذهب أو الفضة أو الحرير على القماش بواسطة غرز دقيقه . مرادف : تحريري

Cretan stitch: See *Embroidery* chapter.

غرزه كريتيه : أنظر فصل التطريز .

Crochet: Kind of knitting done with single hook.

كروشيه : نوع من أشغال الإبره .

Crocus sativus: *Saffron*, plant whose orange-coloured stigmas yield yellow colouring.

كروكس ساتيفس : نبات يحصل منه على صبغة صفراء .

Crore: Indian number, 10,000,000 units.

كرور : رقم هندي ١٠ مليون وحده .

Crotch: Garment part to fit fork of body where legs meet trunk.

كروتش : لباس داخلي .

Cuff: Finish on sleeves and trousers at wrists and ankles.

كفه : تطريز على الأكمام وأطراف البنطلون .

Damask: Reversible textile whereby a pattern is produced that appears on the face and on the back in reverse positions.

دمشقي : قماش تظهر الزخرفه فيه على الوجه وعلى الظهر .

Dart: Tailoring technique taking in small section to shape.

دارت : طريقة خياطه .

Diamente: Glittering object cut as a brilliant diamond from paste or mirror-backed glass. Also known as a "brilliant".

ديامنت : فصوص من الزجاج تشبه الماس .

Dotting: See *Embroidery* chapter.

التنقيط : أنظر فصل التطريز .

Dresslength: Section of textile, sufficient to make a gown.

قماش عريض : مقطع من القماش يكفي لعمل ثوب .

التخريج : طريقة خياطه على حاشية الثوب للزينة أو الوقايه .

Facing: Section of textile cut to fit outer edges of garment pattern, and extending inward for several inches. Facing is a tailoring technique to take the place of a hem and give strength to the garment.

فريسلي : مرادف جاكار .

Fairisle: Syn. with *Jacquard*. See *Jacquard*.

غرزة الريشه : أنظر فصل التطريز .

Feather stitch: See *Embroidery* chapter.

غرزة اللفقه : أنظر الغرزه المنبسطه .

Felling: See *flat fell*.

تلبيد : عملية تلبيد الخيوط .

Felt: Fabric-making technique whereby shrinking, pressing and rolling damp fibres of wool, fur, etc. create an interlocked and matted material.

غرزه منبسطه : طريقة تطريز بها صفان من الغرز .

Flat fell: Tailoring seam requiring two rows of stitches. The first row is followed by *grading* to allow a flat seam by removing bulk when the wider width is folded over the narrower width and stitched down. Also known as a flat seam.

غرزة الفراشه : أنظر فصل التطريز .

Fly stitch: See *Embroidery* chapter.

جاليوم : نبات يحصل منه على صبغه حمراء .

Gallium: Plant providing red dye.

جوديت : قطعة قماش مثلثه .

Godet: Long triangular-shaped section of garment pattern which allows shaping.

جور : قطعة قماش مثلثة .

Gore: Long wedge-shaped section of garment pattern which allows a skirt to flair sufficiently to ease movement, yet does not add restricting additional textile to the bodice.

التدريج : طريقة تفصيل .

Grading: Tailoring technique whereby each layer of a garment seam is trimmed to a different width.

البنيقه : وصلة قماش مثلثه تزاد على ثوب لتوسيع جزء منه او لتقويته .

Gusset: Small diamond or triangular-shaped section of a garment pattern, let in to enlarge or strengthen some part and give ease of movement to the wearer.

الفى : (١) طريقة تفصيل .
(٢) أنظر فصل التطريز .

Hemming: *1* Tailoring technique whereby the garment edges are turned up and hemmed. Also known as felling.
2 See *Embroidery* chapter.

غرزة ضلع السمكه : أنظر فصل التطريز .

Herringbone stitch: See *Embroidery* chapter.

النيله : صبغه يحصل عليها من نبات انديجوفرا ، لونها أزرق إلى أزرق يميل إلى الأسود إذا وضعت الصبغة في وسط قلوي ، وإذا كان الوسط حامضي يكون اللون أحمر ، انديجوفرا أرتكيولاتا .

Indigo: Dye obtained from plants of the genus *Indigofera*. Generally known as a blue colour that ranges from blue to dark bluish/black when the dye is developed with an alkaline medium. A red colour is obtained when it is developed with an acid medium.

جاكار : طريقة تطريز ونسج وفيها يضاف إلى النسيج خيوط من عدة ألوان لتكون أشكال متنوعة ، قام باختراعها جوزيف ماري جاكار (١٧٥٢ — ١٨٣٤ م) وهو رجل فرنسي قام بتطوير النول الميكانيكي ، وهذه الطريقة كانت معروفة للعرب في الماضي ، كما تشتهر بها جزيرة شيتلاند الاسكتلندية حاليا حيث أخذتها في الماضي عن أحد البحارة الأسبان الذي تحطمت سفينته على شواطئها ، وقد تعلمها الأسبان من المغاربه .

Jacquard: Knitting and weaving technique whereby additional threads of different colours are introduced to form patterns. Invented by Joseph Marie Jacquard (1752–1834), a Frenchman who improved the mechanical loom for weaving figured patterns by means of an endless belt of cards punched with holes arranged to form the required pattern. The knitting technique was previously known to the Arabs, and the Scottish Shetland Island of Fair is now famous for this knitting technique introduced there by shipwrecked sailors of the Spanish Armada who took it from the Moors.

جمداني : نسيج قطني رقيق له ألوان زاهية (الموصلين) وهو نسيج هندي تقليدي ، ينتج حاليا في باكستان .

Jamdani: Traditional Indian brightly-coloured figured silk muslin, now produced in Pakistan.

قيراط : مقياس مقسم إلى ٢٤ جزء يقدر به درجة نقاوة الذهب مثلا السبيكة التي تحتوي على ٢٢ جزء من الذهب ، ٢ جزء من سبيكة أخرى يقال عنها أنها ذهب ٢٢ قيراط .

Karat (abbrev. kt.): Measure of 1/24, stating the fineness of gold, eg. a mass containing 22 parts of gold and 2 parts of alloy is 22 carats fine or 22 carat gold.

خرزة السلم : أنظر فصل التطريز .

Ladder stitch: See *Embroidery* chapter.

أعمال التطريز : مرادف كوشينج .

Laid work: Syn. with *couching* and *tahriri*. See *couching*.

طيه : طية الثوب أو حاشيته .

Lappet: Flap, fold, loose or overlapping piece of garment.

لاسونيا إنرمس (حناء) : نبات دائم الخضرة ينبت في مصر وينتج عطر للإستعمال في العطور ومواد التجميل وعند طحنه ينتج البودره .

Lawsonia inermis (henna): Egyptian evergreen privet; shoots, leaves, flowers yield essence for perfumes and cosmetics. Dried berries are crushed to provide powder.

الطماق : كساء للساق .

Leggings: Pants section beginning anywhere from knee to mid-calf and ending at the ankle.

لوركس : قماش يحتوي على ٥٠ بالمائة من خيوط معدنية براقه .

Lurex: Textile containing 50 percent of glittering metallic weft thread.

مادر : الفوه ، نبات متسلق (روبيا تنكتوريم) يؤخذ من جذره صبغه حمراء .

Madder: Herbaceous climbing plant (*Rubia tinctorum*), the root of which supplies a red dye.

ممرسر : طريقة تجهيز يعالج فيها القطن بمحلول من البوتاسا الكاويه قبل الصباغه ، لإعطاءه مظهر حريري ومتانه ، اخترعها جون مرسر (١٧٩١ — ١٨٦٦) .

Mercerised: Textile finishing process which prepares cotton for dyes by treatment under tension with solution of caustic potash, imbuing a silky lustre, strength and receptiveness. Inventor: John Mercer (1791–1866).

تطريز المولا : طريقة تطريز ، أبليك ، تستخدم فيها أشرطة رفيعة من النسيج لتكون زخارف .

Mola work: Embellishment technique, a type of *appliqué*, colourful reverse appliqué wherein designs are cut through various layers in step fashion giving a contoured effect.

مثبت اللون : مادة كيماوية تثبت الصبغه ، بواسطة التفاعل معها وتحويلها إلى مادة غير قابلة للذوبان .

Mordant: Chemical for fixing a dye in or on a substance by combining with the dye to form an insoluble compound.

ناكر : الصدف الذي يحصل عليه من المحار .

Nacre: Syn. with mop and mother-of-pearl, obtained from moluscs which yield pearls.

غرزة السلسلة المفتوحه : أنظر فصل التطريز .

Open chain stitch: See *Embroidery* chapter.

الخياطة الظاهره : أنظر فصل التطريز .

Oversewing: See *Embroidery* chapter.

الخشخاش : نبات مخدر ، يحصل منه على صبغه حمراء .

Papaver: Poppy that yields red dye.

بيست : زجاج براق به نسبة عاليه من الرصاص تصنع منه الحلى الزائفه .

Paste: Brilliant glass of high lead content used for the manufacture of artificial gems.

البركال : قماش قطني عريض بدون لون .

Percale: Fine plain-woven wide cotton textile.

شريط تدكيك : شريط لتضييق فتحة الفستان .

Placket: Additional narrow strip attached to slit openings of garments to hide the gap.

البليد : نسيج صوفي نقوشه مربعه ، ويمكن أن يكون النسيج قطني أو صناعي .

Plaid: Long piece of twilled woollen cloth with checkered pattern. Sometimes applied also to checkered cottons and synthetics.

طريز مرتفع : تطريز أعلى من سطح القماش مثل الصارما أو بندالي .

Raised work: Embroidery that is padded or raised above the surface of the ground cloth, as in the case of *sarma* and *bindali*.

نسيج معاد تطريزه : نسيج أعيد تطريزه مرة ثانية ، أو ثبت عليه شريط أو رباط .

Re-embroidered: Embroidered textile that already exhibits a woven pattern. Sometimes the additional embellishment involves applied ribbon or lace.

رسب : البركال الهندي .

Rhassab: Indian *Percale*.

روج : مادة تجميل حمراء لإعطاء لون أحمر للوجنات .

Rouge: Red cosmetic for colouring the cheeks.

الأرجواني الملكي : اللون الأرجواني مرادف الأرجواني الصوري .

Royal purple: Syn. with *Tyrian purple*. See *Tyrian purple*.

روبياسي : نبات من عائلة المادر، ينتج صبغة حمراء .

Rubiaceae: Plant of the Madder family which yields red dye.

كيس : كيس لحفظ الأشياء .

Sachet: Fabric envelope for storage of soft goods.

القرطم : صبغة حمراء ، أنظر كارثمس تنكتوريس .

Safflower: See *Carthamus tinctorius*.

الزعفران : صبغة صفراء ، أنظر كروكس ساتيفوس .

Saffron: See *Crocus sativus*.

خشب الصندل : خشب طبيعي معطر يحصل عليه من أشجار السانتل .

Sandalwood: Naturally scented wood obtained from species of Santal tree, native to India and Pakistan.

الصارما : أنظر فصل التطريز .

Sarma: See *Embroidery* chapter.

ساتان : نسيج مصقول لامع ، من الحرير أو صناعي .

Satin: Textile with glossy surface on one side, produced by twill weave in which weft threads are almost concealed by warp. Usually silk or synthetic.

غرزة الساتان : أنظر فصل التطريز.

Satin stitch: See *Embroidery* chapter.

غرزة الساتان كوشينج : أنظر فصل التطريز.

Satin stitch couching: See *Embroidery* chapter.

التطريز بالخرز: طريقة تطريز يستعمل فيها الخرز أو ما يشبهه في عمل أشكال زخرفية .

Seed beading: Textile embellishment involving the application of very small beads of uniform size to form patterns.

البذر: أنظر فصل التطريز.

Seeding: See *Embroidery* chapter.

تلوين ذاتي : أعمال تطريز يستخدم فيها لون القماش .

Self-coloured: Decorative work of the same colour as ground cloth.

تطريز ذاتي : مرادف قصب ، أنظر قصب .

Self-embroidered: Syn. with *cassab*. See *cassab*.

سلفدج : أطراف القماش .

Selvedge: Natural side edge of woven textile.

السكوين : (١) نقد ذهبي تركي وإيطالي . (٢) قطعة ذهبية تستعمل عمله . (٣) ترنز.

Sequin: *1* Old gold coin of Turkey and Italy.
2 Thin gold disc used as currency.
3 Garment embellishment medium in the form of small shiny ornamental circular disc with a hole at one side.

سيشا : طريقة تطريز، تثبت أشياء صغيرة لامعة مثل المرآة على القماش .

Shisha: Embellishment technique whereby tiny mirrors or shiny objects are affixed to the ground cloth with embroidery stitches.

سوتيش : شريط مجدول يستخدم في التطريز، ويثبت حول الجيوب والرقبه والأساور.

Soutache: Narrow flat or round ornamental braid for garment embellishment. Usually affixed with fine stitches into cracks of seams and around pockets, necklines and cuffs. Also used to form decorative work such as looped buttons.

ترتر : قرص صغير جدا لامع به خرم يستخدم لتطريز الملابس .

Spangle: Garment embellishment medium in the form of small shiny ornamental circular disc with a central hole.

بيت العنكبوت : أنظر فصل التطريز .

Spiders web: See *Embroidery* chapter.

خرزة الساق : أنظر فصل التطريز .

Stem stitch: See *Embroidery* chapter.

غرزة الساتان السطحية : أنظر فصل التطريز .

Surface satin stitch: See *Embroidery* chapter.

تحريري : طريقة فلسطينية في الكوشينج ، أنظر كوشينج .

Tahriri: Palestinian style of *couching*. See *couching*.

طمبور : أداة تستخدم في التطريز مشابهة لمثقاب الجلد الذي يستخدمه صانع الأحذيه .

Tambour: Hooked tool used for embroidery, similar to shoemaker's awl. Syn. with *arhi*.

تطريز رباني : مرادف أغاباني ، أنظر أغاباني .

Tatriz rubani: Syn. with *aghabani*. See *aghabani*.

صنع المخرمات : عمل مخرمات بها عقد على شريط .

Tatting: Kind of knotted lace made from sewing-thread with small flat shuttle-shaped instrument.

التطريز السطحي : طريقة تطريز فيها لا تدخل الخيوط في النسيج ولكن تثبت في الزخارف السطحية .

Threading: Embellishment technique whereby threads do not enter the ground fabric but are incorporated into surface embroidery.

ذيل الفستان : أن يكون الفستان طويل من الخلف ويتدلى على الأرض .

Train: Back section of garment longer than the wearer, thus it must trail behind.

تللى : نسيج رقيق ناعم من الحرير .

Tulle: Thin, soft and fine silk netted textile.

التويل : نسيج مضلع .

Twill: Textile with surface of diagonal ribs produced by passing weft threads over one and under two or more warp threads.

الأرجواني الصوري : مرادف الأرجواني الملكي ، صبغة أرجوانية يحصل عليها من المحار، اكتشفت في صور وكانت تصدر قديما إلى الإغريق والرومان القدماء .

Tyrian purple: Syn. with *Royal purple*. Purple stain extracted from a certain shell fish. Discovered by the Tyrians (Phoenicia) and exported by them to ancient Greece and Rome.

مخمل : نسيج من الحرير أو القطن أو صناعي له خيوط بارزه .

Velvet: Silk, cotton or synthetic textile with short, soft, dense, smooth warp pile surface on one side formed by loops of additional weft threads which are usually cut through during the weaving process.

السداه (وارب) : ما مد من خيوط النسيج طولا .

Warp: Lengthwise threads set up in a loom on which weaving is achieved when they are crossed and interlaced by *weft* threads.

الغزه الموجه : أنظر فصل التطريز .

Wave stitch: See *Embroidery* chapter.

اللحمه : ما نسج عرضا من الخيوط .

Weft: Threads interwoven with *warp* threads by crossing from side to side on a loom.

الراوند البري : نوع من النبات ينتج صبغة صفراء .

Wild Rhubarb: Plant supplying yellow dye.

ورستد : طريقة لعمل النسيج الصوفي ، من صوف طويل التيله وتكون فيه الألياف موازية لبعضها .

Worsted: Textile woven from fine smooth-surfaced yard spun from long-staple wool combed so fibres lie parallel.

مخنق : جزء من الثوب يطوق العنق .

Yoke: Section of garment that lies around the neckline.

زجزاج : أنظر فصل التطريز .

Zigzag: See *Embroidery* chapter.

سحَاب : زمام منزلق (سوسته) .

Zipper: Slide fastener. Device consisting of two flexible strips with interlocking metal or plastic projections that close or open as sliding clip is drawn along them.